December 1, 1960, five months after the opening of the Lower Dauphin Joint High School, freshman Dale Berkebile was sent by Coach Cassel to the LD home mat at 98 pounds in the Falcons' inaugural wrestling match. Freshman Gary Barb at 103 pounds and junior Jay Kopp at 112 pounds put the first points in the win column for the Falcons via forfeit wins over their East Pennsboro opponents. Both were winning when the forfeits were awarded. Senior John Clemens at 127 pounds was the first Falcon to record a complete six-minute match victory with a hard-fought 2-0 decision.

The LD Wrestling Journey

Randy Umberger
Wrestler, Coach, Administrator

The beginning and the ending of the Falcon Wrestling Story (to date), covered in these pages, eclipses 64 years or six plus decades of team, individual and coaching accomplishments. The beginning and the ending of this record have some interesting comparisons. Both the first and last dual meets in these writings were VICTORIES on the Falcons' home mat. Our first win was over East Pennsboro High School by the score of 51-14 on December 1, 1960. Our last regular season league dual meet in this 64 year span was a 42-16 win over Palmyra on January 2, 2024. Our successes would not be limited to just dual meets as individual performers emerged and recorded firsts in our school's history.

Sophomore **Randy Kahler** in February of 1962 became the first Falcon to win a District 3 Title and advance to the state championships at 165 lbs. and became the Falcons' **first PIAA State Finalist.** In February of 2020 senior **Clayton Ulrey** battled his way to the top of the Lower Dauphin Wrestling Podium by becoming the Falcons' first ever **Four-time District 3 South Central Regional Champion.** He then advanced to an unprecedented four appearances at the PIAA State Championships. Clayton's amazing run was accomplished in three different weight classes; once at 138 lbs, once at 152 lbs and twice at 160 lbs.

The head coaching position has not been spared a similar beginning and ending. **Cleon Cassel,** a first year teacher coach, a product of South Hanover Township, was chosen to start what would become a wrestling dynasty and tradition by the end of the first decade of the sport. In the early decade of 2020 another South Hanover product, **David Wuestner, Jr.** was named to succeed his mentor and coach **Kemal Pegram** to reignite the Falcon Legacy. **Ed Neiswender** and Cleon's son **Craig Cassel,** also products of South Hanover Township, navigated the Falcon Grapplers through successful championship seasons. South Hanover Township can boast of producing five of the nine head coaches in the storied Lower Dauphin Wrestling Program.

December 1, 1960, five months after the opening of the Lower Dauphin Joint High School, freshman **Dale Berkebile** was sent to the mat at 98 lbs. by first year coach Cleon Cassel in the Falcons' inaugural wrestling match held on the Falcons' home mat. Freshman **Gary Barb** at 103 lbs, and junior **Jay Kopp** at 112 lbs. put the first team points in the win column for the Falcons via forfeit wins over their East Pennsboro opponents. Senior **John Clemens** at 127 pounds was the first Falcon to record a complete six minute match victory with a hard fought 2-0 decision over his East Pennsboro opponent. The Falcons prevailed by a score of **41–9** which marked the beginning of a sport that would help unite and bond the families of the five communities in this newly formed school district.

From December 1960 thru March 2024 Falcon Wrestling Fans have witnessed, enjoyed and been part of a wrestling program that established a culture of success that has endured. The program has had its victories and disappointments but has never lost sight of its direction and history.

Many factors have contributed to the successful history and traditions of the **FALCON WRESTLING STORY**. First and foremost only the right persons, at the right time, in the right place could have made all this possible. The hiring of home-grown **Cleon Cassel,** a Hershey High graduate fresh off the campus of Franklin and Marshall College, by Superintendent of Schools **David Emerich,** was the first and most important step. No one could have imagined at that time the immediate and lasting effects it would have on the newly formed school district. That single personnel decision started the momentum for a program that would serve to include the diversity of the five communities and unite them as one. Administration, school board, faculty, community, parents and alumni have seen and enjoyed the lasting effect that inclusiveness has brought for Falcon Matmen.

The young men, and now women, who have entered this uniquely developed program have shared and are part of a tradition and spirit of competition, success that was created the first years under Coach Cassel.

Another important piece to the ongoing success can be attributed to the alumni returning to their alma mater to join the coaching ranks, to pay back what they had learned and enjoyed. That tradition was started by alumnus **Frank Neiswender,** a 1963 graduate. Coach Neiswender, a Bloomsburg State Teachers College Graduate, returned to his alma mater to teach junior high science and contribute his talents to the junior high wrestling program.

The present day sport of wrestling has evolved as a result of many changes over the past 64 years that have significantly affected individual and team records as they are presently recorded. One of the major changes that has impacted individual records has been the increase in the number of matches a wrestler has been permitted to wrestle in a given season. Early on 14 matches made up the dual meet season schedule with a four-team Christmas Tournament during the holidays. Today individual dual meets have given way to in-season, multi-team events as well as individual and team tournaments which allow competitors the opportunity to wrestle up to 4 bouts in a single day. The number of qualifiers that could advance in post season tournaments has increased dramatically from one to four from Sectionals to Districts; one to four from Districts to the Regional and State Tournaments. The State Wrestling Tournament expanded from a four man bracket to an eight man bracket to a 16 man bracket to the present day 20 man bracket. Each time the brackets and qualifiers were changed it created more opportunities for individuals as the sport continued to grow locally and statewide. In 1999 a team championship was added to the post season tournament schedule. District and State Team Championships were scheduled between the end of the regular dual meet season and the beginning of individual sectional tournaments.

Individual match scoring saw the one point takedown for each take down after the first takedown go to 2 points for all takedowns. One or two points were added to an individual's score for riding time advantage over an opponent was abandoned. Five team points for a second or third period pin came to an end in favor of six team points for a pin at any time during the match. The number of weight classes was increased from 12 to 14 to encourage and accommodate the number of participants that joined high school rosters. Due to the number of forfeits that were occurring during a dual meet with the 14 weight classes, the number of weight classes has now been reduced to 13.

Female wrestling will take its place in the Pennsylvania Wrestling Story as the PIAA has approved and adopted the inclusion of female wrestling to the state's list of sports, beginning officially in school year **2023-24**. Whether female wrestling will add its chapter to the Lower Dauphin Wrestling Story is yet to be determined. Over the past decades Lower Dauphin has had females wrestle in the boys program with some success.

With all the changes that wrestling has seen over the last 64 years there is one thing that has remained constant throughout the Lower Dauphin Wrestling Story, the NAMES. Faces have changed but not the NAMES. Brothers, fathers and now sons have been a large and important component of a spirited movement driven by tradition.

I have been privileged and proud to have served and contributed to the ongoing and expanding success of the Lower Dauphin Athletic Program, as a student competitor, assistant coach, head coach, athletic director, assistant principal, and presently in retirement as a spectator and booster. On behalf of all those that have taken to the LD Mats a thank you to our families, teachers, coaches, mentors, administrators, classmates, boosters and athletic friends that gave us the inspiration and encouragement to do better and return and contribute to keep the tradition of Falcon Wrestling alive.

Some say it is hard to maintain the same pace and traditions for 64 years but Lower Dauphin Wrestling's greatest success has been to keep the 1960 vision for Lower Dauphin Wrestling by Cleon Cassel alive and well. That vision has not only served the wrestlers well but has contributed to a committed theme of inclusiveness in all that our school community undertakes.

YESTERYEAR PUBLISHING

www.yesteryearpublishing.org

Lower Dauphin Wrestling
An Uncommon Heritage
1960–2024

ISBN 978-0-9977956-6-0

EIN 26-3987880

Published in the United States by Yesteryear Publishing.

Books are available through www.**amazon.com**. Search *Lower Dauphin Wrestling*.

Cover and Book Design by E. Nan Edmunds

Lower Dauphin
Dauphin
WRESTLING

An Uncommon Heritage
1960–2024

Lower Dauphin Wrestling does not have a list, guide, or an instruction book on "how to be a wrestler." What we do have, however, are adults who **encourage** young men to **find** something in the sport of wrestling that they had not found elsewhere and to **guide** them to see the skills that wrestling provides, including the opportunity for positive changes and for opening many doors, beginning with confidence in competition and ending in lifelong friendships.

Lower Dauphin Coaches live by rules that have been confirmed by experience. They train with a quiet passion and strong belief in their sport and with a clear sense that in their own lives it was **wrestling** that had made the difference. The fact that many of our coaches are graduates of our high school is also a tribute to our successful program . . . and this is what has given Lower Dauphin Wrestling its Uncommon Heritage.

Dr. Judith T. Witmer, Author
Faculty and Administration, 1960–1992

Dedication

*To all whose lives were changed through the
dedication and support of coaches,
faculty, and teammates in their becoming
Lower Dauphin Wrestlers*

Of course, we will have wrestling . . .

In the fall of 1960 the first announcement heard over the public address system was "Of course, we will have wrestling."

▸ Yes, there were wrestlers—here, there, and everywhere—in the gym, in the hallways, in the cafeteria, and years later, even in the newly designated orchestra rehearsal space.

▸ Some believed that football was designed to prepare young men for wrestling and that study halls were designed to be dismissed **from** in order to go to the "mat room."

▸ **Late busses were designed** to take the wrestlers home to finish chores. **"Catching chickens" was created**—or so we thought—as an event by which the wrestlers raised funds. We never asked "catching for what," as it somehow was assumed that we already knew: if the wrestlers were catching chickens, obviously there had to be a good reason.

▸ **Being addressed** by "Yes, M'am," was a sign that the responder was a wrestler.

▸ **Dozing off** in a first period class was a sign of a wrestler who (the night before) had been wrestling many miles away.

▸ **Trying to remember** what the protocol was for asking if the team won the meet (or if they won the **match**) and not to ask *anything* if their faces revealed a negative outcome of the event.

▸ **Seeing Wade** jump out of his corner seat in the last row on the first day of class when the teacher pointed to the two seats in the center front row and casually mentioned that often students who sat at these particular desks earned "A's." Wade and Craig made a mad dash for the seats. And, no surprise, they worked hard to earn their English Literature "letters."

▸ **Watching** wrestlers stand in pride as the National Anthem was sung by John Book and welcoming their interest in joining the cast of the high school musicals with the understanding that we would hold their "spot" on stage if the wrestling season had to be extended—these young men took the theater experience seriously, and stayed in character the entire time on stage.

▸ These **Lower Dauphin Wrestlers** became **champions in life** because they had tasted possibilities for successful adulthood offered by the understanding coaches who cared deeply for their welfare and led them in having personal pride in accomplishment.

Wrestling at LD: The 21ˢᵗ Century

The Dynasty We Have Become

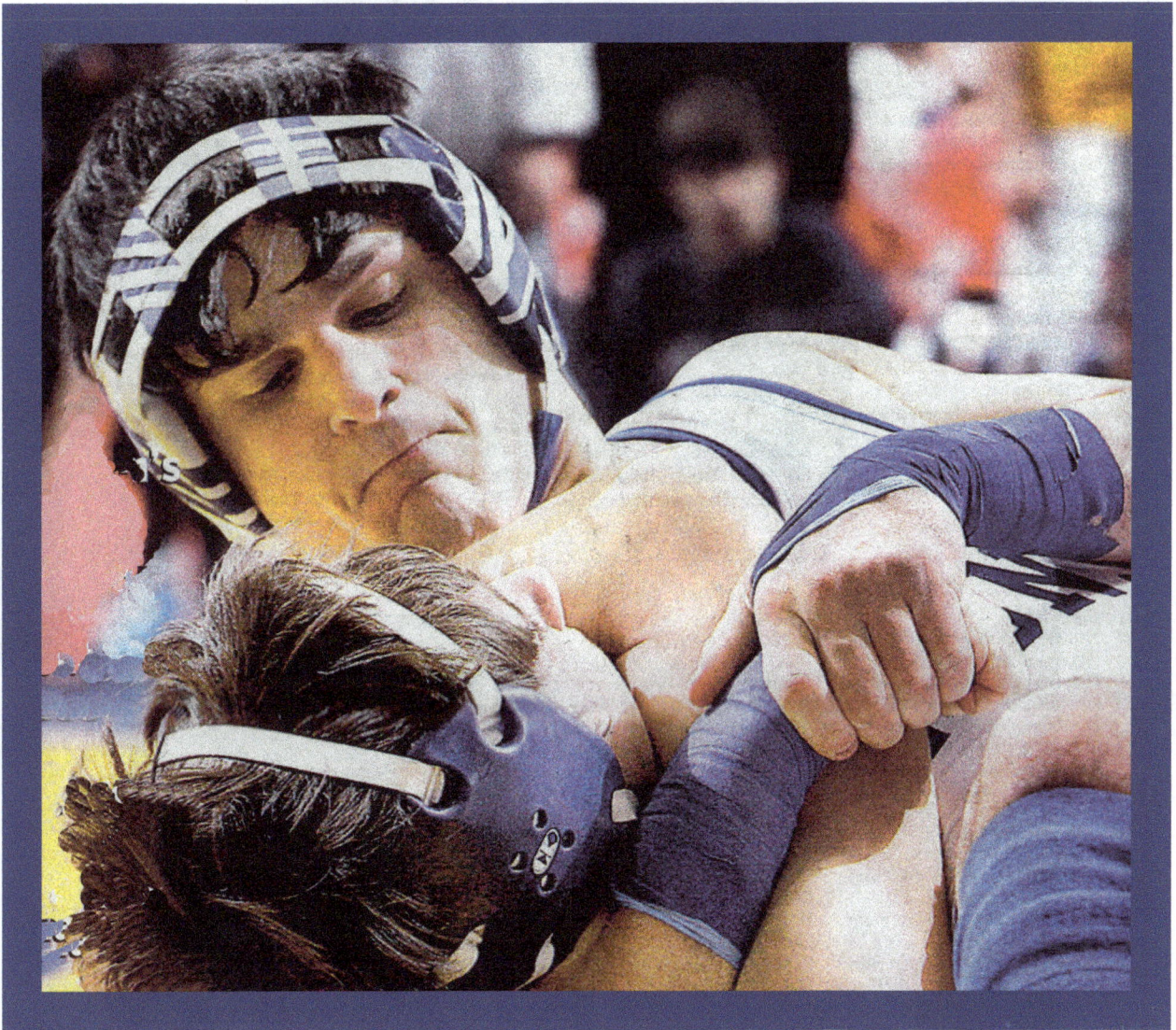

Featured above is **Jarred Kane**, first 100 match winner. Many of the photographs in this section are from Legacy Imagez by **Dannette B**, Photographer. Most others in this section are from **Gino Simonetti,** and *The Patriot News,* who unflaggingly provides coverage of LD Sports, along with our anchor for sports news, *The Hummelstown Sun.*

13

19

Foreword

It took four years to produce this book, but many of its wrestlers and contributors have been working toward it since 1960.

Whether writers, photographers, wrestlers, coaches, administrators, parents of wrestlers, or just fans and scrapbook collectors, scores of collborators have been working toward this volume for more than 60 years.

Why a book about wrestling?

Why write about a sport that typically, at the varsity level, lasts six minutes?

Because their efforts, sacrifices and lessons learned should not be forgotten. More particulary, the human stories not widely known deserve to be seen in retrospective daylight. The triumphs and defeats of the wrestling mat are, in many cases, not even the most compelling part of the story. The athletes of these pages climbed a mountain of effort, emotion, and sacrifice before ever stepping onto the mat or hearing a referee's whistle.

We asked them to tell us their own stories, and many did.

We are LD wrestlers...

Randy Umberger

Ed Neidig

Matthew Werner

Carl Espenshade

Lynn C Grimm

Joseph C Stut

Jason Dupler

Joel C Umberger

Dan Douskow

Chris Cassel

Chuck Koser

Ryan W. Koser

Alec Sweeney

Bill Baer

Tom Whiston

Ike Fullerton

Jeff Hollenbush

Jim Shutt

G. Don Kopp

Ron Kopp

Brian Geeser

Chris Camasta

Leon Koser

Craig S Cassel 82

Keith Camasta

Sam Dupler

Greg Etnoyer

David Wuestner Jr.

Melvin Watts

Ronald Myer

Larry Gingerich

Ron Cruys

George C Kline

L. B. Koser

Earl White

✓ "I was six or seven years old. I was one of those little kids you see running around at matches." *(Wrestler and Coach Ed Neiswender, page 232)*

✓ "In eighth grade a decision to participate in junior high intramural wrestling would become one of the most important decisions I would ever make in my life." *(Randy Umberger, page 41)*

✓ "The evening that I won my first tournament, I actually got a hug from both coaches. They told me that I did a great job. A compliment was something that I had never experienced from a man in my earlier years of life." *(Bob Hess, page 89)*

✓ "There was a sense of belonging to an elite group that honored hard work, toughness, sacrifice, and a degree of shenanigans." *(Craig Tritch, page 97)*

✓ "Unfortunately, shoulder injuries and times I tried to lose too much weight too fast would spoil the end of my season. Also, after practice I had to take the long bus ride home, walk a mile to my house, and then milk the family cow." *(Carl Espenshade, page 86)*

✓ "Coach Cassel, an unassuming, soft-spoken man said to me, 'I want you to wrestle for me, but you have to give me your word that you will commit no acts of violence and keep your grades up.' …I said 'You have my word,' Those four words…completely altered my life." *(Michael Mazerolle, page 216)*

✓ "So it ended at 26-14. The final score failed to reflect the competitiveness of the match. Eight of the eleven bouts contested were decided by two points or less." *(Ron Cruys, page 91)*

✓ "…Their floors were heated. I fell into a deep sleep and when the lights came on, I…could not wake up.…I began to panic, terrified I would lose the match. Finally, I was able to regain stability five minutes before I wrestled and I won…." *(Mike DeMuth, page 95)*

✓ "I always got my best grades during the wrestling season." *(Dr. Craig Camasta, page 212)*

✓ "What I will remember most…is how the team had no hidden agendas, how we were all one when we took to the mat and how we were also all one off the mat. Even though we were all very different people we had a common goal that was TEAM. A valuable lesson we learned was that it isn't always about talent; sometimes it's about HEART." *(Claudio Valeri, page 218)*

The 2000s: Continuing the Wrestling Dynasty

Wrap-Up 379

Review, Records and Rules 395

About the Author 413

Launching a Wrestling Program
From Destiny to Dynasty

"A sport that is as old as the earliest history...... where character is the result. ...a full body chess game of ferocious beauty in which brains count a lot more than muscle."

So opened an article by Kenneth Turan in *Gentlemen's Quarterly* (March 1989), describing the dynamics of amateur wrestling. Turan's description holds as well today as it did some years ago, a wink in time considering the origin (circa 2400 BC) of the sport.

Turan continues, "Each man probes, pushes, and punishes the other with an unforgiving intensity that is both painful and exhilarating to watch ... think of six minutes in hell.

"The experience of watching a wrestler fight off what looks like a dead-sure takedown can be awesome, like watching someone put the temple back together after Samson has pulled it down...

"This is an unforgiving sport, with no breathers and not even a millimeter of tolerance for error ... a fierce test of wills, an elemental ballet for control and mastery....

"It is a kind of chivalry, but with no armor.

"Think of wrestling as the Last Pure Sport because it is so relentlessly individualistic that athletes compete on equal footing. It is a sport that is compelling to watch...."

Initiating a Wrestling Progam
Glenn Ebersole '61, L. D.'s First Wrestling Captain '60-61

While "scholastic wrestling" is the determining term for the style of amateur wrestling that is used at the high school level in the United States, most participants simply call it "wrestling" and the uninitiated might use the term "schoolboy wrestling." To those curious enough to attend the first call for interested boys to attend an introduction meeting prior to the opening of Lower Dauphin High School in the spring of 1960, the definition didn't matter.

This brand new school would be opening in the fall and for many of the boys who would be attending it, there were many unanswered questions. They didn't know the coach—just that he had a good record as a wrestler at Hershey and at Franklin and Marshall College in Lancaster, a highly regarded small college not too far from Hummelstown. This first-year coach lived with his parents in South Hanover Township, but he and his siblings were graduates of Hershey High School, not Hummelstown High School, the local school that had graduated its last class in June 1960.

There had been no wrestling program at Hummelstown High. The young men there had made their mark in football, basketball, and baseball, and most likely had never seen scholastic wrestling, their only exposure being the adult professional wrestling shown on the black and white television set some homes had. Thus, the boys who were in Hummelstown High School had had very little understanding of schoolboy wrestling.

On the other hand were young men who had spent their years of secondary school in Hershey. Some of them knew this new coach for the new high school in Hummelstown, because he was a Hershey High School graduate who had been on the wrestling team not only in Hershey, but on the collegiate team at Franklin and Marshall College.

The other factor, not widely known nor remembered sixty years later, is that the boys from several of the townships surrounding the new high school named Lower Dauphin were given the choice of attending the new school in Hummelstown or finishing their senior year at Hershey High School. I was one of these athletes in the senior class who had that difficult choice to make…

So how were Lower Dauphin wrestling and football teams successful right out of the gate? How did we have a ready-to-roll football team when Lower Dauphin first opened its doors in September 1960, and, by early December, how did we have a wrestling team "ready to roll?"

Since Hummelstown High School did not have a wrestling program, Lower Dauphin's program could be styled to parameters determined by the leadership. It did not share any likeness to the handful of schools in the state who offered the sport of wrestling, least of all Hershey High School who had built a very successful program—one that had been "up and running" for at least 30 years before Lower Dauphin High School was formed.

Building a Team

In the late 1950s, Mr. David J. Emerich, the Principal of Hummelstown High School and newly appointed Superintendent of a new high school to be named Lower Dauphin High School, had a plan...an idea that could overcome the barriers of the size of Hummelstown High School and where there could be interest to field a brand new sport—wrestling, one that had intrigued Mr. Emerich after watching matches in other schools and seeing the enthusiasm for it in those schools—in a new school with new administrators, new teachers, new students and, in most sports, new coaches.

Thus, in the spring of 1960 Superintendent Emerich invited the coaches of all sports to meet with the male students who might be interested in any sports that would be offered by the new school district—a very astute move by this appointed superintendent.

To those curious enough to attend the first call to a meeting about wrestling, the details of the arrangement didn't matter—yet. Many just wanted to hear more about wrestling.

There were many questions. The boys didn't know the new wrestling coach—just that he had a good record at Franklin and Marshall College in Lancaster. This first-year coach lived with his parents in South Hanover Township, which had its own elementary school and had sent its secondary high school students to Hershey High School. This new coach and his siblings were all graduates of Hershey High School.

There had been no wrestling program at Hummelstown High School. The young men there made their mark in football, basketball and baseball, and likely had not seen much scholastic wrestling. Thus, Mr. Emerich suggested that all coaches hold a meeting to introduce themselves and the sport they were offering to students.

Coach Cleon Cassel was the only coach who was recruiting for a sport that was unfamiliar to those currently attending Hummelstown High School. Cassel remembers that day well, "When I arrived at the High School to talk about wrestling there were only five boys present, three of whom were told by a Hummelstown teacher/coach right there before the meeting to leave because wrestling was not for them. Being left with only two boys with possible interest in wrestling was not a spectacular way to initiate a new sport."

Soon after, a second invitation was extended to the students, this time including those boys who would be transferring to Lower Dauphin from Hershey. One of these Hershey prospects was **Glenn Ebersole** who vividly recalls the circumstances: "While Hershey High was detaching its surrounding townships to allow for the rapid growth of homes and industry in Derry Township, Hummelstown was taking on those same townships to create its new school district[1]. Its new high school would have its own identity. Like most students from the outlying areas, I had mixed feelings about leaving Hershey for my final year. I had only my senior year

---

[1] Interestingly the land for the new high school was in Derry Township, not Hummelstown Borough.

to complete and initially I had a strong feeling against making the change from Hershey for just my last year. I even considered paying my own tuition to remain in Hershey, but that idea was short-lived once it became clear that most of my classmates, now living in areas included in the new school district, would be attending Lower Dauphin."

At Hershey High School rising Seniors **Glenn Ebersole** and **John Snavely**—along with Junior **Carl Espenshade**—had been essential members of the Championship Football Team as well as the Varsity Wrestling team at Hershey High. In the 1959 season Glenn had been the only starting-junior, first-team player on what is remembered as one of Hershey High's best football teams, competing in the South Penn Conference for the Championship.

All three wrestlers (Ebersole, Snavely, and Espenshade) made the choice to leave Hershey and to enroll in Lower Dauphin.

According to Ebersole, "When I walked into the meeting for the wrestlers of Hershey who might attend Lower Dauphin in the fall I saw that **nearly the entire Hershey High team** that would have been returning to Hershey the following year would instead be going to Lower Dauphin: **Jay** and **Galen Kopp, Carl Espenshade, Eugene Hertzler, John Snavely, John Clemens**, and **Lynn Grimm** were all there.

"During the meeting Coach Cassel quickly set the tone, and the feeling I sensed made me look forward to coming to Lower Dauphin where there were amenities Hershey did not have. Hershey did not even offer gymnasium seating and, thus, held their home games at the Milton S. Hershey School (on the hill not far from the Hershey Hotel).

"Once the reality that the new school definitely would be ready to open in the fall for my senior year, trading in the old for the new started to feel more like trading in a favorite old automobile for a new one. My thinking was much like weighing the plus and minus to rationalize the inevitable. Further, I realized that starting a new school would be an equal opportunity for everyone and we who lived in the surrounding townships would not be treated as outsiders, the situation that typically occurred at Hershey.

"Leaving Hershey High and going to a new school with a new team became clear. For one thing, I was honored to have been the only underclassman starter on one of the best football teams that had come out of Hershey High. I realized that without the players from the surrounding townships returning to Hershey for their senior year, it would be a rebuilding year for Hershey for sure. The head coach at Hershey also realized the likely outcome of losing his starters; he resigned his position at Hershey. Thus I made my decision—a new school, new friends, new team, new coaches, new friends. Why not?"

Glenn noted, "**Bruce Wyld**, a sophomore from Hummelstown, became the starting quarterback for the first football game of Lower Dauphin against Cumberland Valley after **Junior Dick Summy** came down with mononucleosis and was out for the rest of the season.

Mike Shifflet started the 1st game at quarterback for Junior Dick Summy who was ill. Summy was replaced the 2nd game of the year by Wyld who remained the quarterback for the remainder of the year. This first year team won all of our games and we went on to win the first CAC Championship. Even we knew that was something special.

"It is very important to note that this first football team brought together its three dozen players, molding us from strangers into loyal teammates. We dramatically won our first game against Cumberland Valley 7–0 in the last second of the game. We then went on to **win every game in our conference.** What a way to begin a school year—and what a foundation upon which to build a sports dynasty—from a group of boys whose members were becoming a team for the very first time! We boys—many of whom had not known one another—quickly bonded into a strong football team. This camaraderie carried over to the winter sports of basketball and wrestling.

"Although there was no high school newspaper as yet at Lower Dauphin to provide details for the events of the first year of this new high school, **we all knew** that its first year football team (with **Co-Captains Glenn Ebersole** and **Ken Epler**) was undefeated in conference play, and Lower Dauphin could become the **first Capital Area Conference Champion.** This was a sweet victory over Hershey and was a major factor in bringing the new Lower Dauphin School Community together. We were now, indeed, a team—and one to be reckoned with. This boded well for Wrestling.

"Many of us had met our wrestling teammates for the first time in August at football practice. Our winning season in football had done much for team-building and it was this united team effort that was the major factor in the success of Lower Dauphin in their first fling in the newly formed Capital Area Conference. The careful attention of the coaches, support from faculty, and a determination by all resulted in a championship team and season. And, as I recall, **wrestling practice** started on the Monday after the last football game of the season."

The Hershey Legacy

It is only fair to acknowledge what Hershey contributed to the wrestling program that provided a singular foundation for Lower Dauphin's stellar program. *The Grappler* provided some very telling history of the role Hershey played in LD's success.

It should also be remembered that **Doug Cassel** and **Al Fasnacht** matriculated at Penn State where they further developed their wrestling skills and then shared what they had learned with the Hershey High School teams. In Fasnacht's case, he not only continued sharing his skills with Hershey High, but also founded and coached the Hershey Community Club Wrestling Team, through which Dick and Doug Cassel, as well as **Don Heistand,** wrestled post high school. All of these various experiences benefitted Lower Dauphin.

Another interesting point is that from 1963-73, all of the LD postseason wrestlers who progressed to the sectional level and higher lived in one of the four townships that previously had been part of Hershey High School.

The Grappler[2] (a grass-roots publication) also included some very telling history of the role Hershey played in the success of Lower Dauphin. Hershey's wrestling program had begun in the 1930s with **Coach A. O. Brittain**, a man who was replaced by **Coach Young** during Brittain's service in the Navy in WWII. Upon Brittain's return in 1946, he resumed his coaching at Hershey and during the remainder of the 1940s and into the 1950s coached Dick, Doug, and Cleon Cassel along with Al and Don Fasnacht, and others who were all district champions or runners-up. These included Donald Heistand who had been part of that superior group as a district champion.

Don Heistand notes, "In all of my years with the wrestling program, I never heard any coach use profanity." And very few wrestlers (or football players for that matter) created discipline problems at school.

Wrestling's Initial Challenges

Coach Cleon Cassel recalls, "When Lower Dauphin opened in the fall, we found the new school had only one 25-by-25-foot felt mat—square, not round, and not near regulation size. When I brought this to Mr. Emerich's attention he replied, "That's correct, but what I mean is, if more than 20 boys come out on the first day of practice, I will buy a new mat."

That first day of practice Mr. Emerich walked into the gymnasium and saw more than 150 boys! (Likely he was smiling to himself.) That many boys, of course, could not begin to fit on this one small mat that would be crowded even with only two wrestling.

Cassel notes, "This unexpected need for a larger, regulation-size mat brought School Board Member Mr. Marshall Mountz to the first wrestling match to see why we thought we needed to spend money on a mat for wrestling. A new mat was ordered. From that date and for as long as he lived, Mr. Mountz rarely, if ever, missed a wrestling match."

Mr. Emerich submitted to the School Board a request for the regulation-size mat at the projected cost of $3,000—a huge amount at that time, especially since it specifically had not been budgeted for in advance.

During the opening days of LD when an announcement was made to everyone that any 7th or 8th grade boy interested in hearing more about wrestling should attend a meeting in D-Audion, one hundred boys of all sizes answered that call.

[2] This was a publication initiated by Ed Neiswender for the purpose of keeping former wrestlers engaged in the wrestling program. It replaced *The LD Mat.*

Testament to a Program, a Life Style, a Coach

— Dan Dorsheimer '66

I was in 7th grade in the fall of 1960 and none of the Hummelstown kids had ever heard of high school wrestling. Among ourselves we thought it would really be neat to "wrassle" and jump off ropes and gouge eyeballs!!! How cool would that be! Unfortunately, our coaches, **Clem Cassel, Homer Gelbaugh,** and **Don Heistand,** wouldn't allow any of this, and I'm still looking for the ropes and turnbacks I can jump off!!!

When you think of Coach Cassel starting this program from scratch in 1960, and taking it to the powerhouse program it rapidly progressed into, it indeed is quite amazing. My personal enduring memories started when I was in 8th grade. My all-time favorite and personal choice as LD's most dominating wrestler ever was **Jim Sanders,** a 4-year varsity starter who never lost a dual meet. At that time, you never got a second chance. Once out of sectionals, if you lost, you were done. And for whatever reason, Jim could not get out of districts until his senior year of '65, when he went to states at Rec Hall and tore up his knee. What a frustration.

We had so many fantastic wrestlers during these early years. **Harold "Buster" Shellenhamer** was in the same mold as Jim, one year behind him, wrestling the same four weight classes, and again, never losing a dual meet. And I don't recall **Bill Crick,** a three-year starter, ever losing a dual meet.

Randy Umberger also was a three-year starter. I remember some of his matches very well, such as with Fred Schaeffer of Cedar Cliff, Dave Laboskie of Springfield-Delco, and Jesse Rawls of Harrisburg. Randy won over Jesse on a referee's decision for a district championship in '65.

Bill Pinkerton, Class of '65, 103/120/127, could do everything except beat Jim Sanders.

Carl Espenshade, Class of '62, during a match with CD, took his opponent down, and somehow when this wrestler fell back onto Carl's arms, a compound fracture at Carl's elbow occurred. The broken bone actually protruded through the skin. With equanimity Carl noted, "To this day I've never seen any wrestling injury as severe as this."

In the early years, there was no weight limit for heavy weights. Hershey and Middletown each had men at 300+ lbs. Our heavies typically were under 200, so they didn't have much of a chance.

Others I recall in particular are **Eddie Neidig '65; Ron Cruys '66,** one of my best friends; **Jay** and **Galen Kopp,** light wt. in the early '60s, very strong farm boys; the **Mutek boys, Fred** and **Tom** and **Ken; Frank Neiswender '63,** Eddie's older brother and a very good wrestler.

Jay Ebersole and **Leon Koser** were both multi-year starters. Leon lost on a referee's decision or overtime to eventual state champion Allen Uyeda of Conestoga Valley.

We also had brothers **George '71, Mark '73, Eric '76,** and **Ed Stauffer. Fred Foreman '72** was, in my opinion, the best heavyweight Lower Dauphin ever had; he lost in State Finals at the Farm Show to giant Chuck Correal who later played pro football. For 10 years Fred Foreman went back to LD and worked with their heavyweights. Two words best describe **Roger Witmer '74** on the mat: Intense animal!!!

There is no way possible to mention LD wrestling and not incorporate the name **Ron Michael '72,** perhaps the most forceful wrestler ever at LD. I have always put Jim Sanders on a pedestal of LD wrestlers, but Ron Michael is right there with him. He just never believed that any opponent was better than he and that is how he wrestled. When Coach Cassel told me that he had a wrestler coming up that was as good as Ron Michael, I didn't believe him. All this kid had to do was get healthy. Well, that kid was none other than **Ed Neiswender,** and what a wrestler he was.

In 1973 LD had three wrestlers in the state finals—all going for state championships. Tom Mutek, Mark Stauffer, and Neiswender. ALL THREE LD wrestlers lost, one after the other....**It was unbelievable!!!**

I don't believe any LD wrestler ever had the fan appreciation that Big George Stauffer did. We would sit on the bleachers and roar for George. He never let us down. It was always the highlight of the match. George would fly out onto the mat, cross over and shake hands, the whistle would sound and the next thing you would see were two bodies flying across the mat. He would bring the house down.

What was wrestling? It was hard work; it was exhausting; it was invigorating; it was a challenge we learned to love. The Harrisburg Novice Tournament was our baptism....

The wrestlers won the Junior Division over twenty other teams. **Bob Hess** became L.D.'s first champion in this division at 70 lbs. It was quite an experience for all of us.

The First Season . . . and Beyond

In the lower right corner is a reminder of that very first season for football. In the lower left is a schedule for the first basketball season, the upper right is the wrestling team of the 1963 season and in the upper left is a priceless **original listing of names** (author's memorabilia) of those who **bore the distinction of being regarded as the First Wrestling Team at Lower Dauphin High School.** Over sixty years ago, those named on this hand-typed list began the journey that, in almost every case, changed their lives.

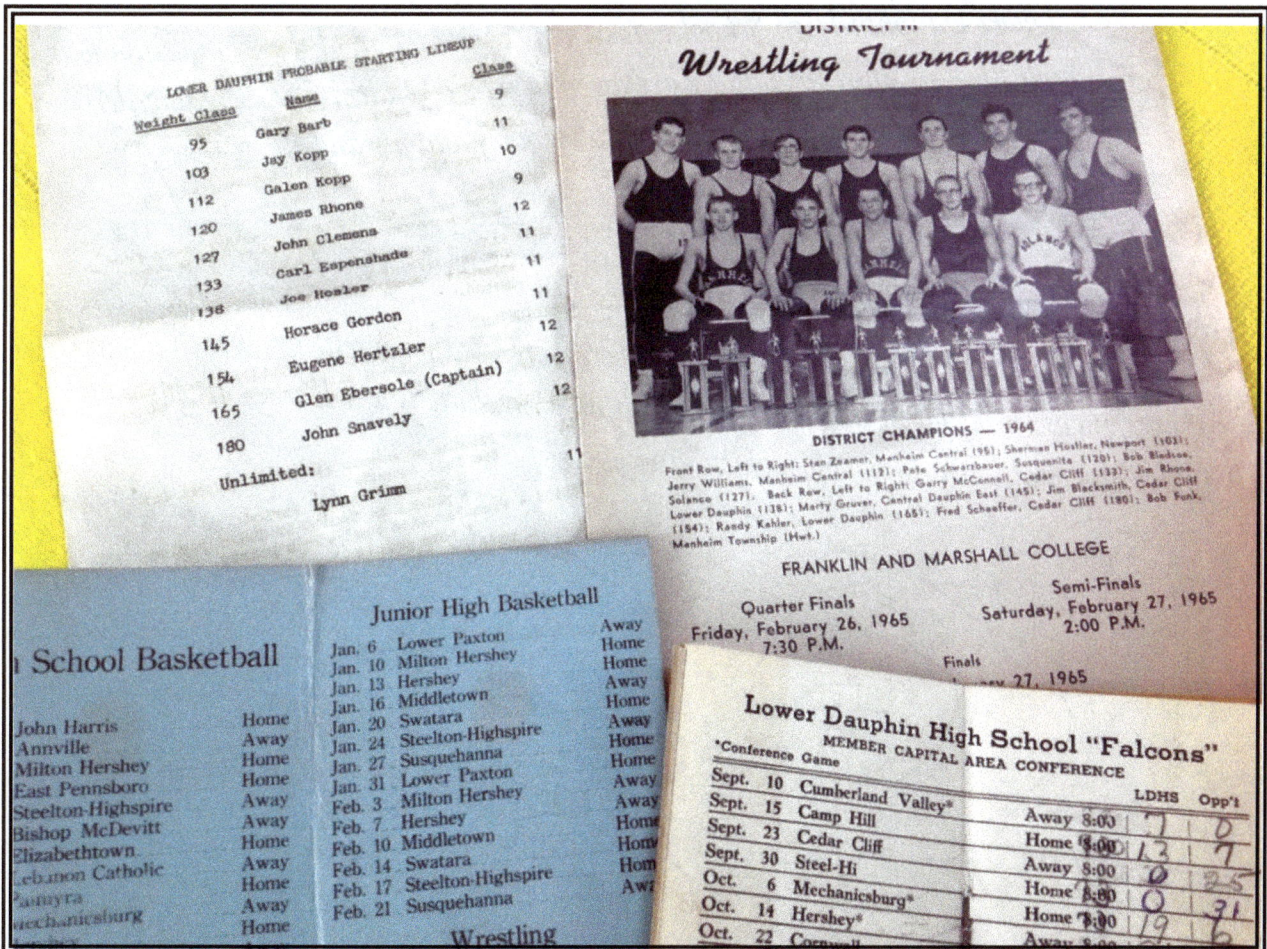

DISTRICT CHAMPIONS — 1964

Front Row, Left to Right: Stan Zeamer, Manheim Central (95); Sherman Hostler, Newport (103); Jerry Williams, Manheim Central (112); Pete Schwarzbauer, Susquenita (120); Bob Bledsoe, Solanco (127). Back Row, Left to Right: Garry McConnell, Cedar Cliff (133); Jim Rhone, Lower Dauphin (138); Marty Gruver, Central Dauphin East (145); Jim Blacksmith, Cedar Cliff (154); Randy Kahler, Lower Dauphin (165); Fred Schaeffer, Cedar Cliff (180); Bob Funk, Manheim Township (Hwt.)

Randy Umberger notes, "Being on the wrestling team made me a part of a community of parents, teachers, friends, and classmates who were there supporting me—and every wrestler— who ever stepped on the mat." In eighth grade, he remembers that "A decision to participate in junior high intramural wrestling would become one of the most important decisions I would ever make in my life. **It changed my world like nothing else could have.**"

What's wrestling?

"Like most wrestlers in our group, I attended a one-room schoolhouse where there were no organized sports available." (Many students had never heard of wrestling before attending LD.) [see page 85]

Three moves:

Lower Dauphin High School was so new, construction of the gymnasium was not finished until the middle of November. As a result, initial LD wrestlers were taught only three moves: two takedowns and a stand-up. [see page 45]

Getting burned:

"In those days, horsehair mats with canvas covers were used for wrestling. Well, I got a lot of mat burns on my face going the season with no wins. Later on, I learned it was more fun to give mat burns to my opponents." [see page 85]

HIGHLIGHTS OF THE MEETS

1960–1961: *(Record 6-4)*

Row 1: Martin Remsburg, Gary Barb, Jay Kopp, Galen Kopp, Jim Rhone, Don Deaven, John Clemens, Jerry Wampler.

Row 2: Coach Gelbaugh, Carl Espenshade, Joe Hosler, Horace Gordon, Eugene Hertzler, Glenn Ebersole, John Snavely, Fred Harner, Lynn Grimm, Coach Cassel

These young men had not all known one another, but they came together with powerful leadership as the First Wrestling Team of Lower Dauphin High School. Aside from the few who had spent their first years of high school in Hershey High School, *most of the team members had never wrestled before entering Lower Dauphin.*

As **Glenn Ebersole** recalls, "It helped that Coach Cassel made the transition as easy and fun as possible, with levity when needed. After he had been hired at Lower Dauphin, Cassel met with the Hershey High wrestlers to inform us that he would be our new wrestling coach. That personal contact confirmed my interest in leaving Hershey High and going to the new school for my senior year."

Still high on our successful championship football season, **many of us on the football team became the wrestling team** and recorded a most impressive initial wrestling season, achieving an extraordinary objective which continued through many years."

Among the noted wrestlers of the first year was **Frank Neiswender** who was the first of many LD wrestlers who would later return to coach at their Alma Mater. Frank remembered, "I will never forget how difficult it was for us to be accepted at the long-running Christmas tournament that year."

Randy Kahler had never seen a wrestling match when the football and wrestling coaches first talked him into coming out for wrestling after a successful football season his freshman year. As a sophomore, Kahler won Sectionals, Districts, Regionals, and competed at the State Finals. The coaches convinced him that if he did a good job he likely would be a four-year letter winner. And he was.

At the end of the first school year the *Falconaire* noted, "Under the excellent coaching of Mr. Cleon Cassel and his assistant Mr. Homer Gelbaugh, the Falcons displayed initiative to earn a name for the wrestling team that would be remembered for many years:

Freshmen: Jim Rhone, Randy Kahler, Gary Barb, and Don Deaven. Sophomores: Galen Kopp[1]. Juniors: Jay Kopp, Carl Espenshade, Joe Hosler, Lynn Grimm, Horace Gordon, and Fred Harner. Seniors: John Clemens, Eugene Hertzler, John Snavely, and Glenn Ebersole."

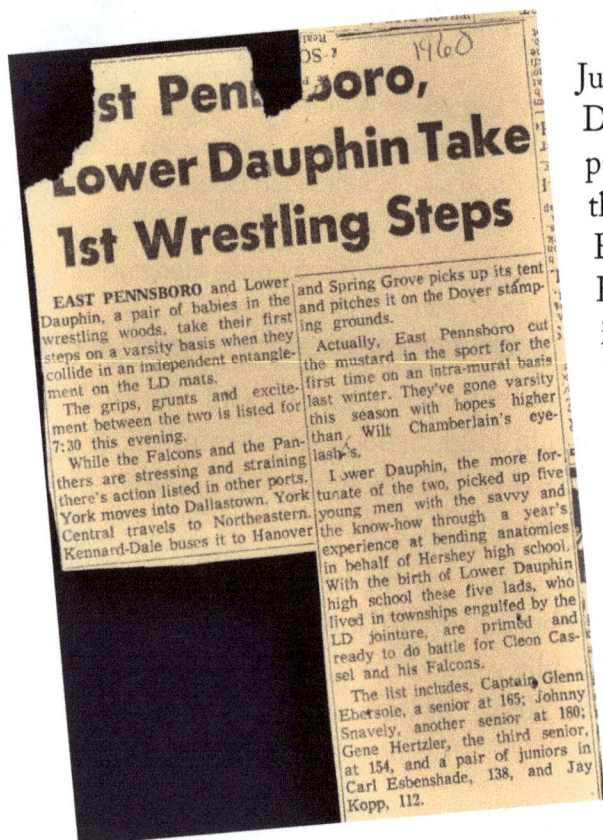

st Pen...boro,
...ower Dauphin Take
1st Wrestling Steps

EAST PENNSBORO and Lower Dauphin, a pair of babies in the wrestling woods, take their first steps on a varsity basis when they collide in an independent entanglement on the LD mats.

The grips, grunts and excitement between the two is listed for 7:30 this evening.

While the Falcons and the Panthers are stressing and straining there's action listed in other ports. York moves into Dallastown, York Central travels to Northeastern, Kennard-Dale buses it to Hanover

and Spring Grove picks up its tent and pitches it on the Dover stamping grounds.

Actually, East Pennsboro cut the mustard in the sport for the first time on an intra-mural basis last winter. They've gone varsity this season with hopes higher than Wilt Chamberlain's eyelash's.

Lower Dauphin, the more fortunate of the two, picked up five young men with the savvy and the know-how through a year's experience at bending anatomies in behalf of Hershey high school. With the birth of Lower Dauphin high school these five lads, who lived in townships engulfed by the LD jointure, are primed and ready to do battle for Cleon Cassel and his Falcons.

The list includes, Captain Glenn Ebersole, a senior at 165; Johnny Snavely, another senior at 180; Gene Hertzler, the third senior, at 154, and a pair of juniors in Carl Esbenshade, 138, and Jay Kopp, 112.

Seniors **Glenn Ebersole, John Snavely,** and Junior **Carl Espenshade** were members of the Lower Dauphin Championship Football team and also part of the successful Varsity Wrestling team just as they had been at Hershey High the previous year. Ebersole, Wrestling Captain, also had competed on Hershey High School football and wrestling teams in both his sophomore and junior years and had been the only junior starting as a first-team player on one of Hershey High's best football teams in 1959, competing in the South Penn Conference for the Championship.

The neophyte Lower Dauphin varsity wrestling team included four freshmen: **Jim Rhone, Randy Kahler, Gary Barb,** and **Don Deaven.** There was only one sophomore on the team, **Galen Kopp.** Juniors included **Jay Kopp, Carl Espenshade, Joe Hosler, Lynn Grimm, Horace Gordon,** and **Fred Harner.** Seniors dominated the heavyweight classes with **John Clemens, Eugene Hertzler, John Snavely,** and **Captain Glenn Ebersole.**

---

[1] Galen and Jay Kopp were the first brother combination to wrestle for L.D. This became a notable trend of LD wrestling with almost every team having wrestlers with at least one younger brother who first had been taught to wrestle by his older sibling.

Because the construction of the gymnasium would not be finished until the middle of November and sports practice space was limited to say the least, the wrestlers initially were taught only three moves: single leg, double leg, and stand-up. The coaches encouraged the wrestlers by telling them that while they didn't know much yet about wrestling, what they did know they would **know better** than anyone else! Ten days later this confidence-instilled team finished **third out of twenty** teams in the Harrisburg Novice Tournament and won the Junior Division over twenty other teams. All in their first year!!

The wrestlers and the coaches were in uncharted territory. They wasted no time and, in this first year, took second place in Sectionals, with Ebersole going undefeated in the season.

Captain Glenn Ebersole, Senior '61

Glenn Ebersole preparing to pin, '60-61 Season

The three experienced upperclassmen helped to institute a winning tradition at Lower Dauphin with a team that went 6 and 4 in its first year, competing against schools that had seasoned wrestling teams. LD garnered more than 40 wins. (For the next three and a half years LD Wrestling was successful both in its league and in competition throughout the state.)

Once the wrestling season was underway, Ebersole claimed 9 pins and one decision in dual meets.

All of the pins were made in the 1st and 2nd periods; three of the pins were won in the first minute; Glenn's only decision occurred in the Milton Hershey match. As of this writing and after all these many years, **Glenn still holds the PIAA State Record for the fastest pin @ :12.**

Ebersole's statistics: Tournament record: 4-1; Sectionals: 1st place; Districts: 2nd place; Regionals: Glenn's qualifying as a District finalist was forfeited due to a knee injury sustained in the District finals.

Lower Dauphin picked up five young men with the savy and the know-how through a year's experience at bending anatomies on behalf of Hershey High School. With the birth of **Lower Dauphin High School** these five lads, who lived in townships engulfed by the LD jointure were primed and ready to do battle for **Cleon Cassel** and his Falcons. This included **Captain Glenn Ebersole,** a senior of 165; **Johnny Snavely,** another senior at 189; **Gene Hertzler,** the third senior at 154, and a pair of juniors in **Carl Esbenshade,** 138, and **Jay Kopp,** 112.

Bill Favinger, Mechanicsburg 112 pounder, appears to be in a helpless position during his bout with Lower Dauphin's Jay Kopp. However, the Wildcat matman lasted out the period and gave Kopp a real test before bowing 3-2 in the third bout of last night's match won by Mechanicsburg, 30-12.

JUNIOR HIGH TEAM ROSTER		
(Original 1961 taken from a scrapbook)		
7th and 8th Grade Wrestling		
Weight	**Team I**	**Team II**
Heavy	*Jack Ruggles*	*Bob Plouse*
145 lbs.	*Randy Umberger*	*Barry Lehew*
127 lbs.	*Bill Stump*	*Joe Hill*
120 lbs.	*George Wagner*	*Barry Boykin*
112 lbs.	*David Scheaffer*	*Dennis Coffman*
103 lbs.	*James Sanders*	*Norman Orbaugh*
100 lbs.	*Paul Weaver*	*Norman Keim*
95 lbs.	*Barry Heffelfinger*	*Martin Remsburg*
90 lbs.	*Randy Riffey*	*Arthur Goodling*
85 lbs,	*Mike Remsberg*	*Dan Dorsheimer*
78 lbs.	*Ed Boyer*	*Steve Lower*
75 lbs.	*Bob Hess*	*Aaron Neidig*
Richard Lyter vs. the winner		

	LD	Opp.
East Pennsboro	51	14
Carlisle	36	15
Cumberland Valley	27	29
Hershey	28	20
Steel High	32	16
Central Dauphin	29	21
Milton Hershey	13	32
Mechanicsburg	13	26
Susquehanna	29	17
Cedar Cliff	17	25

What a great way to promote the sports record: Book Marks!

LD is sporting a 6-1 record, their only defeat a one point match to first place Cedar Cliff.

The tournament was represented by outstanding teams from all over the state. Individual LD champions were Jim Sanders (103) Carl Espenshade (138), Randy Kahler (165), and Richard Walters (180).

Other place winners were Bill Pinkerton, Jay Kopp, Galen Kopp, Jim Rhone, Lloyd Palmer, and Lynn Grimm.

This year's team has scored 217 points to their opponents 92. Cassel's top point-getters are Kopp, 7-0; Espenshade, 10-0; Kahler, 9-0-1 and Walters 10-0. Trailing with only one loss are Sanders, Galen Kopp, Palmer and Rhone. Most of the boys are underclassmen wit only three seniors. The balance is 3 juniors, 3 sophomores, and 3 freshmen.

Central Dauphin's Tournament included individual LD champions Jim Sanders, Carl Es;penshade, Randy Kahler, and Richard Walters.

Falcons Point For Tremendous Season In '62

Lower Dauphin matmen who compiled an enviable record last year have started the second year of competition with high hope of bettering last year's standings.

Coach Cleon Cassel's Falcons are sporting a 6-1 record this year and their only defeat was a one point 23-22 match to first place Cedar Cliff. Last year they finished fourth in the league and second in the sectional tournament.

The school wrestlers won the Central Dauphin Christmas tournament by defeating second place Dover by ten points. The tournament was represented by outstanding teams from all over the state. Individual LD champions were Jim Sanders, 103 lbs; Carl Espenshade, 138 lbs; Randy Kahler, 165 lbs and Richard Walters, 180 lbs. Other place winners were Bill Pinkerton, Jay Kopp, Galen Kopp, Jim Rhone, Lloyd Palmer and Lynn Grimm.

This year's team has scored 217 points to their opponents 92. Cassel's top point-getters are Kopp, 7-0; Espenshade, 10-0; Kahler, 9-0-1 and Walter, 10-0. Trailing with only one loss are Sanders, Galen Kopp, Palmer and Rhone. Most of the boys are underclassmen with only three seniors. The balance are 3 sophomores and 3 freshmen.

Also encouraging is the outstanding record of the Junior Varsity team with a 7-0 record. Seven of the JV boys have already seen varsity action. Undefeated are Aaron Neidig, 88; Dale Berkebile, 95-103; Jay Brandt, 112; Oscar Clair, 127; Al Sutcliffe, 138; Randy Umberger, 154 and Bob Plouse, unlimited.

With experience from the returning varsity boys and added depth from the JV team, Cassel can look forward next year to a much stronger team and a tremendous season. Lower Dauphin also has an outstanding Jr. High Intramural program conducted by Jack Goepfert and Frank Capitani which resulted in 6 novice tournament champions in the Jr. Division.

Goodbye to horses:
LD originally had an old horsehair wrestling mat. The superintendent said that if more than 20 boys showed up for the first wrestling practice, he'd request a new mat. According to Coach Cassel, Mr. Emerich "walked into the gymnasium and there were more than 150 boys!" LD bought the new mat which confirmed a firm foundation for a fledgling sport. By year two, 240 students (high school and junior high) came out for the sport.
[see page 37]

Loyal fans:
Those early years were closely followed by a huge fan base, whether at home or on the road. At one match overcrowded fans were seated on the mat itself! At another sold-out match the gymnasium was quickly packed and LD filled the auditorium with people who bought tickets to watch the match on TV. At another match LD filled every nook and cranny with 1600 paid admissions and the cars "backed up" to the surrounding streets. [see page 74]

Barbed wire in use:
Many early matches were sell-outs. At one point barbed wire was used on the lower side of C-Wing to prevent fans from climbing onto the roof to watch matches through the gym windows. [see page 70]

The Second Year: 1961–1962 (Record 10-3-1)

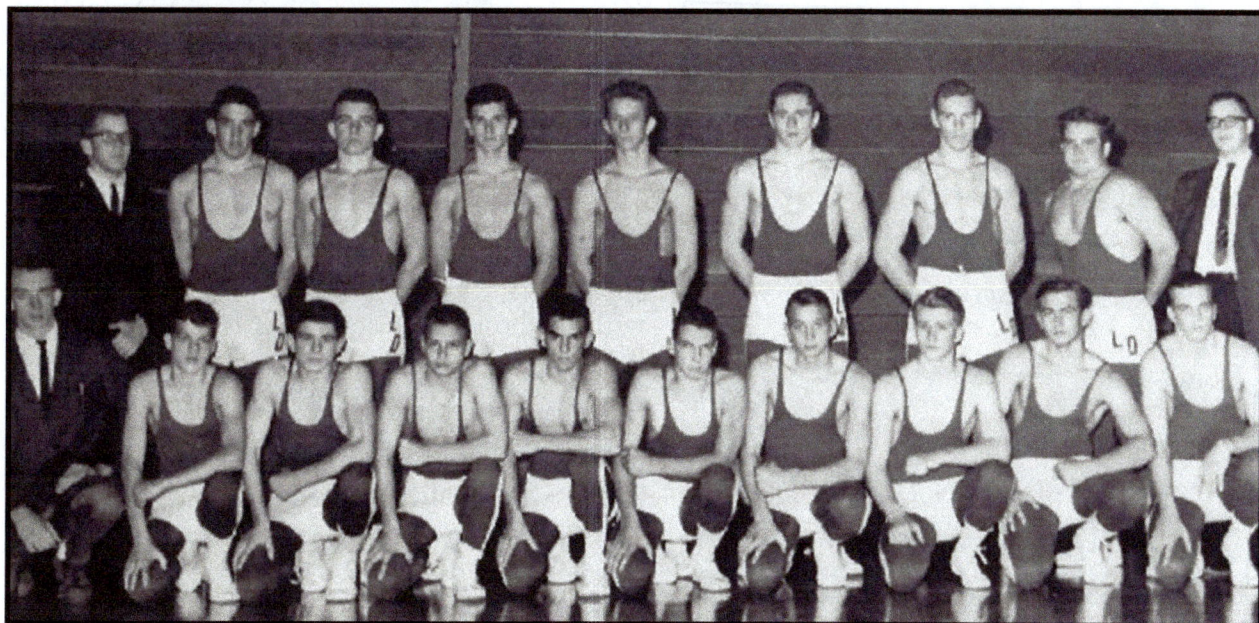

Row 1: Joe Hosler, Bill Pinkerton, Jim Sanders, Gary Barb, Jay Kopp, Galen Kopp, Pete Palmer, Jim Rhone, Donald Deaven, Carl Espenshade.

Row 2: Coach Cassel, John Hutton, Randy Umberger, Frank Neiswender, Carl Patrick, Randy Kahler, Rich Walters, Lynn Grimm, Coach Gelbaugh.

Returnees included Gary Barb (103), Jay Kopp (112), Galen Kopp (120), Jim Rhone (133), Carl Espenshade (145), Randy Kahler, and Lynn Grimm, heavyweight.

Entering its second year, LD wrestling had earned its groundswell of support, and 240 students came out for the team (counting both high school and junior high school) and wrestling quickly became Lower Dauphin's biggest sport. The Superintendent ordered several additional wrestling mats to accommodate the explosion of interest and its success. Our main goal this year was to become noted around the state. Central Dauphin admitted us to their Christmas Tournament at the last minute when one of their experienced teams dropped out. **We won the team title to the surprise of all except ourselves.**

According to the *Evening News,* "Lower Dauphin matmen compiled an enviable record, … finishing fourth in the league and second in the sectional tournament, with most of the team underclassmen…outstanding record of the JV team with a 7-0 record, seven of whom have seen varsity action." For example, this emerging powerhouse was handily taking on established schools such as Camp Hill, in this case defeating them, 35-8.

The goal for wrestling's second year, according to Coach Cassel, was to become established around the state—and the guys were ready and eager to travel to get as much experience as possible. While the "regular season" was already determined, Coach Cassel wanted his team to wrestle in tournaments to gain more capability at every skill level. Thus, when a last

49

An Invitational Wrestling Tournament

(Note the now familiar names of wrestlers, cheerleaders, and spectators who signed the program.)

minute invitation came from Central Dauphin to compete in their Christmas Tournament, Lower Dauphin grabbed the chance, entered the tournament and **won the team title.**

The Harrisburg *Patriot News,* March 12, 1962, noted, "Schoolboy wrestling in the Harrisburg area must now definitely be classified with the best in the state. ...it is no longer in the novice stage. ...(and) the junior high school wrestling programs in most schools are starting to take shape, which means that we will have an even better quality of high school wrestling in this league in a few years."

Physical conditioning is the basis for wrestling as attested to by Coach Cassel, "What helps us is that we are in better shape than most of our opponents," explaining the importance of conditioning....

"We practice every night to go three full 15-minute periods. That makes the 2-2-2 regular bout time seem like nothing. ...Endurance is what a wrestler must thrive on, and the only way to get in shape is to be able to go over the limit of a match by working at it in practice. We also spend a lot of time on push-up exercises since we are strictly **a power club who uses mainly arms rather than the legs."**

The *Sunday Patriot News* summarized this well, "LD had the balance and power to sweep last night's tournament with a total of 69 points. Cassel's Club, who picked up four individual championship titles and 3 consolation crowns, also had sufficient runner-up and fourth places to move into the title ranking. **Jim Sanders, Carl Espenshade, Randy Kahler,** and **Dick Walters** won champion titles; consolation winners included **Bill Pinkerton, Jay** and **Galen Kopp.**

The team took first place in Central Dauphin's Christmas Tournament with a total of 69 points, crushing their opponents, then losing in only one weight class to powerhouse Cedar Cliff—and by only ONE point, and tying with Central Dauphin.

The Christmas Tournament trophy was LD's first in this competition.

On the following page are excerpts from a 1962 interview with the Coach at the end of the second year in response to *The Harrisburg Patriot,* when asked if boys from "farm areas make better wrestlers..."

"…This can't be true; the team with the longest winning streak is from Long Island. …if a boy is not strong but is willing to work, we can give him physical strength. …we work more stand-up, shoulders away from the mat…arm against arm type of wrestling which is not as dangerous (for a pin). We attempt to figure what a boy can do and build around it. …our style is 90% from the waist up.

"This team is especially wonderful. I have never heard the word 'No.' It is always, 'I'll try' or 'Yes,' the only words they use in reply. We also carry a card on all boys in the league—how strong they are, how nervous before a match, do they ride on their legs… We try to know the opponents as well as their coaches.

"We also have situation drills in which we tell our wrestlers to take ten minutes to overcome a particular move.…

"**Co-Captain Carl Espenshade '62** held a 9-3 Season Record and was the Central Dauphin Christmas Tournament Champion. He later coached wrestling and then served the sport as a wrestling official. Another notable LD wrestler is **Frank Neiswender '63** who was the first of many Lower Dauphin wrestlers who later returned to coach at their Alma Mater."

Lower Dauphin, being new and untried, had a difficult time finding tournaments in which to participate because the school was not yet a proven. Coach Cassel gives much credit to **Athletic Director Jack Goepfert** who swept the state seeking places for LD in tournaments.

"Lower Dauphin …to sweep…with a total of 69 points…down to the wire…picked up four individual championship titles and three consolation crowns…sufficient runner-up and fourth place points to move into the title room."

The crowning moment of the season was Sophomore Randy Kahler's winning Sectionals, Districts, and Regionals—and going all the way to State finals. Randy was only one of many LD students who had never seen a wrestling match

Carl Espenshade using a cradle on a wrestler from Hershey. The referee is about to call the pin.

when he was given the promise that if he did a good job, he likely could become a four-letter winner.

Indeed, he did, making a major mark for LD Wrestling.

A later issue of the newspaper reported, "Coach Cassel's Falcons are sporting a 6-1 record to date and their only defeat was a 23-22 match to first place Cedar Cliff."

Co-Captain Jay Kopp '62 (top) 10-2 Season Record; Sectional Tournament Runner-up and Champion

Kahler's loss at States (recall that Randy was only a sophomore in the second year of a new wrestling program!) came through a point loss for stalling in the first period, followed by a scoreless second period. In the third period his opponent escaped for a point and took Randy down for a 4-0 advantage. Kahler finished the season 17-2-1.

Lower Dauphin Cops Central Dauphin's Wrestling Tourney

LOWER DAUPHIN had the balance and the power to sweep the Central Dauphin Invitational Wrestling tournament last night with a total of 69 points.

It was a nip and tuck battle right down to the wire with Dover, a member of the York County circuit, furnishing the Falcons trouble.

Cleon Cassel's club, who picked up four individual championship titles and three consolation crowns, also had sufficient runnerup and fourth place points to move into the title room.

JIM SANDERS, 95; Carl Espenshade, 138; Randy Kohler, 165; and Dick Walters, 180, were the Falcons who took the championship titles. Consolation winners were Bill Pinkerton, 95; Jay Kopp, 112; and Galen Kopp, 120.

Lon Senft's Dover team could manage only one individual champion in Steve Bower at 154. Dick Remmey picked up the consolation 127-pound title for the York County team.

Philipsburg's Ed Myers, 127-pounder, was voted the Outstanding Wrestler in the tournament by the eight coaches. Myers went through the two-day meet in undefeated fashion. He opened with a first round pin win over Central Dauphin's Mike Mellinger in .56 seconds. In his second match he scored a 7-2 decision over Gary Shenk, Elizabethtown. In his championship bout he decisioned Jim Rhone, Lower Dauphin, 6-1.

It was also during these early years that Lower Dauphin began its tradition of garnering huge fan support, both at home and on the road. Many of the same adults who had doubted the team in the beginning became the sport's most avid fans. As noted, "The team and its coaches never felt like they were on the road because of the large (later huge) number of fans who traveled to support and to cheer on their team." Falcon fans continued this practice for years—and with most home games a sell-out.

More than sixty years later, Lower Dauphin wrestling is as exciting as ever, with wrestling team that has created a strong winning tradition and a "family-like" alumni wrestlers' pack.

RNAL— THURSDAY, JANUARY 25, 1962 —THE PRESS AND JOURNAL

Lower Dauphin Wrestling Team Compiles Enviable Record In League Competition

VARSITY SQUAD:

Row 1: Bill Pinkerton, Jim Sanders, Jay Kopp (Captain), Galen Kopp, Pete Palmer.

Row 2: Jim Rhone, Carl Espenshade (Co-captain), Frank Neiswender, Carl Patrick, Randy Kahler.

Row 3: Harold Shellenhamer, Mike Remsburg, Dick Walters, Gary Painter, Calvin Barb, Steve Lower.

Back Row: Cleon Cassel, coach, and Homer Gelbaugh, assistant coach.

    (Not pictured are Jon Hutton and Lynn Grimm.)

In Memory of Jay Kopp '62

Jay Kopp and his brother Galen were the first set of brothers to wrestle for L.D.

This became a notable trend of LD wrestling with almost every team having wrestlers with at least one younger brother who first had been taught to wrestle by his older sibling.

Jay wrestled for LDHS during the years of 1960 to 1962, wrestling in the 112 weight class, and was also Co-Captain during his senior year.

We are so very proud of you, Jay, and your wrestling years at LD.

We will always love you.

Ann '65

1961 – 62   Record   10 –3 –1
Row 1   Joe Hosler, Bill Pinkerton, Jim Sanders, Gary Barb, Jay Kopp, Galen Kopp, Pete Palmer, Jim Rhone, Donald Deaven, Carl Espenshade   Row 2   Coach Cassel, John Hutton, Randy Umberger, Frank Neiswender, Carl Patrick, Randy Kahler, Rich Walters, Lynn Grimm, Coach Gelbaugh

Always a FULL HOUSE at the events!

The Third Year: 1962–1963 *(Record 12-2)*

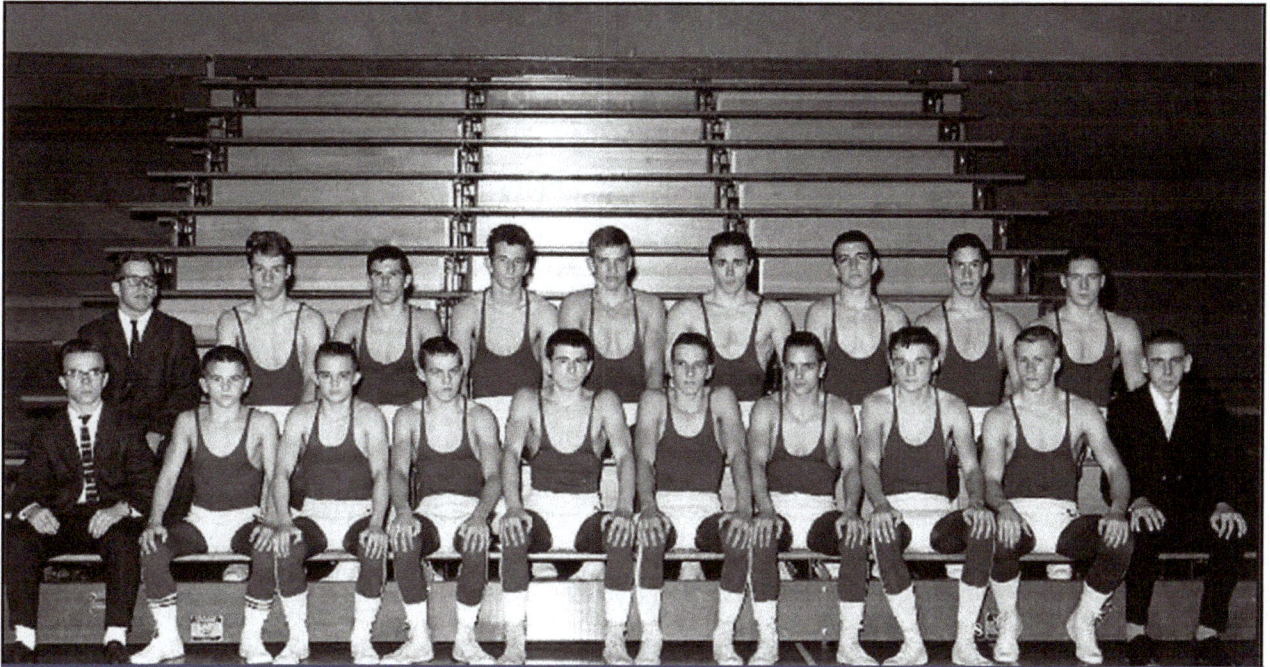

Row 1: Bob Hess, Buster Shellenhamer, Bill Pinkerton, Jim Sanders, Galen Kopp, Gary Barb, Dennis Neidig, Jim Rhone.

Row 2: Coach Cassel, Al Sutcliffe, Frank Neiswender, Carl Patrick, Jim Hertzler, Randy Kahler, Randy Umberger, Jim Erb, Jack Ruggles.

The Mechanicsburg Adventure

According to Coach Cassel, "When the team arrived at the high school, a police escort met us. We were told to follow the driver around to the back of the school because the crowd in the front was too large to navigate. Police officers held the crowd back while we were rushed off the bus and led into a back door before the crowd could force their way into the building. Inside the entrance in the front, there was a crowd in the line for tickets and hundreds of people were actively trying to force open the doors to gain entry to the gymnasium.

"Later, the crowd did break the doors off the hinges and the host school had to chain the gymnasium doors from the inside. There was not a single square inch of open space, not even in front of the team benches that spectators had been permitted to use! Some spectators were even sitting on the wrestling mat itself! The wrestlers had to walk around eight to ten rows of spectators just to get on the mat to wrestle. When wrestlers were forced out of bounds during the match itself, they often landed on the spectators. We tried to ignore the crowd and just do what we had come for. We won the match and the league championship."

Ann Landis Kopp remembers the evening when she had talked her mother into taking her to this wrestling match at Mechanicsburg where the gym was jammed full. Police were turning away cars filled with disappointed fans. *The Patriot*, December 18, 1962 noted: "Mechanicsburg was handed its first Harrisburg Area loss since the inception of the Regional Wrestling League, as Lower Dauphin upset the Wildcats 23-15 last night at Mechanicsburg. Cleon Cassel's Lower Dauphin Matmen swept through four of the first five matches to the surprise of the Wildcats. (Mechanicsburg had won 35 straight since having a previous 49-match streak stopped by Manheim Central in 1960.) Later Jay noted that this match was the beginning of a long run of wins for LD.

The Patriot News — In Section 2 of the Harrisburg Area Tourney, "Lower Dauphin appears to have the over-all power to dominate the division. This club has fine individual strength. The bulk of it will be generated from Harold Shellenhamer (6-0); Jim Sanders (7-1); Galen Kopp (5-1); Jim Rhone (6-0); and Randy Kahler (9-2)."

The Wildcats gained some measure of revenge when Steve Sauve decisioned **Randy Kahler,** Lower Dauphin's 1962 PIAA runner-up."

Continuing to improve, the team reached third place in the Harrisburg Area Wrestling Conference. JVs enjoyed an 11-3 season with ten returning varsity the following year.

The Middletown Press and Journal, Winter/Spring 1963: "Last evening fans saw one of the most exciting and spectacular championship contests in the history of the district…a thriller to the last second. **Bill Pinkerton** was the sensation of the tournament, in command of his entire match. **Galen Kopp** easily won his preliminary match and his final match with **Lee Hershey,** the defending district and regional champion; this was one of the outstanding matches. **Jim Rhone** came from behind for two sensational victories in the semi-final and final matches. **Randy Umberger** won a 4-1 first round decision. Pinkerton, Kopp, and Rhone will enter finals."

From an unidentified newspaper, Spring 1963: "At least 2500 wrestling fans jammed the Steelton-Highspire Gymnasium to watch the District 3 contest. LD sent six contenders. Every match was a thriller up to the last second." One example was the 95 lb. weight class between Newport's Sherman Hostler and Lower Dauphin's **Harold Shellenhammer. Jim Rhone** came from behind for two sensational victories in the semi-final and final matches.

The Evening News, December 18, 1962
The third year of wrestling included the last matches LD would lose for the next three and a half years, with more than 40 wins. In this 1962-63 season the team began the winning streak which continued until the end of 1966. One of the most spectacular, according to Coach Cassel, was the match with Mechanicsburg, one many of us will never forget.

At the end of the second period the score was tied 4-4 after two periods; in the third period Rhone clinched a 6-5 decision. **Bill Pinkerton** was also a District Champion.

The Fourth Year: 1963–1964 *(Record 14-0)*

Row 1: Bill Pinkerton, Jim Sanders, Buster Shellenhamer, Bob Hess, Ed Neidig.

Row 2: Norm Updegraff, Gary Barb, Brian Stoner, Dennis Neidig, Jim Rhone, John Williams.

Row 3: Stu Wagner, Randy Kahler, Randy Umberger, Jack Ruggles, Bob Plouse.

Early in the season a neighboring newspaper noted, "The ten returning lettermen have among them six sectional champions, three district champions, one regional and one state runner-up."
Bravo!

In this 1963-64 season Lower Dauphin began its **40-match winning streak,** which ran through the end of 1966. LD began the season with a **32-16** dumping of arch rival Cedar Cliff. (While this match had no bearing on league standings, nonetheless it was LD's **first win** over defending champion Cedar Cliff, who before this year had inflicted two straight one-point defeats on the Falcons.)

This victory gave the LD team standing which was a morale boost, and led to a record 13 straight wins, including decisive wins over both Hershey and Milton Hershey. The team went undefeated (the only undefeated team in the Greater Harrisburg area to do so) and captured the Division I title of the Harrisburg Area Wrestling League.

The team had **FIVE individually undefeated wrestlers**, including **Ed Neidig, Harold Shellenhamer, Jim Sanders, Jim Rhone,** and **Randy Umberger.**

Undefeated LD captured the Division I title of the Harrisburg Area Wrestling League with the Falcon matmen dumping arch rival Cedar Cliff 32-16, as noted above. **This was LD's first win over the defending champions,** who had inflicted two straight one-point defeats on the Falcons. This victory led to a **record 13 straight wins,** including decisive wins over Hershey (**35-10**) and Milton Hershey (**29-12**). We also had five champions from the Upper Darby Christmas Wrestling Tournament: **Bill Pinkerton, Jim Sanders, Harold Shellenhamer, Jim Rhone,** and **Bobby Hess.**

Individual Sectional Champions this year were **Bobby Hess (95), Harold Shellenhamer (103), Jim Sanders (112), Jim Rhone (138), Randy Kahler (165),** and **Randy Umberger (180).** District Champions were Rhone and Kahler, both seniors, with runner-up Umberger, a junior. The Central Pennsylvania Old Timers' Athletic Association named Cleon Cassel "Coach of the Year" for his outstanding work in leading the Falcons to a perfect **14-0** record this season.

The season's printed wrestling program added an incentive to recruit wrestlers by including information and photos of champions to date: (1) **Glenn Ebersole,** 10-0 season record: Sectional Tournament Champion; District Runner-up and (2) former captains and co-captains in action, including **Carl Espenshade** (Co-Captain, 61-62), **Jay Kopp** (Co-Captain, 61-62), **Galen Kopp** (Captain, 62-63), and a half page newspaper coverage on L.D. Wrestling.

Jack Ruggles (on top)

Also the victory gave the team a great confidence boost, and led to a record 13 straight wins, including decisive wins over Hershey and Milton Hershey as well as boasting the **five champions** from the Upper Darby Christmas Wrestling Tournament named on adjacent page. (*The Falconaire*, 1964, narrative by John Neidinger)

60

Six men remained undefeated throughout the season: **Ed Neidig, Jim Sanders, Harold Schellenhamer, Jim Rhone, Randy Umberger,** and **Randy Kahler,** who had been undefeated since his first match.

"Lower Dauphin won **Six Sectional Championships: Randy Kahler, Randy Umberger, Harold Shellenhamer, Jim Rhone, Bobby Hess,** and **Jim Sanders.**"

As reported by Charley Frey, well-known sportswriter for the *Patriot-News,* "Umberger, the husky LD 180-pounder, was the only wrestler in the two-day show to go through three matches with consecutive falls. He won his title with a 3:24 flip of Dick D'Anna of Hershey. In the semi-finals he pinned George Stauffer, Palmyra, in 2:57 and he opened his preliminary round on Friday evening with a 5:10 pin over Wayne Witter, CV."

(L to R from back row) Umberger, Kahler, Rhone, Sanders, Shellenhamer and Hess. Regionals included these L.D. Sectional Champions.

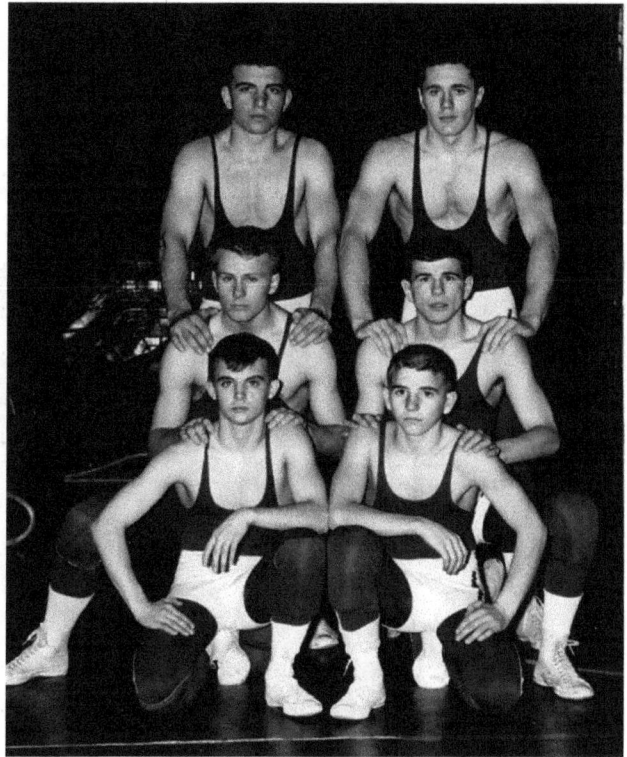

Left, Randy Kahler, Sectional Champion

(Who remembers that Stoner had scored the big upset of the tourney on Friday night when he defeated top-seeded Al Hepford, 3-2 in overtime?) While there was no official team title, LD walked off with the honors, having compiled 87 points. Another point of LD history is that in the total of 83 bouts during the two days, only 17 pins were recorded with LD registering six of them. We also took **three sectional second place wins: Bill Pinkerton** (120); **Brian Stoner** (133); and **Jack Ruggles** (unlimited).

The Falcons sent two contenders (Kahler and Rhone) to **States** where both were semi-finalists. Rhone lost in finals by a very close decision and Kahler lost a highly contested referee's decision that continued to be debated for years.

Pennsylvania Interscholastic Athletic Association

DISTRICT III

Wrestling Tournament

DISTRICT CHAMPIONS — 1963

Front Row, Left to Right, Sherman Hostler, Newport, (95), Bill Pinkerton, Lower Dauphin (103), Bernie Lomman, Cedar Cliff (112); Lee Hershey, Manheim Central (120); Don Hollinger, Manheim Central (127); Jim Rhone, Lower Dauphin (133); Back Row, Left to Right: Jere Herr, Penn Manor (138); Steve Peters, Newport (145); Jim Blacksmith, Cedar Cliff (154); Steve Suave, Mechanicsburg (165); Roy Miller, Manheim Central (180); Glenn Metzler, Manheim Central (Hwt,).

STEELTON–HIGHSPIRE HIGH SCHOOL

Quarter Finals	Semi Finals
Friday, February 28, 1964	Saturday, February 29, 1964
7:30 p.m.	2:00 p.m.

Finals
Saturday, February 29, 1964
7:30 p.m.

OFFICIAL PROGRAM — 15 Cents

Undefeated!

RONALD CRUYS, 15, son of Caroline Cruys, Industrial Engineering secretary, has ended the 1963-1964 wrestling season undefeated. Ron attends Lower Dauphin Junior-Senior High School. Also shown is Jayvee Coach Heistrand. Ron wrestles in the 95-pound weight class.

Caroline Cruys Proud To Admit That She Knows A Wrestler

Although he has been wrestling only three years, Ronald Cruys, 15, made it through the 1963-1964 season undefeated. Ron, who attends Lower Dauphin Junior-Senior High School, is the son of Industrial Engineering Secretary Caroline Cruys. He wrestles in the 95-pound class.

His interest in wrestling began in junior high when the varsity coach, Mr. Cassel, suggested that he try out for the wrestling team. Ron's dream is the dream of all high school matmen: to win the sectional, district and regional wrestling tournaments that lead to the state championship.

Caroline has been with TRW for a year and a half. As a conscientious mother with a serious scholastic wrestler for a son, she finds that attending matches adds up to a lot of evenings away from home.

Cruys Clips

Ron Cruys, 103 pounds, left, and Lester Ratcliff, 95, are pictured in a stand up. Cruys, incidentally, just won the Sectionals and will wrestle at the Farm Show this weekend. The stand up is the move used to get up from the mat, and many variations come from this move. The inside leg is used as a "brace" to keep the wrestler from being pulled down. The elbow is also used to "loosen" the man up.

A Big Win for LD (below) at Williamsport

Lower Dauphin Capture

Defending Champ Hughesville 2nd; Millionaires 6th

Lower Dauphin captured the Williamsport High School Invitational Wrestling Tournament title, lock, stock and barrel last night with 89 points as four boys won individual championships and two others finished close seconds.

Hughesville, the defending champion, placed second with a total of 60 points, and Montgomery won the third place trophy by tallying 45 points. Rounding out the top six were Warrior Run with 38, Danville 36 and host Williamsport 33.

Following in the footsteps of the Millionaires were Loyalsock 32, Lewisburg 25, Montoursville and South Williamsport 24, and Mifflinburg 19. At the bottom of the pack were Milton with 18, Lake Lehman and Dallas 15, Muncy 12 and Wyalusing five.

Milton's Denny Reich received the tournament's outstanding wrestler award for his performance in the 127-pound class. He reached yesterday's semifinals by routing Wayne Dangle of Loyalsock, 16-0, and he won his quarterfinal match by decisioning Vollman of Montgomery, 6-2.

Reich gained the finals by decisioning Lake Lehman's Mark McDermott, 5-3, and he won the 127-pound title by outpointing Bill Pinkerton from Lower Dauphin, 3-1, in an extremely close match.

Lower Dauphin's first winner was Ron Cruys at 95 pounds. He outfought Millionaire Lenny Carson, 11-6, after edging Roger Campbell from Muncy, 8-7, in the afternoon matches.

This was the first varsity loss for Carson in two years of competition. Last year he won the Invitational 88-pound title by pinning all his opponents, and he emerged as the District Four 88-pound champ later in the season. Carson had reached this year's finals by virtue of a forfeit and two falls.

Harold Shellenhamer, Lower Dauphin unbeaten, won his title by beating Hughesville's Dave Snyder at 112. Snyder knocked off Jerry Gold, a returning champion from Warrior Run, in the afternoon via a 6-3 count.

Lower Dauphin's Jim Sanders, another unbeaten, knocked off Big Green 120-pounder Denny Shultz, 4-1. Sanders gave Cherry

grappler Mike Bell a rough 7-0 defeat in the semifinals to gain his crack at the title.

In a battle of the unbeatens at 180, Randy Umberger, another Lower Dauphin standout, snapped Lancer Bob Bower's current streak, 2-0, in a hard fought battle. Bower had reached the final session by posting three tournament pins. He also was a defending champion from last year's inaugural.

Jim Peterman from Hughesville routed Warrior Run's John Gast, another returning title-holder. Peterman won the 165-pound match 10-4, and he had earned his shot by recording two earlier falls and a shutout decision.

Loyalsock's 133-pound Charley Brewer was the only returning champ to repeat his past performance. Brewer ruined Red Raider Gary McQuay's hopes for an upset by beating him, 5-3. He advanced to the finals by pinning Reese Finn of Dallas in 45 seconds of the second during the semifinals.

Ernie Lundy of Montoursville won the 145-pound title by decisioning Jim Wallace of Danville in the closest match of the evening. He pulled it out with a 4-0 overtime victory after the two ended the regular match in a 3-3 deadlock.

Rodney Watts, the Montgomery 103-pounder, decisioned Lower Dauphin's Ed Neidig in another extremely close battle. Watts captured a 2-0 victory over Neidig, a previously undefeated grappler.

Williamsport lost all hopes for an individual champion when Danville's Ted Thilly outpointed Flip Lamade at 154, 6-2. Thilly entered the finals with two falls and an impressive 11-0 decision.

INDIVIDUAL CHAMPIONS—First row, left to right, Shiffler (Lewisburg) 88, Ron Cruys (Lower Dauphin) 95, Rod Watts (Montgomery) 103, Harold Shellenhammer (Lower Dauphin) 112 and Jim Sanders (Lower Dauphin) 120. Second row, Dale Reich (Milton) 127, Charley Brewer (Loyalsock) 138, Ernie L Thilly (Danv man (Hughe (Lower Dauph Williamsport)

Tourney Results

LD winners in the Tournament included **Ron Cruys, Jim Sanders, Harold Shellenhamer,** and **Randy Umberger** and runners-up Ed Neidig and Bill Pinkerton.

The Fifth Year: 1964–1965 (Record 14-0)

Row 1. Ron Cruys, Ed Neidig, Harold Shellenhammer, Jim Sanders, Bill Pinkerton, Dennis Coffman.

Row 2. Coach Cleon Cassel, Marty Remsburg, Frank Petroski, Mike Dean, Bill Crick, Errol Wagner, Randy Umberger, Bob Plouse.

During this season:

▸ **Randy Umberger** pinned 12 of his 14 opponents and **Jim Sanders** had only 9 points scored against him during the entire season.

▸ At the Williamsport Christmas tournament, LD's first winner was **Ron Cruys** at 95 pounds over Lenny Carson who had not lost a match in two years. **Harold Shellenhamer,** at 112 and unbeaten, over Dave Snyder; **Jim Sanders,** another unbeaten, knocked off 120-pounder Denny Shultz. In the battle of the unbeaten at 180, **Randy Umberger** snapped Bob Bowers' current streak.

▸ "Pressure Type Wrestling," *Press and Journal*, January 21, 1965. In an interview (about the Christmas tournament) Coach Cassel responded to a question from the reporter, "Jim had his ribs broken in football this fall and he couldn't wrestle at all until his physician gave his permission. We got the okay the day of the tournament. Jim had had no workout . . . no practice of any kind prior to this. We taped up his ribs, and he won 6-2, 8-3, 7-9, and 3-1 in the finals, missed being named Outstanding Westler of the tournament by one vote."

▸ The headline on the sports page of the *Williamsport Sun-Gazette* on December 31, 1964, shouted Lower Dauphin Captures WHS Mat Invitational: "Lower Dauphin won the Williamsport High School Invitational Wrestling Tournament—lock, stock, and barrel with 89 points, as four LD wrestlers won individual championships and two others finished close seconds. LD Falcon winners were Cruys, Shellenhamer, Sanders, and Umberger."

▸ From the Middletown *Press and Journal,* January 14, "…the Blue Raiders received a trouncing to the tune of 35-12 at the hands of a powerful Lower Dauphin squad as the Falcons swept through the first seven bouts to take a 30-0 lead. **Ron Cruys, Harold Shellenhamer, Jim Sanders, Frank Petroski,** and **Randy Umberger** pinned, while **Ed Neidig, Bill Pinkerton,** and **Jay Ebersole** decisioned.

▸ From a newspaper account, February 11, 1965: "LD overcame Mechanicsburg's team balance as the Falcons clipped the Wildcats, 31-14, to win the Division I title for the second straight year. A capacity crowd of 1,447 cash customers jammed the Mechanicsburg gym to see the two unbeatens tangle. **Ron Cruys** opened at 95 with a 4-0 decision over Bill Baker who had entered the bout with a perfect 13-0 mark. Then, a first period fall by Ed Neidig (103) gave the Falcons a shot in the arm. **Harold Shellenhamer** came from behind in the second period to win 7-2. **Bill Pinkerton** (usually wrestling at 127) at 120 took a 6-0 decision. **Jim Sanders** (typically 120 lbs.) scored a 9-0 decision at 127. (The sportswriter added, "Sanders who was out of school several days this week with a virus, didn't show any effects of it last night.") **Bill Crick** at 154 came from behind to win 3-1. **Randy Umberger** at 180 (with a record of 17-0 going in) "sewed it up for keeps" with a 4:23 pin. **Bob Plouse** scored an upset over previously undefeated Mefford, who had tied it at 4-4, but Plouse won on riding time."

District 3 Qualifiers

Sectionals - Randy Umberger scored three impressive wins by way of falls. Other winners included the following: **Ron Cruys** opened at 95 with a 3-1 decision, gaining a reversal midway in the second period while **Neidig** gained a first-period takedown in a 4-0 win. An early take-down, a third-period reversal and riding time gave **Shellenhamer** a 5-0 victory. **Jim Sanders** scored a 9-0 decision, then an 8-0 shut-out. **Bill Pinkerton** won 4-3 over Spike Temple of Mechanicsburg. **Jay Ebersole** was 9-6 over Carmany of Mechanicsburg.

Districts - Sanders had no trouble, chalking up a 9-0 victory, becoming the third LD wrestler to move to state competition after winning regionals. He holds the **school scoring record** for all four years with 186 points in 49 dual meets and has had only nine points scored against him all season.[*] Also in the District Finals **Pinkerton** won 4-0 and **Randy Umberger** won in an overtime referee's decision.

On the right, Jim Sanders '65

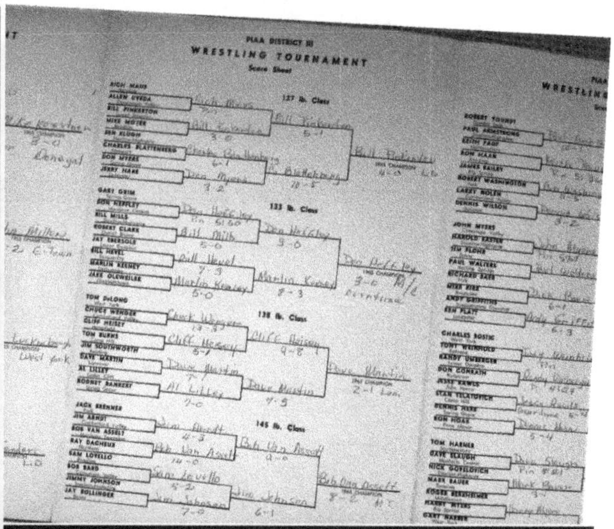

Bill Pinkerton '65

[*] According to Coach Cassel, "Jim has three of the quickest takedown moves I've ever seen . . . This bested even the outstanders—Randy Kahler, who had made it twice to states, and Jim Rhone who made the big one once."

Highly regarded Coach Bob Craig of Cedar Cliff noted that Lower Dauphin had the greatest High School wrestling team he had ever seen after the team scored 492 points to their opponents' 156 points. Further, only one LD varsity starter was pinned during the entire season.

Years later Coach Cassel noted, "The 2006 and 2007 teams in many ways remind me of LD's 1964 and 1965 teams when the Falcons dominated everyone by winning every tournament and had the longest winning streak in the state—45 wins!"

It wasn't all wrestling!

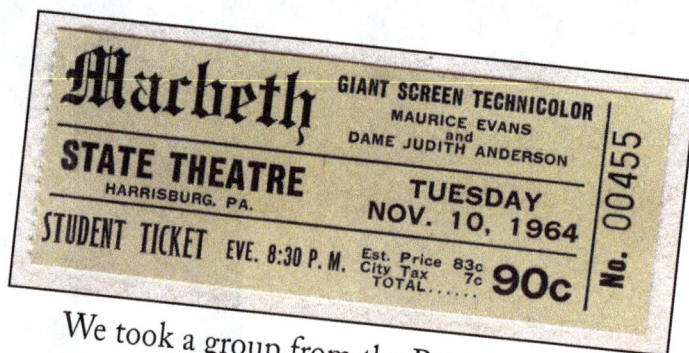

Macbeth
GIANT SCREEN TECHNICOLOR
MAURICE EVANS
and
DAME JUDITH ANDERSON

STATE THEATRE
HARRISBURG, PA.

TUESDAY
NOV. 10, 1964

STUDENT TICKET   EVE. 8:30 P. M.   Est. Price 83c
City Tax   7c
TOTAL...... **90c**

No. 00455

We took a group from the British Literature Class to Harrisburg one evening with no thought for parental permission slips.

Years later Dame Judith Anderson appeared in person (in the role of Hamlet) in our auditorium.

1965–1966 *(Record 13-1)*

Row 1: Jay Ebersole, Leon Koser, Paul Grubb, Buster Shellenhammer, Jason Reed, Ron Cruys, Lester Ratcliff, John Knaub.

Row 2: Brad Weirich, Dave Beinhauser, Jack Ruggles, Bill Crick, Marty Remsburg, Dan Dorsheimer, Robert Shellenhamer, Frank Petroski.

The Outstanding 1965-66 Wrestling Team
—Cleon Cassel

According to Coach Cassel, the 1965-66 team was as tough as any team in LD history. As he noted, "Only two team points in 1965-66 kept the team from being undefeated. We were riding a 30 match win streak going into the 1965-66 season. This team was a great bunch of kids, most of them had wrestled on two undefeated teams and they knew what it takes to be a winner. We breezed through all of the early matches. Mechanicsburg scored 17 points on us—the most of any team. It came down to the last league match of the season with undefeated Cumberland Valley. Bad Luck struck, and we had a snow storm that week and the match was postponed. Cumberland Valley called and said the match could not be rescheduled even though all other teams would have to wait at least a week to wrestle. I protested to our administration because the only way they had a shot at us was to move their 103 lb. wrestler away from **Ron Cruys** and wrestle him at 95 lbs. This is the match I can remember that we used closed circuit T.V. The gym was sold out early and they filled the auditorium with people who paid to watch the match on TV.

"I lost the protest to balance the weights and GUESS WHAT? When we arrived the next week **their wrestlers were down one weight.** This meant that our undefeated **Lester Ratcliff** would wrestle their undefeated Bruce Palmer. If it came down to brains we would win, Lester had straight A's, K-12. The problem is that the match wouldn't be determined by grades. We lost the match 4-3 riding time. **Ron Cruys,** who had never lost a dual meet, pinned their substitute in 50 seconds but the damage was already done. L.D. lost the match 22-20 and our 45 match win streak came to an end.

"Two nights later we redeemed ourselves by stopping Manheim Central's 72 match winning streak. Even though **Harold (Buster) Shellenhamer** beat their team captain (a young man who later became the College Division National Champion) 2-0, we were behind 14-8 going into 145 lbs. **Mike Remsburg** won a hard fought 1-0 match and **Jake Williams** was inserted at 154 lbs. and won a great 5-3 match. Undefeated **Bill Crick** won over their undefeated Nelson Hershey 1-0 period with an escape in the 3rd period.

"This left the match up to **Jack Ruggles.** Jack was an original member of the Class of 1965, but had suffered a serious motorcycle accident. While Jack was in the hospital Mr. Staver went to see him to arrange home-bound instruction so he could be graduated with his class. Jack declined the offer so that he could come back the following year, compete in wrestling, and graduate a year late!"

From an unidentified newspaper report: "A wrestling rivalry started this year with Manheim Central when Lower Dauphin stopped Central's lengthy winning streak. During these matches **LD had to lock their gym doors prior to the Junior Varsity match** as soon as the bleachers and designated floor areas were filled with fans. The school district even had installed **barbed wire** on the lower side of C-wing when it was noticed that during these sell-out matches, ingenious (but unlawful) fans were using ladders to get on the roof of the school to look through the windows above the bleachers."

For the third consecutive season, **the LD Grapplers captured the Sectional Tournament Championship.**

Displaying mat savvy and team spirit, the '65-'66 squad compiled a fine 13-1 record and gained the **Capital Area Co-Championship.** The highlight of the wrestling season came just two days after the lone loss to Cumberland Valley, when the Falcons bounced back to check Manheim Central's winning streak at 72.

The Falcons placed second to Cedar Cliff in the fifth annual Harrisburg **YMCA Novice Wrestling Tournament** with a team score of 27 (to Cedar Cliff's 47) and had champions in **Jay Reed** (88), **Ron Cruys** (95), **Dan Dorsheimer** (112) **and Leon Koser** (127).

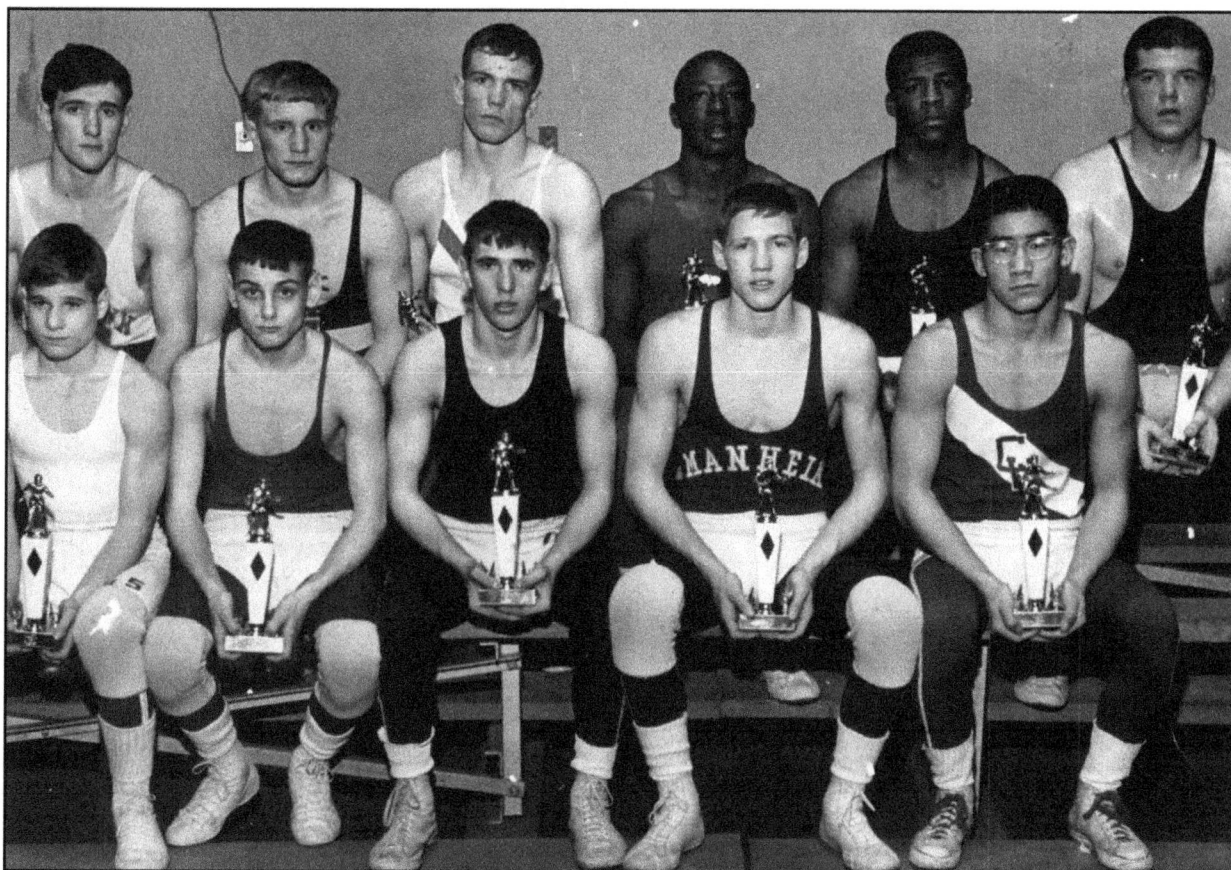

Ron Cruys, front row, second from left; Jesse Rawls, John Harris High School and now good friend to Lower Dauphin, is third from the right in the back row.

On February 15, 1966, the *Daily Intelligencer* of Lancaster wrote, "Lower Dauphin High School accomplished here what no Lancaster County wrestling team has been able to do all season—defeat Manheim Central in a dual meet (**26-14**)."

The *Lancaster New Era* reported: "It looked like the Barons were on their way to their 71st win in a row. *Then something happened.* Lower Dauphin won two key matches to tie the score; after losing the next two matches, the Falcons captured the last five in a row for an easy 29-14 victory. **Les Ratcliff** lost after going into the last period tied. **Ron Cruys** was held to a draw (only his second draw and no defeats in 68 dual bouts; Ron had been the District runner-up last season). **Shellenhamer** won 2-0 on a penalty point and an escape. **Koser** won a decision. **Mike Remsburg** had an escape, **Jake Williams** won, **Bill Crick** won 1-0 following an escape, and **Jack Ruggles** decisioned—and outmatched—his opponent." Quite a tale!

According to the Harrisburg newspaper:* "There is no question. The best team in Division 1 **is Lower Dauphin with their second straight Division 1 title for Coach Cleon Cassel's Club. The Falcons can boast 28 straight dual meet victories in two years.**"

---

* Likely *The Evening News.* In 1996, T*he Patriot* and *Evening News* merged into a single morning paper. *The Patriot-News.*[4] Manheim's winning streak would have been their 73rd.

The city newspaper wrote "**Cruys…sports perfect 21-2 at year-end**" Ron's record was actually 21-2-1 at year end. For the third consecutive season, the LDs *Grappler* captured the Sectional Tournament Championship. The *Falcon Flash* added, "… **action on the Lower Dauphin mats was without equal in central Pennsylvania.**"

The 1965-1966 Squad compiled a fine 13-1 record and earned the **Capital Area Co-Championship.**

Ron Cruys was LD's only District Champion and State Qualifier this year: The spectacular wrestling career; … fulfilled the fondest dreams of every school boy grappler…with the journey to States, climaxing his finest season; has never lost a dual match; and in '65 had won Sectional, District, and Regional crowns.

Cassel added, "As to this year's team—I have never heard the word 'No.' It's always "I'll try" or "yes." …the only words in their vocabulary.

… and **Harold Shellenhamer** is LD's only wrestler with three perfect seasons.

Charley Frey of *The Patriot News* presented a profile on Shellenhammer on December 19, 1965: as "one of the finest wrestlers he has ever handled. He has everything. He's always working on the other guy. Coach never lets him take it easy and it proved out."

Mike Remsburg, Harold Shellenhammer and Ron Cruys.

Mike Remsburg, Dan Dorsheimer, Keith Smith. Mrs. and Mr. D.J. Emerich are seated.

1966–1967 *(Record 13-1)*

Row 1: Bill Smith, Gene Boyer, Bo Glocker, Mike DeMuth, Dan Sanders, Dave Smoyer.
Row 2: Gary Wallish, Keith Smith, Fred Mutek, Ron MacLeod, Paul Matrisian, Jay Ebersole, Leon Koser.
Row 3: Coach Cassell, Brad Weirich, Dave Beinhauer, Craig Tritch, Glenn Snavely, Fred Espenshade, Phil Oller, James Geesaman.

There were four sophomores on this team: **Dave Smoyer, Dan Sanders, Fred Mutek,** and **Craig Tritch,** all carrying outstanding records. Led by **Jay Ebersole,** the team ended their season with a 13-1 record, but lost the championship to Cumberland Valley in a 20-19 squeaker.

The Patriot-News noted, "**Dan Sanders** has his work cut out for him in what can probably be labeled the toughest weight of the upcoming tournament at University Park. Dan is holding a record of 24-1 this season." The newspaper also reported that "**Randy Umberger** is one of seven sophomore starters on the University of Maryland wrestling team. In high school he had captured the 1965 District III title and was undefeated in his Junior and Senior years."

The Patriot News, January 13, 1967 noted that LD wrestlers swarmed over Palmyra 42-3, with pins in the Palmyra meet by Demuth, Boyer, Bush, Mutek, and Tritch.

On January 20 the newspaper announced that "by attending any of the LD matches you will see a team that is never to be put down."

First place winners at the Carlisle Invitational Wrestling Tournament include Dan Sanders, Gene Boyer, Leon Koser, and Jay Ebersole.

The city newspaper noted on January 20, "LD matmen are into another season with every possible chance of capturing the CAC Championship for the fourth consecutive year."

On Jan. 22 the *Patriot News* reported: "Aggressive Jim Rhone, one of the finest matmen in the history of the sport, is Captain of Pitt's Mat Team with a brilliant 25-1 record."

On Jan.26 this same newspaper reported: "The Lower Dauphin Falcons, with Jay Ebersole, Leon Koser, and Brad Weirich, are setting records that are making them one of the finest wrestling teams in the area."

The wrestling program bought a videotape recorder for $1,750—quite an investment for the time. Rick Landis was the first trained to use this.

"Glenn Snavely and Gary Wallish are defending this undefeated season. Seven Juniors are noted for their scoring: Mike DeMuth, Gene Boyer, Bill Smith (defending the title of sectional champion), David Beinhaur, Fred Espenshade, Ken Kuntz, and Steve Wrzesniewski. Four freshman round out the team: Dave Smoyer, Dan Sanders, Fred Mutek, and Craig Tritch."

"The meet with Cumberland Valley gave CV a one-point lead over LD, while a record crowd for any event ever held at LD filled every nook and cranny with 1600 paid admissions, and cars backed up to surrounding streets."

Jay Ebersole was a District 3 Champion.

1967–1968 (Record 12-2)

Welcome to the Home of the CAC Wrestling Champs
1964, 1965, 1966, 1968[1]

Row 1. Bill Smith, Bill Bush, Ken Kuntz, Gene Boyer, Mike DeMuth, Dave Smoyer.

Row 2. Fred Espenshade, Fred Mutek, Dan Verdelli, Craig Tritch, Geoffrey Webber, Dave Beinhaur, Steve Wrzesniewski. (Not pictured: Tom Burrows, Rodney Young, Dan Sanders, Roger Arndt.)

"It's nice to be remembered," the *Harrisburg Evening News* wrote on January 12, 1968. **Randy Kahler** and **Jim Rhone,** who began varsity wrestling together as freshmen in high school, were complimented by their high school coach, "Kahler was a smooth, quick wrestler who was a good take-down man; Rhone, on the other hand, would shoot for the fall. Both were always ready to learn something new."

And Coach Cassel was about to add several additional names to this growing number of memorable LD wrestlers with his 1968-69 team.

"Lower Dauphin's high-flying Falcon matmen retained their unblemished CAC record after defeating East Pennsboro (44-2) with pins by **Bill Smith** and **Craig Tritch.**"

[1] This sign later was erected near the high school… and said it all.

According to the brief account in the 1968 yearbook, "…by hard work, the wrestlers brought the CAC championship back to L.D. Proven team spirit, determination, and wrestling skill, combined with the oversight of Coach Cassel, led to a combination for a winning team."

One example of that winning spirit was the match against Cumberland Valley. After losing a 20-19 heartbreaker to CV the previous year, LD was facing a tie at 18 all. It was coming down to the heavyweight bout when Craig Tritch said to Coach Cassel, "The only way we will take their heavyweight is catching and pinning him. He is an absolute brute and 'Spare' Weber can do it." Weber was sent in as LD's heavyweight and the CV wrestler took the bait, rushing Weber three or four times and throwing him out on the floor. When the fifth rush came, "Weber hit the most beautiful throw I have ever seen," Tritch says, "so high and hard that it knocked his opponent silly with only 13 seconds left." LD won the pin and the match (23-18).

"LD qualified all four sectional champion wrestlers for the District 3 Championship and walked off with all four: **Dan Sanders, Gene Boyer, Fred Mutek,** and **Craig Tritch**—the only grappler to score three straight falls at the event."

On February 25, 1968, the city newspaper announced in its headline: "District Peers: Twelve of Them." **Dan Sanders** (13-3), Lower Dauphin, and Lee Dobyns (17-3), Newport, scored the upsets that were heard around the District 3 wrestling world last night before 2,750 paid followers at the Farm Show Arena. Sanders came up with the first shocker in the championships when he took previously unbeaten Dave Yohn (21-1) of Manheim Central. It was the first loss in Yohn's two-year wrestling career."

L.D. continued its monopoly for Sectional Championships with the Fab Four, and Sanders won Districts and Regionals right up to the semi-finals of States. …

Know Your Schools, March 1968, featured Dan Sanders who, as a junior, had just competed at States. Dan had won Sectionals with a decision of 7-0 by "defeating Mechanicsburg's Ray Yohn (who had conquered every wrestler who had defeated Dan during the season)" and beat him (with a record of 22-0) at Districts.

One of the local newspapers on February 29 notes that "**Lower Dauphin's Jay Ebersole '67 is 15-1 in wrestling at Wheaton College.**"

And, with a little icing on the cake, "LD's Girls Basketball, under Coach Barbara Macaw[2] swept the Susquehanna League title with a perfect season."

Know Your Schools, May 1968, in wrapping up the highlights of the year, complimented this very successful team, "…there is little doubt that something outstanding has once again been accomplished. This is the only team in the state to have both District and Regional Championships for 7 consecutive years."

[2] Coach Macaw (later Atkinson) was a basketball standout at Lebanon Valley College and a 1990 inductee into their Hall of Fame. So noted as another example of the high quality of LD coaches.

"L.D.'s total points for the season: 447. Total points of opponents: 176."

And who remembers that Penn State's head football coach, Joe Paterno, was the guest speaker at the Sports Award banquet held at Lower Dauphin High School on May 28?

The first ever Lower Dauphin Wrestling Clinic was held in June 1968 with top college coaches as instructors.

In July five former Lower Dauphin wrestlers were selected to attend the **U. S. Olympics Camp:** Randy Kahler, Jim Rhone, Jim Sanders, Randy Umberger and Bill Pinkerton.

In their three years at LD these latter three had lost a **combined total of only three dual meet bouts** and were named to the *Wrestling News* honor roll. **The Falcons were the only high school in the nation** to have more than one wrestler make this list.

1968 District 3 Champions

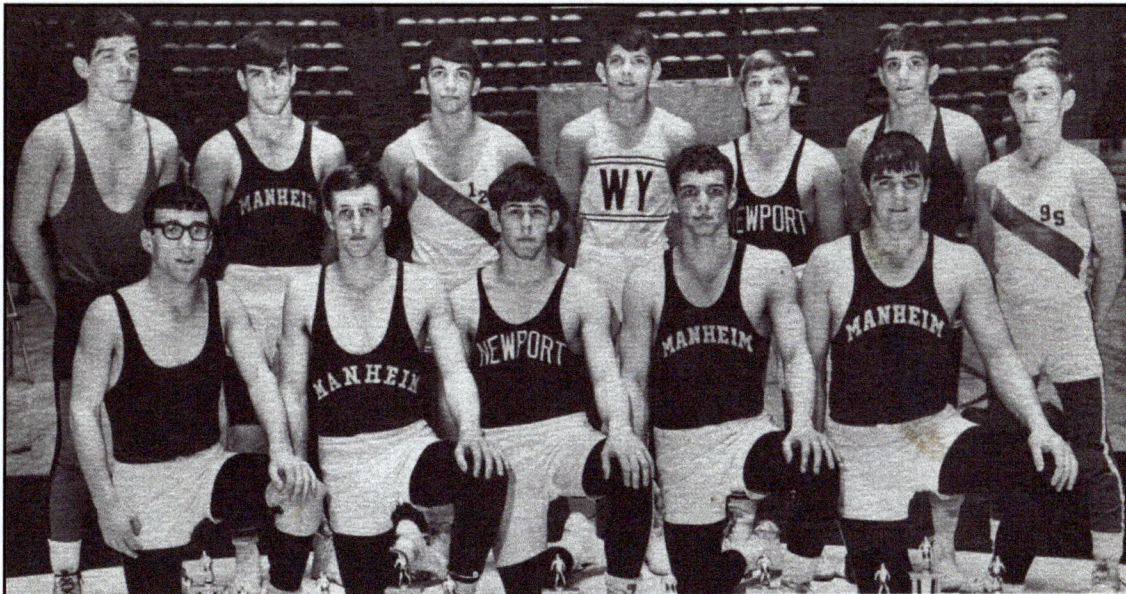

Front Row, (left to right): 145, Bill Thomas, York; 154, Dennis Ibach, Manheim Central; 165, Bruce Jones, Newport; 180, Mike Loercher, Manheim Central; Unlimited (Hwt.), Karl Ginder, Manheim Central. Back Row, (left to right): 138, Phil Conlin, Warwick; 133, Steven Thompson, Manheim Central; 127, Bill Pascarella, Cumberland Valley; 120, Bill Luckenbaugh, West York; 112, Lee Dobyns; Newport; 103, Dan Sanders, Lower Dauphin; 95, Rick Swanger, Cumberland Valley.

Coaches Don Heistand and Cleon Cassel

"Did we fully realize just how phenomenal

the high school wrestling program was!"

1968–1969 *(Record 13-1)*

Row 1. Sam Dupler, Joe Umbrell, Roger Arndt, Jim Hoffer, Dave Smoyer, Dan Sanders.

Row 2. Larry Matincheck, Ron Goodwin, Mel Hyde, Steve Dowhower, Jeff Zitch, Fred Mutek, Scott Gleim.

Row 3. Coach Cassel, Jim Michael, Denny Robertson, Doug Walters, Dan Verdelli, Craig Tritch, Dale Stoner, Rick Landis.

December 20, 1968, *Hummelstown Sun.* George Cruys '70, covering wrestling for *The Sun*, noted, "…Some interesting things can be concluded. First, **Craig Tritch,** one of the team's star wrestlers, was unable to wrestle on Saturday. As expected, **Doug Walters** was able to demonstrate great back-up ability of the Falcon second string."

Falcon Flash, February 1969. "At the end of the season three area wrestling notables were **first** seeded in the Capital Area Conference: **Dave Smoyer, Bill Smith,** and **Craig Tritch.**" *The Patriot-News* Wrestling Season 1969: "…in one of the closest battles of the night, unbeaten Craig Tritch clinched a victory for the Falcons."

Lower Dauphin's **100th victory** came early in the season on January 14, 1969 when the team defeated Palmyra **37-6**, with pins by **Sam Dupler, Denny Robertson,** and **Craig Tritch.** An essential part of this success included Dan Sanders (10-1) and Dan Verdelli (7-5). Sam Dupler began with a 7-0 victory and Dan Sanders edged out his opponent. Fred Mutek and Steve Dowhower also won. Following a tie, the team scored again with Doug Walters, and the stage

was set for the evening. Craig Tritch faced Bill Brown and, after six minutes of very tight wrestling, defeated the previously undefeated Brown, 4-3. The final team score was 20-17.

As if that were not enough, in only eight days, the Falcons won three hard-fought battles against 1. East Pennsboro (**24-19**), 2. Manheim Central where they broke Manheim's 27-game-winning streak (**25-20**), and 3. Milton Hershey (**35-9**).

Craig Tritch (left in adjacent photo) and Dan Sanders were team captains. Last year as a junior, Dan went to States. He had won the Harrisburg Tournament in both 7th and 8th grades and had won the Hershey Tournament as an 8th grader. In 9th grade he took second place in the novice tournament. He won sectionals in 10th grade and as a Junior his "stalwart movement" was marked by the upset win over Swanger in the District competition.

In 10th grade Craig Tritch had taken first place in the Harrisburg novice tournament at the 165 pound class. In 11th grade, Craig won sectionals by **pinning all his opponents.** He also won the Christmas Tournament and took second place in Districts during that year. This year Tritch won the Christmas tournament, bearing the honor of being voted **the first "outstanding wrestler" in Lower Dauphin's nine wrestling years.**

In 1968-69 LD also held an impressive presence in the world of collegiate wrestling:

- **Jim Sanders '65**: Trinidad State Empire Champ, 5th place Nationals
- **Randy Umberger '65**: Captain, U. of Maryland, voted Outstanding Athlete
- **Ron Cruys '66**: Captain, West Chester; Mid-Atlantic University Division Champ
- **Jay Ebersole '67**: Undefeated in dual meets, Middle Atlantic & East Stroudsburg Tournaments; point winner in the National College Championship
- As a freshman at Pitt (1969-70), **Craig Tritch** was Point Winner in Nationals.

Falcon Flash, February 1969. "At the end of the season three area wrestling notables were first seeded in the Capital Area Conference: **Dave Smoyer, Bill Smith,** and **Craig Tritch.**" *The Patriot-News* Wrestling Season 1969: "…in one of the closest battles of the night, unbeaten Craig Tritch clinched a victory for the Falcons."

However, the bigger night was the battle between LD and Cumberland Valley where LD prevailed for the second year in a row. George Cruys, writing for *The Sun,* noted, "The match was expected to be a good one, and the 1,000 fans were not disappointed. So many turned out that once the gym was totally filled, another 400 viewed the match via close circuit TV." It was a very close match. Following the 165 lb. bout, with scores of LD 17 and CV 14, came the match of the evening where, after six minutes of very tight wrestling, Tritch won 4-3. The final score stood at 20-17. This finished the season for the Falcons with a 9-0 record in the CAC.

During the summer Coach Cassel led his 4th Wrestling Clinic with the following headliners as part of the staff:

- **Ed Perry**—Three time National Champion, PIAA State Champion, Eastern Intercollegiate Champion, Coach—U.S. Naval Academy;

- **Larry Lauchle**—National Champion, Two times U.S. Olympic team member, Coach of last year's high school World's Champion team, PIAA State Champion;

- **Ron Gray**—Two-time National Champion, voted outstanding wrestler; Iowa State Champion, three times Big Eight Champion, Coach at F&M;

- **Bob Fehrs**—Two-time National Prep School Champion for Milton Hershey, three times Big Ten Champion, three times NCAA runner-up, Coach at Pitt; and

- **Bill Koll**—three times National Champion, three times Big Eight Champion, Coach at Penn State.

First rate all the way!

Local news coverage noted that Craig Tritch competed in the National Junior Wrestling Championships held in Worland, Wyoming. This was certainly a lesson in endurance: "Craig had four victories under his belt before he tasted defeat. He then was called from the dressing room and was informed that he had been scheduled to wrestle against his fifth opponent in 45 minutes after his previous match." The following year 1969-1970, as a freshman at Pitt, Craig Tritch was Point Winner in Nationals.

Winners from the start:

Even in its first season, LD wrestling had a winning record, establishing a tradition that would remain unbroken for 30 years.

Building stamina:

Coach Cassel: "We practice every night to go three full 15-minute periods. That makes the 2-2-2 regulation bout time seem like nothing." [see page 50]

Breaking in:

Arriving at Mechanicsburg for an early 1960s bout, the Falcon team found a police escort to lead them to the back of the school because the crowd in front was too large to navigate. Eventually the crowd broke the doors off their hinges and some fans had to be seated on the wrestling mat itself.

[see page 57]

Loose as a goose:

According to early Falcon wrestler Ron Cruys, Coach Cassel's final instructions as a wrestler headed to the mat were, "Loose as a goose. Take him down. Work him over. See your chance, put him away." Ron added, "It didn't matter if you were wrestling a fish or somebody really good."

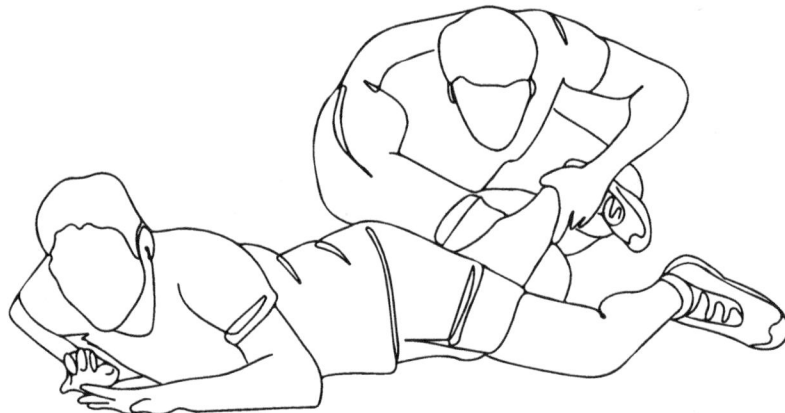

1969–1970 *(Record 13-1)*

Row 1: John Deitz, Jim Hoffer, Larry Kuntz, Ross Rider, Bob Kreiser, Joe Umbrell, Sam Dupler, Mike Kreiser.

Row 2: Bob Ebersole, Paul Maulfair, Tim Patrick, Chet King, Larry Peters, Jeff Zitch, Steve Dowhower, Ron Michael, Ron Goodwin.

Row 3: Jim Michael, Dale Stone, George Stauffer, Coach Cassel, Dan Verdelli, John Nagle, Rick Baer, Bob Freeland.

"LD Wrestles Carlisle," *The Falcon Flash*, December 23, 1969, by George Cruys, Editor-in-Chief: "Led by second period pins by Jim Michael (180) and Dan Verdelli (unl.), LD's grapplers won their first match of the season. The score was a convincing 31-11 trouncing over a scrappy, but out-manned, Carlisle team. Seven decisive choices were posted by the Falcons' lower weights in helping LD pile up an early lead. These included Mike Kreiser (95), Sam Dupler (103), Joe Umbrell (120), John Dietz (133), Ron Michael (138), Steve Dowhower (145), and Chet King (154). Quite a showing! A jubilant, but keen Coach Cassel replied after the match, 'It's always great to win, but we looked sloppy. Part of this is due to faulty conditioning…but it **will** improve.'" And indeed it did. **Their finish shows a league record of 9-0 and overall season of 13-1-0.**

Championships won by this team included the Capital Area League and LD's own Christmas Tournament, with a scoring total of 447 points to the 164 of their opponents.

Achievements by this team include (1) Sectional Champions **Steve Dowhower, Sam Dupler**, and **Bob Kreiser**; (2) National Federation Pennsylvania Champion **Sam Dupler**; (3) Dupler's placing third in the National Junior Championship in Oklahoma.

Individual records included most falls (9) finessed by **Dan Verdelli** and most points scored by Verdelli (60), **Sam Dupler** (60) and **Ron Michael** (43). The team had a good showing all around.

I am a Lower Dauphin Wrestler: This is My Story

*(Wrestlers were invited to contribute to this collection with a tribute, or a memory. . . .
Some of their stories hold humor, some reflect sadness; many are heartbreaking and others
redemptive. All are genuine and reveal humankind at its lowest and at its highest.)*

Falcon Pride is Born

—Carl Espenshade '62

I am proud to be part of the first class of the Lower Dauphin Wrestling Team. The first group
was a mixture of some experienced wrestlers from Hershey High School and some novices who
were recruited out of hallways and had no idea of what wrestling really was. (Hummelstown
High never had wrestling as a sport.)

From day one of the wrestling season, there was a winning spirit and enthusiasm in the
wrestling room. The reason for our success was the hiring of Cleon Cassel as head coach of
the new school jointure. Cleon was an outstanding wrestler both at Hershey High School and
Franklin and Marshall College.

My personal story is not unique and not too different from many others of that generation.
It starts when I was a young boy growing up on a small farm in East Hanover Township. Like
most wrestlers in our group, I attended a one-room schoolhouse where there were no organized
sports available. In 1954 East Hanover Township consolidated its nine one-room schoolhouses
and built East Hanover Elementary School. I attended there from fourth to eighth grade. It
was a drastic move from elementary school to Hershey High. This was quite an adjustment
because we were in a completely new environment. We had to learn to make friends with
people who thought they were our betters. It was not easy, but through sports, I was able to
make some friends.

In the fall of my freshman year, my sister-in-law talked me into going out for wrestling. I
entered the Hershey Novice Wrestling Tournament and did well in it. Against the wishes of
my parents, I decided to go out for the High School team. I had no idea of what I was doing. I
was second string behind a senior co-captain of the team and thought I could learn from him.
However, during the second match of the season he dislocated his elbow and I became the
varsity 112 pounder by default.

In those days, canvas-covered horsehair mats were used for wrestling. Well, I got a lot of
mat burns on my face in each match, going the season with no wins. Later on, I learned it was
more fun to give mat burns to my opponents. I ended my 10th grade season with a .500 record.

In the spring of that year, we learned that everyone who lived in surrounding townships would be going to a new school jointure that consisted of Hummelstown and the four townships. Hershey residents wanted their school to be only for Derry township students. As it worked out, it was one of the best things that ever happened to me.

As classes started, September 12, 1960, I was amazed to find everyone warm and friendly. From that first day of school I could tell this new school was going to be special. The joining together of former Hummelstown and Hershey students went smoothly. I made so many friends and earned the nickname "Smiley."

Almost everyone on the Lower Dauphin wrestling team was from the townships. Therefore, we started our first season with a good nucleus of wrestlers. Coach Cassel did a great job of recruiting some new boys to complete the team. After our first practice, I knew this was going to be a winning program. Coach Cassel instilled confidence in his wrestlers. He taught us the mental aspects of the sport: Stand tall, look your opponent in the eye and carry yourself with confidence. He had his wrestlers believing they could beat anyone. A good example was Randy Kahler, a State finalist in his first year on Varsity. It was hard for me to achieve that confident mindset. Coach made wrestling enjoyable; even practices were fun. I remember drilling with freshman Jim Rhone, and we would continue wrestling beyond the end of a drill. That earned us push-ups after practice. Many of the younger boys were curious and came to watch us practice. I think they could sense the camaraderie and became future Falcon wrestlers.

I felt it was an honor to put on the blue and white three piece uniform and wrestle in our magnificent gym. Hershey did not have a home gym. Our gym was even equipped with a nice rubber mat on which to wrestle. I still get a thrill when I walk into the Lower Dauphin gymnasium as I recall the support of the community, our cheerleaders and students. *(My only personal disappointment was that my parents never came to see me wrestle in high school or college.)*

Our first year, our team earned respect from other schools; we could compete with all our competitors. Entering my senior year, we competed in the Central Dauphin Christmas Tournament. Our team won first place, placing the first wrestling trophy in our trophy case, and I got a pin in the finals. The tremendous spirit was started and would continue to build in the future. Jay Kopp and I were co-captains in our senior year. We finished the season with 10 wins, 3 losses and 1 tie.

I had a great start as I loved going for the pin money (which was an award for the fastest pin.) Unfortunately, shoulder injuries and times I tried to lose too much weight too fast would spoil the end of my season. Also, after practice I had to take the long bus ride home, walk a mile to my house, and then milk the family cow.

As I reflect on my wrestling career, I give Coach Cassel and Lower Dauphin credit for being a major part in my development as a person. I was the only one in my family to go to college. I do not know if I would have gone without wrestling. I became a teacher, a head wrestling coach and for 18 years a PIAA wrestling official. I went on to get my Master's degree and became a Guidance Counselor.

I am happily married and my wife and I have three wonderful sons and nine grandchildren. Wrestling helped me mature from that poor, bashful country boy. I have been fortunate and blessed to live a very successful life. Thanks to Coach Cassel, there are many boys with similar stories. As stated earlier, I am proud to be part of the Lower Dauphin wrestling family and part of the team that built the foundation for winning that would follow.

Carl "Smiley" Espenshade

Kopp Brothers: Jay and Galen Kopp
—Ann Landis Kopp '65

September 1960. My 8th grade Social Studies teacher, Mr. Cleon Cassel, was one of the many new teachers when Lower Dauphin first opened its doors in the fall of 1960. It was Mr. Cassel's first year in teaching as well as starting a wrestling program. We were all interested in and focused on what this new teacher was doing in bringing a new sport to a new high school. The wrestling matches took place on Thursday nights in our new gym. As an incentive for his students, Mr. Cassel gave "extra credit" for those who attended the matches. I thought this was a good way to attract fans to the bleachers.

My own eye was on two high school boys who were a hold-over from my days at South Hanover. Coach Cassel identified them as "Kopp Incorporated," made up of Jay and Galen Kopp, 11th and 10th graders. He was sure that one of these brothers would catch my interest since they were farm boys and I was a farm girl. By the following year, my 9th grade, I was hooked on Jay. However, he was a senior and I knew my parents would not agree to me dating a senior. Thus, for some time I had them believing my eye was on Galen who was a junior.

My dad and Jay's dad both belonged to the Y.F. (Young Farmers), an organization guided by Mr. Carl Herr, the vocational agriculture teacher, and before long my parents realized it was Jay who had captured my interest.

Strict coach and good man that he was, Coach Cassel "spot-checked" on his wrestlers, calling their homes around 9:00 p.m. just to see that they were home! Coach's discipline included push-ups at practices when the guys were goofing off. Those who were overweight, and had to lose a pound or so, put on a rubber suit and crawled under a rubber mat. Often, on the nights before a match, the wrestlers' supper would be a boiled egg for added protein.

Jay had to lose weight to wrestle at 112 or else beat his brother at the weight they shared. In order for both to wrestle, they could not be the same weight. Jay did better at this. Jay enjoyed wrestling and, because it was a winter sport, both brothers could participate. However, there were always the cows to milk when they got home after practice.

Coach expected a lot from his wrestlers. During practice a match would be much longer than six minutes and they worked through many matches at a practice.

Best of all, Mr. Cassel was spot-on in thinking Kopp, Incorporated produced good farm boys! Seven years later at our wedding, Coach said, "I knew from the beginning that you two were a match!" As usual, **he was right.**

Remembering Orange Peels
—Bill Pinkerton '65

It was the 1964-65 season. We were undefeated and wrestling Middletown on a Saturday night. They weren't a big rival, but we didn't like them for some reason. At weigh-in, Jim Sanders and Harold Shellenhammer were overweight. They both put on rubber suits and went into a hot shower room to work off the weight. Both of them scalded their feet, but they made weight. During the match we could eat sliced oranges when not wrestling. Some of the guys got a bit frisky and started throwing orange peels around. Yes.

At Monday's practice Coach reminded us of Saturday night and that since we were so frisky we could do a few pushups to his count. However, he had a different kind of count in mind: 1. From the up position, hold for thirty seconds: ONE. One quarter of the way down, hold for thirty seconds. TWO: half-way down and hold for thirty. THREE: Hold three quarters of the way down. FOUR: All the way down. ONE: One quarter of the way up and hold for thirty seconds. And so on. We did TWENTY of those in what felt like an hour. To this day I am careful about orange peels.

From Chicken Coop to Cassel
—Bob Hess '65

I was about ready to enter 8th grade when Lower Dauphin High School opened her doors. For me, life was about to change. My family life was difficult. My mother worked hard to raise three of us children on her own. I was the oldest of the three.

Some of the things I experienced in those first years of school, before entering Lower Dauphin, were not things that most children would be going through. Some of these actions involved a lot of fear. Male leadership in the right direction was something that I lacked.

I thought 8th grade was just going to be "another year of being bored to death" doing something that I just hated. I did not like school. Nor did I like anything that school offered me. Most sports were not something that I felt that I could do well in. That all changed one morning as announcements were made about something called "wrestling." Wrestling in junior high school? I never realized there was such a thing. So, after school I headed over to the gym for the meeting. A new life began.

My first year on the team was encouraging. I found something that I could do, and something that I could succeed in. I wrestled in a tournament that year. I won a gold, first place medal. I had finally succeeded in a sport!

I learned much in this great sport that I came to love. Most wrestlers look back and consider their "wins" and "losses" as the most important part of the years they wrestled. I, however, learned about something that was even more important.

During that first year of wrestling, I came into contact with two great men. They were my wrestling coaches, Mr. Cleon Cassel and Mr. Homer Gelbaugh, both who encouraged me, supported me, and taught me how to WIN a wrestling match. The evening that I won my first tournament, I actually got a hug from both coaches. They told me that I did a great job. A compliment was something that I had never experienced from a man in my earlier years of life. *Something new began taking place in my life.*

As my 8th grade year was ending, I found out that I was going to move away from Lower Dauphin because of family problems. Coach Cassel gave me what I had not experienced very often when he called me aside and told me that he had heard what was taking place in my life. I often felt that he really cared about what was happening in the lives of his wrestlers, but he shocked me with what he told me that day. "If you ever need my help, contact me and I'll be there for you." I thought a lot of him. But I had been promised many things in the past and when it came time for help, there was no one there.

Some months after my wrestling coach made this promise, my younger brother, sister, and I were living in what I call a "chicken house that the chickens had moved out of." We also found out that we were going to be without any adults living with us for a while. The police had picked up my father, with whom we were living at the time, and who had left us there alone. Yes, this is true. I walked about two miles to try to make some phone calls. A kind bartender gave me money to make the calls, which all had the same answer. "I'm sorry but we don't have the room for you."

Somehow, someone found out about our situation, came, picked us up, and took us off to foster homes. My first foster home only lasted for about a month or so because the husband (the wrestling coach at Hershey) and his wife found out that they were expecting a baby and didn't have enough room for my brother and me to stay with them much longer.

Soon after that, this wrestling coach came to me and asked me if I remembered Coach Cleon Cassel from Lower Dauphin High School. After telling him that I DO, DEFINITELY, know him, he told me that my brother and I would be going to live with Mr. Cassel and his parents. I was SHOCKED. MY FRIEND. MY WRESTLING COACH. The MAN who was about to fulfill the promise that he had made me a few months earlier.

Great things began happening in my life at that time. The "gold medal" that I earned in my first year of wrestling was not even close to how important the wrestling COACH became to me. My wrestling coach showed me and proved to me, that there was someone in life who DID keep promises that he made. Cleon Cassel took me to his family's home, AND into his family.

His mother and father were fine Christian people who helped me to see what is actually important in life. Because of my wrestling coach's care for me, a young person who needed serious help at such an important time in life, I learned what "work" was all about by taking on responsibilities at the farm and in the Cassel home. Their Christian life taught me, by their actions and lifestyle, what were the most important things in life. Several times, during my 4 years in their home, my coach's mother told me that I wasn't "just a foster child," but I was "THEIR son." They showed me what the word LOVE really meant.

The Lower Dauphin wrestling program changed my life. No, it wasn't because of my gold medal and my two first place trophies. No, it wasn't because I was able to defeat guys who were bigger than me. No, it wasn't because I was recognized by other students as a member of one of the greatest wrestling teams in our area. It was because of a WRESTLING COACH who TRULY CARED about what was happening in my life, kept his promise, and shared a very precious part of HIS life with me.

Because of this coach, I stayed in school, instead of dropping out. Because of this wrestling coach, I made it through high school. Because of this coach's love for his country which I saw as we sat down together and went through some books that he had, I developed a love for my country and, later, even became involved in politics. Because of this, I was given the opportunity to meet and work for Barry Goldwater's campaign.

Three years after graduation from high school, I surrendered my life to God's ministry during my time of duty in the Air Force while stationed in Germany. After serving nearly 6 years in the Air Force, I wound up attending Missionary Baptist Seminary in Little Rock, Arkansas. While there, I pastored a church for 3 years. And to the surprise of many who had known me in my school years, I actually earned my theological bachelor's degree through Eastern Baptist Institute. (NOTE: For someone who hated "English class" in high school, part of my degree program was not only taking English, but also Greek and Hebrew.) I pastored churches for 20 years and now assist our pastor. I also teach Bible Studies online and teach a class each week on the subject.

That is the important role that being involved in wrestling had upon my life. God has richly blessed me in my 77 years of life and Coach Cassel was a very important and fruitful part of that blessing.

LD Snaps Manheim Central's 72-match Winning Streak
—Ron Cruys '66

Most wrestlers remember one match that stands above all others. The following is one example. Only those who are not wrestlers may have difficulty realizing that, yes, the grapplers do remember every detail.

It was Monday night, February 12, 1966 when the Manheim Central Barons took on the Lower Dauphin Falcons for the first time ever on a wrestling mat. Manheim was riding a 72 straight match unbeaten streak. The Falcons' own winning streak of some 40 matches had ended two nights before in a 22-20 loss at Cumberland Valley. This match would be on the Falcon mats in Hummelstown.

Prior to the match, Captain Buster Shellenhamer gathered the team in the locker room for a first ever discussion of how we let our coaches and fans down with the loss to CV. We thought we were ready to do something special this night. However, we got off to a rather slow start, losing two of the first three bouts, with only a disappointing tie by Ron Cruys avoiding a sweep for Manheim through those weights.

Seeing this, Buster must have felt that he had to demonstrate how it's done. It wouldn't be easy. His opponent that evening was Stan Zeamer. Stan was something of a legend in District 3, winding up being a 2-time champion and a 2-time runner-up in that tournament. He had beaten Buster, 6-5, the year before in the District 3 tournament, the only time they had wrestled. We knew the bout would be close.

Buster took a 1-0 lead into the third period. With Zeamer in the down position, he needed an escape to tie. Stanley controlled the action in the period, which seemed to last at least 10 minutes. He kept getting to his feet, then switching or rolling or peeling hands, but never let the action last more than a few seconds before taking it out of bounds to get a fresh start. It was dizzying. No matter what Zeamer attempted, Buster was on him like a leech, following every move and hanging on for a 2-0 win, including riding time. The crowd was in an uproar.

Buster's win had an immediate inspirational effect on Leon Koser, our 127 pounder. In a toss-up match, Leon wrestled better than I'd ever seen him and he prevailed 4-3 to bring the overall match score even at 8-8.

Manheim fought back. Heavily favored in the next two bouts, the Barons once again took a 6 point lead into 145. At this time, Coach Cassel's ability to maneuver his wrestlers in the lineup to get the best match-ups possible started to show. He was a master at that. He had moved our 154 pounder, Mike Remsburg, down to 145. This was no easy weight cut as Remsburg had wrestled 154 in the CV match two days earlier. Having a penchant for keeping things close, thereby upping anxiety levels for all of us, Mike prevailed 1-0.

With Remsburg down a weight, the question was "Who would we wrestle at 154?" Whether he is psychic or just had a gut feeling, Coach Cassel inserted John "Jake" Williams into the lineup. Jake was a senior, who had wrestled on the JV squad prior to this year and had never wrestled a varsity match. Now he was representing his school in the biggest match of his career. Through a combination of self-belief, guts and determination, Jake brought home a 5-3 victory and we were all tied once again at 14.

We felt very comfortable with the next two weights upcoming. Bill Crick, Co-Captain at 165, was unbeaten and as reliable as anyone on our team. He was heavily tested by Manheim's wrestler, though. Crick walked off with a 1-0 win and we had our first lead in the match.

At 180, we had Jack Ruggles. Jack is an interesting story, as he should have graduated with the Class of 1965. However, a terrible motorcycle accident laid him up through that year. He stayed out of school, rehabbing, returning to wrestle his senior year and graduate with us. We're glad he did. Jack was another co-captain. He dominated his Manheim opponent to the tune of 9-1, and we had a six point lead heading to heavyweight. By the way, Jack also came from behind in the sectional finals against his adversary from Mechanicsburg, winning the championship and leading us to that sectional team title over the Wildcats. We wouldn't have had nearly as successful a season without him.

At 20-14, we had earned at least a tie with the Barons. Our heavyweight, Brad "Herk" Weirich, was chomping at the bit to get out on the mat. I'd never seen him so worked up. Athletic director Jack Goepfert and I tried to calm him down. He was furious when the Manheim coach decided to forfeit to him. Their heavyweight had been injured a few weeks earlier and they had a substitute who weighed about 170 to compete against Herk. The coach didn't want to risk injury to his wrestler as Herk was a good-sized heavy.

So it ended at 26-14. The final score failed to reflect the competitiveness of the match. Eight of the eleven bouts contested were decided by two points or less. Fans on both sides of the gym had certainly received their money's worth. We had started a new winning streak and Manheim's bus trip home would have had a much more somber tone than any in the last 5 years. It was a great night to be a Falcon.

A Tribute to the Early Wrestlers

—Dan Dorsheimer '66

George Stauffer ✦ Fred Harner ✦ Lynn Grimm ✦ Buster Shellenhamer

Ed Neidig ✦ Jim Sanders ✦ Randy Umberger ✦ Fred Foreman ✦ Kevin Ricker

I don't believe any LD wrestler ever had the fan appreciation that Big George Stauffer did. We would sit on the bleachers and roar for George. He never let us down. It wasn't just the students and former wrestlers. The parents and other adults were just as boisterous as we were. It was always the highlight of the match. George would fly out onto the mat, cross over and shake hands, the whistle would sound and the next thing you would see were two bodies flying across the mat. He would bring the house down. We loved it. The opposing wrestler never knew what was coming. There was very little scouting done and tape-recording a bout was practically unheard of. Only later did we have a camera.

In the early years there were not weight limitations on a heavyweight. Hershey and Middletown in the early '60s each had a 300 pound beast, Bel Seaman from Hershey and a fellow from Middletown whose last name was Pickle. I don't believe our heavies, Fred Harner and Lynn Grimm, were even 200 pounds. It was rather terrifying watching our "big boys" squash over the light heavies.

In some very interesting early bouts with our arch rival Hershey (who could never beat us), hard feelings occasionally surfaced. In '66 a 120-pounder from Hershey boasted what he would do to our 120-pounder, Buster Shellenhamer. The wrestler from Hershey had to have known Buster's reputation but he still opened his mouth. The match was at Hershey and the crowd was boisterous. Buster came out and beat the crap out of his opponent. Coach Cassel was so mad at Buster for wrestling like this that I thought he was going to pull him off the mat. Maybe coach didn't know what had been said by the Hershey wrestler, but he was mad at Buster.

In the '60s I recall four LD wrestlers one did not bad mouth before the match, especially if you wrestled for Hershey. Eddie Neidig (103), Buster Shellenhamer (112 & 120), Jim Sanders (120), and Randy Umberger (180). Let's just leave it at that.

I believe the year was 1971, Hershey at LD, the gym was packed. Hershey came up thinking they could beat us; Hershey went home with 1 team point. I don't recall what class they won, but I do remember Fred Foreman decking Hershey's heavyweight in something like 30 seconds; the kid got up and took a swing at Freddie, the official stepped in, the Hershey wrestler's father, a former pro football player, came up flying out of the stands. Coach Cassel and Hershey's coach, Red Campbell, managed to get things calmed down, but "wow," what a match to remember. It got pretty hairy. Regarding Foreman, he is arguably the greatest heavyweight LD ever had. He lost in the state finals in 1972. Legend has it that for ten continuous years after being graduated from high school Fred returned to his Alma Mater and worked with the heavyweights.

Hershey High had a middleweight for three years (145, 154, 165) who was an outstanding wrestler, but every year he lost to a (different) LD opponent. In 1972 he wrestled Kevin Ricker (at a Hershey home meet) under the lights! At this time Hershey was a very good wrestling team and most weights were a toss-up. Every bout was huge!! As Kevin was a personal favorite of mine I offered him a steak dinner as an incentive (not that he needed one). This particular match was going back and forth with the wins and I am there screaming my head off. With about 20 seconds left in the match, Kevin leading by a point, the wrestlers went out of bounds. The Hershey wrestler dragged himself back to the center where Kevin was waiting and I was going nuts watching. Just then, he looked up into the stands and—while I am sure he can't see me—raised three fingers signaling to me that everything was under control. Kevin won the bout and LD won the match, Yes, Kevin got his steak dinner.

The Best Excuse Ever

—Gene Boyer '68

While attending Lower Dauphin High School, one of the activities I participated in was the wrestling program. I really appreciated Coach Cleon Cassel's instruction to help me improve my wrestling skills to become a better member of the Falcon Wrestling Team.

There were many good times spent in the wrestling room. Coach Cassel required strict discipline during his program of instruction which was evidenced by Lower Dauphin's excellent wrestling program and record.

There was one incident I will never forget and I still tell this story today. It was during my junior year in wrestling when the first day of buck deer season began and school was closed on that Monday, but we still had wrestling practice in the evening. After being up before dawn, out in the cold all day and hiking in the mountains looking for deer, I was exhausted by evening. So, I decided to skip wrestling practice (as did some other members of the team).

During the next practice, Coach Cassel called out those who had missed practice and wanted a reason for missing. When he came to me he asked why I didn't attend practice last evening. I told him that my father (a funeral director) got called out and I had to go along with him to pick up a body. I will never forget how Coach Cassel about rolled with laughter and then said, "That's the best excuse I have ever heard!" Needless to say, those who missed Monday's practice had to do at least 100 extra pushups. Coach Cassel's goal was achieved because I never again cut another wrestling practice.

Kangaroo Court

—Mike DeMuth '68

As I think about Lower Dauphin wrestling, two personal memories come to mind. The first happened my Junior year and our first meeting with Manheim Central High School on their territory. A few weeks before, the Manheim team had been featured in a national publication. While we were impressed, this didn't faze us. Following our usual routine after weigh-ins, I was lying on the floor waiting for the lights to go out, anticipating time for preparing mentally for the match, when I realized their floors were heated. I fell into a deep sleep and when the lights came on, I stood up with my eyes open but I could not wake up. I was in a trance. This was such an odd sensation that I asked Phil Oller to slap my face to bring me around. It didn't work and I began to panic, terrified I would lose the match. Finally, I was able to regain stability five minutes before I wrestled and I won my match.

The second most impressive memory was our Kangaroo Court, named by the Coach after one of our team did a "dastardly deed" and coach thought he should be tried in front of the entire team. While part of me knew this was done in fun and to break up the monotony of practice, there still was a reason, in this case something I had done. I had been having trouble making weight and should not have gone sledding with Danny Sanders, but when Dan mentioned something about girls being there I was out the door. Monday morning, tired from the adventure, I decided to bag school, sleep in, and rest my body. Little did I realize Danny had decided to do the same thing....

The next day the talk among teammates was not about missing school, but about our missing practice. We were summoned to Court where each of us would have a teammate as a lawyer. I decided to represent myself. My defense including Danny's calling me, my refusing, his persistence in our going sledding, and my agreeing in a moment of weakness. I added that the entire time of our sledding, I was thinking about the team. Of course I lost the case, and the verdict was unanimous with even Danny's lawyer voting against us.

Once a Wrestler

—Steven Wrzesniewski '68

I wrestled at LD from 1964 to 1968 with Billy Smith, Jay Ebersole, Ron Cruys, Jimmie Sanders and his younger brother Dan, Craig Tritch, and many other great wrestlers.

They called me "Rez" back then.

I was graduated in 1968 and spent the next 26 years in the Air Force. I did do some wrestling while I was in the Air Force. Upon my retirement from the Air Force in 1995, I became a teacher for the Knox County School System in Knoxville, TN where I taught Aerospace Science and became the Assistant Wrestling coach. I held that position for three years. During that time I coached two State Champions, Jason Bault at 171 lbs. and Tim Frills 189 lbs. They were great wrestlers and great young men.

I now work for the National Nuclear Security Administration and the Office of Secure Transportation as an Instructional Designer and Lead Instructor. However, three years ago I was asked to be a non-faculty wrestling coach at the Alcoa High School. This year I have had to drop back to assistant coach due to the travel requirements of my full-time job.

This year our school will be hosting the Region Tournament at Alcoa HS. We will host 24 schools for a two-day tournament. I will be serving as the tournament director.

My involvement with wrestling in Tennessee came about with my teaching my son how to wrestle and I was asked to coach with the local AAU Wrestling program. I have taught these young wrestlers the same moves that I had learned while I wrestled at LD under Coach Cassel and Don Heistand. What they taught has served me well while I served in the USAF and as a AAU and high school coach here in Tennessee. To my wrestling coaches, I say Thank You for all that you have taught me, but especially for teaching me to love the great sport of wrestling.

A Fellow LD Wrestler, Steve Wrzesniewski (Rez) Class of 1968

Off the record . . .
—Craig Tritch '69

No measure of any program can be quantified unless there is a standard of success. To name only one standard as a measure misses the greatness of LD wrestling, its wrestlers, and its coaches. They made us what we were. There was a sense of belonging to an elite group that honored hard work, toughness, sacrifice, and a degree of shenanigans. Our best was expected and sloth or laziness was called to task daily with hundreds of extra push-ups, and, ultimately with heart-to-heart talks about our participation in what was a great fraternity of athletes.

Weight loss was part of the character-building. Tongue out, tired, dry-mouthed and ready for tomorrow honed the toughness and determination which we took into every match. Somebody, our opponent, was going to pay for this misery, and they did!

I, along with some others, could not take this constant, intense strain, so I contrived all sorts of "horseplay" which may have made me the "most-punished wrestler in LD history." It didn't seem right to labor continually without some fun, so some teammates might get whacked with a rope, or jumped on out of the collapsed bleachers. In turn, every sin was judged and punished by additional push-ups or continued wrestling with one opponent after another.

Sadly, I don't think I ever "got away" with any indiscretion. My closest teammates would turn me in just to see the suffering I had to take. In turn, when asked to defend a teammate in our wrestling court, I stopped my beautifully crafted defense, to throw my teammate on the mercy of the court—crying "He's guilty as hell! Punish him!"

Somehow I always had colorful language—each utterance punishable by after-practice push-ups. One night miraculously when I had not sworn—I was given push-ups for swearing. When I protested, and was backed up by the team that no foul words had left my lips, Coach gave me permission for a swear word. Seizing this chance I launched into one of my hyphenated-mixed curse words and filthy language to address my best friend and teammate. This outburst was (of course) judged excessive and the number of push-ups I would have received was doubled or tripled.

Thankfully I was never dumb enough to disrespect a coach. I saw one idiot, who was beating on a second team JVer, get his comeuppance when Coach stopped that match and stepped in to rectify the situation. My own worst punishment came from calling out like Tarzan (high in a tree in the Gettysburg National Cemetery on an 8th grade class trip sponsored by our teacher—yes, Cleon Cassel). Coach's paddle was legendary and I can attest to that. Hell, this wasn't even part of wrestling protocol....

The '70s: Refining a Wrestling Dynasty

The Rice Brothers: Wrestlers and Equestrians

While history will rank these brothers under the category of very successful horse trainers and/or jockeys, their mark in Lower Dauphin Sports is as wrestlers.

Brian, the older brother of Wayne and Curt, is not an LD grad but wrestled in the State Championship Tournament in West Virginia before the family moved to East Hanover Township in Dauphin County and became part of Lower Dauphin School District. Both Wayne and Curt were members of the wrestling team at LD.

Clyde Rice (father of Wayne, Curt, and Brian) had been a biology teacher and wrestling coach who moved to be near Penn National in 1972 when the racetrack gates first opened for business—racing horses! Clyde Rice's love for and skill with horses influenced sons Wayne and Curtis to become jockeys, and Brian a horse trainer.

Wayne '80 and Curt '81 at ages 18 and 17 wrote the record books at Penn National while still in high school. **Curt became the winningest apprentice jockey in the country in 1979,** as a sophomore in high school at LD, recording earnings of over $1,374,000—the youngest rider to purse over a $1 million at Penn National in a single season. Curt had amassed career totals of 2,400 mounts, 347 wins, 342 seconds, and 262 thirds. And that was just the beginning.

Wayne finished a successful wrestling campaign for the Falcons and Curt logged a 10-3 career wrestling record while competing in his sophomore year. With all of their success out of school, the brothers consistently remained responsible, low-keyed students. Very few of their classmates knew of the brothers' lives as jockeys. They are of interest here as representative of Lower Dauphin's welcoming whoever wanted to play a sport and was willing to follow the school guidelines. Many accommodations were made for any student who had an earnest interest in scholastics and any other school activities.

Athletic Director "Burr" Rhoads noted at the time, "Wayne and Curt are well-liked in the school and handle their responsibilities with ease." Coach Randy Umberger echoed the message, noting that "In the seven years I've been coaching, they are the most dedicated and disciplined athletes I've ever had the pleasure of coaching. They are unselfish and do not take advantage of their scholastic situation (and altered attendance schedule) as both are on work-study, and at the track at 6:30 a.m. By 10:30 both boys are in school, taking a full load of classes. During wrestling season both remain after school for wrestling practice until 6 p.m. and make post time as jockeys at Penn National Race Course at 7:30.

Perhaps the Best Dual Match Ever for LD

Lower Dauphin Wrestlers Win Fourth CAC Crown

A tribute in summary for the wrestling team's phenomenal 70-71 season

"Hershey's Trojan grapplers invaded Lower Dauphin gym last Thursday night, determined to be the one to knock off the high-flying Falcon wrestling team, which was aimed toward their unprecedented fourth straight Capital Area Conference wrestling championship.

When the shouting faded after this particular event, so had the Hershey Grapplers who limped back up Route 422 with a 48-1 drubbing administered by the Lower Dauphin champions. After scoring a win in the opening 95 pound bout, Hershey High's Trojans were shut out by Lower Dauphin for the remainder of the evening.

The win brought Lower Dauphin an undefeated season in CAC matches, with only powerful Manheim Central a possibility to mar a faultless season.

"Hershey's Neal Fasnacht decisioned **George Kline** at 95 lbs. LD's **Sam Dupler** (103) finished off Craig Keprer in the second period. Twenty-four seconds into the first period, Dupler took Keprer down, and from there controlled him to his finish.

"**Joe Umbrell** (112) accumulated a 4:47 riding time before putting away Hershey's Mike Yasson at 5:45 in the third period.

"Falcon **Bob Kreiser** (120) didn't waste any time putting away Harold Becker. The time was 1:25 in the first period.

"**Larry Kuntz** (127) won big in a decision over Dean Huebner, 13-2.

"**Tom Mutek** (133) had to wait until 2:32 in the second period to show Jim Brandt the lights.

"Undefeated **Ron Michael** (138) scored his eighth pin of the season against Duane Bungs.

"**Ed Neiswender** (145) surprisingly could not get the right combination for a pin, but decisioned Tom Arndt, 8-0 for a different kind of shut-out.

"**Ron Verdelli** (154) decisioned Ed Arndt 6-1.

"**Chet King** barely pulled off a tough match win against Hershey's Tom Stadulis at 165. As the closing seconds ticked away, Stadulis fought for the tying escape point, but King denied him.

"Undefeated **George Stauffer** (180) surprised Don McCorkel 14-4. McCorkel's four points were penalties against Stauffer. He was trying a little too hard for the pin.

"**Fred Foreman** gave his opponent, and the crowd, a real surprise in the unlimited bout. Forty-two seconds and the match was over. Foreman put on the quick move and the Hershey wrestler was still looking for the next move."

…*from a Cumberland Valley Fan*

While I have been the "historian" for Cumberland Valley wrestling for the past 43 years, my recollection of the mat rivalry goes back to the early 1960s when CV's coach was Rick Cassel, whose brother Cleon was the coach at Lower Dauphin. Both Cassels laid the foundation for what would become the mat protocol **in this area** that remains today.

The wrestling rivalry was fueled by the three coaches of CV, CC, and LD—namely, Don Humes, Bob Craig, and Cleon Cassel. Most dual meets were sold out when any of these three teams were the headliners, with CV and LD in the former Capital Area Conference and Cedar Cliff leading the Harrisburg Area League. Usually one of these three teams would have an undefeated season, and often one of the other two would have only one loss. Most years the team with only one defeat had lost to one of the other two teams. (All of this, of course, was before the advent of the PIAA Team Championships.) Cleon Cassel, Dick Cassel, and Don Humes all had a number of undefeated teams who would have been able to compete on the mat with anyone—and no doubt all three would love to have seen the outcome of that kind of match-up, pun intended. As it was, many of the LD-CV matches were won by 3 to 5—or even fewer—points. For many seasons the Capital Area Conference Championship was won by one or the other of these three teams—for it was rare when any other school except these **three** "won Conference."

In 1973 Cumberland Valley crowned Eric Carr their second PIAA Champion, while Cassel, in the rarest of coaching feats, placed three wrestlers in the PIAA finals. What made this almost unprecedented was that these three wrestlers were in sequential weight classes: **Stauffer, Mutek, and Neiswender.** Their names still roll off the tongue as if it were only yesterday.

Because of wrestling, I have developed many friendships through the years with Lower Dauphin affiliates—the Cassels; Ron and Ed Michael; Bill Linnane (LD's first Junior High coach); Paul Shirk (long-time score-keeper); Ed Neiswender; Carl Espenshade; and Craig Tritch—as well as others.

One of the important things I've come to realize as I've become older is that wrestling is a rare sport. When you are competing, regardless of your dislike for the opposing team or the guy you're wrestling, there is a great deal of respect shown. And, in later years, it becomes all respect.

A Cumberland Valley Wrestling Historian

Tribute to a Wrestler of the 1970s
Fred Foreman: One of a Kind
—by Dan Dorsheimer '66

The year was 1971, Hershey was at LD, and the gymnasium was packed. Hershey came up thinking they could beat us; Hershey went home with one (1) team point. I don't recall what class they won, but I do remember **Fred Foreman** decking Hershey's heavyweight in something like 30 seconds: the kid got up and took a swing at Freddie, the official stepped in, and the Hershey wrestler's father, (formerly a professional football player) came up flying out of the stands. Coach Cassel and Hershey's coach, Red Campbell, managed to get things calmed down, but "Wow," what a match to remember. It got pretty hairy. (See previous *Best Dual Match*.)

Regarding Foreman, he is arguably the greatest heavyweight LD ever had. He lost in the **state finals** in 1972.[*] Legend has it that for ten continuous years after being graduated from high school Fred returned to his Alma Mater and worked with the heavyweights. **True blue!**

[*] On his route to the State Finals Fred had defeated two wrestlers who were so outstanding in size and skill that they later played professional football.

HIGHLIGHTS OF THE MEETS

The seventies were very successful years for Lower Dauphin, placing three wrestlers in the state finals: Ed Neiswender, Tom Mutek, and Mark Stauffer. Even more prestigious is that Lower Dauphin received attention as the **Number 1 high school wrestling team in the state of Pennsylvania.**

During this decade **Lower Dauphin Star Ron Michael** lit up the country. After a 37-2 career at LD, Ron wrestled for Kent State University and became **our only NCAA Division I, All-American** when he placed fourth at the **1978 National Championship.** He was two-time Mid-Atlantic Conference Champ and posted the third best winning percentage when at Kent State…winning the prestigious Joe Begala Award in 1979 and earning All-American status with a fourth-place finish at 158 in the **1978 NCAA Championships.**

One of the most spectacular feats in LD's overall dual meet history is **Rick Kelley's** 1972-73 drive to break into the line-up. His story is found below in the 1972-73 section. His teammates will never forget this exploit!

LD also proudly salutes its ENTIRE wrestling brotherhood with its large number of families who have had **more than one son on the wrestling teams.** As one example, in the 1970s we had the Fluman Brothers Decade. The Fluman Family (Al, Eric, and Brandon) is the only family to this date whose three sons were on teams over-lapping **six consecutive years.**

Al: 1974, 1975, 1976, 1977
Eric: 1975, 1976, 1977, 1978
Brandon: 1976, 1977, 1978, 1979

Tape him up

Still recovering from broken ribs due to a football injury, Jim Sanders received a last-minute approval from his doctor to wrestle in a tournament. With no workout and no practice, Coach Cleon Cassel remembers, "We taped up his ribs, and he won his next four matches and missed being named Outstanding Wrestler of the tournament by one vote."
[see page 65]

I just want to say one word— plastics:

A wrestler trying to make weight was discovered in an attic crawlspace, apparently "wrapped in plastic." [see page133]

No sulking . . .

Of the 1986-87 team, Coach Cassel said: "This is a fun team, a loose team in practice.... It is evident they hate to lose, but they don't sulk. They work." [see page 201]

Ouch . . .

Trauma for one LD wrestler prompted Dan Dorsheimer to write: "To this day I've never seen any wrestling injury as severe as this." [see page 38]

1970–1971 (Record 13-0-1)

"The Great 1970-71 Team"

(…as the fans named them and as their wrestling record supports)

Row 1: George Kline, Mike Heagy, Mike Kreiser, Sam Dupler, Joe Umbrell, Bob Kreiser, Larry Kuntz, John Koser.

Row 2: Tom Mutek, Coach Don Heistand, Ron Michael, Jere Zitch, Mark Stauffer, George Stauffer, Ed Neiswender, Fred Foreman, Steve Ricker, John Neagle, Kirk Lehmer, Dale Goodwin, Ron Verdelli, Coach Cleon Cassel, Bill Divel.

This 1970-71 team had "…eight returning starters: Mike Kreiser, Sam Dupler, Joe Umbrell, Robert Kreiser, Larry Kuntz, Ron Michael, Chet King, and George Stauffer. There were two seniors, Kirk Lehmer and Steve Ricker, along with three juniors—Fred Foreman, George Kline, and John Neagle. Sophomores who gave the team great depth were Mark Stauffer, Tom Mutek, and Ed Neiswender."

The Birds won their first three matches of the decade, and it appeared nothing could stop them. On December 16th the LD matmen took a 38-3 win over Palmyra and on December 18th they pinned a 52-2 defeat over Central Dauphin East.

Hummelstown Sun, Dec. 23, 1970

"Falcons Remain Undefeated in Pair of Matches"

George Kline had the first pin. **In just 31 seconds,** Kline scored a take-down and stacked up his opponent. **Mike Kreiser** followed suit and flattened his opponent in 5:16 to give the Falcons a lead of 11-0. Not to be outdone, **Sam Dupler** tallied 6 more points for the team with his first period fall in 1:01. **Joe Umbrell's** 7-1 decision was followed by **Bob Kreiser's** 9-4 win which gave LD a 23-0 lead. …**Tom Mutek** then won a 7-0 decision which provided the Birds a 26-3 lead. The fourth Falcon fall of the evening went to **Ron Michael** who flattened his man in 2:52. A 7-1 decision by 154 lb. **Ron Verdelli** made the score 34-3." The colorful description here by its original sportswriter continued with "**George Stauffer** scored the fastest fall of this match in just 29 seconds—his fourth fall in as many matches."

In the conflict with Cedar Cliff, **George Kline** decisioned his Colt competitor 7-2. **Mike Kreiser** got stacked. **Dupler** lost his first match in two years. **Joe Umbrell** pinned Brian Smith, tying the score. After the Colts took the lead, **Ron Michael** "whooped the stuffing" out of his opponent 11-2. At the end, an 11-0 decision for **George Stauffer**, along with **Fred Foreman's** stalling and predicament points, tied the bout.

Here again is a headline we all loved, referring to the wrestling team after only three meets: "**Unbeaten As Usual.**"

As **Dan Dorsheimer** remembered, "We would sit on the bleachers and roar for Stauffer. He never let us down. It was always the highlight of the match when George would fly out onto the mat, cross over and shake hands, the whistle would sound, and the next thing you would see were two bodies flying across the mat. He would bring the house down. We loved it. I felt sorry for the opposing wrestlers, because most never knew what was coming. There was very little scouting at that time and taping the bout for later review was practically unheard of."

Lower Dauphin Wrestling

Home of the Champs

Have team will travel

95 lb. G. Kline	138 lb. R. Michael
103 lb. S. Dupler	145 lb. E. Neiswender
112 lb. J. Umbrell	154 lb. R. Verdelli
120 lb. B. Kreiser	165 lb. C. King
127 lb. L. Kuntz	160 lb. G. Stauffer
133 lb. T. Mutek	UNI F. Foreman

These cards were printed in the school's print shop just for fun and for distribution to the team and their fans.

The Hummelstown Sun, January 6, 1971. "The teams traveled to Cumberland Valley last Saturday night and pinned a 31-19 loss on the Eagles. **George Kline** was wrapped up by the Eagles' Mark Whitcomb in the first period. Our **Mike Kreiser** pinned. Dupler's 5-0 decision provided a 9-6 edge. **Bob Kreiser** pinned. **Larry Kuntz's** bout ended in a 0-0 tie. **Mutek** scored a decision and **Ron Michael** levied another fall, giving the Birds a 24-8 advantage. Sophomore **Ed Neiswender,** in his first dual match on the varsity squad, was forced to settle for a 0-0 tie. …two Falcon Grapplers, **Joe Umbrell** and **George Stauffer,** were honored by area coaches and sports writers by being named to the **Big 12 Wrestling Team.**"

The Patriot-News, January 15, 1971. "Lower Dauphin rolled to its **fifth** Capital Area triumph with a 37-9 decision over Mechanicsburg. There was little surprise. However, a couple of shockers in individual competitions had the fans screaming because of the **two** "Big 12" contenders who went down to **defeat for the first time** this season.

George Kline

"A breath-taking move by **Ed Neiswender** at 145 edged Rod Chamberlain with six seconds remaining."

George Stauffer recorded his ninth win without a loss, using a half nelson to pin Joe Law. The team brought home another **CAC Championship.** A bonus for many matmen was the collection of sharp photography of the wrestlers in action demonstrating various wrestling positions. (See George Kline above and others below.) Such attention to attire and positions was not customary, but the fellows were intrigued with photos that were other than just the team picture.

CAPITAL AREA SECTION OF DISTRICT III

Lower Dauphin grabbed half of the titles in the Capital Area showdown.

RESULTS

95	Mark Whitcomb, Cumberland Valley, pinned Neil Fausnacht, Hershey, 2:31.
103	Sam Dupler, LD, dec. Bob Stumbaugh, Red Land, 13-5.
112	Joe Umbrell, LD, dec. Mike Torchia, RD, 8-0.
120	Bob Kreiser, LD, dec. Eric Carr, CV, 11-0.
127	Elmer Lower, RL, dec. Larry Kuntz, LD, 5-1.
133	Russ Stepp, Mechanicsburg, pinned Mike Hoffman, 4:38.
138	Ron Michael, LD, dec. Ken Dupert, CV, 10-6.
145	Ed Neiswender, LD, dec. Rod Chamberlain, M., 4-0.
154	Terry Destito, East Pennsboro, pinned Ron Verdelli, LD, 2-46.
165	Dan Deichmiller, Susquehanna Twp., dec. Chet King, LD, 11-4.
180	George Stauffer, LD, pinned Joe Law, M., 2:32.
Hvy.	Carl Shields, M., dec. Fred Foreman, LD, 6-1.

Ron Michael

"… January 27, 1971. The Falcons handed the Spartans one of their worst setbacks. The big men iced the cake as **George Stauffer pinned** and 'Fearsome Freddie' Foreman dumped **Joe Berning** to totally destroy Spartan spirits." **George Kline** did everything but pin his opponent, winning at 14-1. **Dupler, Umbrell, Kreiser, Mutek, Michael, Neiswender, Verdelli** and **King** also won.

The Sun, February 3, 1971: "Falcons Still Flying High Toward CAC Crown."

"Yeah, they'll win the CAC, but wait till they meet Manheim" was the first line under this second headline: **Falcons Down Manheim Central –Finish Season Undefeated.**

Fred Foreman

"**Lower Dauphin Wrestlers Win Fourth CAC Crown** (February 17, 1971). When the shouting died, so had the Hershey grapplers, who limped back up Route 422 with a **48-1** drubbing administered by the LD champs." (The entire article is worth a full read, but suffice it to say that 2 separate team points were deducted for Unsportsmanlike Conduct from Hershey's initial score of 3.) See accompanying details in the personal story of "Best Dual Match Ever for LD."

Falcon Flash, February 26, 1971, by Tom Orsini: "On February 16, the team rounded out their schedule by tripping Manheim Central 26-15, after smearing Hershey 48-1 to clinch the league championship and finish the season with a 13-0-1 record. …**Mutek** is the most underrated of all the Falcon matmen and is quite aggressive for a sophomore. **Michael** and **Stauffer** should have little trouble winning."

"Lower Dauphin Matmen Dominate CAC Sectionals," *The Sun,* March 3, 1971. From *The Hummelstown Sun:* "It was a breathtaking array as no fewer than ten Falcons…did battle for Sectionals." Yes. This wrestling team was so good that it is well deserving of much attention in this book that covers highlights of the 64 years of Falcon wrestling history.

The Hummelstown Sun, March 10, 1971: "Lower Dauphin's high flying Falcon matmen came away with **two District 3 titles** as Bob **Kreiser** decisioned Camp Hill's Pete Zurflieh 14-1. Ron **Michael** decisioned Central Dauphin's Dave Selvey in a breath-taking three periods. The Falcons go on to Regionals in Philadelphia."

Bob Kreiser Headed for State Finals—March 17, 1971: "**Kreiser pulled the upset of the night last Friday at Regionals,**" qualifying him for the state tournament.

1971–1972 (Record 14-1)

Row 1: Ted Young, George Kline, Greg Finch, Rich Vogel, Mike Kreiser, Bill Divel, Jerry Kuntz, Frank Zininni, Mark Stauffer, Dan Engle.

Row 2: Coach Cassel, Tom Mutek, Ron Michael, Mike Blouch, Ed Neiswender, Kevin Ricker, Darrel Seaman, Fred Foreman, John Neagle.

LD took on its second consecutive powerhouse season as it claimed one-third of the **Big Twelve** honorees: **Fred Foreman, Ron Michael, Tom Mutek,** and **Mark Stauffer.**

At Hershey **Ron Michael,** after slipping at 3:00 in the second period, regained the lead with an impressive third period, scoring 10 points and pulling the win out 17-10. Also noted was that there were still 5 undefeated Falcons. "All of the Falcons unbeaten in the battle remained and were the strength of the Falcon attack."

In the Mechanicsburg meet the Falcon JVs completely over-powered the Wildcats. Notable was "…the **JV** standout match of **Rick Kelley who made the fastest fall** with a pin at :56."

January 16, *Sunday Patriot News*: "LD took **FOUR** of the newspaper's Big Twelve Honors: **Fred Foreman, Ron Michael, Tom Mutek,** and **Mark Stauffer.**" That is ONE THIRD of the 12 featured sports spots.

In March the team brought home another CAC trophy, one they had captured 9 out of the 12 years, with the cumulative record of 147-15-2 for a **90%** winning average. The team has had amazing consistency in dual match competition despite the fact that the Falcons have never had a state champion.

Both Varsity and JVs closed out their **second undefeated season** as Lower Dauphin notched another consecutive Capital Area Conference title. **Ron Michael** and **Fred Foreman** advanced to semi-finals and **Foreman** went on to the finals. According to the local newspaper, **"1971-72 must be classed as one of the finest years ever for Coach Cassel."**

"Central Dauphin East brought a final score of 33-15, with **Tom Mutek, Ron Michael and Ed Neiswender** recording consecutive pins. Cedar Cliff provided one of the three toughest matches the Falcons faced. Consecutive pins by **Tom Mutek** and **Ron Michael** capped the contest for the Falcons, closing at **32-20.**" At Cumberland Valley **Mike Kreiser** recorded the only pin for the Falcons; it took a close 9-8 decision by **Foreman** to pull out the victory in the final bout. At Mechanicsburg **Ron Michael** recorded the only pin for the team's **31-13 win.**

"It took a pin by **Tom Mutek** at 138 to put the Falcons in the lead at Susquehanna Township and then **Michael** followed with still another. **Neiswender** decisioned and **Foreman** added yet another fall for a win of **35-18.** At Middletown the birds recorded their biggest score and most pins in a match for the year, **50-12.** Hershey was a close contest at **23-19.**"

At the Optimist Club dinner meeting honoring Fred Foreman and Ron Michael, State Finalists

LD kept **five** Sectional Championships with **Mark Stauffer** (133), **Tom Mutek** (138), **Ron Michael** (145), **Ed Neiswender** (154), and **Fred Foreman** (Hwt) taking titles, winning the mythical team championship.

At the District 3 Championships **Ed Neiswender** went all the way to finals, losing in a close overtime, 6-5. **Kevin Ricker** at 165 went to the semis where he also lost a close decision at 4-3.

Ron Michael is **LD's first District Champion** this year as he pinned in his first bout, decisioned 10-0 in his second, 16-2 in his semi-bout, and 13-0 for the championship. **Fred Foreman joined Michael as a LD's District Champion** that year at heavyweight."

PA Wrestling Roundup, a state-wide publication, ran a **feature article on Ron Michael.** That is how good this LD team was! Individuals became icons among a team of celebrities! With the new format of using 14 wrestlers in each weight class from the seven sectional tourneys, things were pretty hectic at the **District III Finals.** Most of the top boys were getting bumped off regularly in the stiff competition, so much so that one coach said, "With all these guys getting beat, I can't figure out who is winning."

The magic for LD continued throughout the season and their wins were legendary.

The Sun, Wednesday, March 22, 1972. "Falcon Grapplers Defeated in State Championships" by John Hartwell. "After a long season of wrestling, the Falcons once again fall one short of bringing home a state champ. The highly successful team was betting on at least one champ and as the post season tournaments progressed, their hopes were boosted.

The most likely Falcon to bring home the state title was Ron Michael at 145 lbs. After a fantastic season of 14-0-0, which included seven pins and several overwhelming scores, the fans were betting on him…. In each regular season match these fans and his teammates could count on Ron to score a win or a fall." Hartwell continued, "Words alone cannot begin to describe the kind of wrestler that Ron is. He won the outstanding wrestler award at the Sectionals when he scored pins in each of his two matches. In Districts he overwhelmed … going on to win his Regional title without any trouble. …but lost States. …However…in the eyes of all Falcon wrestling fans Ron is a champion who **will never be forgotten.**"

Hartwell then turned to "the Falcon to go farthest this year—**Fred Foreman,** who weighed less than many of his opponents, **but was a star with his speed and ability,** always managing to outscore his competition (and) …when it came time for the real matches that counted, he changed from a good wrestler to a fantastic one." (See full article *I Am a Lower Dauphin Wrestler.*)

Each time Fred stepped onto the mat he came away a winner. … He won three matches to become the **Sectional** champion, then won four more to take **Districts** and **Regionals,** even defeating Barkinic who had a 25-0-0 record that included 17 pins. Exhausted after these grueling matches, Fred simply tired in the state finals that evening and fell to Chuck Coryea who had a 24-0-0 record which included 19 pins.

In the first 12 years of the wrestling program the Falcons completed 147 wins, 15 losses, 3 ties. This year they scored **504 points** to their opponents' 192!

John (Jack) E. Neagle '72

When a team is outstanding, with a number of extraordinary young men whose accomplishments are heralded, **we are reminded of those who are part of the success even if their names do not always appear** in the narrative, only on the roster. One such proud and loyal wrestler was **John E. Neagle** (shown here in action), whose sister donated to the Alumni Association what had been precious to John: programs and photos he had kept from his days as a Falcon Wrestler. We found this information helpful in making our case that wrestling has many sides. For a sport in which the wrestler stands alone, it still coalesces the team.

1972–1973 *(Record 13-1)*

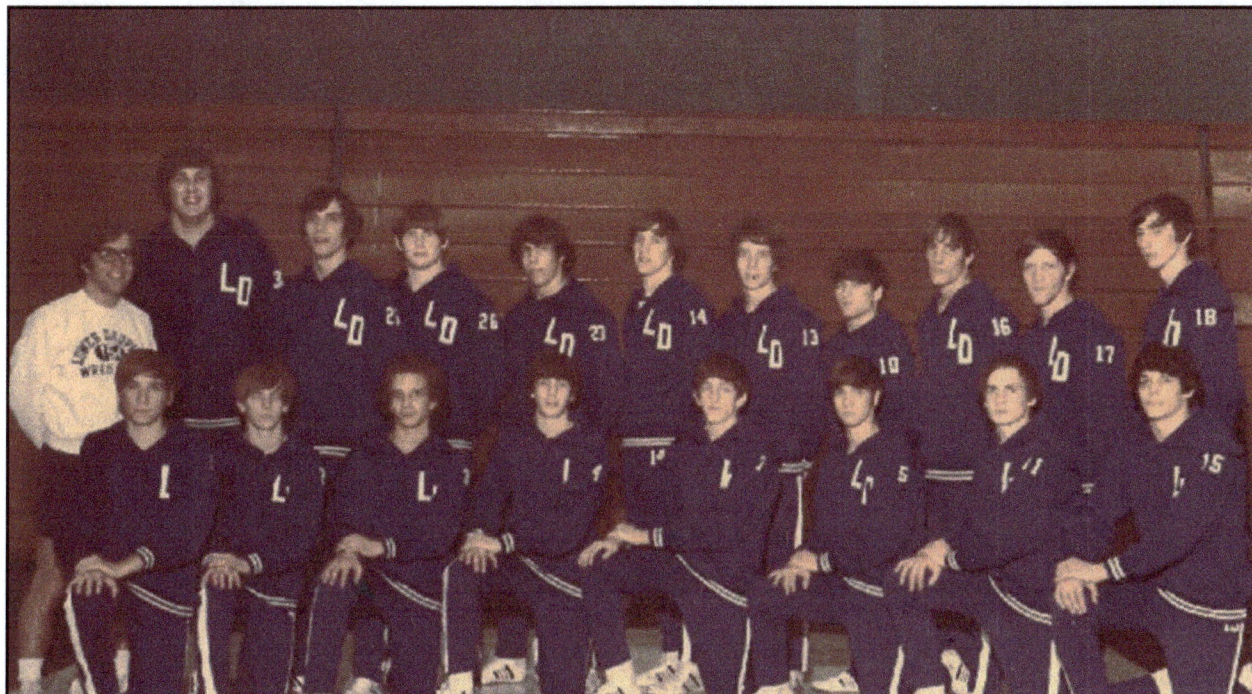

Row 1: Will Etnoyer, Ted Young, Steve Summy, Leon Via, Butch Tonkin, Bill Divel, Mike Heagy, Bruce Rhine.

Row 2: Coach Cassel, Wayne Jockers, Gary Wagner, Darrel Seaman, Roger Witmer, Mark Stauffer, Jeff Felty, Rick Kelly, Eric Deppin, Tom Mutek, Dennis Ebersole, Ed Neiswender, a member of the team, is not shown.

This particular wrestling season gained well-earned attention as an outstanding team to a man. Even though **this team's win records were strong**—and **often dramatic**—the work horses (and **score gainers of the team**) did not see their names in ink as they should have. Its members deserved better and should have been lauded.

On December 9, 1972 with **Bill Etnoyer** at 98 pounds, the Falcons opened the season with a pin. This was followed by **Tom Mutek** making his first pin at 138 pounds, as **Mark Stauffer** at 145 pounds achieved a 9-0 decision. At 155 pounds, **Ed Neiswender** began to earn his "Easy Rider" nickname. The battle ended with the score of LD 43, CD East 13. **The Falcons were up and running again!**

Cedar Cliff was a nail-biter to the end as the squads went into the unlimited bout, tied 20-all—and it was up to **Wayne Jockers,** who won by a 7-5 decision. At Mechanicsburg it was much of the same, a relatively easy **38-13** win as the "wiz-bang" **Tom Mutek** style earned him the nickname of "The Pin Machine." Red Land was the next opponent; the Patriots emerged, leaving Falconland dragging a **29-12** defeat behind them.

Everyone expected the Falcons to be fat cats after the Christmas holiday break, but the birds put these rumors to rest on January 9 when they demolished Reading by a **42-5** score. Mutek overwhelmed his opponent 20-5, as **Mark Stauffer** and **Rich Tonkin** pinned. **Ed Neiswender** remained undefeated by overpowering Gary Otto 12-3.

On January 11 the Falcons took the short trail to Susquehanna Township where they were ambushed. The Indians took the first two bouts, but those two were followed by LD catch-up time. While **Mutek** got his decision, **Mark Stauffer** had one of his toughest bouts and emerged with a 1-1 draw. **Darrell Seaman** was unexpectedly decked at 185 and **Wayne Jockers** needed a pin to pull out a win. Jockers chased his opponent for three periods, but couldn't get the fall that evening—most unusual for him. Thus, this Falcon team suffered their first and **only loss**, a heart-breaking **20-21**.

Rumors started almost immediately after the Palmyra meet that the upcoming Hershey contest would be the birds' version of Waterloo, as the high-flying Trojans were looking for blood, or so they said. Then on the day of the match (January 18) the LD matmen found themselves **locked out** of the Hershey gym. When they finally got in they were insulted enough to defeat Hershey **24-19** before a standing-room-only crowd!

Moving up a weight class, **Mark Stauffer** scored a take-down in the last nine seconds and **Neiswender** rode for over three minutes and then escaped to decision Ed Arndt, 2-0. The match was tough and pins on either side non-existent; however, **Bill Etnoyer, Rich Tonkin, Tom Mutek, Jeff Felty, Mark Stauffer** and **Ed Neiswender** all won, and that was enough for a final win.

LD scored the most falls of the season at Manheim Central, pinning five opponents (**39-14**). At Newport the Falcons stifled any threats by a **33-16** defeat, with **Wayne Jockers** winning his 10th match. **Ted Young** (105) got a fall.

On February 8 the team snow-balled Middletown, **49-12**, with **Bill Etnoyer** getting things "rolling with a pin," as a novice sportswriter noted. **Stauffer** and **Neiswender** remained undefeated.

The Birds crunched the Palmyra Cougars **49-3** with **Bill Etnoyer, Tom Divel, Tom Mutek, Mark Stauffer,** and **Robin Nestler** recording pins.

Manheim Central (39-14) was another pin night for the Birds, with **Bill Etnoyer** winning again and **Rich Tonkin, Tom Mutek, Mark Stauffer,** and **Wayne Jockers** all turning the trick.

Evidently East Pennsboro's heart wasn't in this meet and the final **41-6** score showed it. High scoring decisions by our Birds were the order of the evening as only one Falcon fell.

Middletown's Blue Raiders were on the loss end against Lower Dauphin, **49-12**, with no fewer than six Falcons earning pins.

At Cumberland Valley the Eagles heralded that they would knock off Lower Dauphin and take away their share of the CAC crown. They did win the first two bouts, then **Rich Tonkin** won on a decision while **Bill Divel** was tied, after which **Rick Kelley** upset State Champion Eric Carr on a late reversal. "This win by Kelley led to the impetus to win the next four matches, before a close loss at 185 put the heat on **Wayne Jockers** again to save the day. Wayne did not disappoint and got his happiest pin of the season, giving LD a **26-21** win and the **CAC crown** for another year."

According to Coach Cassel, "Probably one of the most spectacular feats in our dual meet history is **Rick Kelley's** drive to break into the line-up. He had first tried out at 185 and lost the wrestle-off. At 165 pounds, he could not defeat district finalist, Kevin Ricker. He could not beat 154 pound state finalist Ed Neiswender, 145 pound state finalist Mark Stauffer, or 138 pound state finalist Tom Mutek to earn a slot. However, one month later, Rick announced that **he was dropping to 132 pounds** to beat Cumberland Valley's State Champion. That night Rick started his first varsity match. The gym was packed and doors were locked before the JV match started. In the varsity match everything went wrong that could go wrong and by the 132 lb. category we were behind 15-5, and now Kelley was facing the State Champion. He wrestled his heart out but, because of a locked hand penalty, was losing 2-1 with only 10 seconds to go. Then the impossible happened. The crowd went wild. Rick reversed his CV opponent, threw in a leg, and rode him out, **winning the match** 3-2. (As the sports writer noted, "Not bad for a kid who had worked hard for six years of practice but had wrestled only one Varsity match.") Rick's victory inspired the team to win another championship."

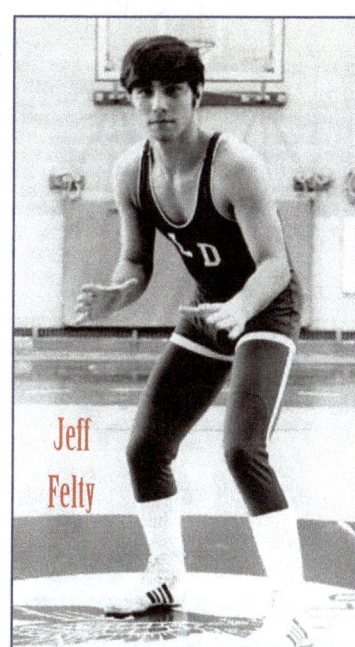

Eric Deppen

Tom Divel

Jeff Felty

At Sectionals LD produced the most individual champs, winning the mythical team championship with five winners: Bill Divel at 119, Tom Mutek at 138, Mark Stauffer at 145, Ed Neiswender at 155, and Wayne Jockers at heavyweight. Districts*, Regionals, and State Championship again pitted the Falcons against many of their previous foes. **LD was the number 1 team in the state of Pennsylvania.** We placed THREE in the State finals, all of whom were **State Runners-up: Mark Stauffer, Tom Mutek,** and **Ed Neiswender.** Quite a feat!

Records for these top three:

Tom Mutek: two-time Sectional Champion; District and Regional Champion; State Runner-up in 1973; posted 17 pins on the way to a 26-1 record this year; his three-year record was 60-4. (Older brother Fred had co-captained the 1967 LD team).

Mark Stauffer: two-year record of 42-2-2; twice Sectional champion; 1973 District 3 and Regional Champion; Runner-up at States the past year; brother of alumnus Falcon George Stauffer, Middle Atlantic champion for Elizabethtown College.

Ed Neiswender posted a 64-4 record for three Varsity years at LD: three time Sectional Champion; 1973 District 3 Champion; Regional and State runner-up; Pennsylvania Federation Champion in 1972; three times Christmas Tourney Champ; and Captain of the LD football team.

During this same decade **Ron Michael** lit up the country! After a 37-2 career at LD, Ron wrestled for Kent State and became LD's only NCAA Division I, All American when he placed fourth at the 1978 National Championships. He was two-time Mid-Atlantic Conference Champ and posted the third best winning percentage in Kent State's wrestling history. His 19 career pins placed him fifth on the all-time Kent list....

Mike Heagy

Bruce Rhine

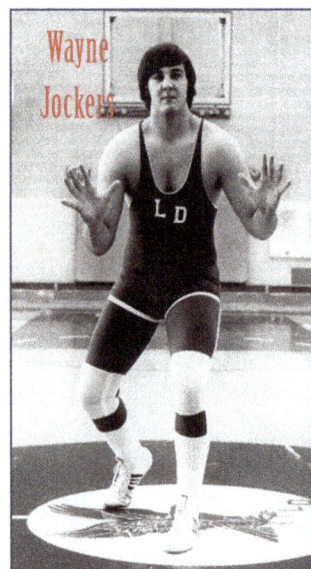

Wayne Jockers

---

* Tom Mutek scored the first Falcon championship win at 138 as he polished off Conrad Weiser's John Santaour 7-0. Mark Stauffer had a 12-2 decision.

There was only one low point during the season when LD's three-year, 38 dual meet winning streak was halted by Susquehanna, but in true Falcon fashion the team turned around and defeated an outstanding Hershey team and a tremendous Cumberland Valley team in two gripping matches to end the season. High among the names that will be remembered from this are **Tom Mutek, Mark Stauffer, Ed Neiswender, Wayne Jockers, Bill Divel,** and **Rick Tonkin!**

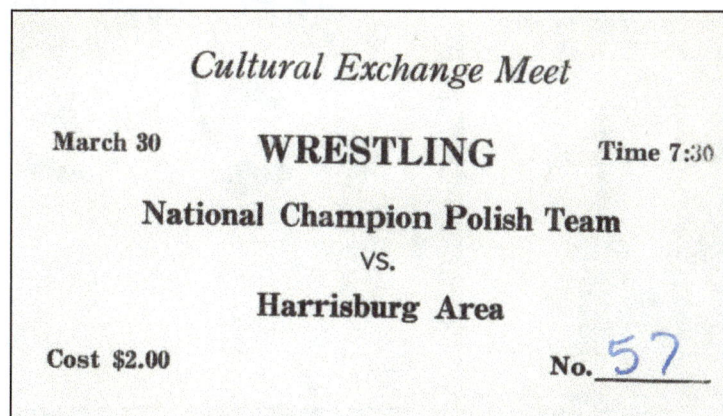

Cultural Exchange Meet

March 30   **WRESTLING**   Time 7:30

National Champion Polish Team

VS.

Harrisburg Area

Cost $2.00   No. 57

In addition to these achievements, on March 30 LD hosted a meet between the National Champion Polish Team and the Harrisburg Area All Stars. LD contenders included Tom Mutek, Mark Stauffer, and Ed Neiswender. Quite an honor!

As the high school yearbook (*Falconaire*) noted, "This year's team again proved to be just as great, if not greater, **than that of any other year** in producing a **season record of 13-1-0 and THREE state runners-up**."

Based on a document that recently came to our attention from the proud Class of 1973, the following are here being acknowledged:

Wayne Jockers had a perfect, undefeated season this, his senior year: 12-0-0.

Tom Mutek had a perfect record of 14-0-0 in 1971-72 and 13-0-0 in 72-73.

Ed Neiswender achieved the same—13-0-0 in 1971-72 and 14-0-0 in 72-73.

Sectional Champions were **Bill Divel, Tom Mutek, Mark Stauffer, Ed Neiswender,** and **Wayne Jockers.**

District Champions included **Tom Mutek, Mark Stauffer,** and **Ed Neiswender.**

State Runners-Up were **Tom Mutek, Mark Stauffer,** and **Ed Neiswender.**

Wrestling finished with a 13-1 record, losing only to Susquehanna Twp. in a thrilling 21-20 match. The team shared the title with Cumberland Valley whom they trounced with the help of an electrifying match between Rick Kelley and the heavily-touted Eric Carr.

Steve Summy

Gary Wagner

Darrel Seaman

Each position shown here (and above) was matched to the move that followed.

1973–1974 (Record 12-2)

Row 1: Dave Yavoich, Ted Young, John Dupler, Leon Via, Lamar Koser, Ken Mutek, Karl King.

Row 2: Jerry Kuntz, Dave Graybill, Bob Keller, Barry Tomazin, Mark Camasta, Roger Witmer, Darrel Seaman, Karl Appleyard, Coach Don Heistand.

With Coach Cassel on sabbatical leave this year the Falcons were ably led by Coach Don Heistand in his first varsity head-coaching assignment. Assistant Coach was Randy Umberger, who was engaged in this wrestling program most of his life. It says a lot for a school when its graduates return to their Alma Mater in coaching positions and when these coaches step up to the mat!

Left to right: Coaches Paul Wolfe, Frank Neiswender, Don Heistand, Dave Epler

December 6: The grapplers won their opener against CD East, **36-11**, winning all bouts from 98 to 155 lb. with **Ted Young** (105) and **Dave Graybill** (138) registering pins.

December 13: Lower Dauphin then defeated Milton Hershey with a big lift from **Roger Witmer** for a **29-16** victory. Witmer had controlled the action, outpointing Jim Hall by 10 for a superior decision, thus erasing Milton Hershey from any chance of winning.

December 15: After an early season loss to Cedar Cliff, the Falcon wrestlers manhandled everyone in sight on December 20 to win over Mechanicsburg: **27-18**.

At a Dallastown Holiday Tourney Lower Dauphin defeated State College for the team title while also out-pointing their JVs.

On January 3, 1974, LD bombed Red Land **41-12**. On January 10 they defeated Susquehanna Township **23 to 18**, and on January 12 it was **LD 42 to Palmyra's 11**.

"Lower Dauphin-Hershey Thriller" was Skip Hutter's title for his article covering LD's match with Hershey in the January 17 issue of *The Patriot News*: "It might have required nerves of steel to take in last night's Lower Dauphin-Hershey wrestling match. …The Capital Area Conference match was deadlocked at 21 going into heavyweight confrontation which sent Lower Dauphin's Darrel Seaman against Bill McCorkle. …with 40 seconds remaining in the fracas, the score was tied, 9-9. Seaman then put McCorkle into a near-fall, ending the match in a take-down for a 13-10 decision." Hershey **21**, Lower Dauphin, **24**.

On January 23 *The Sun* reported that "The LD matmen chewed their way through the East Pennsboro lineup last Thursday night for a **45-5** victory, looking toward a showdown contest with Cumberland Valley in what will undoubtedly be the contest for the 1974 Capital Area Conference wrestling crown. Pins came from **Dave Graybill, Mark Camasta, Roger Witmer, and Karl Appleyard**."

The *Sunday Patriot News* on January 26 reported the following: "Newport battled Lower Dauphin on equal terms during the last seven weights. However, the Falcons won the first five bouts for a 35-14 triumph and the night's big match involved undefeated Steve Rudy of Newport and Dave Graybill of Lower Dauphin at 145 lb. After a scoreless first period, Graybill reversed his opponent to take a **2-1** lead in the third, but it ended in a **2-2** draw."

Roger Witmer and Dave Graybill, displaying their trophies presented at the Lower Dauphin Boosters' Wrestling Banquet April 30, 1974. Both had battled their way to "States" where they ended great seasons.

February 7: "The Falcons won a huge victory over Middletown at 57-3 with pin wins recorded by **Ted Young** (105), **Leon Via** (119), **Lamar Koser** (126), **Jerry Kuntz** (138), **Dave Graybill** (145), and **Bob Keller** (155). Middletown's last two weights forfeited."

On February 14 LD met Cumberland Valley. "This Valentine's Day was recorded as one of the most palpably tense days of the school year. Spirits ran high at the afternoon's pep rally. Skits, cheers and chants sent emotions to a fevered pitch for the most dramatic match of the season— one with two teams, both undefeated in the Capital Area Conference and in the **last CAC meet** of the season." * Unfortunately LD lost (only its second match of the year) by a decisive score, **32-12**.

At the end of the season Lower Dauphin High School was ranked as one of the top ten teams in the state, ranking just below State College (which LD had out-pointed in the Christmas tournament) in wrestling in the entire state of Pennsylvania.

The varsity team's total season was 441 to their opponents 214 – in other words LD doubled the total score of their collective opponents.

*The Falconaire, 1974

Jillian Jacobs and Jean Ball Jacobs '77, Sponsors

"To all of the Falcon Wrestlers whose lives were changed by dedicated coaches, supporting faculty, and the experience of being a Lower Dauphin Wrestler!"

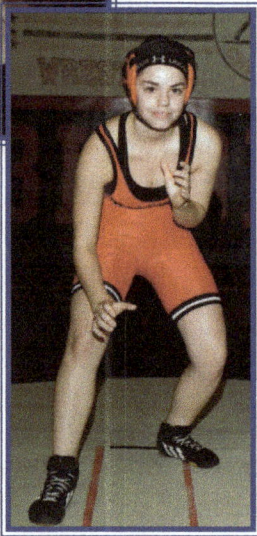

Jillian Jacobs, daughter of 1977 LD graduate, Jean Ball Jacobs, and Honored Academic Commencement Speaker, who became the first female to win a wrestling match in the renowned Clearfield High School Bison Wrestling History in her team's win over Clarion at the Bison Duals in 2008.

In honor of **LOWER DAUPHIN WRESTLING,**

. . . especially Coach Cleon *and* Dottie Cassel *and my favorite wrestler,* George Kline, Class of '72

In memory of my favorite, **LOWER DAUPHIN WRESTLING FANS:** *my father,* Kenneth Imhof, *and my sister,* Nanci Imhof Swistoski.

—*Kathy Imhof Weber*

1974–1975 *(Record 12-2)*

Row 1: Brian Leeser, Don Messick, Mel Watts, Keith Umberger, Larry Cobaugh, Bob Myers

Row 2: Charlie Hammaker, Chris Wallish, Jim Einhouse, John Dupler, Dave Havoich, Greg Etnoyer.

Row 3: Karl King, Ken Mutek, Lloyd Umberger, Tom Sanders, Coach Cassel.
(Missing from the picture is Al Fluman.)

From Skip Hutter, Sportswriter for the Evening News: … "Lower Dauphin whipped Milton Hershey, 35-12. Sophomore Al Fluman won his first varsity match with a **6-4** decision over Rich Schmoel at 119. At 126 Lloyd Umberger advanced the Falcons to a commanding 10-0 lead with a **10-7** triumph resulting from a take-down and predicament."

The Falcons maintained their reputation as a powerhouse, winning important victories over Hershey and Susquehanna. However, the main obstacle the Falcons had to overcome was Cumberland Valley. Coming in, both teams held 8-0 records and both were poised for their annual showdown. Fans were anticipating a memorable victory; however, confidence weakened as the match progressed.…

The Evening News, January 10, 1975, reported, "In Capital Area wrestling Hershey continued its winning ways over Palmyra while Lower Dauphin kept pace with a **38-12** victory over Susquehanna Township. However, injuries marred the Lower Dauphin victory. At 185, Keith Umberger and Susquehanna's Scott Pierce collided head-on 30 seconds into the match."

The Sun, January 15, 1975 noted, "On January 11ᵗʰ the Lower Dauphin gym was ready for its home match. As expected, the young men showed their fans just how the sport of wrestling is well-executed...."

The Sun, undated, reported by Chuck Ercole: "In a battle of the unbeatens last Thursday night, LD topped Hershey, **24–18**. It was an extremely close match that saw six one-point decisions. At the 98 lb. category LD got off on the right foot when **Etnoyer** pinned Pavone. Then **Dave Yavoich** decisioned Gonzales. **Dale Hixon** took down Rick Bechtel midway through the first period. That turned out to be all the points scored, as each wrestler rode the other in the next two periods of a 2-1 decision. With thirty seconds to go, McCorkel had a takedown. He put on a cradle to tilt **Dupler**, but the move was too late and **LD received the decision. Ken Mutek** pulled one of the big upsets of the night winning a one point decision for LD as he edged Hershey's John Campbell 4-3. With six seconds to go, **Karl King** took Dave Coxon down to gain a 4-3 decision. Going into the 145 lb. match, the Trojans **needed** to win the remaining five matches to tie, but won only four of them."

The Falcons defeated East Pennsboro on January 30, **48-6**. Then... "It was all on the line as they hosted undefeated Cumberland Valley with the winner taking home the Capital Area Conference crown. ...**Dave Yavoich, Ken Mutek, Mel Watts,** and **Bob Myers** were the only Birds to emerge victorious, all by **decisions for the Falcons**. The rest was all Cumberland Valley (**36-12**)." **Karl King** at 138 lb. was named to *The Patriot-News' Big 12.*

1975–1976 *(Record 13-1)*

Row 1. Larry Cobaugh, Mel Watts, Richard Bittinger, Dwight Kreiser, Jim Leeser, Don Messick, Eric Stauffer.

Row 2. Ken Mutek, Chris Camasta, Randy Stammel, Blake Bowers, Barry Tonkin, Dale Hixon, Greg Etnoyer, Tim Costik, Coach Cassel. Missing from photo: Lloyd Umberger

The Express, Easton, Pa. Feb. 2, 1976. Lower Dauphin's wrestling team entered the 25th Street Gym in Easton, sporting a perfect record after 10 dual meets. When the 11th meet ended, the Red Rovers had knocked off the Falcons by **27-18**. …LD made the score closer when unbeaten **Mel Watts** at 187 and **Larry Cobaugh** at heavyweight added a decision and a pin at the end. **Eric Stauffer,** described by the Easton sportswriter as "a real slick legger," was ready for DiVietro in one of the top matchups of the event. After a near fall, DiVietro scored a reversal for a 6-2 final. The highlight of the meet, however, was **Barry Tonkin** holding on to Mark Bierei for an entire period.

The following are excerpts from the season written by Jennie Jones in a special report for *The Sun,* April 7, 1976: "This is the team who brought home the **10th CAC trophy.**

After the first few practices in the **brand new wrestling room**, it was clear to see when the season began—off at full tilt.

LD had a group of rough-but-ready young men who headed for CD East on December 6 where three Falcon falls were immediately registered. CD East was left in the dust as the Falcons pushed far ahead, **39-14**."

The next dramatic triumph was an impressive **43-5** win over Milton Hershey. Cedar Cliff, a school that usually dominated, followed. LD took the lead immediately and kept a firm hold on that lead throughout the match, squashing the Colts **31-18**.

The first home meet on December 18 was held in our own arena with three pins by three Falcons—**Don Messick** (155), **Mel Watts** (185), **and Hwt. Larry Cobaugh,** leading the Falcons to an easy win.

The tightest match of the season was Red Land (**28-25**), where, while "touch and go," slick falls were performed by sophomores **Chris Camasta** and **Charles Cole**. Then unbeaten **Eric Stauffer** at 145 registered his own first fall of the year and Mel Watts came through, winning the match for LD, with his close but good enough 7-6 decision win.

The Falcons then slaughtered the Susquehanna Indians (**33-13**), followed by Palmyra (**39-9**) where **Stauffer** and **Watts** won their 11th straight matches, Watts by fall. Next on the schedule was arch foe Hershey; the Falcons demolished the Trojans **30-23**.

A home match against Central Dauphin (**29-17**) provided the 10th Falcon triumph while Easton gave the Falcons their first disheartening loss (**18-27**). Next was East Pennsboro, losing by a huge margin, **39-6**. Likely the most celebrated night of the season was LD squashing with five pins, **earning their 10th CAC pennant at 57-5.**

Ten Falcons went on to Districts, with **Mel Watts** and **Dale Hixon** claiming wins in their weight class. Hixon and Stauffer advanced into the District Championship and earned gold. Ken Mutek and Mel Watts both placed third. **Four went on to States** where **Eric Stauffer** won both the 4th place title and a name for LD at States.

1976–1977 (Record 14-2)

Row 1. Brandon Fluman, Jay Dissinger, Chip Hitz, Charlie Cole, Roger Summy, Mike Barrick, Tim Higgins.
Row 2. Dave Carlin, Randy Stammel, Kevin McCorkel, Chris Camasta, Lloyd Umberger, Tom Martino.
Row 3. Al Fluman, John Kiessling, Todd Walters, Rich Behrendt, Doug Stafford, Steve Wagner, Tim Gamber.

"This 16th year of Falcon wrestling had 70 vying for starting positions with enough to fill in any vacancies. Many of the team members were experienced and LD should again be a serious threat to take the CAC crown from Cumberland Valley."

In the fall of 1976 Skip Hutter, sports writer for the *Patriot-News*, wrote a preview of the upcoming wrestling season. Included was his assessment of Lower Dauphin wrestling, "LD simply wants to hold on to something it already owns…and is back on top. Coach Cassel has 10 boys with varsity experience ready to defend the CAC crown. Leading the veterans is Chris Camasta, followed by Charlie Cole. Also returning are Tim Costick, Randy Stammel, Lloyd Umberger, and Tim Higgins."

Their first time out of the gate the team defeated CD East (**26-18**); the second time they crushed Millersburg.

Brandon Fluman '79 remembers the '77 season: "The wrestling team had begun the year with six underclassmen in the starting lineup. Many fans wondered how the inexperienced Falcons would fare against their opponents. When the season started, the team showed them with three straight victories, the middle weights showing impressive wins.

Wrestlerettes: Jennie Jones '77, Terri Stare '79, Barb Baxter '78, Robin Ebersole '77 (Source: 1977 *Falconaire*)

Arch Rival **Cumberland Valley** then traveled to the LD gym where LD fell behind in the lower weights, but slowly caught up toward the end. **Doug Stafford's** pin at 185 brought LD within one single point. The match came down to the final bout. **Tim Gamber '77** easily took the CV man down, but as the opponent began to stand, Tim slammed him to the mat. **On a very controversial call we lost the final bout** and, thus, the match.

December 8, 1976. Defending champion Lower Dauphin took a milestone victory as the Falcons whipped Hershey 26-16 for the school's **200ᵗʰ dual meet win.** With **John Keissling's** win the meet was stopped to announce, **"Two hundred victories ago on this day Lower Dauphin won their very first match."**

December 11, 1976. **Tim Gamber** thwarted a spirited comeback by Cedar Cliff when he scored a second period fall in a **29-21** victory. Although the Colts won more individual matches (six with one ending in a draw), LD made good use of the fall to pick up the winning points.

December 16, 1976. Many saw this match with Cumberland Valley as having the wrestling title at stake. However, the result wasn't clear until the final match, when LD heavyweight **Tim Gamber** stormed out and took down CV's Steve Stoner after just seconds. In complete control, Gamber drove for the fall which should have left the dual tied but along the way he picked up Stoner and slammmmed him. The six points went to CV.

The *Sunday Patriot News*, January 9, 1977. Among **THE BIG 12** (Midstate's Top 12) Tournament Winners were **Chris Camasta** at 138 and **Charlie Cole** at 112.

January 13, 1977. The Falcon wrestlers are gaining momentum and knocking down each school like a chain of dominoes. In their last win LD destroyed the notorious Susquehanna Indians **32-13**.

January 20, 1977. The Falcons were piling up wins almost faster than they could handle. The match against Red Land (**33-14**) was an easy one for LD. Two days later the Falcons raided the Rams of Central Dauphin (**37-17**); see details below. **Charles Cole** was nominated to the Big 12.

January 22, 1977. At Central Dauphin Dean Seaman won by a superior decision, but LD JVs were still down by 3. Big Blue couldn't manage to score until the 185 pound weight. **When a pin was the only thing that would help, Jeff Watts went in and decked his opponent.** In Varsity, **Chip Hitz** won in a thriller. **Dave Bowser's** bout was eventful from start to finish—all of its **one minute and 16 seconds—ending in a pin.** More victories followed, including a **Tim Gamber** fast fall, his specialty.

LD vs Mechanicsburg. LD weighed in 18 men; yes, 18, with plans for relief for some of the first-line wrestlers. Even at that, **LD prevailed 44-12.** Chip Hitz put in an excellent performance for a pin. **Bill McMinn** came through loud and clear with the second fastest fall of the night. The third pin was by **Dave Carlin. Chris Camasta** finished in a superior decision victory, **Lloyd Umberger's** swift 30 second take-down, **Steve Wagner's** turn-over and half-nelson, and **Doug Stafford's** 6-3 crunch—were all part of the win.

Waynesboro men were wiped off the LD mat (45-3), evidence of a good show by **Brandon Fluman** who earned 4 points, **Chip Hitz** who had a shut-out, **Bill McMinn** who clinched a massacre, **Randy Stammel** who came back strong after an injury, **Brian Klinger** with a 7-3 win, **Fritz Glass** who got the first and fastest fall, **Tom Martino** after a rough takedown, and **Ed Stahl** who showed what wrestling skill is. This also marked **Chris Camasta's** scoring a take-down, after which the opponent was unable to continue, resulting in a fast injury default win.

February 3, 1977. Until this date the Cougars of Palmyra had been undefeated, so the Falcons faced a challenge. **Eric Fluman** led off with a pin. Cole was then decisioned by Palmyra. Smith lost to Barrick (Palmyra). Herrick held a decision over Carlin. Finally we had a pin with **Camasta** at 138. **Umberger** (145) followed suit, decking his opponent in the third period, after completely dominating him. Another pin by **Stafford** clinched the match for LD.

February 10, 1977. The East Pennsboro JV score was 51-0 and the Varsity was **40-5!!** However, one of the matches included one of personal aggression when one East Penn wrestler showed unsportsmanlike conduct as he lunged at our wrestler and missed him, flying off the mat out against the score table!

February 12, 1977. Easton brought its wrestling juggernaut in a **28-17** victory over LD.

February 18, 1977. **Chris Camasta** scored a takedown in 3 seconds through an injury default by his opponent.

LD qualified two men for states, seniors Charlie Cole and **Lloyd Umberger,** who "performed the best of all Lower Dauphin matmen, holding on and fighting like tigers."

On March 4, the *Sunday Patriot-News Sports Section's* lead headline shouted, *L. Dauphin's Fritz Glass Shows Mat Form.* "There's an air about those who excel. They tend to draw attention. ...Kevin Brown found Lower Dauphin's Fritz Glass too much to handle as Glass pinned him at 4:56 at 146 pounds. It was LD's day."

From a letter to Coach Cassel from **Ron Michael,** who had competed at the collegiate level "Nationals:"

Dear Coach,

I'm sending you a picture of me at Nationals. I was really glad that you could be down there with me. I hope the next time I'm wrestling in Nationals you will be there to coach me...I guess it's really rewarding to know that you helped straighten some kid's life up. You taught most of your wrestlers how to be winners by preparing mentally. I help kids during the summer months and they have talent but don't have it mentally. Coach, thanks for everything...you can put the picture in your barn....

The following highlights of 1977 wrestling are from Brandon Fluman '79:

The Falcons rebounded, as we won our final two matches before Christmas at State College where we crowned three champions: **Chris Camasta '77, Al Fluman '77** and **Tim Gamber '77** were all victorious as we tied for the championship with Cedar Cliff. The new year brought us seven wins with only one loss. Six wrestlers survived Round 1 while Charlie Cole, Chris Camasta, and Lloyd Umberger qualified for the District Crown. Both Charlie and Lloyd made it to States, but both lost in the first round. The team finished the year with a 14-2 record.

From the "WE MAKE SACRIFICES" DEPARTMENT (and you thought you knew everything about the wrestling program): Sometime during the mid-to-late 1970s, a faculty member was working in his classroom on a Saturday morning and, in need of supplies, entered a loft on the second floor of his shop/classroom. While familiar with this area, he was taken by complete surprise when he tripped over a body!! Upon further inspection he discovered that it was a wrestler apparently wrapped in plastic. Why? It seems that the young man had gone there in hope that he would lose weight prior to the "weigh-ins" at the match that evening....

Heavy duty:

Several closely-fought dual meets were determined by a Falcon heavyweight fall in the final match of the night—for example, Harry Strawser's HWT pin against Cedar Cliff in 1983, or the meet-clinching fall at 167 by Tom Salus against Mechanicsburg in 1987.

[see pages 191 and 202]

Early winners:

In LD wrestling's fifth year (1964-65), Randy Umberger pinned 12 of his 14 opponents (a record) and Jim Sanders had only nine points scored against him during the entire season. [see page 65]

Not actually a legal move . . .

One Hershey wrestler, pinned in something like 30 seconds, was so angry he took a swing at LD heavyweight Fred Foreman, prompting both coaches to intervene. [see page 94]

Who was that masked man?

There were actually two "Masked Wrestlers" and this Falcon action led to a change in the National Wrestling Rules. [see page182]

1977-1978 *(Record 14-2)*

Row 1. Craig Hetrick, Brandon Fluman, Jay Dissinger, Chip Hitz, Tim Costik, Dave Bowser, Charlie Cole.

Row 2. Bryan Klinger, Bill McMinn, Mike Barrick, Pat Kelley, Coach Cassel, Fritz Glass, Chris Camasta, Brian Good, Farrell Black.

Row 3. Dean Seaman, Todd Gregor, Jeff Watts, Craig Lehmer, Steve Stevenson, Ed Stahl.

December 7, 1977. Seventeen years ago, Cleon Cassel was given the task of establishing a wrestling program. "It was expected the Falcons would put a winner on the mat. They did just that… (and) **haven't known a losing season since.**" That evening they came away with a **45-14 win over CD East.**

Special from the 1977-'78 Season: The Falcons next flew high over the Susquehanna Indians, 40-11 for an 8-1 overall record. Hetrick pinned; Fluman swamped Swartz; Hitz wrestled tough; Bowser decisioned; Cole's opponent was disqualified; McMinn earned a 13-12 victory; Camasta wrapped up with a fall; and Stahl pinned. Writing for the Middletown *Press and Journal*, LD's Martha Costik said it all in her opening sentence, "The Lower Dauphin Falcons chalked up three falls, **two regular decisions, two superior decisions,** and **one disqualification** to send the **Susquehanna Indians** back to the teepee."

THE SUN, WEDNESDAY, DECEMBER 7, 1977

Falcon Grapplers Get 200th Cassel Victory

by Tammy Manoogian & Barb Baxter

In their season opener last Friday night, the Lower Dauphin High School matmen traveled to Central Dauphin East and hung a lopsided 45-14 victory in their column to give head coach Cleon Cassel his 200th match win since his arrival at Lower Dauphin in 1960.

Starting the match off at 98 pounds for the Falcons was freshman Craig Hetrick, who decisioned his 98 pound opponent Paul Moretz by an 8-0 score. At 105, Brandon Fluman pinned John Moretz of CD East in an upset, Moretz having been picked in the top 100 area wrestlers by pre-season polls.

At 112 pounds, Jay Dissinger first scored two points on a takedown, then two more on a reversal for a 4-0 decision win. At 119, Lower Dauphin's Dave Bowser had his hands full, scoring three points in the second period and then coming back for a fourth point in the final to gain a 4-4 tie.

Wrestling at 126 is team captain Charlie Cole, who scored four points in the first period, three in the second and then went on to pin his man in the final stanza. Bryan Klinger, a junior wrestling at 132 for the Falcons, had similar success, but couldn't quite show his opponent the lights, having to settle for a 7-0 decision shutout win.

Fritz Glass, the Falcon entrant at 138 pounds, recorded the fastest fall of the evening in 1:38 of the first period. At 145, co-captain Chris Camasta pinned Kim Biery for six more team points for the Birds.

Falcon sophomore Sam Heagy, wrestling at 155, was the tough luck loser of the evening. Facing CD East Senior Dave Platt, Heagy scored two points in the first period on a reversal, then had another reversal in the second period to lead going into the final, when he got reversed and pinned.

At 167 pounds, senior Dean Seaman wrestled captain Mark Dietz of CD East, losing by a fall.

In the 185 pound class, Lower Dauphin's Jeff Watts did most of his point scoring in the second period, but then showed CD East senior Bill Gigliotti the lights in the final stanza.

Finishing off the night for the Falcons was senior heavyweight Steve Stevenson. Steve scored two points in the first period, then kept wracking up points to win by a decision, 9-5.

JV MATCH

The Lower Dauphin Junior Varsity started their season with a victory for coach Don Hiestand, by a lopsided 50-3 mark.

Wrestling for the Falcons - 98 Mark Watts WBF, at 105 Mark Kiessling WBF, 112 Chip Hitz WBF, 119 Dwight Zitch 13-0, 126 Bob Dupler 6-2, 132 Eryc Christofes 6-4, at 138 Brad Bomgardner 10-6, at 145 Evin Ginn WBF, 155 Bob Hammaker 7-4 at 167 freshmen Joel Umberger LBF at 185 John Book 3-2, Hwt Ed Stahl WBF. The JV team showed signs of expert knowledge in wrestling, winning the match with the final score of 50-3.

Following the match, the LD wrestling Booster Club congratulated Coach Cleon Cassel on his 200th victory with a celebration in his honor.

Many friends, fans and former wrestlers gathered in the Lower Dauphin cafeteria awaiting the return of the successful coach and the wrestlers with an inscribed wall clock.

Bob Myers, along with the 1975 wrestling team, awarded their former coach with a trophy.

Barney Osevala, principal, presented coach Cassel with a watch and two wall plaques, one of which will be displayed in the Lower Dauphin District Office, and the other for Coach Cassel himself. The plaque reads, "You're only as tough as you think you are; you're only as good as you want to be."

December 10, 1977 against Cedar Cliff. The Colts provided their usual tough time and throughout the evening it was up and down, the final victors unclear, not usual with CC. In JVs the Falcons' Mark Watts decked Steve Sauerman in 2:43. With a Falcon forfeit at heavyweight it was up to John Book at 185 to come through and win it! The score gap was three points going into the heavyweight battle. A penalty gave LD's Ed Stahl a first period point, but in the second period he was warned for stalling;* the same happened in third period. In the remaining seconds, "Big Ed" scored a takedown, 4-1. This gave LD the win for this bout. The score was Cedar Cliff **23**, LD **29**.

---

* Was the sports reporter's clever play on words intentional?

December 15, 1977 against Cumberland Valley. Despite herculean efforts, as the match narrowed to the final two, LD badly needed a pair of pins. **Jeff Watts** provided just that. The heavyweight would again be crucial. There was no score in the first period as the crowd came to its feet. In the second, Ed Stahl won two points with an escape and was awarded two more points in the third period on stalling by CV, preventing Ed from winning through action. (**PIAA** notes: **LD 23**, and **CV 22**)

The Sun, January 4, 1978. "Falcon Grapplers Win Last Three Meets, beating Chambersburg **43-13**." At **Elizabethtown Fluman** went undefeated, **Gregor** at 167 wrestled a superb bout with the superior 16-6 score and with a final team score

Ed Stahl

of 38-6. At Middletown the Falcons won. The final match at 167 was a close win for Todd Gregor. The mighty Falcon machine blew the Blue Raiders completely off the mat with a **67-0 win, according to PIAA records.**

The Sun, January 11, 1978 by Barb Baxter. "The mighty Lower Dauphin Falcons planned to start the New Year off right, traveling to **Milton Hershey** as scheduled. As usual, Craig Hetrick began with a first period fall (this time of 1:44) over his Spartan combatant. At 105, Brandon Fluman accumulated 2 points each period for a 6-0 score over Jim Truax. Coming back after 2 losses for LD at 120 was Co-Captain Charlie Cole. After a 6-0 lead, our Falcon proceeded to pin Fred Fouad in 3:03. The Score was **LD 36 and Milton Hershey 13.**

Next, the varsity marched onto CD East's mat and became complete owners of it, **LD 45, East 14,** beginning with **Freshman Craig Hetrick's** 10-0 superior decision over T. Moretz. From there it was practically all LD! Jay Dissinger took his first victory of the season by controlling the 112 lb. class with a 4-0 decision. Dave Bowser's match came to a 4-4 draw. At 126 Charlie Cole pinned J. Harris in 4:21. Brian Klinger (132) defeated Chiaucttia, 7-0.

At 138, Fritz Glass decked J. Harris in 1:38, which was the quickest fall of the night. Veteran Chris Camasta pinned K. Biery in 1:55. At 155 and 167 came the only Falcon losses of the evening, but LD retaliated at 185 when Jeff Watts took the last pin by decking Gigliotti at 4:15.

The surprise to follow occurred when the team returned to the high school where they were just in time for the surprise party in celebration of **Coach Cassel's 200th win.**

On February 2 the Falcons took **Susquehanna 40-11.** Dave Bowser at 119 won his match with the superior score of 25-10 while Craig Hetrick added another pin in the record time of 3:07.

Chosen for the "Big 12" by the *Patriot News* at 126 was **Charlie Cole** who, in the second home match, with a lead of 10-1, suffered an intentional eye gouge from his Susquehanna opponent who had come to the match with a record of six pins. Soon thereafter the Susquehanna wrestler used the same stunt again and the bout was stopped. Six points were added to the Falcon scoreboard and a minus 1 was charged to Susquehanna.

Bill McMinn had an escape with 21 seconds remaining, and in the very last second he reversed. **Another oddity found Chris Camasta wrestling Evin Ginn who just three days before the match had left Lower Dauphin where he was on the wrestling team, moving back to Susquehanna and was now an LD opponent.** With losses at 155, 167 and 185 for LD, the match ended when Ed Stahl put the move on Derrick Brodfield and decked him in a time of 2:33.

At **Central Dauphin**, February 4, **Charlie Cole** won in a fast 1:40 fall. McMinn had a superior 17-8 Falcon score; Brian Klinger won 9-1. Camasta ran into a reversal but came off the mat with the 11-9 win; Farrell Black finished 6-4; Dean Seaman gathered an escape, takedown, and 2 back points for a final 8-4 win. Jeff Watts showed Stan Gingrich the lights in 3:48 and Ed Stahl won the 8-0 victory. In typical LD style, this sums up the Falcons and their practical coach. **Lower Dauphin 36, Central Dauphin 13.**

Charlie Cole

Coach Cassel and his young athletes appeared to be at a low point and the tough four-team tournament hosted by Dallastown was ahead of them, but that didn't keep them from plugging away at practice. **It paid off.**

The Sun, February 8. The Falcons went against the **Panthers** of East Pennsboro with **Craig Hetrick scoring a superior 9-0 victory.** Brandon Fluman had a 6-3 win against Dave Frantz, Charlie Cole gathered 14 points, Bill McMinn stood over his Panther opponent with a 9-3 score, and Brian Klinger maneuvered combatant Rick Daub for a swift fall. Co-Captain Chris Camasta gained LD six more points. Jeff Watts' power led to another 6 points. The last bout ended in a tie, but LD won the meet, **42-13.**

The Falcons next flew high over the **Susquehanna Indians, 40-11** for an 8-1 overall record. Hetrick pinned; Fluman swamped Swartz; Hitz wrestled tough; Bowser decisioned; Cole's opponent was disqualified; McMinn earned a 13-12 victory; Camasta wrapped up with a fall; and Stahl pinned.

January 15, the *Sunday Patriot-News* announced two LD grapplers for the BIG 12, Charlie **Cole** (126) and Chris **Camasta** (138).

Chris Camasta, back row, first on left; Charlie Cole, front row, third from right

1978 District III AAA SC

Regional Champions

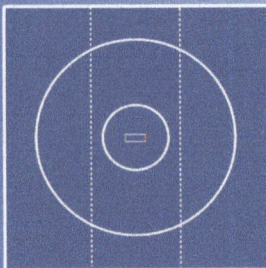

1978–1979 *(Record 14-2-1)*

Row 1. Mike Kelley, Dave Bowser, Jay Dissinger, Brandon Fluman, Scott Lloyd, Curt Rice, Chuck Diebler.

Row 2. Bryan Klinger, Sam Heagy, Chip Hitz, Craig Hetrick, Wayne Rice, Jeff Witmer, Bob Dupler.

Row 3. Coach Umberger, Eryc Christofes, Dick Stokes, Jeff Watts, Ed Stahl, Fritz Glass, Joel Umberger, Dwight Zitch, Coach Cassel.

Asst. Coach Randy Umberger was elevated to the top spot to serve as Co-Head Coach with Cleon Cassel. Karen Camasta, sports reporter for LD, wrote: "The Lower Dauphin grapplers were off to a winning start after earning their first win of the season by destroying Central Dauphin East **45-17**. With eight lettermen returning, the recapturing of the CAC Championship looked promising. The Junior Varsity followed suite, slaughtering their opponents 55-12."

And so the season went, win by win, **led by a dynamic pair of coaches, Randy Umberger and Cleon Cassel,** to an impressive record of 14-2-1. And with such a wrestling roster of familiar names of students who were winners in their own right, the record looks about right!

Here, too, is evidence that our bona fide high purse-winning jockeys (brothers Curt and Wayne Rice) were, indeed, also successfully engaged in wrestling on the LD team with classmates who were members of entrenched LD families well-established with familiar names of the Hummelstown and Lower Dauphin conglomerate, all of them vested in the community and its school district, a modern tableau of "Our Town."

Following a successful season the *Patriot-News*, March 4, 1979 reported, "At the **District Wrestling Tournament** Kevin Brown, Manheim Central, found L.D.'s Fritz Glass (145) too much to handle. Glass pinned Brown at 4:56 of their preliminary match. Waynesboro's Brian Smith had to go to overtime before defeating Wayne Rice (112) of L.D., 5-0. At 126, Mike Kelley (L.D.) was the lone entry to come away victorious. Both champion Larry Kostelac at 132 of Cumberland Valley and runner-up Brian Klinger of Lower Dauphin were easy winners in the quarterfinals. The lone area winner at 167 was **Jeff Watts** of Lower Dauphin.

The *1979 Falconaire* notes that Senior **Mike Kelley** was the only Falcon selected to the Big 13 squad. Kelley, along with Bryan Klinger and Jeff Watts, also advanced to States.

Again, it was a Kelley who provided a spectacular match. With the score locked at 10-10, **Kelley pinned Rico Chiapparelli** who later was four-time Maryland State Champion. This match was the only bout Chiapparelli lost in high school prior to winning the National Championship.

The Wrestling Season record was **14-2-1**. Coach Cassel's Note: The seventies finished on an outstanding note when LD tied Mt. Saint Joseph of Maryland, 27-27. Prior to facing Lower Dauphin, Mt. Saint Joseph had won 125 straight matches in five different states.

1979–1980 *(Record 16-1)*

Row 1. Chuck Deibler, Steve Reeder, Craig Cassel, George Coble, Wayne Rice, Craig Hetrick, Don Farr, Craig Camasta.

Row 2. Charlie Ritrovata, Mark Kiessling, Joel Umberger, John Book, Ken Hosler, Eryc Christofes, Rhys Myers, Sam Heagy.

This decade had begun as one of the most successful in Lower Dauphin history and the teams were 117-32-1. We defeated Shikellamy in 1980, snapping their 45 match win streak, followed by also cracking the long winning streak for Warwick.

Three sophomores (Craig Cassel, Ray Fogleman, and Craig Camasta) were promoted to the Varsity Team. There were also three juniors (George Coble, Craig Hetrick, and Joel Umberger) along with 13 seniors on varsity.

At East Pennsboro Wayne Rice collected 17 points, adding to the 5 superior decisions. The team scalped the Indians and gave Warwick its first loss in a string of **38** matches.

LD also **shattered three lengthy win streaks** this season: Cumberland Valley's 25 wins, Warwick's 30, and Shikellamy's 32.

Below is a truncated account by Skip Hutter, polished sportswriter for *The Patriot:* "**After defeating CV for the first time since 1976,** the team watched fans run onto the mat at the end of the win. A highlight of that win was John Book's take-down of Collins five times, letting him escape four, and ultimately winning, 16-10. The meet had also provided **a tide-turner by Joel Umberger** against Joel Ondrejicka, knowing he needed to win if the Falcons were to have any hope at all.

From the outset Ondrejicka looked like he was going to make matters extremely difficult. An unforgettable situation, Ondrejicka took Umberger down just 12 seconds into the match and maintained control until the closing seconds. Umberger did score a penalty point when Ondrejicka locked hands. Then with 14 seconds left in the opening period, Umberger suddenly reversed and took the lead and controlled the second period with time running out. He worked into a cradle and then a half, before surprising the crowd by **pinning Ondrejicka with just three seconds left in the period.** This set up hope for Book's masterful performance, leading the LD fans to go wild with the win. In the midst of this breath-taking match, Rice remained unbeaten."

Another perfect touch to the evening was the battle of sophomores at 112, in which Craig Cassel, son of Coach Cassel, escaped with 26 seconds left in the match to gain a 1-1 draw with Steve Sauve, son of former Mechanicsburg coach Steve Sauve. What more could anyone want?

This LD team also was the Christmas Tourney Champions, defeating Dallastown, Cedar Cliff, and State College. And they were the **first team ever** in District 3 to win all titles:

- AAA Top Team in District 3 (Dual Meets)
- Sectional Champions
- District III Tournament Team Champions with a new scoring record of 85½.

The story-book, major match that everyone had been waiting for was the heavyweight battle that culminated the meeting of Lower Dauphin against **Milton Hershey School;** it bears a place in LD history. From *The Sun's* account: "The match had long been decided, but just about everyone was awaiting the heavyweight bout, and with good reason. Squaring off were Lower Dauphin's Joel Umberger and Milton Hershey's Carlton Bleiler, two of the top heavyweights in the Capital Area Conference, and, in all probability, all of District Three. It turned out to be quite a showdown, finally won by (Joel) Umberger by a 6-3 count, nailing things down as the Falcons posted a **42-13 victory.**

Umberger and Carlton had been wrestling at both 185 and heavyweight this season, and both had been big winners thus far. Bleiler opened the scoring here by taking Umberger down 20 seconds into the bout, but he managed to maintain control for less time than that before Umberger reversed him to make it 2-2.

Bleiler escaped with just under a minute left in the period to go ahead 3-2, but with 18 seconds left, Umberger scored a takedown to make it 4-3. The score stayed that way throughout the second period, with Umberger on top and in control for the entire two minutes. Bleiler was on top in the third period, and while in control for most of the frame, couldn't turn Umberger and wound up opening himself up for counters. With six seconds left, Umberger finally succeeded in reversing Bleiler for the final two points."

The win boosted Umberger's record to 8-0 in dual meet competition and to 9-1 on the season. Craig Hetrick, Lower Dauphin's 138-pounder, ran his record to 10-0 on the season as he pinned Dave Pinkney in 4:30. Other winners for the Falcons were Sam Fallinger at 105, Craig Cassel at 112, Mike Mazerolle at 119, Craig Camasta at 138, Paul Eyster at 155, Joe Radwich at 167 and Kevin Rogers at 185. The win boosted the Falcons to 5-0 in the CAC and to 6-2 for the season.

In early March, Chuck Deibler, Eryc Christofes, and Craig Hetrick earned a place at States where Craig took a third place victory.

In a feature article in *The Sun*, Karen Camasta noted, "Never in Falcon history has LD produced a team who has captured as many awards as the 1979-1980 team. With 15 sophomores, 11 juniors, and 13 seniors, from lightweight Chuck Deibler to heavyweight John Book, much was achieved, including Eryc Christofes' being chosen as a member of the

District Winners: Craig Hetrick, Craig Camasta, Wayne Rice, Craig Cassel, Chuck Dibeler, and John Book (at right edge of the photo).

Above: Eryc Christofes, Wayne Rice, Chuck Dibeler, and Craig Hetrick.

Patriot News "Big 12" squad. As a team, the Falcons won all four of their club tournaments."

Coach Cassel commented, "… we were again ranked as one of the top teams in the state. The team took on everything there was to win and won it."

On April 20, 1980, the *Sunday Pennsylvanian* did a feature story on Rice brothers Curt '81 and Wayne '80, "both successful wrestlers at Lower Dauphin High School and jockeys at Penn National. Wayne had completed a successful campaign for the Falcons over the winter and Curt logged a 10-3 career record while competing in his sophomore season."[*]

Our students are versatile, indeed, and John Book, varsity wrestler (see adjacent page), not only had a successful sports season, but also delivered the National Anthem at the beginning of the home wrestling meets. In addition, he took a leading role in the annual school musical in 1980, as the Captain in "The Sound of Music."

The musical sponsorship on the following page appeared in the 1979-80 Wrestling Program.

---

[*] At LD both Curt and Wayne Rice were on work-study, at the race track at 6:30 a.m. and in school by 10:30, taking a full load of classes. During wrestling season both remained after school for wrestling practice until 6 p.m. and then made post time at Penn National at 7:30. See "He's My Brother" in this book (*Lower Dauphin Wrestling*.)

Standing in 2nd place is **John Book.**

The Lower Dauphin CAC Wrestling Champs would like to congratulate their versatile teammate, JOHN BOOK, for his latest endeavor, the role of Captain Georg Von Trapp in this year's production of

THE SOUND OF MUSIC

April 10th - 7:30 p.m.
April 11th & 12th - 8:00 p.m.

ADULTS - $2.00   STUDENTS - $1.00

Lower Dauphin Wrestling
Home of the Champs
Have team will travel

95 lb. G Kline	138 lb. R Michael
103 lb. S Dupler	145 lb. E Neiswender
112 lb. J Umdrell	154 lb. R Verdelli
120 lb. B Kreiser	165 lb. C King
127 lb. L Kuntz	180 lb. G Stauffer
133 lb. T Mutek	UNL. F Foreman

John Book, left, as Captain Georg Von Trapp in LD's presentation of "The Sound of Music."

Craig Hetrick, Champion '80

1st Place

Joel Umberger

2nd Place

Randy Umberger and Cleon Cassel named District III and PIAA State Co-Coaches of the Year.

Coaches Randy Umberger and Cleon Cassel with Ron Kanaske, PIAA* — March 26, 1980

The Class AAA Wrestling Championships was the perfect event for this award, with LD being **named the top team in District Three, along with winning the District Championship,** even with not placing a wrestler in the state finals. That fact was evidence of the esteem in which these two coaches were held, marking the first time that a coach from District Three had been so honored. The coaches even shared longevity at LD, both having arrived in the fall of 1960, Cassel then as a teacher and coach and Umberger as an eighth-grader. What made the award even more of an honor was that it marked the first time that a coach from District Three has been so noted. (See more on these two exemplars in this book's section, *Lower Dauphin Falcon Coaches and Athletic Directors*.)

*Kanaskie himself had been inducted into the National Hall of Fame in State College with 662 career wins.

Wrestlers' Stories of the 70s

Falcon Pride Expands
— George Kline '72

Wrestling has been typically represented as a character-building sport for individuals. And part of that is certainly true. At Lower Dauphin in the early 70's, wrestling built self-discipline, respect for authority, perseverance, and an appreciation for hard work. A lot of the credit for that goes to Coach Cassel, but he also created a sense of personal accountability and leadership.

Wrestling at Lower Dauphin definitely was a team sport and the leaders of the team and Coach Cassel held all members accountable to "work hard, give your best effort and always conduct yourself accordingly." The practices could be demanding and Coach expected the best effort from everyone whether varsity, junior varsity, or third string.

As we practiced, Coach would roam the mats, offering advice, encouragement, and sometimes a verbal "kick in the pants." The practice-ending, timed sit-outs routine could be especially tough, yet it all served to create a camaraderie and true sense of a team family.

The best memory I have of my two years of varsity is that the team did not lose a match. The only blemish on our record was a tie with Cedar Cliff, the outcome of which hinged on what Coach would politely refer to as a questionable call by the referee. (Ironically that referee would turn out to be my college assistant wrestling coach.)

My fondest individual memory was of a match with East Pennsboro. In those days the team had a "kitty" for each match and the wrestler with the fastest fall would win the pot. I was not the most accomplished member of the team and rarely was in the running for the money.

East Pennsboro was not a wrestling powerhouse and, as the lightest weight in the match, I led it off, pinning my opponent in thirty-one seconds. As the match progressed, it appeared that time (31 seconds) would hold up as the fastest. That is until the next to last match when George Stauffer, our 180 pounder, pinned his opponent in twenty-nine seconds. The "razzing" that followed was classic….

Two Memorable Kelleys, '78 and '79

— Coach Ed Neiswender

Rich Kelley '78 came out for wrestling after football his senior year, determined to win a slot. He tried out at 185 lbs, losing to seasoned Darrell Seaman. He next tried out at 165, but lost to Roger Witmer '74 who was tough as nails.

The next three weights were Murderers' Row with Mutek, Stauffer, and Neiswender, all District Champs and State Finalists—impossible to beat in try-outs. These three had kept Rich from wrestling Varsity the first three years (of the four in high school).

One night late in the season Rich walked into the wrestling room and announced, "Coach, I am going down to 132 and beat the state champ Eric Carr from Cumberland Valley." CV was the last match of the year and the 1973 League Championship would be decided on this match. The gym was packed and doors were locked before the JV match started. In the Varsity match everything went wrong that could go wrong and by the 132 match we were behind 15-5 and now Kelley was facing the State Champion. He wrestled his heart out, but because of a locked hand penalty he was losing 2-1 with 8 seconds to go. Then, the impossible happened and the crowd went wild. Rich reversed Carr, threw in a leg, and rode him out and won the match 3-2.

As a coach I will never forget **Mike Kelley '79** as the lone entry from LD to come away victorious at Waynesboro at the District Wrestling Tournament, being described in the Sunday Patriot, as "completely dominating his opponent." Mike was wrestling Rico Chipparilli who had never lost a match (his high school record was 125-1) and, not unexpectedly, Rico proceeded to tear Mike apart. Halfway through the second period, Rico led 10-2, but Mike kept coming back and closed the gap to 10-10. Then, just like in the movies, in the third period Kelley pinned Rico. This is just one indication of a great season with Mike, along with Bryan Klinger and Jeff Watts, who all advanced to states. Mike was also the only Falcon that year selected to the Big 13 squad.

Nothing Stops Us
— *An Adventure with Steve Dowhower '70*

One day, as he often did, Steve went squirrel hunting with a friend. As they were seeking their prey, Ed's hunting buddy, who had forgotten his glasses, saw something move at a distance and fired. **The bullet struck Steve.** In the medical emergency unit the attending physician was able to extricate several BBs from Steve's head, but X-rays showed some of the BBs were still lodged in Steve's skull. These could not be removed at that time, but to be scheduled following the wrestling season.

During a later match (which Steve insisted on wrestling, but today would probably be barred), Steve suddenly grabbed at his forehead and went to the side of the mat with blood running through his fingers. He came to the edge and Coach asked him what had just happened. Steve calmly told him that he had just had BB's knocked out of his head!

As the official was becoming irritated before giving the expected team points for "loitering," Coach Cassel saw a loose BB on the mat. He picked it up and presented it to the official who replied, "I'll be darned; only at L.D." Two more BBs were found on the mat while the team physician (the Coach's brother) wrapped surgical tape around Ed's head and sent him back on the mat where Steve pinned his opponent. Indeed, only at L.D.

The Best Team
— *Eric Stauffer '76*

I love all this talk about which team is the greatest of all time. The guys from the 60's were and still are awesome men. But being undefeated doesn't mean that you have the best team of all time. I witnessed the match where they brought Manheim Central's amazing win streak to an end. Those guys were flat out tough as nails. They thrived on the Cassel triangle offense; single leg, stand up, and the half nelson, still good stuff.

Without a doubt the great teams of '71, '72 and '73 were awesome and could easily state their case for having the best team of all time. We qualified 4 guys to go to states, but we also had 3 underclassmen who competed and went to states. Count them—**7 wrestlers who competed in states from one team: Dale Hixon, Ken Mutek, Eric Stauffer, Mel Watts, Lloyd Umberger, Charlie Cole, and Chris Camasta.**

When you then add the accomplishments of Greg Etnoyer, Barry Tonkin, Jim Leeser, Dwight Kreiser, and Larry Cobaugh you have a very well-balanced team. If they had had team championships in '76 I firmly believe that we would have beaten Easton in a re-match and won it all.

Only a Sophomore Would …

When Ed Neiswender was a sophomore he sustained a football injury which caused his arm to dislocate when it was raised above his head…

When the football season became the wrestling season, Ed's injured (and vulnerable) arm was taped to his side during practice to encourage it to heal; in addition he sat out the first five matches of the season. By the sixth match it was determined that he was ready to compete, although not many people thought this was wise. A visiting coach, scouting Ed's first match back with the team, approached Coach Cassel, and said, "…I didn't think you would throw Neiswender to the wolves." Without missing a beat, Coach calmly replied, "We're not; we are going to win the match."

The match began with our sophomore getting an unbelievable take down, but in the second period Ed's opponent returned the action and almost pinned him. In the third period Ed rode his opponent and the match was tied with 15 seconds left to wrestle. Ed turned his opponent loose, then **took him down at the buzzer** and won the match!

Ron Michael '72 and Fred C. Foreman '72
— *John C. Hartwell of* The Sun

"After a long season of wrestling, the Falcons once again fall one short of bringing home a state champ. The highly successful team was betting on at least one champ and as the post season tournaments progressed, their hopes were boosted. The most likely Falcon to bring home the state title was **Ron Michael** at 145 lbs. After a fantastic season of 14-0-0, which included seven pins and several overwhelming scores, the fans were betting on him. From the beginning of the season it appeared that Ron was on his way. In each regular season match the fans and teammates could count on him to score a win or a fall. His expert ability and speed, along with his strength and great conditioning, made him look like a champion every time. Each time he took to the mat one could sense the pride and determination he held when he represented Lower Dauphin on the mat. His opponents would wrestle him in hope that he might make a mistake and they might win; but **in regular season it never happened.**

"It is difficult to describe the kind of wrestler that Ron is. He won the outstanding wrestler award at the sectionals when he scored pins in each of his two matches. In Districts he overwhelmed each of his four opponents and went on to win his Regional title without any trouble. With the pressure building to a tremendous level, Ron lost 11-3 to Duane Fossler of DuBois in the state semi-finals.

"Ron was up against the very best without doubt. It appeared that he was concentrating on his second match more than his semi-final match. Counting on a win over Fossler, he was worried about Don Rohn of Saucon Valley, the two-time State Champ. Rohn, with a 25-0-0 record which included twenty pins, was certainly something to worry about! He was almost a sure bet to win except that Dave Rogers wasn't told about it. Rogers, with a cradle, pinned Rohn at 3:36 in the second period. On another day Ron might have worried about his opponents one at a time; nevertheless, in the eyes of all Falcon wrestling fans, **Ron Michael is a champion who will never be forgotten** and continued to prove it at the college level.

"**The Falcon to go farthest this year was Fred Foreman,** who wrestled in the heavyweight class. Fred, who weighed less than many of his opponents, was a star with his speed and ability. Fred scored only a few pins through the season but even so, he always managed to outscore his competition. Fred was a good wrestler all season long, but when it came time for the real matches that counted, he changed from a good wrestler to a **fantastic** one.

"Each time he stepped onto the mat he came away a winner. He won three matches to become the sectional champion; then he won four more to take the district title. In regionals, he won 5-3 with his speed to take the heavyweight crown. When Fred took on George Barkinic of Lehighton, he surprised many who had doubted his ability. Barkinic had a 25-0-0 record, which included seventeen pins. Fred, with all of his ability, completely demolished Barkinic 13-3. He was all over him and scored several near-falls and predicaments. After a match like that, it looked like we had a champ in the making; however, after such a grueling match in the afternoon, Fred finally tired in the finals with a packed house of 10,900.

"Chuck Coryea of Reynolds, with a 24-0-0 record, which included nineteen pins, was simply too much for the wiped out Fred who had won in the afternoon. Coryea was without doubt the biggest wrestler (250) in attendance and held a definite weight advantage over anyone. Coryea scored a quick takedown in the first period and rode for the remainder of the period. Fred was helpless to do much of anything against the fresh and ready Coryea. That command took the match, but not our peerless Falcon. **Fred earned the respect of everyone that evening and brought honor to his school, teammates and himself.**"

Reflections from the Edge of the Mat

George Cruys '70

Driving into Harrisburg with my brother Ron a few years ago… I talked about how we used to go to the farm show when we were kids—the smell of prize cows and popcorn.

"This is where I wrestled districts," he said.

We had different memories of the same place.

It is not possible to live near the wrestling world, as I have, without admiring its participants. No other sport requires so much of the individual, both on and off the mat.

Practice after school was routinely exhausting—straining to hold the backward arch of a bridge when someone steps on your stomach. Home on the activity bus after dark, my brother didn't talk about the struggle to make weight, even when he'd been working out in a rubber sweat suit. But I do remember tears at a Thanksgiving dinner when he had too much discipline to eat.

Wrestling is not a fun sport. Of all the athletic contests—baseball, basketball, skiing—wrestling offers the least recreational diversion. I never wrestled a single competitive match in my brief experience when I wasn't scared to death. To meet a wrestler, in uniform or in street clothes, is to face your own destruction. Only a set of rules and social conventions limit the potential violence.

Once you step on the mat, you are facing a person who is very much in the moment, whose sole thought is to beat you, possibly to humiliate you. What this can mean to the team, your friends, your reputation, are all in the back of your mind. In six minutes of total exhaustion, subject to immediate retribution for any mistake, you use every bit of energy, every trick you know, to have your arm raised at the end. In some cases those six minutes are among the longest of your life. I've seen wrestlers so tired at the end of a match it seemed they could not raise their arm without the ref's help.

But for all its physicality, there is grace. A difficult move, well executed, is a thing of beauty. A clean takedown, the transition to a winning (pinning) combination—these are not a triple salchow or a toe loop jump, but they share something in artistry. A wrestler's repertoire is the tight waist, the cross face, the chicken wing, the fireman's carry. But you need to know how to use them. I was almost pinned once in a JV match because of inept use of a simple figure four.

I had few wrestling accomplishments, more comic than athletic. I once won a fourth-place ribbon in a weekend tournament without winning a match: a forfeit, a bye, and a loss. This is not Achilles circling Troy with Hector's body. In another match, to my enduring shame, I won fast fall money by mistake. Warned in advance that the JV wrestler I'd be facing was new to the sport (it was his first match) Coach Heistand told me to "go easy" on the guy. That was my plan. But after a takedown I heard the coach shout "Shoot the half!" He was only pointing out an opportunity for my further training. But the half nelson is a pin combination, and I, in the moment—adrenalin flowing—did what I was told. In 37 seconds, a time I still regret, the match was over.

I was, all-in-all, a terrible wrestler. My brother's many victories rippled through our family with sometimes embarrassing results. I remember my petite mother crawling on the gym floor at one match, her head against the wood to see the opponent's shoulders better, shouting "Pin!" "Pin!" When I told my brother about that recently he said he was glad he didn't know it at the time. We have my nephews and me to demonstrate that a good wrestler is not only the result of informed coaching, but also of hard work and dedication. My brother's two sons eventually left the sport—one after comic results like my own, the other after a concussion and a broken arm.

You need a fire inside to combine with the training, strength and endurance. My brother had that, as did so many LD wrestlers of this storied period: Two-time district champs **Jim Rhone** and **Randy Kahler,** both state runners-up. **Jim Sanders** and **Randy Umberger,** known for pinning their opponents—Umberger with something like 18 falls in 24 matches. In one memorable bout Umberger picked up his man and shot the pinning combination while he was still holding him in the air. Two-time district champ **Bill Pinkerton**—who used to dance onto and off the mat—didn't pin opponents nearly as often and used to joke that Sanders and Umberger pinned their men because they were too weak to go the full six minutes. Memorable years included the 14-0 undefeated squad of 1963/64, the seven sectional finalists of the also undefeated 1964/65 squad—all of whom won, and the 1970/71 team with **9 sectional finalists** out of 12 weight classes—six of whom won. I remember that **Danny Sanders** (Jim's brother) always seemed to have an odd grin on his face as he went to the mat against even his toughest opponents. I always just assumed **Craig Tritch** would be in the win column at 165, often with a pin. **The more you dig into LD wrestling, the more there is to discover and admire.**

We can't all be legends. But I still think of LD wrestling when I do leg lifts in the morning. These guys inspired us. Tough, physical people can weigh 95 pounds. Someone who looks like Jackie Gleason can have the strength of a bull. You can win, no matter where you're ranked (in the time it takes to drink a cup of coffee). These are great things you can learn from the sport: self-reliance, individual effort, discipline, and sometimes accepting defeat with no one to blame but yourself.

I have a house in Hummelstown and once in a while a wrestler will stop by and say hello. They remember my brother. Only at LD would he be just one of many.

The Bridge of Alex Stone

(A short story)

by George Cruys '70

Two wrestlers are out on the mat in the high school gymnasium. The one on the bottom is flailing excitedly and rocking back and forth on his shoulders. His face is bright red, glistening with sweat. A thick, purple vein stands out among the strained muscles of the neck, and his teeth are bared all the way to the gums in a contorted grimace.

A referee in black and white stripes lies on the floor beside the struggling pair. The side of his head is flat against the mat; he is looking only out of his lower eye. His right arm is pressed against the mat like his body; his left hand is raised slightly with the thumb and index finger spread apart about two inches and closing slowly.

Even from the edge of the mat you can smell the bodies of the writhing pair: the hot, suffocating smell of human effort. You can hear their frenzied puffing, just audible above the din of the crowd. The wrestler on the bottom sobs as he gasps for air. He throws his right arm skyward. It hangs there limply, uselessly, for a moment then slams down as he shifts to his other shoulder. His left arm soars up and dangles over the back of the wrestler on top, limp wristed. The shoulders are shifting every few seconds. The cries escape as he forces the air out of his lungs and because there is a moment, between the thrusts, when both shoulders are touching the mat together.

The crowd is roaring now as the fingers of the referee tremble just out of touch. A whistle gleams in his teeth. The boy on the bottom can see the rafters clearly as he thrusts his head wildly from side to side. The bright argon lights shine in his eyes. He grunts and rocks on his shoulders with increasing rapidity, gasping for air. The crowd seems insignificant above his own breathing and he is still struggling, rocking, kicking, when the grip of the wrestler above him suddenly loosens and lets in the cool, fresh air. The referee's hand has fallen. The whistle has blown. Alex Stone has been pinned again.

Like the man with the whistle in his mouth, I too wear a black and white shirt. I am the official timer of these matches and I sit at a large table at the edge of the mat behind two sturdy red clocks and a panel with toggles that run the electronic scoreboard.

I know Alex Stone only within the circle. I see him only at matches within the large, twenty-eight foot circle that serves as the out of bounds line for the wrestling mat.

When this first bout is over, Alex's team, the Eagles, forms two solemn lines at the edge of the mat. As Alex shuffles between the lines, a few wrestlers offer listless handshakes or a sharp whack on the behind.

Alex wrestles in the ninety-eight-pound class, the lightest varsity weight category. When he loses, which is every match, Alex sits on the bench in personal torment, his elbows on his knees, his chin on his chest. When he is pinned, which is almost as often as he wrestles, you can see his humiliation as he sits there trembling in view of everyone.

When Alex goes out on the mat for a bout, everyone on the team, including Alex, is hoping he will just lose by a hefty margin.

When Alex loses a match on the basis of points, a maximum of five team points are awarded his school's opponents. But when Alex gets pinned, like tonight, a full six team points are awarded to the opposing side—the same number the team would have received if the weight class had been forfeited. Alex needs to lose once in a while—as opposed to being pinned—for it to make any difference at all that he showed up.

I admit that sometimes I secretly hope Alex will actually win, but the grizzled old scorekeeper beside me—a man whose face calcified years ago—has made it clear that no partisan emotions are permitted at the officials' table. And in any event, Alex leaves you very little to cheer about.

A week later, with my fingers again on the toggles of the scoreboard, I am the quiet observer of his world. There are a minute and seventeen seconds to go in the second period of his bout. The opposing wrestler is gripping Alex in a cradle, an almost inescapable pinning combination.

A big cheering section has arrived with the visiting team and the gymnasium thunders with stamping feet, whistles, and catcalls. Alex's bench and the Eagles' stands are studiously silent. The opposing team's cheerleaders—young, good-looking girls with firm thighs and shiny hair—want Alex to be pinned. "Turn him over and show him the lights," they chant, as if they had been rehearsing all week just to get Alex. Alex's own cheerleaders prefer to attend basketball games at this time of year, and they are talking about this as they stand together at my left.

The mixed calls from the visiting fans exhort Alex's opponent to finish his man quickly. A middle-aged woman, probably the mother of the opposing wrestler, has slipped from the first row of bleachers to the floor. She yells and shakes her tightly clenched fists as she wiggles toward the mat on her knees. She is only a few feet from the mat and I can see the spittle fly from her mouth as she shouts. "Pin him!" she screams, her voice straining. "Pin! Pin! *Pinnnn!*"

The noise in the gym is deafening. We keep a knotted towel at the scoring table because sometimes, in situations like this, the crowd is so loud the referee can't hear the buzzer ending the match. When time runs out, I throw the towel into the circle to prevent any late pins from being called.

But within the circle tonight, there is plenty of time. Alex's opponent appears to be calmly following his mother's instructions. The cradle in which he holds Alex is very tight; one arm behind Alex's neck, the other circling his left leg. As the cradle tightens, Alex's leg and head are bent together at an unnatural angle. I can almost feel the vertebrae of Alex's neck popping as he is rocked back onto his shoulders. The woman on the floor spreads out both hands flat and presses the side of her face against the wood. The referee, in a similar posture, holds his fingers up again to mark the narrow margin of Alex's continued life in this bout. The fingers come together, he slaps the mat twice, quickly, and it is all over again for Alex for another week.

This is the way the season goes for Alex, as it did last year, bout after bout, one painful loss after another. I see Alex rise up from the mat before me—a red, stretched thing; his hair tousled at odd angles. I see the Alex of previous matches wavering there too, his legs spread painfully in a split scissors, his body twisted in a guillotine, his features smeared weirdly by a cross-face. I see the Alex of the whizzer, the chicken-wing, the tight-waist, the arm chop, the hammerlock, and it seems to me that his body is just so much clay for the violent sculptors who await him each Thursday night, when others from his school are, perhaps, out for a milkshake and a movie.

It's a difficult life for Alex and I know, from knowing the sport, that he does not come by it easily. Alex, a junior, is the only wrestler in the school capable of making the ninety-eight-pound weight class. At a time when every muscle and bone in his body is calling for growth, Alex limits his intake to the bare essentials. A three-hour workout, in rubber suit, nets about three pounds of liquid. Alex has to drink part of that back to maintain his water balance. He can eat about a pound of something—perhaps a can of fruit cocktail—in the evening after practice. His body burns about one pound, six ounces in a normal day's activities, much of which is eaten back to maintain strength. In bed at night he'll lose another eighteen ounces from overtime put in by his birdlike metabolism and from the damp sheets that result from hours of thinking about the next Thursday night.

The next Thursday night arrives and it's back to the cradle for Alex as his shoulders swing alarmingly close to the mat. Beside me at the officials' table the scorekeeper has just written down three more points for a near pin. The referee is on his stomach again, as if he were looking for something beneath Alex. I should be used to this by now, but for some reason this particular bout bothers me and I watch the orange numbers on the scoreboard changing shape; one twenty-seven, one twenty-six, one twenty-five....

There is a point of humiliation beneath which one stops blaming the world and starts blaming the individual. As Alex rocks back again on his shoulders, I reflect that he is nearing that point. Up on the scoreboard the numbers keep changing–one-fifteen, one-fourteen, one-thirteen–it's all a matter of time.

Third period, in the center of the mat, Alex's mouth hangs open and he gulps for air. The ref aligns Alex with the big, central arrow which points in an arbitrary direction and the bout resumes. What Alex gets for his extraordinary effort is the chance to go through it again. Tonight the other wrestler tries another cradle, finally gets it right, and pins Alex with fifteen seconds left on the clock.

There are six hundred and four thousand, eight hundred seconds between Alex's bouts. I figured that out one night with a dull pencil, while Alex was getting pinned. And tonight, the last home match, I know exactly what Alex has been thinking about in all those seconds since last week.

Tonight the Eagles wrestle Mechanicsburg, the strongest team in the district. As usual, the Eagles have tied them for first place. Also as usual, the winner tonight will be the champion for another year. Last year the big district trophy came out of the glass case by the gymnasium and went to Mechanicsburg. This year it might come back.

On the official scoresheet beside me, the Eagles' coach has written "E. vs. Mechburg," followed by a list of his wrestlers by weight class. To the right of each name, a single digit with a plus or minus gives the coach's best guess at the outcome of each bout. At the bottom of the page, which looks like it has been worked over a lot, some numbers are crossed out: E21, M27. Further up the page, next to "Franklin" (one hundred and sixty-seven pound class), the minus three is marked over and a plus three is in its place. Later, in another pen, a bottom score of E24, M24 is crossed out again and further up the page, next to Hetrick (one hundred and fifty-five pound class), a plus six has miraculously replaced a plus three. The final numbers at the bottom of the page are tentative "E27, M24?" At the top of the page, next to Alex's name, the coach has written minus six with no question mark.

The wrestlers file out by weight class and stand facing their opponents across the mat. They look like one of those "Ascent of Man" diagrams, with the little chimpanzees at one end, the stooping Neanderthals in the middle, and tall, upright modern man towering among the heavyweights. Somebody plays the national anthem. Alex is at the chimpanzee end of the line facing a considerably more muscular ape.

Alex has wrestled this one before. "Wrestle" is the wrong word for it. The guy's name is Spyder Barret. He went to the state championships last year and won third place. This year they expect him to go all the way.

When Barret paired off with Alex last year, Alex was pinned in twenty-three seconds. Barret won the fast fall pool on his team that night and I've been told by other wrestlers that Alex colors when you even mention Spyder's name. This is a year later. Spyder is stronger. Alex has been pinned more times than the entire cheering squad. I cannot imagine what gave him the nerve to show up for tonight's match.

After the national anthem, Alex and Spyder come out on the mat. The ref stands between them with the whistle in his teeth. He signals for the wrestlers to shake hands. Alex looks into Spyder's face. Spyder looks over Alex's shoulder. Everybody in the gym knows what is going on. Spyder intends to pin Alex even faster than last year. Alex has to know this too.

The whistle tweets and I hit the toggle to start the display clock. Spyder steps forward and gives Alex an open-handed rap on the forehead, knowing he can stun him. Alex's head jerks back but instead of shooting for Alex's legs and the takedown, Spyder steps right up to Alex, holds his left arm tightly and shoots the half while they are still standing. A murmur runs through the crowd and a few of the Mechanicsburg wrestlers laugh from the bench. Six seconds of the bout have gone by, both wrestlers are still standing, and Spyder already has Alex in a pinning combination. A groan goes up from the Eagles' bench but the coach stops it with a poisoned look.

Spyder is behind Alex now with the half nelson in tight. He trips out Alex's feet and the two of them go down to the mat. Nine seconds. The visiting bleachers are going nuts. They'd love to start this match off by humiliating the Eagles. Spyder clamps onto that hold like he's kissing his girlfriend, rolls Alex onto his back and lies across his chest. Alex's feet start kicking and I start watching the clock: one forty-seven … forty six…forty-five….

"Nine more seconds," I say under my breath. Stick it out nine more seconds and at least you'll last longer than last year.

Alex looks terrible, his face red and strained. Through the roar of the Mechanicsburg stands I can hear the high-pitched gasps as he sucks in air. Spyder's got Alex's left shoulder down and he's leaning on the right. It dips lower toward the mat, slowly, steadily. I've got my neck hunched forward at a weird angle and my lips are pursed tight, like somebody's going to hit me.

"Hang on!" I say aloud, gripping the red clock before me. The words get out before I can stop them. The scorekeeper looks up at me from his book and I turn a little red. Alex has rocked back on his head now, in a bridge, resting on the soles of his feet and the back of his head, arching his back to keep his shoulders off the mat. Spyder puts all of his weight across Alex's shoulders. Alex is now supporting both of them on his neck muscles alone. Three more seconds … two … yes! I watch the clock click on into the match: one thirty-six … thirty-five … thirty-four. At least Alex has outlasted last year.

I look around me and no one else is celebrating. Alex is in deep trouble. Still bridged on his head. Spyder balanced on his chest, he's going to collapse any moment. Spyder is mad about the time. He's banging up and down on top of Alex to knock the neck out. He wrenches Alex's arm into a painful angle. He knows all the borderline moves: not quite a chicken wing, not really a face slap, not actually slamming—you get to the state championships with things like that. He's working over Alex like tonight's stew meat. The Mechanicsburg bleachers are quieter now, and meaner. "Pin the fish," somebody shouts. Isolated voices pop out of the crowd, disappointed and faintly bored. "Finish 'em!" a man in a dark coat yells. An older woman walks to the edge of the mat, cups both hands to her mouth and shouts: "Put the sissy away!" A murmur of laughter shakes through the visiting stands. Another fan comes forward and leads the woman back to her seat. The Eagles stands are strangely silent.

Down on the mat, Alex is still in that neck bridge. It's a hard position to hold for long, especially with the guy on top of you wiggling his hip bones into your chest and bouncing up and down like he's riding a hobby horse. There are twenty-seven seconds to go in the first period. The storm is starting to quiet down. What is Alex doing? His skinny neck is a little red fireplug, braced against the mat. Twenty-three seconds. The veins of his neck look like dark rubber hoses. Spyder is becoming frustrated and gets warned for slapping. Fifteen seconds. Alex looks like rigor mortis has set in. His back is arched like a Roman bridge and his teeth are clenched tight from the pressure on his neck. Seven seconds. The gym is absolutely silent. Four seconds … three … two …one. The buzzer goes off. A couple of fans on the Eagles side clap self-consciously. The scorekeeper looks up, gives me a long face and raises his eyebrows.

Period two opens with Alex in the top position with Spyder on his hands and knees aligned with the arrow. At the whistle, it takes Spyder all of about ten seconds to pull a standard switch, throw his legs around Alex's waist and squeeze him into a figure four. Alex is really suffering out there. A good figure four can make your lungs come out of your mouth.

Spyder has changed tactics. A figure four isn't a pinning combination. It's a painful ride. He's going to make Alex pay for lasting out the first period. Like Hitler bombing London. I look down and the scorekeeper's tapping his pencil on top of the table.

Alex is crawling around on his elbows and toes. I expect to see him throw up his intestines any time. Spyder looks like an anaconda on top of him. Nearly a minute goes by and the ref warns Spyder for stalling. This makes Spyder even more irritated and he whips in a split scissors for a quick pin. You can see Alex's face go slack as that figure four comes off. The scissors doesn't catch and Alex crawls for the edge of the mat. Spyder grabs him at the waist and drags him back into the middle—the crowd jeering—Alex's hands raking behind with the fingers dug in, like a cat being pulled by its tail.

Spyder shoots the half. Alex rolls out of it awkwardly—not even a move, really, just a roll and then he sits up, spread-eagled, like you might do in your living room. Spyder catches his chin for a snapback, but Alex spins free, gets some foot room and springs for the sideline. Spyder loses his grip for a second and Alex rolls out of the circle by himself. The crowd breaks into general laughter. Alex gets warned for stalling. They're back in the center of the circle again, facing each other on their feet. Spyder shoots a neat single-leg takedown and Alex falls to the mat like something in a sack. Spyder shoots the half, tight, rolls Alex over and is nothing but business when the buzzer sounds and it's the end of the second period.

Somebody in the stands says, "OK Alex." A couple of people applaud. A cheerleader does a silent split. I look over at the scoreboard and Alex is down eight to one. He got a point for the escape. Alex begins the third period like a wrung-out cloth. Spyder breaks him down from the starting position and digs Alex's face into the mat. Alex buttons up, tight, and for a few long moments Spyder looks like a dog sniffing a turtle.

"Go, Alex!" calls a kid with a crew cut. Another Eagles fan lets out a long shrill whistle.

Alex the turtle is lumbering his way toward the sideline again. Spyder is still struggling for a good grip. Alex gets out of bounds and the ref blows his whistle. One minute and forty-five seconds to go. More jeers from the opposing bench. More whistles from the Eagles bleachers.

Spyder dances around in the center of the circle, shaking his fingers. He assumes the superior position, the ref restarts the bout, and Spyder works the tightwaist. Alex crawls for the sidelines again. "Pin the baby," someone yells. Just as Alex nears the edge of the circle, Spyder grabs him by the ankle, stands up, and drags Alex back to the center of the mat, like a cave man bringing home dinner. The Mechanicsburg bleachers break into a loud laugh. The Eagles side is silent but edgy. "Drop dead!" an Eagles fan shouts.

Alex is in real trouble. Red-faced, exhausted, puffing, his limbs dangle limply. The ref warns him a second time for stalling.

Spyder has plenty left. He shoots the half, rolls Alex over and locks in the pinning combination, lying perpendicular to Alex's chest. There is an air of finality about this. A minute and thirty-two seconds. Mechanicsburg cheers. People are yelling, angry, on the Eagles side. The scorekeeper is staring down at his page and is running his pencil around in a big black dot that is not wrestling notation.

Alex strains into a bridge. In wrestling, the bridge is the last thing you try before you get pinned. Feet and neck, with the body a tight little rainbow of school colors beneath the opponent. Spyder bangs his chest against Alex, hard. We can hear a savage "hugggghh" as air comes out of his lungs. He knocks Alex's head out with his left arm. Alex's shoulders splat flat on the mat. The ref is down on his stomach. Alex digs in and gets back into the bridge. Spyder knocks the head out again. Alex gets it back.

There are a minute and seventeen seconds to go. Alex is straining to hold the bridge. His legs tremble as he rises up on his toes, arching skyward.

"Wow" I say to the scorekeeper. "I never thought he'd last this long."

"He's doin' OK," says the old man.

Behind us, in the stands, a lot of people are shouting. The Eagles bleachers are making almost as much noise for their losing wrestler as Mechanicsburg does for the future state champ. "Let's go, AL-LEX," chant the cheerleaders.

Out on the mat you can see Spyder puzzling over a problem in geometry: "Why can't this curve become a straight line? I can't figure it out myself. What holds Alex up there? And for that matter, what made him even show up tonight? Or any night? To come here and take this kind of punishment for this long when the only thing he has to hope for is to lose. And still we see him braced there, using all his strength to hold on—Spyder using everything he's got.

The stands behind us are a riot now; people stomping the bleachers and chanting AL-LEX! AL-LEX! AL-LEX! One of the cheerleaders is down on her knees, her fists clenched, her eyes bright. From here on I see things only in a strobe. A flash of the mat: Alex struggling to hold the bridge. Then the gym clock: fifty-three seconds to go. Then the mat: Spyder digging an elbow into the straining flesh. And the clock: forty-eight seconds. And Alex: the bridge. And the clock: forty-two. A red face. The orange numbers. The ref on his stomach. The clock clicking down. The stands: AL-LEX! And the entire gym shaking from the sound, Mechanicsburg shouting for all they've got. Our side screaming back. And I don't know what it is about a guy who loses all season that makes people get like this. And I don't know why the scorekeeper is biting his pencil. And I especially cannot explain, with twenty-five seconds to go, why I am standing up—way too early—with that knotted towel in my hand and my arm cocked back, but I can tell you that the second that clock counts down to zero, the ref is going to get hit with this thing right in the face.

The '80s: Expanding a Wrestling Dynasty

History

While there were similarities between and among the ten Lower Dauphin wrestling teams in our league during the 1980s, all Lower Dauphin coaches of this decade were seasoned—and all had been winners. All held records of their own, both as wrestlers and as coaches. Together, the ten 1980s school teams were viewed as a proven power and respected for their character. There were no rookies among the teams reviewed and all were so noted by opposing coaches and sports followers.

In fact, before this decade had barely begun and far before this decade's records were collected, Lower Dauphin wrestling was recognized—and final scores were gathered—by the most highly regarded wrestling magazine in America:

Wrestling USA, May 1, 1980

Wrestling USA *is the premier wrestling magazine in the country* and is respected at all levels. Its 1980 May issue featured District III AAA Coach of the Year Honors shared by Cleon Cassel and Randall Umberger. The magazine article covers most of the information found in *Lower Dauphin Wrestling: An Uncommon Heritage* and is here noted as a tribute to the school's impressive wrestling statistics to that date. The team had captured its eleventh league championship and in the process ended District III's second-ranked Warwick High School's thirty-two match win streak and third-place Cumberland Valley's twenty-seven-win run as well as halting Shikellamy, District IV's top team at 32 wins.

"During their first 20 years of wrestling, the Falcons proved themselves against the best; they competed against District XI's Easton and Parkland; District IV's Shikellamy; District VI's State College, in addition to District III champions Carlisle, Cedar Cliff, Central Dauphin, Governor Mifflin, Manheim Central, Warwick, Maryland's State Champions, and Mt. Saint Joseph (the National Prep School Champions). They had won 13 Christmas tournaments including the Upper Darby, Central Dauphin, Williamsport (Top Hat), Carlisle, State College, Dallastown, and Lower Dauphin Invitational.

"Lower Dauphin was also named at that time as the number one dual meet team in the District III coaches' poll and winner of the District III Tournament Team Title with a record 85 ½ points. Lower Dauphin had had a 16-1 season with its lone loss to District XI's Easton and had picked up the Capital Area Conference title as well as the Christmas tournament win.

In addition to the team's eleventh league championship and ending several winning streaks, the 1980s Falcon standouts included 61 Sectional champions, 25 District III champions, 17 South Central Region champions and 6 State AAA finalists, as well as numerous third and fourth place finishers. In 1973 Lower Dauphin had sent three finalists to the State championship matches and the team was named the number one team in Pennsylvania by *Scholastic Wrestling News.* The Lower Dauphin Falcon total record added up to an impressive 256-28-3 which included **a streak of some 40 straight wins and 5 undefeated seasons."**

The Limited Early History of Distaff Wrestlers at LD

At this time there was not yet a history of girls on the LD wrestling teams; however, they do bear notice. Cathy Clark '84 is considered the first female member of L.D.'s team. Cathy earned her place on the JVs in 1981 and quietly fit in without fanfare as a bona fide team member. Unfortunately, she was not in the team picture; nonetheless, she should be noted as **Lower Dauphin's first female wrestler.** Cathy also was strong in academics with broad interests, including a slot as one of the early members of LD's premier English Enrichment Program. Cathy also was active in Student Council and was the editor of the school's creative writing arts publication *Media.*

Some 30 years later, two sisters became rightful members of the Falcon wrestling team. Amanda Vale was a member of the 2014-2015 squad and Brianna Vale was a 106 pound starter her senior year, 2015-16, with a record close to .500. Brianna is remembered as a good athlete and mentally tough, with a record of 8-14, four actual wins with the remaining forfeited. Brianna (Brie) later enlisted in the Marines. The sisters' younger brother Jacob was also on the wrestling squad. However, this military career family was relocated before Jacob was graduated from LD.

This information is a reminder of the trail-blazing for which LD was known. These three young women (Amanda, Brianna, and Cathy—the ABCs of LD's history of female wrestling) were unobtrusive about their choice of breaking ground. They simply wanted to wrestle on the team under the same rules as the boys, no favors asked.

Singlets and Silhouettes ... of Moves and Holds

The wrestling "uniform" worn by the wrestlers is particularly designed for this sport. Typically it is a "one-piece singlet cut no lower in the back or front than the level of the armpits and under the arms no lower than one-half the distance between the armpit and the belt line. If sufficient reason is determined by the referee, a tight-fitting, short-sleeved or sleeveless undershirt of a single, solid color unadorned with no more than one manufacturer's logo/trademark/reference, may be worn under the one-piece singlet; this is accompanied by either full-length tights with stirrups and close fitting outside short trunks or a properly cut one-piece uniform with a minimum 4-inch inseam and a maximum length of above the knee."Uniforms have changed very little over the years. Fabrics have improved with a better fit that has "give." While color combinations may change or the fabric may be an abstract design, the design is basically utilitarian. The school typically provides the uniform and the student wrestler is responsible for the care of his/her own uniform.

3 PIECE UNIFORM 1960

SINGLET WITH TIGHTS, 1972

SINGLET, NO TIGHTS 1979

JAM CUT SINGLET 1994

"Champions don't do extraordinary things, they do ordinary things better than everybody else."

2015 Singlet

2016 Singlet

2021 Singlet

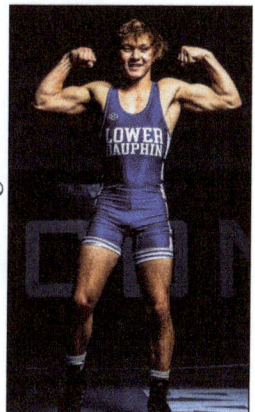

2023 Singlet

Wrestlers Take on the Arts

Wrestlers take on more than opponents-on-mats!

Front cover of the *1982 Falconaire*

1981-82 Season: "For the third consecutive year the CAC wrestling trophy rests upon a shelf in the Lower Dauphin trophy case, thanks to the successful season of 15 wins and 1 loss. Junior Varsity also came out on top, with a record of 14 wins and 2 losses. Coach Cassel notes that this year's team was very well-balanced, with many outstanding wrestlers."

*In 1982, **Craig Camasta**, Varsity Wrestler, presented to the Lower Dauphin School Board a gift of his own creation, a handsome framed charcoal drawing of a falcon.*

Camasta was one of many wrestlers who during LD's third decade of wrestling were surprising themselves as they ventured into the unknown, even taking roles in the high school musicals, when in 1982 this book's author invited our school athletes to be part of the supporting cast in the High School Musicals. This was the first musical to incorporate "extras," and this year featured them as "crap shoot" players in the high school musical *Guys and Dolls!* That musical was the beginning of a run of appearances of athletes on stage. In 1983 some of these athletes became Seabees in *South Pacific*, where they appeared in a male chorus with a lusty rendering of "There's Nothing Like a Dame." In 1984 they again brought spunk and enthusiasm to an unfamiliar playing field, giving their all as "Dogpatch" dancers in the musical *L'il Abner*.

These athletes thus had an opportunity to experience a different kind of athleticism, some even admitting that stage performances aren't all that different from preparing for a match. In 1985's *Bye, Bye, Birdie* the wrestlers were an absolute hoot and in 1986 they splendidly portrayed King Arthur's Knights in *Camelot*, adding authenticity to the production while taking pride in their own involvement in a stage production.

Craig Camasta in "Guys and Dolls"

Space in the sports headlines was shared by the spring musical in which the LD athletes were announced as part of the cast. This custom of LD Athletes taking supporting roles in the musicals began when the director, Judith Witmer, extended an invitation to athletes to experience an arts activity in addition to being engaged in a sport.

The first year's musical cast included athletes Ted Bauman, Craig Camasta, Bernie DeLuca, Tony Dobson, Mike Graham, Dan Jenakovich, Rick Martin, Rick Salus, and Rick Smith. This change of casting added a brand new dynamic to rehearsals!

PRESENT!

1982 Musical: Guys & Dolls

Space in the sports headlines was shared by the spring musical in which the "LD athletes" were announced as part of the cast. This custom of LD athletes taking minor roles in the musicals began when Mrs. Witmer extended an invitation to LD's athletes to experience an arts activity in addition to being engaged in a sport. This year's musical cast included athlete Ted Bauman, Craig Camasta, Bernie DeLuca, Tony Dobson, Mike Graham, Dan Jenakovich, R. Martin, Ron Salus, and Rick Smith. This change of venue added a brand new dynamic to rehearsals.

LOWER DAUPHIN HIGH SCHOOL AUDITORIUM

Early Years:
Finding our way in music, drama, governance, & SPORTS

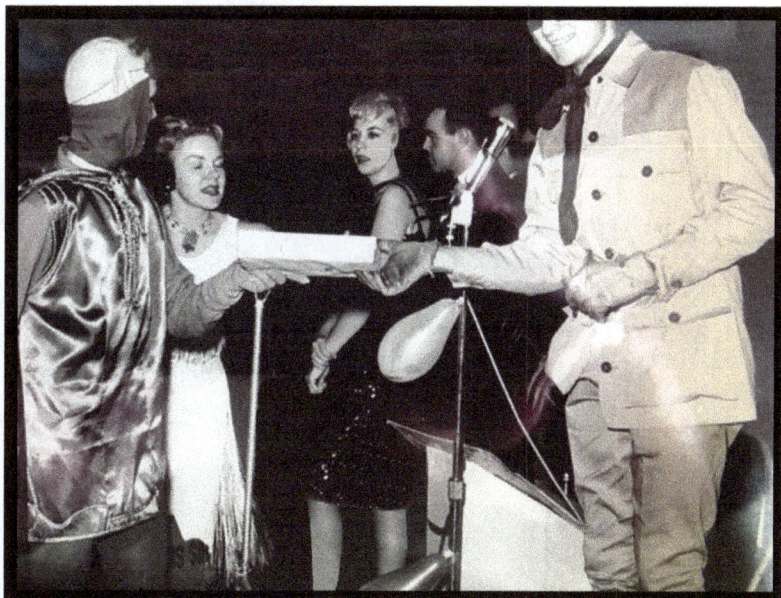

Left: Dave Lidle '67, Student Council President at the Prom. Right: Mardi Gras event with (l to r) Don Green and Jane Mellon Smith (Choral Director).

Present Day:

Hemlock Knob, wrestling retreat

175

The Men of Dog Patch

L'il Abner

Camelot & King Arthur's Court

Can you identify the wrestlers and other sports team members in the casts?

LD's National and International Theatre Stand-Outs

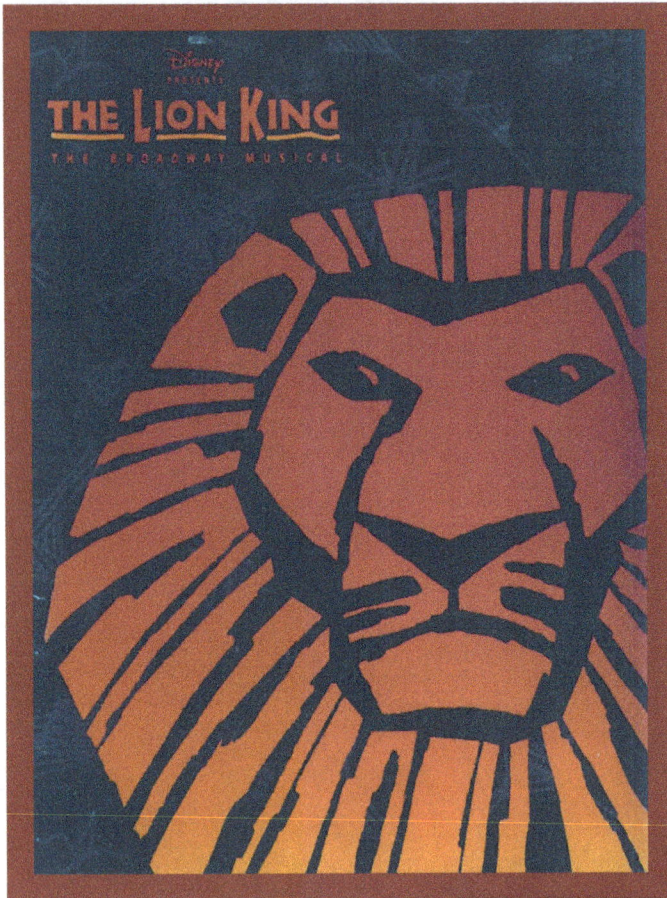

Broadway and

China Stage

Producer,

Don Frantz '69

Technical Theatre

☆ Lighting

Tim Deiling

Within the student body, there are many students whose activities go unnoticed. Often these students dedicate a lot of time to their activity. Tim Deiling is one of these students. He spends his time on lighting design.

Tim has been involved in lighting since middle school when he was on technical crew for productions within the school. Since sixth grade, his interest has grown immensely. He is now the lighting designer and technician for any and all productions on the high school stage. Those productions include fall play, musical, musical concerts, and award ceremonies.

Seeing the colors mix on stage and the gratification that comes on opening night are Tim's favorite part of lighting. Sometimes he has to be quite resourceful since the budget does not always meets his expectations. In the 2004-2005 school year Tim will be attending CASA for technical theatre. In the future, he hopes to be a lighting designer for Broadway or touring music.

Broadway & Europe Stage Lighting Master, Tim Deiling '06

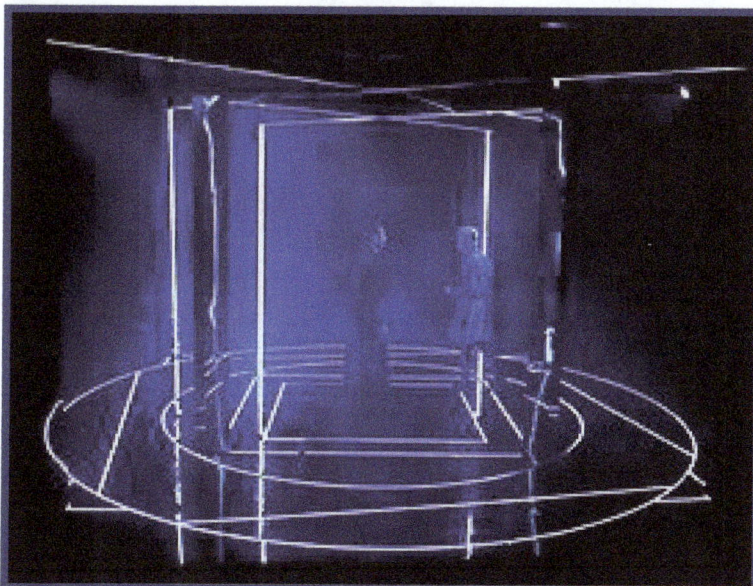

Tim began as one of the **L.D. stage crew** and is now known worldwide.

Even Don Frantz '69 well-known international theatre producer, recently contacted Tim regarding a lighting design when both were doing stage work in Europe!

Never say die

February 3, 1999: "The Falcons dumped the first five bouts against Manheim Central and found themselves at a 22-0 default. LD then turned things around at 135 and motored to a 27-25 victory." On January 27, 2011: "Lower Dauphin spotted Red Land an 18-0 lead through five bouts and then scored 40 straight points for a 40-24 Mid-Penn Conference, Keystone Division victory."

[see pages 274 and 329]

Downtown mugging

An eighties sportswriter wrote: "Wrestling against Lower Dauphin High School is sort of like being mugged by a businessman in a three-piece suit in broad daylight...." [see page 195]

Successful streakers

The 2006 and 2007 teams in many ways remind me of LD's 1964 and 1965 teams," Coach Cassel has said, "when the Falcons dominated everyone by winning every tournament and had the longest winning streak in the state!" (40 wins)

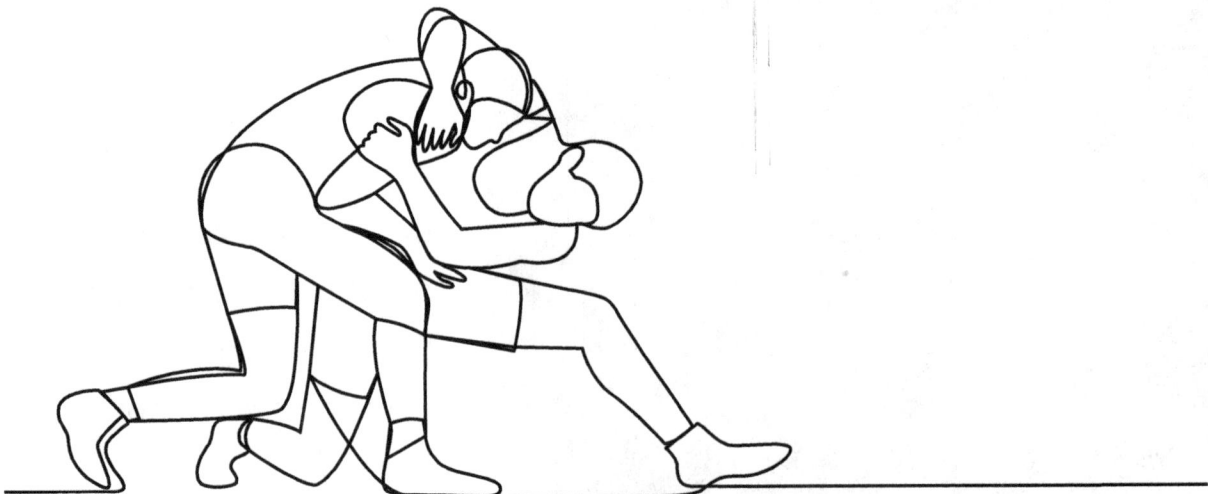

[see page 305]

HIGHLIGHTS OF THE MEETS
1980–1981 (Record 13-4-1)

"The characteristics of strength, power, determination, and stamina led to winning seasons."

Row 1. Cary Gray, Sam Fallinger, Craig Cassel, Mike Mazerolle, Ray Fogelman, Chris Bath.

Row 2. Craig Hetrick, Doug Seaman, Craig Camasta, Rick Salus, Steve Costik, Paul Eyster.

Row 3. Tom Stumpf, J. D. Miller, Joe Radwick, Joel Umberger, Kevin Rogers.

In December the road ahead of this team was said to be rough and unending; however, victory was their reward with a 38-14 win over Hershey. Craig Cassel, making his first appearance in the varsity line-up, had a third period pin at 112. Tom Stumpf and Hershey's Bill Demmel battled to a 0-0 deadlock; the Falcons closed things out with two decisions, boosting the Falcons to 2-1 for the season and 2-0 in the league.

These wrestlers also were the **first team** (as verified by our records) **to include a female member on the team:** Catherine (Cathy) Clark '84, as previously noted.

The team's total record for this 1980s decade was 116 wins, 32 losses, and one tie. These 80s teams snapped the winning streak of Shikellamy (The previous season the score was LD 32 and Shikellamy 23) and with Warwick 22-17. The Falcons also were ranked as one of the top teams in the state.

This **1980-81** team also won the CAC Championship and the District III team title with Coaches Cleon Cassel and Randy Umberger being named **Pennsylvania Co-Coaches of the Year.**

Nothing stopped this team, and the varsity scored, on average, twice as many points as those of their opposition, reaching their peak in the 13th match of the season. On **January 29, 1981** in the LD gymnasium, which was overflowing with eager fans, the remarkable Falcons clinched the CAC championship title by winning against the Eagles of Cumberland Valley. And they seemed to have had fun doing it.

In January the school newspaper shouted this headline: **Falcons unravel CV Wrestlers.** Only those who had been at the match understood the headline. The Falcons certainly did "unravel the opposition" when the wrestler from Cumberland Valley reached the mat from their side and stared across the mat at two Falcon wrestlers wearing face masks! Yes. Facing the CV wrestler and the crowd were two masked Falcon wrestlers—**Kevin Rogers** and **Joel Umberger.** The CV coach was confused, wanting the LD wrestler selected to be the best opponent for Cumberland Valley to defeat. How could the CV coach tell which of his wrestlers to choose, as he faced two masked men both wearing Lower Dauphin singlets and otherwise unidentified?

The visiting Cumberland Valley coach had to make a quick choice and he took a chance, guessing that the masked man he chose was Joel Umberger, thus committing his own 185 pound wrestler to face who he thought was Umberger. However, when the mask came off, everyone realized that the CV wrestler was facing Kevin Rogers, not Umberger! The bout began and Rogers (LD) proceeded to pin CV's Turban.[1]

---

[1] Yes; this is a true incident; one of those "you had to see it to believe it" and then you might not believe it. For a detailed account, see "Lower Dauphin Falcon Wrestling, 1960-1993" (which was published in the souvenir program in celebration of the 400th Wrestling Victory.) For Coach Cassel's account of this event, see *The Falcon Grappler*, May 2006.

This is the masked wrestler.

Using two masked teammates, identical in outward appearance in their singlets and masks, was a brilliant strategy for LD. Of course, The CV coach was dumbfounded, if not annoyed, as were some of the spectators in the stands. No one had ever seen anything like this.

LD won the meet. (No one knew until later that this stunt was a personal pay-back from Coach Cassel for an earlier prank perpetrated by CV's coach against Cassel himself).

The crowds on both sides were perplexed but thoroughly entertained. (We can only imagine what the CV coaches, to say nothing of the referees, were thinking!) Not surprising, it was this match that caused a change in the **National Wrestling Rules** by which every wrestler ever after was required to report to the Score Table to identify himself before each match.[2]

On a note with a more decorous tone, the *Sunday Patriot News* named two wrestlers from Lower Dauphin for their Big 12 Wrestling Team: (1) Craig Hetrick, who had a senior wrestling record of 8-0, and (2) Joel Umberger, whose record was 10-0.

An unidentified newspaper on February 6, 1981 had this to say, "…Last evening Lower Dauphin earned a share of its second straight **Capital Area Conference crown.** LD, who is the defending CAC champion, spotted Middletown a 98-pound decision, but ruled the remainder of the evening in their recent 59-3 win to extend their conference mark to 8-0. There is a good chance the Falcons can clinch the title outright next Thursday in their match with Palmyra."

---

[2] The '81 season in its mask match with Kevin Rogers and Joel Umberger against CV will never be topped, according to John Rozanski in a comment placed on Facebook in 2022. Nor has the prank ever been forgotten.

March 1, 1981. Upsets were few and far between at Lower Dauphin when the Falcons and arch rival Cumberland Valley shared the Section IV team crown. A tough Steve Sauve (CV) finished with a first-period fall, using a headlock to pin valiant Mike Mazerolle of LD. Craig Hetrick defended his title and Keith Youtz of Hershey took a 6-2 decision from Lower Dauphin's Craig Camasta. Joe Radwick came from behind and won at 167. Best of all, LD gained the team tie when Joel Umberger (185) reversed his opponent.

March 8, 1981. Class AAA Sectional Champions included Craig Hetrick and Joel Umberger, both of whom scored falls the whole way through.

March 15, 1981. A victory over Hershey was earned when back-to-back forfeits in the first two weight classes gave the Falcons a quick 12-0 lead, and the team never looked back. Craig Cassel, in his first varsity appearance, executed a third period pin. (Further, and just as engaging, at the District 3 AAA Championships Craig Hetrick staged a big comeback in the final period and won 12-4.)

Keith Youtz of Hershey took a 6-2 decision from Lower Dauphin's Craig Camasta; LD's Joe Radwick reversed his opponenet at 185 lbs.

Additional Sports Power Stars of the 70s & 80s

Field Hockey

When **Field Hockey** earned its first championship season, it was the first distaff **powerhouse** team at Lower Dauphin. Top seniors included **Carole Engle, Julia Staver,** and **Linda Kreiser—all legendary Class of 1970**—with many records in various areas. Staver and Kreiser later became International standouts in their sport.

Track and Marathon Runner

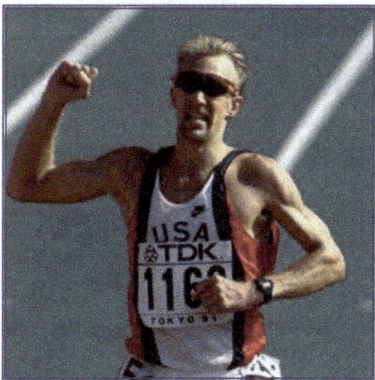

Runner Steve Spence (Class of 1980) is the holder of **International Marathon** records and is a successful track coach at Shippensburg University.

On May 11, 2024, two days after his 54th birthday, Steve Spence ran a 4:54 sub-5:00 mile streak for an astonishing 41st consecutive year.

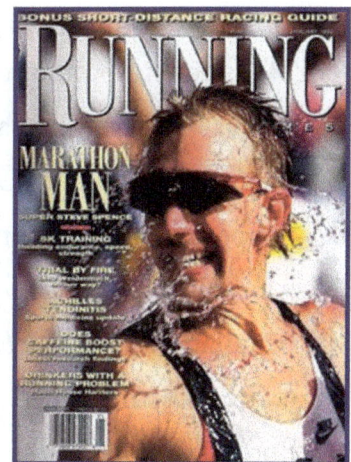

—A sample of LD's many exceptional athletes

Congratulations Wrestlers and Coaches

"Watch for forthcoming database and communication system for all alumni!"

Founded April 15, 1989
Celebrating 35 years of Service

Supporter of
Lower Dauphin Wrestling
An Uncommon Heritage

Sampling of our work:

▶ Fund-raising for and installation of the large Alumni Showcase
  ▶▶ Frequent promotional and celebratory displays therein
▶ Annual College Scholarships
▶ Sponsorship of LD's Golden Jubilee event
▶ Support of homecomings and alumni recognition
▶ Alumni cheerleaders for special events
▶ Installation of *Falcon Pride* signage
▶ Noting Distinguished Alumni
▶ Books focusing on the history of LDHS
  ▶▶ *Loyal Hearts Proclaim: The First 50 Years* (**2013**)
  ▶▶ *The English Students of B-1* (**2018**)
  ▶▶ *Remember LDHS* (**2022**)
  ▶▶ *Memorable Moments of Your Class* (**2022**)
  ▶▶ *Lower Dauphin Wrestling* (**2024**)

Email: ldalumni@ldsd.org
Address: LDAA, Box 255
          Hummelstown, PA 17036
Website: lowerdauphinalumni.org
          facebook.com/LDAlumniAssn

1981–1982 *(Record 15-1)*

Row 1. Joe Felegi, Cary Gray, Troy Bathhurst, Warren Dodson, Ed Fischl, Sam Fallinger, Craig Cassel, Mike Mazerolle, Ray Fogleman.

Row 2. Jim Stahl, Kevin Rogers, Tom Stumpf, J.D. Miller, Rick Salus, Craig Camasta, Jamie Kiessling, Dan Sadler, Chris Bath.

In the fall of 1981 the PIAA acted to shorten the scholastic wrestling season, effective the following year, to avoid the overlap of one sport season on another. These calendar boundaries were to be clearly stated and enforced statewide.

Listings from *The Sun*, April 14, **1982**, include the following achievements for this Lower Dauphin Wrestling Team:

- CAC Champion, Section IV Champion, 15-1 Record
- Craig Cassel: 14-1 Sectional Champion, Patriot-News Big 12 Selection
- Sam Fallinger: Undefeated 11-0. Sectional Champion, Dallastown Champion, *Patriot-News* Big 12 Selection

- Carey Gray: 11-4 Sectional Champion
- Craig Camasta: 15-1 Sectional Runner-up, Patriot-News Big 12 Selection
- Ray Fogleman: 14-1 Sectional Runner-up
- Rick Salus: 15-1 Sectional 3rd Place
- Mike Mazerolle: 13-2 Sectional 3rd Place
- Kevin Rogers: 10-3-1 Sectional 4th Place
- J.D. Miller: 12-2-1 Dallastown Tournament Champion
- JV Team Record: 14-2.

Undefeated Junior High Team: 8-0

CAC Champions – Section IV Champions – (15-1 Record)

Weight	Name	Grade	
98	Carey Gray	12	
105	Warren Dodson	11 (or Ed Fischl)	9
112	Sam Fallinger	12	
119	Craig Cassel	12	
126	Mike Mazerolle	12	
132	Ray Fogleman	12	
138	Dan Sadler	11 (or Chris Bath)	11
145	Craig Camasta	12	
155	Rick Salus	12	
167	J. D. Miller	12	
185	Kevin Rogers	12 (or Tom Stumpf)	11
UNL	Kevin Rogers	12 (or Jim Stahl)	12

1982–1983 *(Record 15-1)*

Row 1: Ed Arnold, Claudio Valeri, Warren Dodson, Ed Fischl, Greg Denk, Chris Bath, Ron Stammel, Steve Ulrich.

Row 2: Kevin Kotchey, Trevor Hershey, Mike Saich, Steve Rider, Harry Strawser, Tom Stumpf, Oliver Maxwell, Craig Wallace, Duane Geesaman.

We Loved these Headlines!!!

LD Trips Red Land, January 9, 1983

LD Grapplers Win Two, Still Unbeaten, January 12, 1983

Lower Dauphin Takes C. Cliff on Mats, January 14, 1983

Lower Dauphin, CD Continue Win Ways, January 21, 1983

Lower Dauphin in Key Win, January 28, 1983

L. Dauphin Grapplers Keep Rolling

With spot-on reporting by Amy Wallish:

December 8, 1982. Against Governor Mifflin High School, the LD varsity team flew to a 42-12 win. With that finished, two days later they sprinted to Red Lion to have their opposition grapplers for dessert.

December 23, 1982. Leading the score from start to finish, LD tacked a 26-18 scholastic wrestling setback on Warwick last night. The triumph was the Falcons' fourth win of the season without a loss.

A prelude to this season is found in the Sunday newspaper: "The Falcons don't have much in the way of household names but with Cleon Cassel directing the traffic, they're sure to be in the race. …Cassel says the group includes the best sophomores he has coached and the candidates beginning in the freshman class were members of Lower Dauphin's **first undefeated junior high team in 15 years.**" An enviable record to carry to senior high!

Dreaming of someday...

Chris Bath '83, Coach Cassel, (David Machamer, Roy Gesford, Jeff Benedict, Clint Etnoyer —all 8th graders), Eddie Hoffman '85, Tom Stumpf '83.

January 6, 1983. The LD wrestlers handily won their match against Carlisle 33-15. Ed Arnold breezed by his opponent with an 8-3 decision to start the winning side of decisions. Falcon grapplers Chris Bath at 132, Dan Sadler at 145, and Tom Stumpf at 167 all registered pins. Claudio Valeri decisioned Carlisle's Keith Blessing at 10-6. LD won seven of the first eight matches and coasted the rest of the way in an impressive opener, thanks to the LD triumph by Tom Stumpf.

January 8, 1983. In the Saturday contest LD squeaked by a scrappy Red Land, 28-21. The Falcons did not register a pin in the match but took eight out of 12 matches. Red Land provided more competition than the Falcons probably expected… "but with the match heading for a draw, Dodson reached back for some old-fashioned Falcon spirit. He reversed and put Zimmerman on his back for two near-fall points, all in the last four seconds, resulting in a 10-6 victory." Harry Strawser bunched four points deep into the final period for his 5-3 victory, locking up the meet.

January 13. Lower Dauphin heavyweight Strawser battled back from an 8-3 deficit to pin Cedar Cliff's Frank Wilson with 90 seconds left in the dual meet as the Falcons pulled out a wild 26-18 victory. The triumph kept the Falcons unbeaten overall in the season as well as in Division I.

January 20. At home the Falcons exploded into the match with a pin by Ed Arnold in 1:02 followed by a six-point forfeit for Claudio Valeri. Chris Bath's win at 9-2 and Tom Stumpf's first minute pin ("Seventeen seconds into the match he took Brian Shives down and 26 seconds after that, it was over.") at 167 pounds clinched LD's 32-18 victory over Chambersburg. Craig Wallace earned a decision, Ed Arnold had a take-down, then a pin. Stalling violations from Chambersburg gave Ron Stammel (138) the margin of victory; Dan Sadler '83 held back, then escaped with 11 seconds to go.

January 27. Lower Dauphin broke open a tense struggle with Central Dauphin by winning the last three matches on the way to a crucial 32-18 Mid-Penn Wrestling triumph. Tom Stumpf's superior decision at 167 lb. and Craig Wallace's pin at 185 shattered the 18-18 tie and locked up the Falcon victory in the showdown battle between Division I's two unbeaten teams. LD now topped the circuit with a perfect 4-0 log, hard-won but perfect.

February 3. LD Matmen easily won 54-3 over CD East. The match began with an impressive fall for sophomore Ed Arnold and a 9-5 win by Claudio Valeri, followed by a series of falls and pins.

This triumph kept the Falcons unbeaten overall in the season as well as in Division I of the Mid-Penn. Their late-match heroics provided plenty of fireworks and some crucial points—in three of the Falcons' six victories of the evening they came from behind in the third period. …With the meet still up for grabs at 185, LD's Craig Wallace trailed Tate in the last period. Wallace escaped and set Tate up for a takedown which resulted in a pin. …The Falcons earned a fall from Ed Arnold '85 and superior decisions from Dan Sadler and Tom Stumpf. …The outcome left LD the only unbeaten team in Division I.

February 16. "Falcon Matmen Take Mid-Penn Division Title," defeating Milton Hershey. Right before the winter blizzard struck, LD had done just that. Coach Cassel said he never had expected the championship to be nailed down before the end of the season. He noted, "The young team is heavy with sophomores and juniors, undefeated, which was surprising, as at the beginning of the season they had looked like a bunch of rookies." The 1983 Yearbook shows the score as 31-18.

Coach Cassel and the Varsity Wrestlers brought home the Division I Championship from the newly formed Mid-Penn Conference. The team's record of 15-1 brought LD its fourth successive league championship and sent two seniors—Tom Stumpf, with a record of 25-5, and Dan Sadler '83 (23-5)—to the State Championships in Hershey.

Claudio Valeri reflected on this season: "What was special about the 1983 team?" His reply was clear and can be seen in his own story in this book.

Tom Stumpf '83

He noted that LD had some tremendously close matches like our 22-21 against CV. "We pinned Cedar Cliff's heavyweight for the win. Harry Strawser was the hero that night and I still have that match on tape. We broke Murderers' Row to beat Northern when Chris Wallace was trailing 3-1, his lateral dropped CD's 189 pounder for a fall, clinching the victory for the Falcons."

Among the many notes of congratulation received by Coach Cassel, he kept the following letter from Craig Tritch, then in Arizona, "Please send me any orphans who may want to wrestle. I was able to fill only nine slots on my team and we still placed 15th in the state tournament. ... also please give my regards to the team for upholding the fine tradition of LD wrestling."

1983–1984 *(Record 8-6)*

Row 1: Chris Cassel, Claudio Valeri, Joe Felegi, Ed Arnold, John Saich, Ed Fischl.

Row 2: Eric Oakley, Brian Costik, Matt Fallinger, Keith Camasta, Rodney Stammel, Bob Early, Matt Hahn.

Row 3: Glenn Kohr, Trevor Hershey, Kevin Kotchey, Troy Light, Craig Wallace, Matt Moore, Tony Castanzi, Roger Swisher. Missing: Harry Strawser.

Coach Cassel had been on sabbatical, returning to a team feared by most of its rivals to be this year's powerhouse. (Easy enough to do when LD, more often than not, is the powerhouse.) Cassel noted, "There's no question we have a pretty well-balanced team this year, but it's hard to pick a frontrunner when you see how strong our league will be. It is, of course, a bonus to have returnees in every weight class."

The LD varsity team was Champion of the Cedar Cliff Christmas Tournament, followed by two impressive victories, beating Carlisle soundly on January 5 at home, 47-11, with Chris Cassel launching the event with a win (13-0).

The match against Cedar Cliff (January 12) started badly when Cassel and Valeri both lost. Arnold won at 112, but for every successful bout LD took, the Colts took two with a final score of 31-16.

The Falcons lost against Susquenita on January 21 at a home meet with a packed house. Coach noted, "Eric Oakley held on to win at 9-5 followed by a major decision for Camasta." Score: LD 14, Susquenita 34.

Winning against Chambersburg, LD had four falls: Camasta in 5:05, Matt Hahn in 45 seconds, Kotchey at 4:43, and Swisher in 1:13. Cassel received a 4-point decision. Arnold, Saich, and Strawser each contributed 3 points.

The Birds then took a shocking loss from Central Dauphin on January 26 when they were scoreless, until Matt Hahn (145) won his bout. Our other two wins were from Strawser (185) and Geeseman (Unl). In JVs, Wade Alexander contributed a superior decision and Moore took a 5 pt. superior decision for a victory of 45-6.

Even with only one senior in the lineup, the season ended with a record of 8-6 with five wrestlers qualifying for the first round of the District III Championship.

1984–1985 *(Record 14-2)*

Row 1: Pete Valeri, Doug Pavone, Chris Cassel, Claudio Valeri, Jeff Mathias, Ed Arnold.

Row 2: Ed Fischl, Eric Oakley, Jim Mehaffie, Ed Hoffman, Keith Camasta, Tom Salus.

Row 3: Matt Hahn, Trevor Hershey, Rodney Stammel, Brian Englehart, Jim Crist, Mike Crick, Harry Strawser, Duane Geesaman.

The wrestling season began with what sportswriter Amy Wallish described as "an impressive victory" (35-17) over the Wilson High School Bulldogs on Saturday, December 15, 1984. The Falcon Grapplers then took first place in the LD Christmas Tournament, following their win (45-19) over Harrisburg in a December 20 match. On December 22 Bob Black wrote, "The crowd was minimal. The action was maximal. The battle for second was intense." However, to Cleon Cassel the tournament was a success. "This tournament gives people who appreciate good wrestling an opportunity to see some of the best before we get into league season."

On January 5 Lower Dauphin, described as "tough and talented," defeated the Hershey Trojans, 40-12. On January 10 they defeated the Central Dauphin Rams (34-13), followed by the Mechanicsburg Wildcats (51-12). LD's Mike Crick (185) earned a fast fall for both matches, pinning within seconds.

Bob Black, *Patriot-News*, wrote, "Wrestling against Lower Dauphin High School is sort of like being mugged by a businessman in a three-pieced suit in broad daylight…. Wrestling with businesslike precision last night at Central Dauphin, the Falcons cruised to a 34-13 victory."

What was not expected was the loss (14-44) to undefeated Shikellamy, where LD lost all bouts until the 167 weight class when Trevor Hershey pinned Shikellamy's Bill Lytel in 22 seconds. The Falcons then went on to beat Chambersburg, 50-11. Another victory came from Cumberland Valley, with a final score of 40-10 in our favor.

At the end of the next meet—one that was divided into three rounds and included a bit of everything, including a frightening injury incident, a sincere "gentlemanly response" was demonstrated at the end of the meet: Coach Cleon Cassel stood up from his chair and walked directly over to Waynesboro's Kurt Bowman who had had a brilliant match and, in fact, one in which Trevor Hershey got away with a reversal (one of the few against Bowman in the past two years). Reaching the mat, Cassel extended his hand to Kurt, offering congratulations.

Overall it was a very successful season, with a pause to celebrate on February 16, an event that few coaches—or wrestlers—reach: **"Eleven Falcon grapplers went to the Section I Tournament…"** and came away with five fourth place finishers, three third placers, two second places and one first place champion, Senior Ed Arnold, who was seeded first in his weight class. Good work! Bringing home **11 Total!!**

1ˢᵗ place: Ed Arnold
2ⁿᵈ place: Mike Crick, Harry Strawser
3ʳᵈ place: Keith Camasta, Eric Oakley, Trevor Hershey
4ᵗʰ place: Matt Hahn, Chris Cassel, Claudio Valeri, Tom Salus, Ed Fischl.

The victory on February 16, 1985 marked Coach Cleon Cassel's 300ᵗʰ career win. *Below is an excerpt from one of many congratulatory messages sent to Coach Cassel, this one from Newville:*

"Again—Congratulations on winning #300! The more I reflect on that feat, the average wins per year, the longevity involved… and the many young men you have influenced positively—the more I came to appreciate just what you have accomplished!"

With all of the accolades being sent to them, this wrestling team still took on the mundane job of "Mat Crew" on Wednesday, March 13 through Saturday evening, March 16, for the State Wrestling Championship held at the Hershey Arena.

A big change in wrestling came in 1985 with the **Technical Fall rule** that when an individual match reached a 15 point difference in the score, the match was stopped, and the winner was awarded 6 team points. Needless to say, not everyone was pleased with the rule.

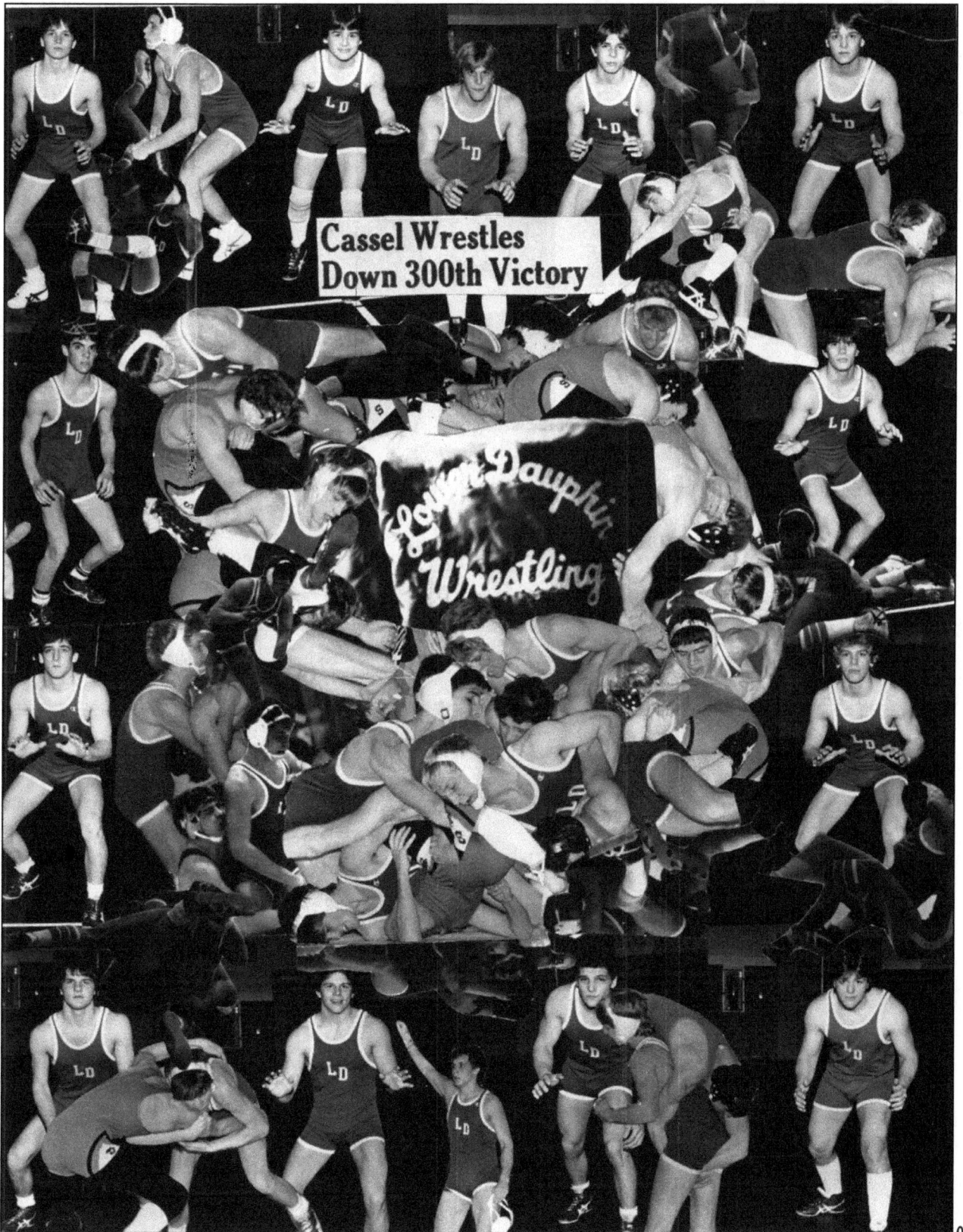

In honor of sons Matthew '87, Andrew '90 and Nathan '94

Carl '62 and Joan Espenshade, Sponsors

Carl Espenshade, member of the legendary First Wrestling Team, attributes wrestling as the path to a college education.

Matt and Andy followed Dad to the wrestling arena.

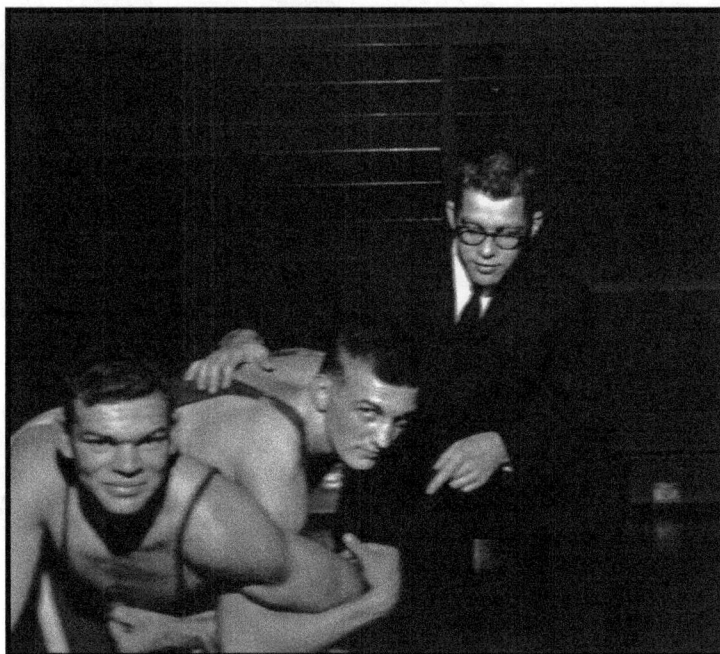

Richard Walters '63, Carl Espenshade '62, Coach Cleon Cassel

Coach Cleon Cassel

…To Coach Cassel, who asked every ounce of devotion from us, and returned the same. He never forgot us—providing guidance and support far beyond the wrestling mat—and we will never forget him.

Heartfelt thanks from all the wrestlers you aided and inspired.

Tribute to Coach Cassel by an Anonymous Sponsor

1985–1986 *(Record 11-5)*

Row 1. Kevin Wolfe, Pete Valeri, Clint Etnoyer, Chris Cassel, John Saich.

Row 2. Wade Alexander, Scott Alexander, Tim Shutt, Roy Gesford, Jim Blouch, Tom Salus.

Row 3. Andy Weaver, Jeff Gruber, Matt Moore, Brian Davis, Kirby Kuntz, P. J. Kolaric.

Lower Dauphin is very proud of its reputation as having a fine wrestling program. The record of the wrestling teams to this date was 310 wins, 38 losses and 4 ties. The 1986 team came away with a remarkable win over defending District III champion, South Western, and they lost only to the toughest teams. Matt Moore remained undefeated in dual meet competition.

On January 4, the Falcons downed Hershey 38-15; LD winners by pins included Kevin Wolf, Chris Cassel, and Tom Salus. Other Falcon wins included Pete Valeri, Clint Etnoyer, John Saich, and Matt Moore with superior decisions, and Wade Alexander with a win by default. It all counted.

On January 9 the team recorded two wins against strong opponents. On Thursday they went 32 to 20 against the Central Dauphin Rams where our wrestlers had two pins and one technical fall on points to garner the victory. Valeri and Cassel both had pins while Tom Salus registered a technical fall. Other winners were Kevin Wolf, Clint Etnoyer, Wade Alexander, and Matt Moore.

Against Mechanicsburg on January 11, the Falcons had two pins and one technical fall to capture the match, defeating Mechanicsburg, 39-13. Winners included Valeri, Cassel, Alexander, Salus, and Gruber – all with decisions, plus Moore by forfeit.

On January 16 Cedar Cliff pinned a 41-12 loss on the Falcons. Only three LD grapplers won their bouts. At 119 Chris Cassel pinned his opponent at 3:11 while Tom Salus at 155 had a 4-2 decision. Matt Moore won his bout, 10-3. Two days later, the Falcons overcame South Western, 39-21, taking two pins, two technical falls, and four decisions to win. Those winning by pins included Kevin Wolf at 98 in 1:04 and Cassel at 119 in 4:12. Pete Valeri and Salus both had technical falls. Clint Etnoyer, Wade Alexander, Roy Gesford, and Matt Moore won decisions.

On January 25 the grapplers easily won a tri-meet against Waynesboro and Big Spring and on January 30 the matmen took on Chambersburg and came away with a big 50-12 win. Kevin Wolf earned a fall at 5:21 with 17-1 points. Pete Valeri followed with a forfeit and Etnoyer with a technical. However, on February 1 against Susquenita, the Falcons came away with a disappointing 24-37 loss.

On February 6 the Falcons downed Northern 32-21. Unfortunately, Shikellamy was overpowering and only Brian Davis and Matt Moore earned decisions there.

In a match-up with the Rams, Valeri and Cassel both had pins while Tom Salus registered a technical fall. Other winners were Kevin Wolf, Clint Etnoyer, Wade Alexander, and Matt Moore.

The Falcons had two pins and one technical fall against Mechanicsburg to capture the match with LD winners Valeri, Cassel, Alexander, Salus, and Gruber, with Moore winning by forfeit.

On the 13th LD defeated Carlisle and on the 15th crushed Red Land.

Coach Cassel noted, "We rely a lot on tradition—tradition of toughness and confidence. We don't do any of the 'rah-rah' stuff. We just want the kids to be calm and believe they are going to win. Toughness in our view means to not give an inch to anyone. And if you do, get back in, and do more. …hard work is a tradition at LD. We have always been known for being in as good a shape as can be." However, LD's inexperience limited them at Wilson. Of their five wins, three were falls and two were by decision.

1986–1987 *(Record 13-3)*

Row 1: Pete Valeri, Mike Weneck, Kevin Wolfe, Neil Wychock, Clint Etnoyer.

Row 2: Chris Pavone, Dave Machamer, Chris Cassel, Ryan Gray, Tim Shutt, Tim Heimbach.

Row 3: Jamie Eberhard, Roy Gesford, Tom Salus, Keith Kotchey, Jeff Hollenbush, Ken Buchanan.

While the 1987 Falconaire noted that initial expectations had not been high for this season, the team members were determined to be recognized as contenders. According to Coach Cassel, "This is a fun team, a loose team in practice. Don't get me wrong. It is evident they hate to lose, but they don't sulk. They work."

LD and Hershey faced off on January 3rd and the night belonged to LD. Mike Weneck pinned at 1:12; Chris Pavone won by forfeit; Pete Valeri won by technical fall; Chris Cassel pinned Curt Cash; Matt Becker decisioned. Tim Shutt also decisioned against Eric Ruhl, and Jamie Eberhard decisioned Davy Roush; Tom Salus won over Brad Rhine; Keith Kotchey decisioned Jerry Look and unlimited Jeff Hollenbush decisioned at 9-1. A lot of decisions!

January 8 brought a hard-fought victory over perennial powerhouse Central Dauphin. The *Patriot News* sportswriter Rod Frisco[*] wrote, "A month ago, Lower Dauphin looked anything but tough when it lost all of its semifinal bouts in the four-team State College tournament. However, the Falcons have since molded nicely as a dual meet team and are among only a handful of unbeaten teams in the Mid-State."

On January 10 the Falcons' strong lightweights carried the team to a lead over Mechanicsburg that ended the dual "about 10 minutes after the meet started" and ended 32-21. Coach Cassel noted, "Mechanicsburg won four of the last five bouts, but LD's lone win in the heavies was the **meet-clinching fall at 167** by Tom Salus, who is even bigger and better than he was last season."

As typical, the Falcons were on the right path and, as a result, the wrestling team was dubbed the best group of No-Names in the mid-state by *The Patriot News*, which noted "… Hall of Fame Coach Cleon Cassel turned the team into a formidable group that continued the strong wrestling tradition at LD."

Not in the record books is the back story that Cedar Cliff came within one victory of wrapping up Division I with a triumph over LD in a showdown. However, the Colts fell behind 15-3 when Pete Valeri made a drop to 98 lb. and defeated Khoi Tran 15-0 for a technical fall. LD's Kevin Wolf (at 105) had a fall and 119-pounder Dave Machamer upset Brian Hannen 9-8.

At the end of the season **LD's Pete Valeri** was the only area scholastic wrestler to compete in the PIAA Championships.

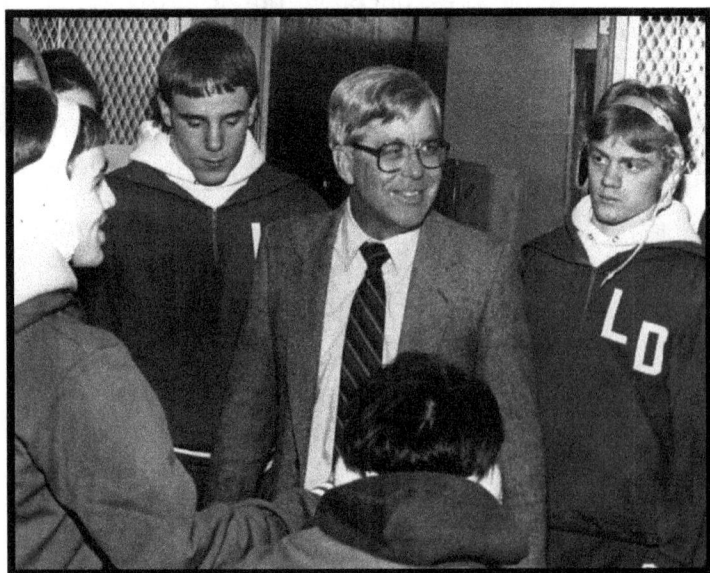

For Gesford and Macamer, 1987, the "Dreaming of Someday" came true.

[*] Named by Tom Elling's *PA Wrestling Handbook, 2021* as a Top Wrestling Writer.

202

On April 4, The Patriot-News *posted this headline:* **Cassel Resigns:** "...
——*ending one of the most durable and remarkable coaching careers in the state."*

- Cassel's team had captured 13 CAC titles and two Mid-Penn Conference Division I championships.

- The Falcons were undefeated in 63-64, 64-65, 70-71, and 71-72.

- Nine of Cassel's teams were defeated only once.

However, the most impressive figure among Lower Dauphin's wrestling numbers is ZERO. That's how many losing seasons the Falcons have had since the fall of 1960.

Coach Cassel closes his coaching career with an outstanding 324-42-4 dual meet record.

This same year (1) the wrestling team was teased by *The Patriot News* as being the best group of "unknowns" in the entire mid-state and (2) Pete Valeri made a successful run to the state tournament.

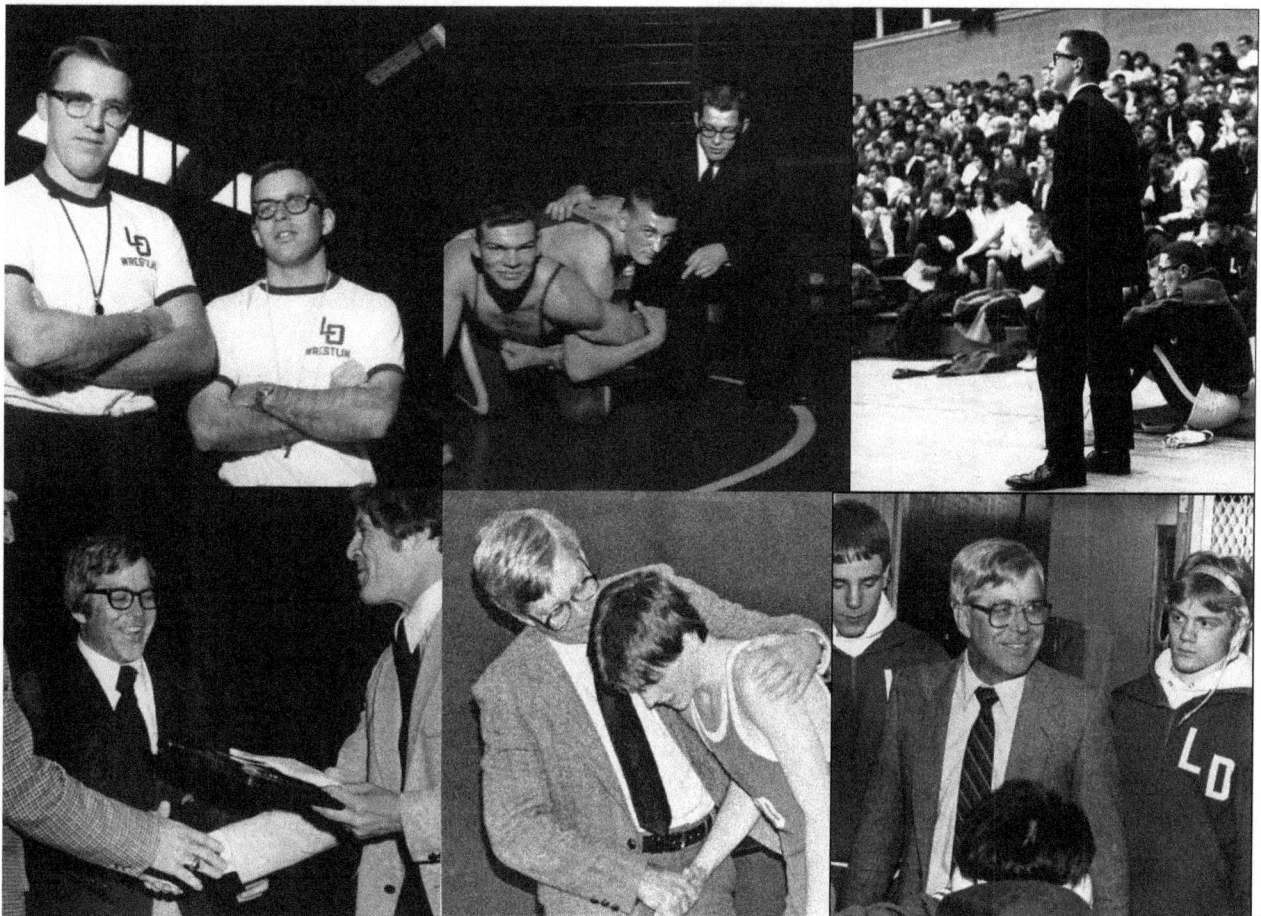

Donna Walmer Shutt

Tim Shutt

An example of LD's many three-generation sports families!
Donna Walmer Shutt '64: mother of Tim;
Tim Shutt '87: father of Blaine '10 and Bailey '16

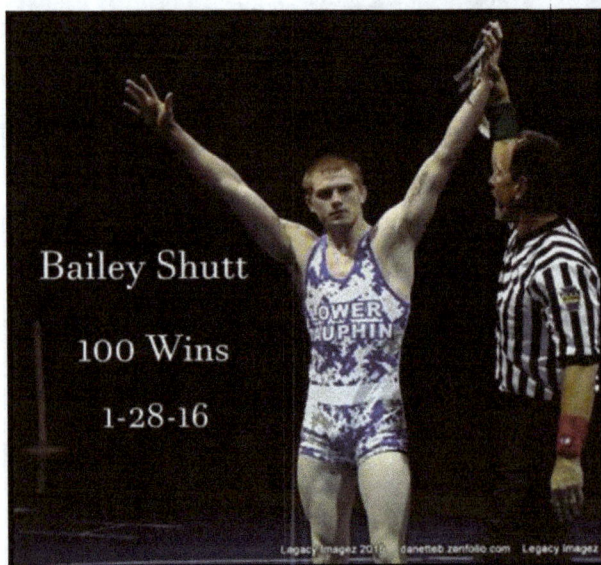

Bailey Shutt

100 Wins

1-28-16

Bailey Shutt, Class of 2016
Son of Tim Shutt

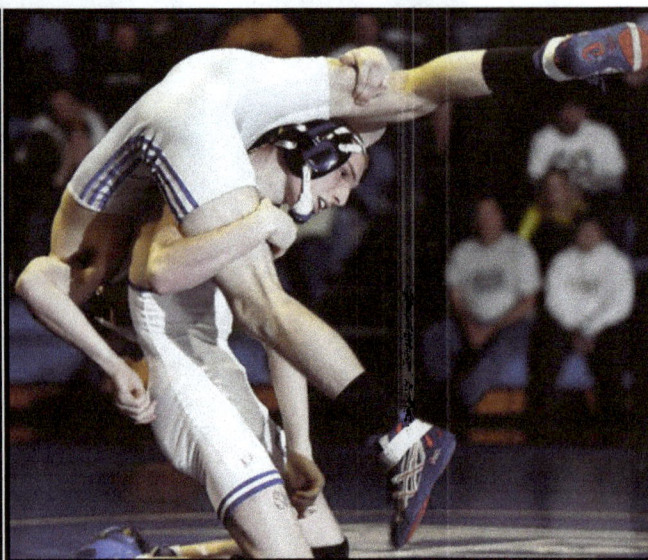

Blaine Shutt, Class of 2010
Son of Tim Shutt

1987-1988 *(Record 11-3)*

Row 1. Randy Lutz, Nick Cargas, Rick Cargas, Chris Pavone, Mike Weneck.

Row 2. Ben Lerew, Neil Wychock, Kevin Wolfe, Mike Kriner, Chuck Via, Ryan Gray.

Row 3. Curt Hosler, Todd Conz, Jamie Eberhard, Andy Klahr, Keith Kotchey, Jeff Hollenbush.

According to the 1988 Falconaire, "Our well-trained Falcons placed second in the tough Mid-Penn Division I. A key part in their success was a skilled coaching staff, led by head coach Ed Neiswinder '73 and assistants Ron Michael '72 and Don Reese. Even though the Falcons suffered setbacks against Cedar Cliff and Shikellamy, the Birds won big victories over strong teams such as Dover, Central Dauphin, and Susquenita."

The pride always shines through...."

Snapshots of the Meets:

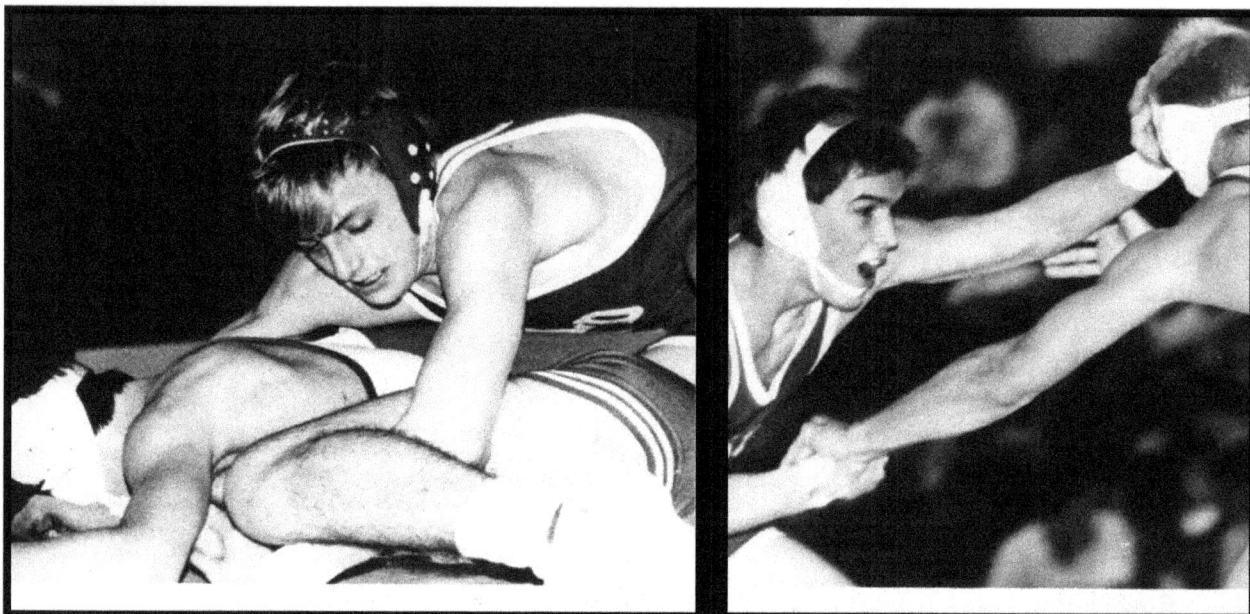

Above left, Randy Lutz going for the pin. Right: Neal Wychock full of determination.

Above: Jeff Hollenbush (Big 13) crushing his opponent.

1988–1989 *(Record 10-7)*

Good Luck to the reader in matching names in rows with wrestlers here!

From left to right should be Randy Lutz, Chris Wallish, Neal Wychock, Andy Espenshade, Rob Wallish, Tom McMullen, Chuck Via, Andy Klahr, Scott Baker, Keith Koncir, Jamie Eberhard, Nick Cargas, Tim Rhine, Ron Hostetter, Jeff Hollenbush, Chad Nolte, "Woody" Woods, Kevin Wolfe, Steve Lutz, Rick Cargas, Mark Goodman, Norm Hurst, Scott Sadler, and Jason Dupler.

The Falcons continued their winning tradition with a successful year. While crushed by power house Cedar Cliff (57-12), they strongly out-wrestled Harrisburg, Central Dauphin, and their nemesis Cumberland Valley, as well as Carlisle. Falcon Senior Jamie Eberhard was rated 1st in District III and Jeff Hollenbush was named to the Big 13. This team smashed Harrisburg (48-15), Central Dauphin (45-24), Chambersburg (40-23), Cumberland Valley (35-18), Milton Hershey (24-20), and Carlisle (25-0).

Sometimes we just need reminders of how good we are!

1989–1990 *(Record 10-4-1)*

Row 1: Eric Strunk, Shawn Strange, Randy Lutz, Jason Dupler, Steve Lutz, Mike Smoyer, Terry Dobbs, Norm Hurst.

Row 2: Brad Meloy, Steve Frelich, Nick Cargas, Rick Cargas, Andy Espenshade, Todd Noel, Tim Rhine, Chris Wallish.

Row 3: Coach Strawser, Brandon Weber, Scott Baker, Chad Shell, Josh Lininger, Chad Nolte, Steve Goho, Chuck Via, Andre Lewis, Steve Messick, Ken Baker, Conan Tollett, Woody Woods, Coach Umberger.

As wrestlers know, their sport is a combination of individual skill, team dedication, and the dynamics of trust. In this case the trust was found through the leadership of new head coach Randy Umberger who had been a part of Lower Dauphin wrestling since the fall of 1960. As a member of the first wrestling program in the newly formed high school, Umberger had been an outstanding wrestler at his Alma Mater as well as a very successful college wrestler at the University of Maryland, highly regarded by his peers at all levels.

Under Umberger's leadership this year, a fresh start for the wrestling program led to a fulfilling year. With an overall record of 10-4-1, including Central Dauphin and Cumberland Valley, the LD wrestling tradition of excellence was recharged.

Sectional Winners included Steve Lutz (103) who battled through three matches, pinning his opponents in the first two and winning by a four-point decision in the final match. Ending his regular season with a 13-1-1 record, Lutz would be a top wrestler in his weight class in the arena the following year.

Jason Dupler (112) also captured a title, defeating Jeff Depew of Red Land 15-6, followed by defeating Eric Fegley in overtime. Dupler advanced to beat Dave Stambaugh of Mechanicsburg for the head spot, ending with 13-1-1. Senior Nick Cargas also left the mat as an undisputed victor as he finished off three opponents to take the number one seat at his weight class of 125.

The fourth LD title belonged to Senior Chuck Via who, at 145 pounds, won his first match by a crushing 13-5, continuing on to beat Fred Williams of Middletown with a 16-6 decision victory. To seize the final victory Via defeated Ty Kreamer of Central Dauphin and finished the regular season with a 14-0-1 record.

LD Pep Rally

And who remembers the All-Sport Pep Rally when sports teams were introduced and supporters were invited to arrive in costume (in this case the author as Darth Vader)?

I am a Lower Dauphin Wrestler . . .

A Woven Thread:

Lower Dauphin Wrestling 1982

—Dr. Craig A. Camasta, A Family Affair

The Camasta family was introduced to wrestling when eldest brother Mark tried his skills on the mats at Bishop McDevitt high school. He transferred to Lower Dauphin his senior year, and received a scholarship from the University of Maryland. Brother Chris was next, and a natural talent at that. He placed 3rd in the state his senior year, and followed Mark to Maryland on a wrestling scholarship. Thus, it was an assumption that little brother Keith and I would follow the trend.

Wrestling was a family ordeal that spanned 15 years for Mom, Dad, Karen, and Adrianne, all in support of our family sport. It was common for our family to start a Saturday in Maryland and finish it in Hummelstown, between collegiate and high school matches. This trend continued for many years but it morphed into a Millersville-Hummelstown and then Millersville-Elizabethtown affair.

Wrestling for Lower Dauphin was also a family affair—with many families generational in their participation. This naturally meant that we would interact as a community, through sports, building social connections, friendships, and life-long relationships that continue on.

Junior High. The wrestling room was a bustling place where little kids interacted with high school seniors, in awe of their size, strength, and skills. It was a place to learn by observing and then trying moves and maneuvers. It was a place for "getting in shape," but the early years were not as intense as what was yet to come. There was always fun to be had—and this was led by some really big kids who disguised themselves as teachers/coaches. Craig Tritch led the bunch in junior high school, along with Al Hershey, Ed Neiswinder, and the Bittenbender brothers. On a daily basis, someone was going to get pegged in the face by a volleyball playing dodgeball, someone was gonna get a wedgie, someone was gonna get pounced on, the likes of a professional wrestling stunt flying through the air. We had fun!

One stand-out event that will forever live in the memories of all in attendance occurred during a winter sports pep rally, with a full student body in attendance. And this was masterminded and executed by my buddy Craig Tritch. We were individually called to center-court, lined-up by weight class, when coach's lair was set. We were in street clothes but concealed beneath was our wrestling outfit. Coach gave the charge – "OK Boys, SHOW THEM YOUR NUTS!" So, we stripped our street clothes off!!! All I remember beyond that was Principal Linnane shaking his head and covering his eyes…. We had fun!

Senior High. The stakes grew more intense as each year passed, and we were fervently proud to be Falcon Wrestlers. Our graduating class won the league championship all three years. Nothing made us more proud than to see the big blue banner in the gymnasium, memorializing our years of success. And it still stands, and we're still just as proud. A standout match that made the newspaper's front cover page was the perennial championship match-up against Cumberland Valley. Critical to our success was how the last two matches would play out. We had Joel Umberger and Kevin Rogers both weighing in at 185 lbs., so one would wrestle the 185 lb. class and the other would wrestle heavyweight, the decision to be made based on the line-up of the opposing wrestlers. Our preference was to have Rogers line up with their 185 pounder. Earlier in the week, Umberger broke his nose and was using a face mask. The home team was required to present their wrestler on the mat first, and the opponent could then send out their favored man. We were all huddled-up and we sent out Rogers, masked! The match started, Rogers was sidelined, and he removed the mask, revealing the ruse! We got our desired match-up, both Falcons won, and we secured another championship!

Nothing in this world can take the place of persistence. Talent will not: nothing is more common than unsuccessful men with talent. Genius will not; unrewarded genius is almost a proverb. Education will not: the world is full of educated derelicts.

Persistence and determination alone are omnipotent.

—Calvin Coolidge

College & Life Lessons. I continued wrestling at Millersville University at the 134 and 142 lb. weight classes. This was at a whole new level of competition. As with many small state universities in Pennsylvania, we were Division I and in the Eastern Wrestling League. The likes of Penn State, Pittsburgh, Cleveland State, and Univ. of Maryland rounded out our schedule.

Studying pre-medicine, this routine demanded discipline greater than any other time in my life up to that point. This was a preamble to what I would face in medical school. I learned to manage time and balance life. I had classes, practice, and then the library. Lots.. of.. time .. in the library. And I always got my best grades during the wrestling season.

Wrestling is a rarity among sports—all sports require intense physical activity, tough mental strength, and an unwavering devotion. But wrestling also involves weight loss and control. Of the three basic human drives, the desire for food is second only to the fight/flight response (survival). The ability to voluntarily starve one's self is unique to wrestling and an aberration among the world of sports. The discipline required to "make weight" is incredibly empowering to the mind. It is a self-lesson in conquering something so basic that lends itself to other life challenges.

A few years ago, I faced a cancer diagnosis—six months of chemotherapy followed by a month of radiation. This time I lost weight, but not by my choosing. During this journey, I got a message from Cleon Cassel, my childhood wrestling coach, to "stay tough, it's the 3rd period, you're behind by a point, and you've got to pull this off!" Wrestling coach, life coach, life lessons, character challenges—the common thread that weaves the fabric framed around a sport.

When We Weren't Wrestling, We Went Hunting

—Dr. Craig A. Camasta '82

It was a Monday morning in early winter which was the "opening day" for trapping (coons, muskrats, foxes, or anything else that we could lure in), and (Craig) Cassel and I went on our morning rounds checking the traps at 3:30 a.m. This task had to be completed twice a day, before and after school. Excitement was in the air as we knew that the first day was going to be a haul!

Luck struck with a red fox (which was bringing around $70 back then), so we dutifully shot it with the .22 rifle between the ears (dare not put any holes in the pelt), and brought it home to the farm. We were prepared with an empty chest freezer in the basement of the house (no time to skin the animals until the end of the season). We put the fox inside and went to school. In second period across the PA system came an unusual beckoning: "Craig Cassel is to go directly to the Principal's Office." Craig's mother was on the phone and she was angry! She had heard a noise in the basement of the Cassel home and found the fox jumping and bouncing inside the blood-coated freezer!!! That summons ended with us carrying the freezer that night to the barn for the rest of the season...

And we did catch lots of chickens (along with pheasants, quail, and like birds). At that time we were obsessed with fly fishing, and, being kids, we could not afford to buy the flies.

This is where the trapping money intersects a particularly memorable affair. Too poor to buy the flies, and not having enough funds to buy commercially available feathers/pelts, we got into the business of killing our own chickens for the feathers. We had to skin them from butt to eyes and stretch the hides upside down on a board, stretch and tack with small nails, then coat with salt, and wait a few weeks. This would produce a neck that would last a long time (I still have some and still use them!). Well, the supply around the farm was very limited, and the best feathers came from old roosters, the older the better, as their hackles were fully mature and served us in tying dry flies. Then the game got serious, and we had a plan....

On a Friday night we got a ride to Root's Market (in Manheim) where they auctioned livestock. We went early, with notepad and pencil, and scouted the birds that we wanted. We plucked a feather or two from select birds, "Yep, that one will do!" So the auction commenced, and we bought 12 very old roosters. Our plan was to do all the work the next morning. We were prepared with our gear. To kill the birds, without causing any damage to the feathers, we would put a bird in a cardboard box, and affixed one of mom's vacuum hoses to the end of the tail pipe of the truck, and asphyxiate the birds with the carbon monoxide. This produced a dead bird unscathed and ready to skin out... We did not get home from the auction until around midnight, and put 6 roosters in each of 2 crates. At 7:00 am we went to start a day's-long chore, armed with a good sharp pocket knife. Well, we learned a very important lesson that morning, as all the roosters were dead (spare one nearly dead, one in each crate—the winner), having fought the entire night to the death. All of the feathers were plucked out, there was a floor of blood-matted feathers, and the winner was not even useful... We looked at each other and cried... And being old birds, there was no use for the dinner table. So those birds made it to the dump. Lesson learned... It was a good metaphor for life...

I could go on and on like this—all true, revealing, and sometimes scary. There was the bartender who pulled a gun on us, the time when we had a policeman shoot his gun through the woods when he came upon 8 kids 12-16 years of age camping on Conewago Creek, the nearly disastrous forest fire we barely averted, and getting pulled over by the cops. How we survived is a small miracle. But we knew the boundaries of the time....

I remember when there would be a fight in school. It was usually a coach who broke it up and he had the boys meet in the wrestling room after school, where he would give the boys boxing gloves and let them duke it out. That produced a winner and a loser, an affirmed pecking order, and that was it.... (You who were there know the details.) I truly believe that much of the current state of school violence is a product of pent-up anger that has no outlet.

LD Wrestling: Cause and Effect
—Michael Mazerolle (Maz) '82

The reader should first understand that this story is not meant to glorify violence and is a part of my life that is not easy for me to write about. The early teenage years of my life dredge up memories of things which are truly better left in the past. However, without a foundation, the reader has a lack of knowledge and information to understand how good and honorable men and an athletic program based on solid fundamentals can change the course of a life from negative to positive.

I spent four years in a Boys' Home. When I first entered the Home in 1976, my violent tendencies already existed. Many boys in this Home came from rough backgrounds and had violent tendencies such as I did. In this environment, physical violence was not uncommon and could happen without words or challenges exchanged.

For example, one day I was walking down the hallway, towards the metal shop and was punched in the face so hard I almost lost consciousness. The assault had come without warning. I was able to maintain my faculties and I fought back until my assailant started to get the worst of it. At this point my assailant's cohorts—five of them—jumped in and beat the hell out of me. Several weeks later one of the cohorts, a football player, approached me with menace in his eyes. I immediately hit him in the throat and the fight was over. I could fill a book about the fights I was involved in at the Home, but that's not the purpose here. Rather, it is to show the reader a mere glimpse of who and what I was when Lower Dauphin Wrestling and Coach Cleon Cassel entered my life and changed negative to positive.

I was a member of the Lower Dauphin Wrestling Team from 1980 to 1982. I came to the team as an outsider during my Junior year and I came with anger management baggage. I mention "outsider" and "anger management" because what follows is a portrait of All-American Management, Leadership, Discipline, and Compassion displayed by unique individuals, all of which led to success both on and off the mat.

When I first came to Lower Dauphin I was angry and prone to physically violent behavior towards other people. I wanted to wrestle, but knew that my fierce past and tendencies were no secret. I tried out for the Wrestling Team and didn't know what to expect. The two primary coaches were Coach Cleon Cassel and Coach Randy Umberger.

So there I was thinking, "Look at all of these wrestlers who are from here and grew up here and know everybody; what chance do I have?" Then one day I was approached by Coach Cassel, an unassuming, soft-spoken man who said to me, "I want you to wrestle for me, but you have to give me your word that you will commit no acts of violence and keep your grades up."

I don't know what type of crystal ball this Coach Cassel had or if he was a natural at judging character. I believe the latter, and he knew that if I gave my word I would honor it at all cost! I looked at Coach Cassel, who was still looking at me, and this went on for several minutes. Giving my word meant changing who I was and how I had dealt with physical confrontation all my life up to this point. Looking at Coach Cassel I said, "You have my word." Those four words given to Coach Cassel completely altered my life.

The wrestling was fantastic, win or lose. Even though I was an outsider I was never treated as such and was accepted as a member of the team, which cleared a path for friendships, camaraderie, and teamwork, esprit de corps. This kind of atmosphere would not have been as effective if not for the promotion of it and the leadership of the coach.

I considered myself to be a good wrestler, but there were many times when I rose to the challenge and above my ability to win and overcome my opponent because of the knowledge that my teammates and coaches needed me to do so. That shows the strong ties that loyalty, friendship, support, and leadership can accomplish.

Off the mat the friendships continued—going to events such as parties, movies, camping, hunting, fishing, swimming, visiting Coach Cassel—where all are treated like family with a sense that you belonged there.

What I have mentioned here may seem normal to the reader. But, trust me; it is not normal for everyone. This comment is coming from someone who knows first-hand the difference between poor management, poor leadership, lack of discipline, and lack of compassion. With solid management, fair and consistent discipline and compassion, a person is enabled to achieve excellence and success in his personal life after wrestling.

It was Lower Dauphin Wrestling—the experience and Coach Cassel challenging me to give my word and honor it, that allowed—and opened—the path for me to become a United States Marine, member of a Nuclear Special Weapons and Tactics Unit, and Retired Law Enforcement Officer of 25 years.

As evidenced, Lower Dauphin Wrestling and proper leadership can and does result in much more than only good wrestlers and championships. It results in solid Americans who continue the legacy. I am proud to be part of the exceptional Lower Dauphin Legacy.

Reflections on Legacies
—Craig Cassel '82, LD Wrestler and Coach

As the son of the "Father of Lower Dauphin Wrestling" and arguably one of the greatest high school coaches ever, it is hard for me to top the stories and histories of my father. However, the last match against Central Dauphin made me realize that all contributions are important to the continued excellence of Lower Dauphin Wrestling.

The feeling of excitement throughout the match and the final outcome made me realize why we all love to hear the stories from the past. That match made my memories more vivid than ever, and this recent flood continues as my son, then in his 1st year of wrestling in the elementary program, continues to ask me to tell him stories of when I wrestled. I think of my heroes on the mats in the wrestling room and gyms of my childhood and how I tried to emulate their moves and character. I still have autographs from Jockers, Young, Neiswender, Mutek, Stauffer and Michael somewhere in a shoebox in the basement.

After Saturday's match, I felt the excitement that I had felt as a wrestler wearing the Lower Dauphin singlet, knowing all the screaming and cheering was for my teammates and I who had put in the time and pain in sweat and blood for the Thursday and Saturday nights when we could step out on the mat to do our best. As Lower Dauphin Wrestlers we looked up in the crowd at parents or girlfriends and knew we had made them proud. Last Saturday night throughout the match I felt a part of that pride. There was a piece of me on the mat each time an L.D. wrestler sucked it up and came out on top in a tight spot. I felt inspired by each and every wrestler whose win, loss, or draw came off the mat knowing he had given everything there was. They had given their best.

That evening as I watched my son on the mat at the Lower Dauphin Elementary Practice, I could feel excited for his potential and knew that after practice when he asked me to tell him another story about when I wrestled there would be plenty of stories to tell. I also knew that from now on, each match would inspire me to continue this tradition so that he could share the stories and memories that he also will likely accumulate.

The Miracle Season
—Claudio Valeri '85

The 1983 wrestling season was a very special year in my life, starting varsity as a tenth grader, something that was never assumed by any of us.

This was the first year of the Mid-Penn Conference, a new and exciting time for sports in the South Central Region. Lower Dauphin had only two returning starters—Dan Sadler and Tom Stumpf. It looked like it might be a long year. I remember Coach Cassel telling me later that if we had achieved .500 he would have been happy. Well, not only did we go .500 but we also achieved a record of 15-1, with a very close 30-15 loss to Shikellamy as our only blemish.

So what was so special about the '83 team? First off, we had some tremendously close matches like 22-21 over Cumberland Valley. We pinned Cedar Cliff's heavyweight to defeat them. Harry Strawser was the hero that night and I still have that match on tape—25 years later from when I am writing this. We broke Murderers' Row to beat Northern and Craig Wallace's lateral dropped CD's 189 pounder, losing 3-1 to beat them.

What I will remember most, however, is how the team had no hidden agendas, how we were all one when we took the mat and how we were also all one off the mat. Even though we were all very different people we had a common goal and that was TEAM. A valuable lesson we learned was that it isn't always about talent; sometimes it is about HEART.

A brief conversation with Claudio . . .

Former LD wrestler and experienced coach Claudio Valeri, as an enthusiastic follower of LD wrestling offered the following tidbits:

- ✓ Jeff Watts wrestling with a broken jaw — and winning.
- ✓ Beating Northern's "Murderers' Row."
- ✓ Harry Strawser's "I'm winning" promise to the coach before a must-win bout against Cedar Cliff (quickly fulfilled).
- ✓ A coach's warning at a heatedly competitive match: "Don't anybody go back to the locker room without at least one other guy with you."
- ✓ The full story of Neiswender's victory in a States bout that prompted a lengthy ovation. Coach Cassel said "made the hair on my neck stand up."
- ✓ Overhearing a fan with a Pennsylvania Dutch accent at a Mechanicsburg match saying: "These guys from Lower Dauphin are serious!"

Confirming the Dynasty: The '90s

History:

Athletic Directors

1960-2024

Lower Dauphin has been endowed from the beginning with Athletic Directors who have a history of success as athletes and as coaches—upstanding and outstanding in the positions. All have demonstrated their allegiance to and love for Lower Dauphin wrestling. The role of Athletic Director is a position that requires stamina, dedication, understanding, and, at times, the wisdom of Solomon. The School District has also been fortunate that the service terms for this crucial position have been of length.

John Goepfert	1960–1978	18 years
Wilbur Rhodes	1978–1987	9 years
Randy Umberger	1987–2007	20 years
David Bitting	2007–2022	15 years
Kaylor Kulina	2022–	

Kaylor Kulina is the newest appointed Athletic Director for Lower Dauphin. He began his tenure on August 1, 2022, as the successor to long-time athletic director David Bitting. Kulina returned to his Alma Mater, the ambition of many athletes who respect such a position and often view serving as A.D. an objective. Kulina himself admitted, "I always had aspirations of getting back into athletics, getting back into sports with my master's degree in sports administration."

A product of Millersville University, Kulina had worked in a sales role for an IT staffing company and coached Hummelstown's American Legion baseball team. He admits that coming back to his Alma Mater was his "dream" job. According to *The Sun*, Kaylor noted that he was looking forward to working with his father, Ken Kulina, who continued as the baseball coach and added, "I am looking forward to the opportunity to work alongside all of our great coaches as I think that's what makes Lower Dauphin and our athletic department so special. We have so many skilled people."

Mr. John (Jack) Goepfert

LD's First Athletic Director, 1960-1978

The right man at the right time!

Jack Goepfert

Following college and prior to tenure at Hummelstown High School, Jack Goepfert served in the Navy during World War II (1945-46) with the Special Forces Scout Raider Division in the China Theatre. During the war he was a member of the Black Hawk Basketball Championship Team in Shanghai, China. Following his military service, in **1947** Jack began a professional **basketball career** with the Sunbury Mercuries and the Harrisburg Senators/Caps where he averaged 7.1 points per game in his 106-game career which continued through the **1950** season.

According to the information found in the *1960 Tatler* (Hummelstown High School's final yearbook), "In **1948** the Bulldogs hired a new coach in the person of Jack Goepfert who had come to the Harrisburg area to make his mark." In his initial season at Hummelstown, he ended the year with 4 wins and 6 losses in football. In his second year, he turned in a 7-2-1 log and earned the Class B Championship in the Lower Susquehanna Conference. He was honored by this Conference as Coach of the Year.

In the fall of **1950** Jack Goepfert coached the Harrisburg Senators during their 1950 season.

At Hummelstown High his **1953** football team was runner-up in the league with a 5-4 record. In **1954** the Bulldogs had their first ever undefeated season with a 10-0-0 record, scoring 302 points against a mere 32 for their opponents. "The Team that Jack built" won the overall L.S.C. Championship. In **1955** Hummelstown had its second undefeated and untied season scoring **336** against their opponents' **34**. Goepfert was again voted Coach of the Year.

In **1956** Coach Barney Osevala took over the football coaching reins at Hummelstown High and in **1957** coached his team to a 6-4-0 season and another championship. In **1958**, and for the fourth time in five years, the team won the

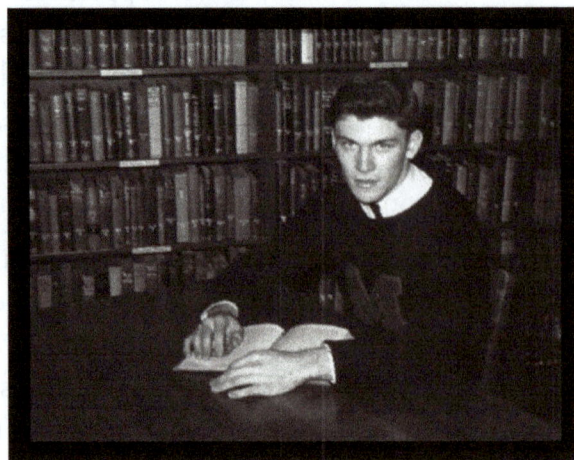

John "Jack" Goepfert, Jr., Mahanoy City High School
1941 - Senior Class Vice President

Conference Championship yet again, this time with a record of 6-3-1.

With the opening of Lower Dauphin High School, both Mr. Osevala and Mr. Goepfert joined the faculty, Osevala as a Social Studies Teacher and football coach and Goepfert as Athletic Director and Physical Education Teacher.

Wrestling was a sport new to even Jack Goepfert but that did not deter him from agreeing to scout for the Lower Dauphin teams. In fact, while he had never seen a wrestling match prior to his arrival at

Mahanoy City High School
(with thanks to Paul Coombe, MAHS, Historian)

Lower Dauphin, he offered to attend matches and "rate each wrestler, home and visitor," thus providing invaluable information to Coach Cassel. "We carry a card on every wrestler in the league," Cassel noted, "… starting it from their being placed on the team. We have everything on it—how strong he is, how nervous before a match, does he ride back on his legs, and other valuable information, thus providing advance notice to our own wrestlers about their opponents. We are, however, careful not to make our boys dependent on the information. We don't want the wrestlers to participate in a tournament that has been impossible to scout, and have them be nervous because there is no scouting card." Coach continued, "We also have situational drills in which we say to our wrestlers, "This kid has done this, which makes it impossible for you to do this. How do you block it? We tell them to take 10 minutes to work out a method to overcome the move. It usually works."

Jack's Plymouth, (restored and now owned by Mike Miller '82).

Goepfert also introduced a 4th-6th grade program to augment and improve Lower Dauphin's future wrestling programs.[*] Jack was astute at determining how to make things better without fuss, quietly improving various elements.

And some of our wrestlers may recall one of Jack Goepfert's many kindnesses when he transported those participating in the District Tournaments—in his personal car—the first being a red station wagon and later a **blue and white Plymouth.** (pictured above is Jack's car, now restored.)

[*] Lower Dauphin wrestling program, December 19, 1963.

Randy Umberger

Wrestler, Coach, Athletic Director
Six Decades with Wrestling

No other coach has the longevity garnered, the awards won, or the diversity of positions nobly filled than Randy Umberger. His is the name associated with Lower Dauphin at each level, with Athlete, Coach, Athletic Director, Librarian, and Assistant Principal being the Defining ones.

Teammates 1964:

from the top: Randy Umberger, Randy Kahler, Jim Rhone, Jim Sanders, Buster Shellenhamer, and Bobby Hess (bottom right)

January 2023

Still Teammates of Lasting Friendship

Randy Umberger, a man for all seasons!

In Randy Umberger's own words—

"My life's journey was created by the confidence and determination I gained by participating in the LD Wrestling Program. Home grown, born and raised in East Hanover Township, I attended East Hanover Elementary School, grades 1 -7, from 1953 through 1960.

"In September 1960 came a big change, moving from elementary to junior high school at the newly opened Lower Dauphin Jr/Sr High School. An announcement the fall of that first year invited 7th and 8th grade boys interested in wrestling to attend a meeting in "D Audion." Approximately 100 boys of all sizes answered the call, mainly out of curiosity. What was wrestling? No one really knew. We soon found out. The Harrisburg Novice Tournament was our baptism. What a lonely feeling I had with my first trip to the center of the mat. **That was the last time I would feel alone when on the mats.**

"Being on the wresting team made you a part of a community of parents, teachers, friends, and classmates who offered support every time you stepped on the mat. I am proud to say that I contributed to the popularity and growth of a recognized sport in the community, throughout the area and the state. I would spend five decades in the sport of wrestling at Lower Dauphin, as part of two championship teams—as a wrestler in the '60's and as an assistant, co-head, and head coach in the '70s and '80s. Many team and individual accomplishments (8 varsity letters, 3 each in Football and Wrestling and 2 in Track and Field) were realized during those years, but none as rewarding as having the opportunity to work side by side with fellow alumni coaches." (Randy also co-captained football and wrestling in his senior year, setting a goal for those who followed.)

"The individual student athletes were always my focal point, hoping they could gain from the Lower Dauphin Experience that had afforded me so many opportunities that guided me. In 1987 I was fortunate to be appointed Athletic Director at my Alma Mater, a position I held for the next 20 years, serving the student-athletes, until retirement."

One of the many improvements Umberger brought to the school's sports program was expanded opportunity in the following:

Year Initiated	Sport	First Year Coach
1988	Girls Soccer	Randy Behney
1996-97	Girls Volleyball	Sharon Barlet
1996-97	Boys Volleyball	Mark Painter
2004-05	Girls Lacrosse	Carrie Brown
2005-06	Boys Lacrosse Club Team	Larry Thomas
2006-07	Girls Swimming & Diving	Cari Zelko
2006-07	Boys Swimming & Diving	Cari Zelko
	Ice Hockey Club Sport	Royal Dimond

"Some of my most memorable moments include having my three brothers follow me onto the Lower Dauphin Mats and being able to contribute to and share their successes and disappointments; our teams defeating Central Dauphin High School two years in a row in front of a packed LD Gym where two different LD Wrestlers defeated the same state finalist to seal the win; as athletic director expanding athletic opportunities for Lower Dauphin's students; selecting, assisting, and supporting a highly successful coaching staff. Thirty-five years well spent and enjoyed."

And it should be noted that, prior to becoming the Athletic Director, Randy had moved from Librarian to Principal, where it is notable that he remembers as a highlight that LD was one of the first schools to use a computer to track circulation and inventory books using the now ancient "floppy disk."

Randy earned the following academic degrees and designations:

- B.S., University of Maryland
- M.S., Shippensburg University
- Secondary Principal's Certification, Penn State

He holds membership in the following:

- District III Wrestling Coaches Association
- Pennsylvania Wrestling Coaches Association
- District III PIAA Athletic Directors Association
- Pennsylvania Secondary Principals Association
- Pennsylvania State Athletic Directors Association

While Athletic Director he served and chaired the following:

- District III Board of Directors—Elected (14 years 1993-2007)
- Baseball, Field Hockey, Football, and Wrestling Committees
- PIAA Wrestling Steering Committee
- Mid-Penn Conference Athletic Directors

Recognitions:

Tri Captain, 1964 LD Football Team

Co-Captain, 1964-65 LD Wrestling Team

1969-70: Omicron Delta Kappa, Men's Leadership Honorary, University of Maryland

1970:   Outstanding College Athletes of America

1969-70: Atlantic Coast Conference Academic Honor Roll; Co-Captain, University of Maryland Wrestling Teams, Jr. and Sr. Years

1970:   Charles LeRoy Mackert Outstanding Wrestler Award, University of Maryland

1979-80: District III & Pennsylvania Co-Coach of the Year (w/Cleon Cassel)

1979-80: Co-Coach National High School All Star Team vs PA All Star Team, Dapper Dan Classic

1993:   District III Wrestling Hall of Fame Inductee

2005:   Pennsylvania Athletic Director of the Year, Mid-Penn Conference, District III, PIAA, Region IV

2007:   Lower Dauphin Alumni Association, recipient of the First Distinguished Alumnus Award

2011:   National Wrestling Coaches Hall of Fame PA Chapter, Lifetime Service Award

2012:   Resilite Top Performing Dealer

2018:   Pennsylvania Sports Hall of Fame, Central Pennsylvania Chapter Inductee

2019:   PIAA Beverly Owens-Gaither Meritorious Service Award

2020:   Resilite Top Ambassador

2021:   Resilite Dealer of the Year

Positions Held after leaving Lower Dauphin School District:

- Resilite Sports Products, Inc., Eastern & South Central Pa Dealer (2007—2022)
- Executive Director, Mid-Penn Conference Athletic Directors (2014—present)

We are proud of the major milestone 700th Victory of Lower Dauphin High School Wrestling. This landmark was achieved through the efforts of the many young men who dedicated themselves to the task of being the best they could be under the guidance of a committed coaching staff who devoted their hearts, their energy, and their skill to the sport. In turn, the teams continue to leave an impressive heritage.

Lower Dauphin wrestling history is rich. We are proud to remember it. And we are dedicated to a continuation of distinction in the future, built upon a novice first year team who didn't know just how good they were, followed by an early powerhouse team in the mid-60s, which, in turn, was built upon by the legendary dynamo coaching team that knew what they were doing, all the while creating history and a legend.

All that happened because of the coaches who provided much more than wrestling skills. Coaching requires expertise as a successful wrestler, respect for the sport, and a desire to "help kids." And so they did, more than any parent or wrestling fan can possibly fathom.

Lower Dauphin Head Wrestling Coaches

Cleon Cassel	1960—1973
Don Heistand	1973—1974
Cleon Cassel	1974—1978
Cleon Cassel/Randy Umberger	1978—1981
Cleon Cassel	1981—1983
Ed Neiswender	1983—1984
Cleon Cassel	1984—1987
Ed Neiswender	1987—1989
Randy Umberger	1989—1991
Craig Cassel	1991—1996
Sean Ahern	1996—2002
Ed Neiswender	2002—2009
Josh Lininger	2009—2012
Ed Neiswender	2012—2013
Kemal Pegram	2013—2021
David Wuestner, Jr.	2021—

Cleon Cassel
The Man and the Legend

Cleon Cassel is applauded, as well he should be. He has the credentials. No one speaks ill of him. He has never had a losing season. Nor has he ever lost a friendship. He remains unassuming. Many have called him A Legend. Others call him Friend. Wrestlers address him as Coach. Some of us have known him as Colleague. All agree he is One of a Kind.

For many years the name "Cassel" has been a synonym for Lower Dauphin Wrestling. At the helm for 25 years, Coach Cleon Cassel engineered the construction of a monumental wrestling program, whose foundation has continued long after his retirement.

From the beginning of his journey as a wrestler, as a member of the Hershey High School Class of 1956, Cassel lettered four years, was undefeated in his junior and senior years as captain of the wrestling team with a career log of 40-2. Crowning his high school achievements was a second-place medal at the **PIAA State Championships.** That match was one of epic proportions, finally decided in overtime via a penalty point. Among his many other earned honors, Cleon was a three-time Middle Atlantic AAU champion and a two time State Finalist.

Following his high school career, Cassel continued to gather acclaim at Franklin and Marshall College as a four-year starter for the Diplomats, competing in the Eastern Intercollegiate level; three of his losses were by only one point, each time to Dave Auble, later to be an Olympian and two-time NCAA champion.

Cassel was recruited by newly formed Lower Dauphin Junior-Senior High School as its First Wrestling Coach. There he initiated and built a wrestling program, at that time a barely known sport in the region. Over his 25-year tenure, Cassel's teams compiled a record of 324 wins, 42 losses, and four ties, combining for an overall winning percentage of 88.1%, **including 26 District Champions and 7 State Finalists.**

According to Coach Cassel, "Probably one of the most spectacular feats in our dual meet history is Rick Kelley's drive to break into the line-up. Rick first tried out at 185 and lost the wrestle-off. At 165 pounds, he could not defeat district finalist Kevin Ricker. He could not beat 154 pound state finalist Ed Neiswender, 145 pound state finalist Mark Stauffer, and 138 pound state finalist Tom Mutek. One month later, Rick announced that he was dropping to 132 pounds to beat Cumberland Valley's State Champion. That night Rick started his first varsity match and with 10 seconds left in his bout, he reversed Carr to win. His victory inspired the team to win another championship."

Sectionals produced the most individual champs, winning the mythical championship with five winners: Bill Divel at 119, Tom Mutek at 138, Mark Stauffer at 145, Neiswender at 155, and Wayne Jockers at heavyweight. Districts,* Regionals, and State Championship again pitted the Falcons against many of their foes.

LD was the #1 team in the state of Pennsylvania, placing THREE in the State finals, all becoming State Runners-up: Mark Stauffer, Tom Mutek, and Ed Neiswender.

Other victories include 15 league championship teams, leading the number one team in the state in 1973. In 1971-72 Cassel was named Coach of the Year in District Three while the 1973 team took the unofficial state championship. In 1980 Cassel was honored as District 3 and Pennsylvania's Co-Coach of the Year, along with Randy Umberger, an honor capped by Cassel's 1986 induction in the State Wrestling Hall of Fame.

The distinctive accomplishments of the Lower Dauphin Wrestling Team and its quintessential coach are known statewide. Lower Dauphin Wrestling earned many honors under Coach Cassel, whose lasting legacy to the program is its very foundation—skill, care, and understanding both of the sport and of the players. This carefully crafted underpinning became the integral factor which continues to give Lower Dauphin wrestlers a unique drive, spurred on by the long standing tradition and continuing excellence in the program.

As the curtain fell on his last season of coaching in 1986-87, Cassel left behind a legacy of both personal and team-wide achievements. Accomplishments of Lower Dauphin Wrestling are recognized throughout the mid-state and further, along with the legend of their coach.

---

* Tom Mutek scored the first Falcon championship win at 138 as he polished off Conrad Weiser's John Santamour 7-0. Mark Stauffer had a 12-2 decision.

Donald Heistand

Varsity Coach 1973–74 and Champion at Multiple Levels

Coach Donald Heistand is a 1950 graduate of Hershey High School and has been involved in sports for as long as he can remember, beginning as a student and wrestler at Hershey High School, where he lettered three years in football and was a District III wrestling champion and a state title contender—all giving him a keen perspective on the sports arena. He then was a member of one of West Chester's most impressive wrestling teams ever. He later was an Air Force Sergeant and holds an advanced degree from Millersville University.

Heistand continued wrestling as a member of the well-known and respected Hershey Community Club Wrestling Team, where two of his teammates were Dick and Doug Cassel. Thus, it is noted that wrestling in Hershey was well established prior to the opening of LD, and Lower Dauphin benefited from Hershey's interest and success in the sport.

Don Heistand's arrival at Lower Dauphin High School in the fall of 1960 puts him in the category of a Lower Dauphin Pioneer with major experience as a wrestler. He signed on at LD as a full-fledged *experienced* adult, who had notches in his belt and not the "deer in the headlight" characteristic of many of his peers who were "brand new."

Heistand also brought a distinctive personal experience with these first years of LD wrestling, noting another interesting point of wrestling history that from 1962 through 1973, all of the LD post-season wrestlers who progressed to sectional level and higher came from families who lived in one of the four townships (and would have attended Hershey if Lower Dauphin had not existed). It can be further assumed that other LD sports and activities— notably football—also benefited from the early Hershey connection. Further, as noted in this wrestling history, sports at Lower Dauphin greatly profited by gaining Carl Espenshade, Glenn Ebersole, Randy Kahler, Randy Umberger, the Kopp brothers, and others who would have been Hershey graduates.

Heistand vividly recalls that Coach Cassel established a grade 7-9 junior high feeder wrestling program, followed years later by an elementary program. "Cassel brought experienced assistant coaches into the program, many of whom had achieved high levels of success in wrestling and all of whom instilled important values through their coaching and interactions with the wrestlers. For example, the coaches noticed that other schools generally scrimmaged among their own wrestlers, often repeating mistakes; Lower Dauphin practiced with an emphasis on drills and moves to improve where we had noticed difficulty.

"Our wrestlers were learning moves and counter moves; they learned what worked for them and then practiced those moves over and over until they became second nature, while we worked on confidence, backed up by the skills to win. Thanks to feeder programs, discipline, and insistence on drill, we quickly joined the ranks of highly successful program."

231

When Coach Cassel took a sabbatical in 1973-74, Don Heistand stepped forward to lead the Varsity team to a very solid 12-2 record in his solo season as Head Wrestling Coach. Don had been the Junior Varsity Coach and Assistant under Cleon for eleven years, unassumingly compiling a record of **129-25-0** and a winning percentage of **.838**. He was indeed growing the future stars for LD. He had undefeated teams in 1963-64, 1970-71, and 1971-72. By the time 1973 rolled around, the JV Falcons had undefeated records against 19 of the 25 different schools they had faced.

Ed Neiswender

The Man Who Came to Dinner... 1974 and Beyond

There is something compelling about Lower Dauphin High School that its graduates become teachers and/or coaches at their Alma Mater and spend a lifetime working with students in the classrooms and on the playing field, or in this case, the wrestling mat. Some of those who have earned success elsewhere, and who may even have coached at another school, return to LD. Most live in the district so that their own children can attend school here and who, in some instances, become wrestlers just like their fathers.

One such example is Coach Ed Neiswender, who is remembered for his own high school wrestling success, as well as collegiate wrestling—maybe even internationally, as he was one who had no fear and volunteered to be on the team that took on a professional team from Poland! And, yes, it is true that he also wrestled a big black bear—**a real one.**

"My association with LD wrestling actually began in the early 1960s. My brother Frank wrestled for Coach Cassel through his graduation from Lower Dauphin in 1963. I would occasionally tag along with him to practices over holiday breaks. I was six or seven years old. I was one of those little kids you see running around at matches. After graduation, Frank moved away to Bloomsburg State College to become a teacher and also to wrestle. I didn't see much of him over this time.

"Fortunately, wrestling did not end there. Coach Cassel began a wrestling program at my elementary school. The program was for a few days a week and lasted a couple of weeks. I started learning moves and how to wrestle. I think I began in third grade and continued through sixth grade. Seventh grade is when I became a committed wrestler. I had Coach (Bill) Linnane during his last year at LD Junior High. I think I got pinned my first match... and I'm pretty sure that was the last time that happened!

"In tenth grade I was Coach Cassel's wrestler. My brother did not abandon me though. He stayed for the high school practices to help us out. Coach Cassel refined us even more, not only as wrestlers but also as people. There was much more than wrestling being taught in that wrestling room! Frank and Coach Cassel are the major influences on the way I would coach for the next 45 years and counting!"

Also as a sophomore Neiswender had a football injury which caused his arm to dislocate when it was raised above his head. The arm was taped to his side in practice to encourage it to heal and this set him out for the first five matches. On the sixth match he was ready to compete, although no one thought this was wise. A visiting coach scouting the match approached Coach Cassel, "…I didn't think you would throw Neiswender to the wolves." Coach replied, "We're not; we are going to win the match."

Ed continued, "After my high school graduation, I was fortunate to have Jesse Rawls (an All-American at Michigan) recruit me to wrestle for the University of Michigan. He came in and wrestled with me my senior year at Lower Dauphin. I signed. We have been friends ever since. I had a great experience as a wrestler and student at Michigan. I also began my coaching career there. I helped out at the local high school and at a large elementary wrestling club.

"After being graduated from Michigan, I applied for a job at Lower Dauphin. I was hired! Along with teaching, I was hired by Coach Cassel as an assistant wrestling coach. I was head junior high coach for a few years, and Coach Cassel would move me around to where I could best serve the program. I also was head coach for about 11 years. Since I had been associated with LD wrestling for so many years, I was acquainted with many wrestling families. That is a very special part of my time at LD. I got to coach many boys from the families of my friends and the LD family's children. I was also fortunate to coach my son Eddie. Every week we made the matches a family affair. I retired from Lower Dauphin after 35 years of teaching.

"I lost my older brother Frank to cancer in 1996. Without him, I may never have wrestled, played football, or even gone to college. It is amazing how someone's influence can chart the rest of your life. I am forever grateful for everything Frank's positive influence had on me."

Ed was head coach twice, for two years in the late 1980s and for the last seven years. Lower Dauphin qualified at least one wrestler for states in each of those past seven seasons. He noted, "I was very proud of the team that won the 3-AAA dual meet championship in 2007."

The wrestling record from 2001 through 2008-09 was 111 wins to 30 losses. Neiswender was awarded the honor of District III AAA Coach of the Year in the **2006-2007** Season, then reached **#100 win during the 2007-2008 season.**

Craig Cassel
Legacy Coach on his Own Terms

The Falcon Flash, May 23, 1995

Coach Cassel has been hitting the mats ever since he was in third grade. In high school he was part of a District III team championship, and in 1982 was a sectional champion at 119. In his senior year, Cassel was team captain and finished his season with a record of 25-3. He continued his education and wrestling career at Franklin and Marshall, starting all four years, and was F&M's team captain for two years.

At Susquenita School District Cassel served as the Junior High wrestling coach for one year with a season record of 8-1. In 1990-91 he was assistant senior high wrestling coach at Line Mountain High School and was part of its AA State Championship Team. He then was invited by Lower Dauphin following the spring of 1991 to accept a teaching and coaching position. He served as coach for four years, leading the Falcons to two Mid-Penn II championships and a District III team title.

...pausing here a moment for the trajectory of Craig Cassel's own remarkable journey in Wrestling Land:

Craig likely has no memory of ever ***not*** being a part of wrestling. Some kids play "cops and robbers" and some "Batman" or "Darth Vader" or jockey. Cassel grew up with all of this; in addition, he was immersed in wrestling, beginning in third grade (as noted).

From this book's author:

> My clearest memory of this high school wrestler is his tenure in the Senior Year College Prep British Literature course. Craig Cassel and his wrestling teammate, (Dr.) Craig Camasta (Internationally known Podiatry Specialist and notable International Guest Lecturer) were both ardent students—if I can just get out of my head the mental imagery of their dragging into their morning class after having been out the night before "herding chickens" (the poultry kind) as a source for making their own fishing flies...

Cassel also was the coach to celebrate winning the school's **400**th win which happened in the 92-93 season. Of the 400 wins, Craig had coached the most recent 25.

As Coach Craig Cassel recalled at one point in the season, "After Saturday's match, I felt the excitement that I had felt as a wrestler wearing the Lower Dauphin singlet, knowing all the screaming and cheering was for my teammates and me—we who had put in the time and pain in sweat and blood when we stepped out on the mat to do our best. There was a piece of me on the mat each time an LD wrestler sucked it up and came out on top in a tight spot."[*]

And it was no surprise when to top it off Craig Cassel was named the District III AAA Coach of the Year.

Rod Frisco of *The Patriot News* had noted, "It will be a big surprise if Lower Dauphin's Craig Cassel is not the Class AAA winner of the 1995 Coach of the Year. Lower Dauphin was dominant this season and the Falcons expected a decent year and a good run at the 3-AAA dual meet title, but an un-beaten season (19-0). That was no sure thing. Craig Cassel—humorous, a little self-effacing and already so successful that no one calls him Cleon's son anymore—**is the man this year....**"

Sean Ahern

Coach: 1997–2002

Sean Ahern was Head Coach at Lower Dauphin for six years, from the fall of 1997 to the end of 2002 with a break-even record of 3–3. A graduate of Camden Catholic High School and of Lock Haven University where he was a varsity letterman, he completed post-graduate work at Millersville University. From 1979 to 1989 he served as head coach at Susquenita High School in Duncannon. In 1984 this team was 19-0 and ranked first in AA wrestling in Pennsylvania.

Ahern's teams at Susquenita won the following honors:

- 4 District III, AA Championships
- 7 Sectional Team Championships
- 5 League Team Championships
- 2 Pennsylvania State Champions
- 12 State Place Finishers
- 10 Individual District II Champions
- 30 Individual Section Champions ...and in 1984 his Susquenita team was 19-0 and ranked #1 in AA wrestling in PA.

In 1984 Ahern's Susquenita team was 19-9 and ranked #1 in AA wrestling in Pennsylvania. The following year he relocated to Lower Dauphin where he coached for six seasons, after which Ed Neiswender returned as coach, 2002-2009.

(After 30 years with the program and the close of his **third** stint as coach, in

the spring of 2009 Coach Neiswender passed the torch to Joshua Lininger until

Neiswender would again find himself home).

Josh Lininger

LD True Blue: 3-Sport Letterman: 2009–2012

Josh Lininger is a graduate of Lower Dauphin, Class of 1993. In wrestling he was a four-year starter, team captain as a senior, and member of the 1992-93 Mid-Penn Championship Team. During his time in LD wrestling, Lininger grew up under the tutelage of Coach Neiswender as well as former Head Coach Craig Cassel and Coach Randy Umberger…and, as he touchingly noted, "in 4th grade by former LD wrestler, Claudio Valeri."

In addition to wrestling, Josh also was a three-year letterman in football and a two-year letterman in baseball. He was on the football team at Susquehanna University where he was a four-year starter and was twice named to the All-Conference team.

He began coaching at LD, working under head coach Sean Ahern from 1997-1999, then coached at Cedar Cliff under legendary Hall-of-Famer Bob Craig.

Josh also served as head wrestling coach at Big Spring for four years beginning in 2000, accumulating a career record of 55-21. That team qualified for District 3 Championships twice and shared the 2004-05 Mid-Penn Championship title, breaking most of the records, closing out the season with two PIAA State medal winners and a Team "State Top 20" finish.

Kemal Pegram

The Engine Who Could: 2013–2021

Kemal Pegram came to Lower Dauphin with credentials. In high school in New Jersey Pegram was a 87-6 record **State Champion**, 6th place winner, two-time **Regional Champ** and three-time **District Champ**. At Lock Haven he added to his laurels where he had a record of 92-46, 2nd All-Time Major Decisions (22), EWL and PSAC Champ, and was a **Freestyle All-American.**

In 2011-12, he guided the Bulldogs of Big Spring to the 2012 PIAA Team State Championships. Big Spring beat Council Rock North 42-30 in the preliminary round at Big Spring High School, but the Bulldogs lost to Easton 48-13 in the first round and North Allegheny 37-27 in the first consolation round. Pegram knew from experience how LD had felt.

At Big Spring Pegram guided Wyatt Keck, Dustin Rook, and Danny Hockensmith to the 2012 PIAA Individual Championships. Pegram left the program at Big Spring after four years with a career record of 52-18.

Coach Pegram arrived at Lower Dauphin with a plan to recapture and rebuild the Falcons back into a District 3 power. "Getting people in and excited about our program now and getting it back where it used to be is probably my most important job. I think I understand now what the surrounding community and Lower Dauphin is all about. It will be the goal to tap into that excitement and determination to be great again. You go anywhere in town and there is a former wrestler or team who was great. When our guys are walking around wearing the blue and white, those guys are patting them on the back.

"This year's team understood they had underachieved last year and are hungry to change that. We are loaded with seniors, and this is their last hurrah. Here at Lower Dauphin the sky isn't falling. We have talented athletes, a great support system and wonderful community. The only thing I hope I can add to the mix is the engine that propels them forward." **And so he did.**

David P. Wuestner, Jr.

Home Grown and Loving it!
Coach: 2021–Present

David P. Wuestner, Jr., who, at this writing, had just completed his third season (2023-2024) as the Head Wrestling Coach of the Falcons, is a 2014 graduate of LD and a former four-year starter as a 285-pounder at Millersville University. He also spent time coaching the Marauders' club team before returning to LD, where he served on the coaching staff for several seasons.

Wuestner—like Umberger, Neiswender, Craig Cassel, Ron Michael, and Josh Lininger—is one of the few who dream of returning to their Alma Mater and actually do it. As he noted, "It has always been my goal to give back to the Lower Dauphin program which is very special to me. I want to help young men shape their lives to be prepared to face the adult world and be contributing members of society. That's really what it's about. I want kids to have a good experience here and to have success."

Hired prior to the 21-22 wrestling season, Wuestner wasted no time in working at the elementary level with a group "super eager to keep growing and increasing their skills," and with preparing the varsity players ready for the season.

He continued, "On January 27, 2022, the wrestling team achieved its 700th win of a proud wrestling legacy, a testament to all of the proud Falcon wrestlers who have been a part of this amazing wrestling tradition since its first season in 1960-61. I am humbled to follow in the line of the many exemplary coaches who have sacrificed much to maintain a proud wrestling tradition."

On a personal note, "I think I connect well with my guys. "I know their lingo. I know what they enjoy doing. It wasn't too long ago I was their age. I think wrestling is an ever-evolving sport, so there are not many young head coaches out there. I count myself fortunate to return to my 'home base' or, in this case, mat," he added.

"My goal is to continue to build on the well-earned respect and the emotional excitement of the program to maintain and advance the love our community has for wrestling. I appreciate the support from the administration and encouragement from former coaches who have built this dynasty."

Ron Michael

Iconic Assistant Coach

Ron Michael, a 1972 graduate of Lower Dauphin and 1979 graduate of Kent State, had a 51-5 record at Lower Dauphin with an 89-7 record at Kent State. At Lower Dauphin, he was a two-time Capital Area Sectional and District Champion and, in 1972, Southeastern Regional Champion at 145 pounds and a **semi-finalist in the PIAA State Championships.**

Following graduation from Lower Dauphin, Ron attended Stevens Trade School in Lancaster, where he compiled a two-year wrestling record of 61-1. At **Kent State** he was a four-year letterman and **two-time Mid-American Conference Champion** at 158 pounds. In 1978 he placed 4th in the NCAA Division I Championships and was inducted into District III Wrestling Coaches Hall of Fame in 1993.

He never, however, left Lower Dauphin, returning after college graduation from Kent State to his Alma Mater to serve as a teacher and a coach ....Ron is an exemplar of what Lower Dauphin does best, first, building fine men to aspire toward a goal and second, creating outstanding wrestlers.

Clovis Crane '98

One Wrestler's Journey

as Wrestler, Jockey, Entrepreneur
National Rodeo Champion
Owner and Manager of Crane Thoroughbreds

Joe Nevills Photo

Clovis Crane is his own success story. A graduate of Purdue University, Crane early on earned national acclaim as a jockey, rodeo cowboy, breaker and consignor of 2-year-olds (horses), dressage rider, and as an off-track thoroughbred trainer.

Leaving high school after his sophomore year at LD to become an apprentice jockey, Crane booted home 95 winners during his first professional season. In his second year, he rode 122 winners and earned more than $2.1 million. — **all of this while still on the LD wrestling team and keeping up with academics.** And yes, perfectly permissible.

Rod Frisco accessed this academic issue in his "Wrestling" column in response to a question raised by a reader questioning Crane's eligibility to wrestle since Clovis also participated in thoroughbred racing as a professional jockey. "The PIAA grants eligibility to athletes who are amateurs *in the sport in which they participate.* Thus, according to public school sports rules, Crane's jockeying is in no way associated with his amateur wrestling status and he was qualified to earn purse money.

When it was determined that a growth spurt would prevent him from a career as a jockey, **Clovis returned to LD, doubling his course load for his junior and senior years.** He was graduated and **recruited by many universities as a *wrestler!***

Crane matriculated at Purdue University where he was a two-time national qualifier and was voted the team captain. By the time he was graduated from Purdue **he ranked fourth in the country in college wrestling.**

After college Clovis joined the rodeo, taking honors left and right—as well as earning the purse money.

Later Crane was a prodigy when he was named the Professional Rodeo Cowboys Association's First Frontier Circuit Rookie of the Year in 2005. Four years later, he won the all-around title at the Dodge National Circuit Finals Rodeo, becoming the first person to qualify in three events in the same year: bareback riding, saddle bronc riding, and bull riding—enduring an almost unbelievable number of injuries. In one year alone he claimed circuit championships in four categories—all around, bareback riding, saddle bronc riding, and bull riding.

Clovis owns and manages **Crane Thoroughbreds** in nearby Lebanon, Pennsylvania. Someone should invite him to teach a high school course in entrepreneurship through physical fortitude and amazing skills, including, of course, wrestling. He is a most interesting, savvy, self-made success.

For more examples of UNTRADITIONAL SUCCESS see *According to the Falcon Flash*, a paperback publication featuring stories of notable Lower Dauphin graduates **who were overlooked by *The Flash* and *The Falconaire.***

Pennsylvania Century Farm: The Cassel Family

*Members of the Cassel Family of Dauphin County were honored at the 2022 Pennsylvania Farm Show for their **Century Farm**,* which has stayed in the family since the land was purchased in 1903. The current stewards of the land, Cleon and Dorothy Cassel, take care of approximately 25 horses while helping the next generation of Cassels operate a vineyard and event venue.

Growing up attending the Farm Show, Cleon has decades of experience showcasing his role in Pennsylvania agriculture. "When I was about eight or nine years-old I used to sleep here every night when we had the dairy cattle," Cleon recalled about those years of experience. "We switched over to horses," he continued, "because you don't have to milk them twice a day."

All of Cleon's unique agricultural ventures have been marked by the amazing farming community the Cassels belong to in Pennsylvania. Reflecting on his family's century old farm, Cleon says, "It's the bond that kept our family together. We've all been involved in it. It's more than just an occupation, it's a life." For Cleon Cassel, "agriculture is a refreshing breath of air," a sentiment which continues to be passed down through the Cassel family for generations.

Undefeated

The Falcon wrestlers were undefeated in 63-64, 64-65, 70-71, 71-72, and 94-95.

[see page 203]

Fortunate break-in

"Probably one of the most spectacular feats in our dual meet history is Rick Kelly's drive to break into the line-up." [see Coach Cleon Cassel, page 117]

Jim class

Jim Sanders was the third LD wrestler to move to state competition. He held the school scoring record for all four years with 186 points in 49 dual meets. Opponents scored only 9 points against him in the entire 1964-65 season.

[see page 67]

You only lose twice

The third year of LD wrestling included the last matches (two of them) that the Falcons would lose for the next three and a half years. [see page 58]

HIGHLIGHTS OF THE MEETS

1990–1991 (Record 1-14)

Row 1: Shawn Strange, Norm Hurst, Eric Strunk, Randy Lutz, Jason Dupler, Bill Welsh, Jamie Lindin.

Row 2: Brad Meloy, Tom McMullen, Josh Lininger, Scott Baker, Jose Sastre, Chad Nolte, Brian McLeod.

Row 3: Joe Stoke, Estaban Villarreal, Bob Ebersole, Jerry Hiller, Tony Bender, Andre Lewis.

Yes, this was the school's first ever losing season, despite Herculean efforts by Coach Umberger, who already had a full plate serving the school district as its Athletic Director. As this coaching position would be only a one-year obligation, the District saw assigning Randy as their best solution and pressed him to help. He reluctantly agreed to this request from the District to serve this year as the wrestling coach in addition to the full-plate, all-seasons duties as AD.

It is always difficult being an inexperienced team and only 20 in number; thus, while not looking for excuses, the author is compelled by fairness to this young team to note that three of the meets were lost by "squeakers." In short, this untested squad of mainly underclassmen simply lacked the necessary depth of power, numbers, and experience to gain the points needed to win.

Desire to win was their consistent hallmark. Eliciting cheers from the crowd and, with only **20** members, they still **never lost the desire and intensity** needed to be the true champions they might have been.

In disbelief after a second loss in the season by LD, one keen-eyed sportswriter noted that "LD played host to a tri-meet with Middletown and Milton Hershey and showed themselves so hospitable that LD came up on the **losing end** of the **19-32** score against **Milton Hershey** and on a close squeaker of **29-31** to Middletown."

Early in the season Jason Dupler took a pin win at **Northern Lebanon** and the team came home victorious, **46-19** over Northern Lebanon where Bill Welch earned a decision win over his opponent.

On January 3 the Falcons flew into an unexpectedly strong Polar Bear grappling team from **Northern York**. The Falcons' difficulty began with the middle weights, until LD's Brad Meloy changed the course with his match, earning a hefty decision of 16-5. Important as this was, the final score was not enough for LD to claim the meet and LD lost, **33-26**.

January 10 brought a **41-21** loss for LD against **Carlisle**. However, a personal highlight for Josh Lininger was his **first varsity win** with a second period pin. LD's Jason Dupler had a default win over his Carlisle opponent in the third period when the coach threw in the towel.

On January 19 LD held a tri-meet where Meloy won by a close 4-3 score, Jason Dupler won 5-4 over Milton Hershey, and Eric Strunk's pin-wins were impressive.

Nevertheless, the team faced adversity the following week when they added a pair of lopsided losses to their record. The team lost (**35-15**) to Cumberland Valley and to Shikellamy (**53-12**), which was a non-league match.

On **January 24** at Cumberland Valley the Falcons had only four wins against the Eagles with Randy Lutz earning a 9-4 decision win at 112, Jason Dupler a technical fall 20-4, Scott Baker a 16-13 decision win at 171 and Andre Lewis a 17-4 decision win at 189.

On January 31 Randy Lutz worked hard for his pin in his 112 bout against CD. On February 9 a highlight in the match with CD East was Chad Nolte's 8-4 decision. However, team losses continued despite Scott Baker's "gutsy" performance at 171, as even with that, East took the match.

The Falcons then lost a heart-breaking 26-25 to Red Land. With all of the disappointments, however, LD's Randy Lutz still completed a pin which put him in the District III championship round where he took a second place by way of a 10-4 decision.

Even with the unexpected set-backs, however, this was an exciting team to watch. In a summary by Steve Summers (Patriot News, May 29, 1991), "There was always something magical about Lower Dauphin wrestling."

1991–1992 *(Record 6-12)*

Row 1. Mike King, Eric Strunk, Ryan Lutz, Brian Moure, Mike Smoyer.

Row 2. Todd Mostetter, Estaban Villarial, Chad Koser, Brent Szymborski, Jason Ely, Joe Stoak, Shawn Strange, Todd Johns.

Row 3. Coach Craig Cassel, Bob Snyder, Jose Sastre, Steve Goho, Shawn Thomas, Josh Lininger, Bob Ebersole, Brad Meloy, Bryan MacLeod, Luke Undelhoven, Andre Lewis, Jerry Hiller, Robert Anderson, Ken Long, Ken Straining, Coach Youtz.

With renewed pride in the fall of 1991—having been kept afloat the previous year (1990-91) by dedicated Athletic Director Randy Umberger serving as coach—the Wrestling Dynasty was pulled out of the ashes, earmarked by their new coach with the familiar name of Cassel.

Coach Cassel sounded just about right, bringing with it a tradition of wrestling. The season was off to a good start with three wins, particularly considering that this was a young team with a number of underclassmen filling varsity weight positions. With a skilled and dedicated coaching staff, this determined team met their goals of (1) keeping the lineup without injury, (2) winning more matches, and (3) establishing a sound record for the season. All three goals were accomplished with dignity and style.

The 1991-92 team was built with determination around senior starters: Lininger, Long, MacLeod, Strunk, and Udelhoven, along with junior stand-outs Hiller and King anchoring both ends of the lineup. With steady performances by all team members, the well-earned result would be the **Mid-Penn Division II Championship**.

It all began on Friday December 21 at Northern Lebanon where Bill Welch took a decision win of 11-5, and Jason Dupler earned a pin to win. **34-30 LD**

Later, *The Sun*, January 15, reported, "The Lower Dauphin wrestling team had a scare from Carlisle on Thursday, January 9, before pulling out a win at the end of the match, **32-30**. The Falcons got out to an early lead with Mike King, Eric Strunk, and Ryan Lutz, all pinning their opponents. Shawn Strange and Josh Lininger also racked up wins, while Joe Stoak tied his opponent."

Sportswriter Josh Orlandi commented, "LD's strong points are in the lower and upper weight classes. Improvement in the **middle** *is needed* to take the Falcons to the elusive next level." Such were the marching orders the coaches laid out and the team followed.

Even so, on Saturday, January 18 the Falcons lost to Milton Hershey **40-24** and then to Middletown by a heart-breaking **34-32**. On January 22 the Falcon matmen took it on the chin, after losing January 16 to Susquenita, **57-10**.

Josh Orlandi (*Hummelstown Sun*) explained in early February, "Despite the team's lack of success, **several individuals** have compiled commendable records. Mike King (12-2), Eric Strunk (7-3), Brian Moure (6-5), Brad Meloy (7-7), and Josh Lininger (9-5) —all have provided **leadership** for this young Falcon squad."

Some would say the season's most satisfying match was the **36-28** victory over Red Land on Red Land's home mats. After our winning the first two bouts, the roof almost fell in as Red Land won the next **six** matches, a most commanding lead. The Falcons were faced with the *need* to win just about all remaining bouts. … and **that is exactly what they did.**

For details of what have been identified as "memorable moments," ask any team member about the following non-wrestling moments: the King-Meloy feud, the boiler room, the forgetfulness of Ken Long, the confusion between the "Barn" or "Bridge" of Waltonville, and the Santa Claus imitator.

More importantly, on the mat the grapplers' motto had been rightly chosen—and fulfilled: **"The Pride is Back!"** And their supporters welcomed it.

1992–1993 *(Record 17-4)*

Row 1. Mike Rozzell, Eric Kessler, Mike King, Bobby Hahn, Eric Strunk, David Tognoni, Estaban Villareal, Rick Good.

Row 2. Penn Almoney, Todd Mostetter, Travis Rogers, Brent Szymborski, Bob Snyder, Jason Gleim, Chris Leppo, Chad Koser, Jeremy Borrows.

Row 3. Joe Stoak, Bob Ebersole, Jamie Lindin, Bryan MacLeod, Luke Udelhover, Josh Lininger, Andy Strite, Ken Long, Jerry Hiller, Bob Anderson, Ron Michael, Mark Woodring.

Indeed the pride was back.

As a team, these young men began with a regimen every day at 3:00 when they met in the mat room ready for the four-mile warmup run. Rain or shine, they ran, vowing **never again** to tease Cross-Country as they had been accustomed to do before becoming wrestlers. At 4:00 p.m. the focused wrestling practice began with endless drilling, conditioning, and motivation—all of which helped to achieve a successful season.

At their pre-season action, the 1992-93 Falcons opened at the Ephrata Invitational Tournament where they took second place with a pair of champions in **Mike King** (112) and **Eric Strunk** (119) who was named the **Outstanding Wrestler** of the Tournament.

The team next met Hempfield where, after losing through the 135 bout, the Falcons won all of the remaining ones—**and the match**—with **seven pins** (Mike King, Eric Strunk, Bob Snyder, Joe Stoak, Bryan MacLeod, John Lininger, and Ken Long). While LD placed fourth overall, there were no fewer than **six Falcons in the finals** and the Birds emerged with the 119 weight title with Eric Strunk's putting away of Cedar Cliff's Dennis Applebury with a pin.

The Falcons then opened their **official 1992-93 season** on December 12 at the Ephrata Invitational Tournament. They finished the tournament with a pair of champions in Mike King (112) and Eric Strunk (119)—who also was named **the Outstanding Wrestler** of the event.

On December 22 the Falcons posted their **400th victory** but were taken to task by Rod Frisco of the *Patriot News*. He boldly stated that the Falcons "aren't one of the best teams in the district—they currently claim the No. 1 spot by accident."

With that gauntlet being thrown, the Falcons next took the team title at the Dallastown Tourney with three individual titles for Ryan Koser, Travis Rogers, and Jerry Hiller, along with six runners-up. Rogers was also named Outstanding Wrestler of the tournament.

The team was on top of the world when, on Tuesday, January 21, they soundly defeated Milton Hershey by a **27-9** score which knocked "The Milt" out of first place.

January 27, 1993, *The Sun:* "Falcons are Flying High with Three Victories!"

February 4, 1993: The Trojans lost to LD, thus spoiling Hershey's chances of winning the Mid-Penn Championship.

February 10 headline: "Falcon wrestlers remain on top with their drubbing of Hershey High."

February 17: "The Falcons were on top with a record of 6-0."

February 18: The Falcons then nailed down the **Mid-Penn Division II championship** with an impressive 46-0 shutout of Palmyra.

March 10: *Harrisburg Patriot-News.* "The Lower Dauphin Falcon grapplers spent Friday and Saturday, March 6 and 7, in the gym at Cedar Cliff and when the smoke had cleared on Saturday night, the Falcons were in **third place** for the team title with 105 points, emerging with one champion—**Eric Strunk** at 119, who then fell to Cumberland Valley's Tom Donnelly in a close 2-0 match."

Team members continued to build on what they had accomplished last year and then, for good measure, as noted, won the **Mid-Penn II Championship.**

No fewer than **seven** Falcons were in the consolation round for third place and a trip to the Districts the next week-end, and no fewer than four of them made it through with victories, and thus landed a slot as **District Qualifiers:** Eric Strunk, Bryan MacLeod, Ken Long, and Jerry Hiller. At 103 Ryan Koser decisioned Cumberland Valley's Cory Benner, 8-0. At 112, it was Mike King with a pin win over Central Dauphin's Greg Celesky at 2:20. Bryan MacLeod at 160 got a close 7-6 decision win over Jason Benkowitsch and at 189, Ken Long pinned Mechanicsburg's Ken Kenes at 4:42.

In the end, the Falcon team, led by four captains (Strunk, MacLeod, Lininger, and Udelhoven) was 8-0 in the conference and 17-4 overall... becoming **Mid-Penn Division II Champions** with **Eric Strunk a State Qualifier** at 119 lbs.

With memories of pre-practice runs, the Punisher, Cedar Cliff, Power Net 2000, Sunday fun-runs, and mat-mopping championships, these LD matmen indeed took satisfaction in their success of **bringing back** Lower Dauphin wrestling.

The Sun, **March 31, 1993**

Randy Umberger, Ed Neiswender, and Ron Michael (All **alumni,** all noted **wrestlers,** all winning **coaches**) were inducted into the **PIAA District III Hall of Fame.** Overall, it was a very good year for Lower Dauphin.

Coach Cassel noted, "The decade of the 90s has revived with a new strength and thrust with a Mid-Penn Division II Championship (while the Junior High earned the Mid-Penn Division IV title). Continued dedication in the years to follow could make it one of the strongest decades of our history."

If you are among those who wrestled in this Decade of the Nineties and haven't seen the 50-page program, **The 500th Victory History Book,** *Lower Dauphin Falcon Wrestling 1960-1993 and published in Celebration of the 400th Wrestling Victory, December 23, 1993,* **do** try to find one. It is a gem filled with records and off-the-record stories! The book was produced by the Lower Dauphin Wrestling Booster Club under the authorship of Bill King.

1993 Coaches Hall of Fame

Not ONE, not TWO but THREE HONOREES

Page 20

THE SUN, WEDNESDAY, MARCH 31, 1993

Three L.D. Coaches To Hall Of Fame

The PIAA District III wrestling contingent held their annual AA-AAA All-Star Meet and Coaches Hall of Fame induction ceremony on Wednesday, March 24, at Lower Dauphin High School.

Three former Lower Dauphin High School wrestlers and coaches were inducted into the PIAA District III Wrestling Coaches Hall of Fame on Wednesday, March 24, as part of the 1993 Wrestling All-Star Meet held at Lower Dauphin. Those honored were, from left, Ed Neiswender, Ron Michael and Randy Umberger.

. . . the following year (1992-1993) the strong voice of the new team resonated clearly in the Susquehanna Valley, resulting in earning the position of **Mid-Penn Division II Champions**. The 92-93 team scored 93 falls against 38 by their opponents. "This team earned themselves a place in history through both its performance and its heart (and) when *the championship was on the line* against Palmyra, the Falcons beat the Cougars 40-0." **How's that for determination?**

1993–1994 *(Record 12-4-1)*

Row 1. Bill Van Winkle, Joe Kulp, Ryan Koser, Eric Kessler, Bobby Hahn, Mike King, Steve Polshuk, Brent Szmborski, Brian Moure, Travis Rogers, Ryan Lutz.

Row 2. Coach Cassel, Penn Almoney, Chad Koser, Jason Gleim, J.D. Shuman, Rick Good, Matt Weaver, missing name, Mark Woodring, Mike Lehrman, Ron Michael, Jeremy Burrows, Mike Minto, Jerry Hiller, Coach Youtz.

In his own distinctive prognostication, Ron Frisco reports, "Lower Dauphin can start strong and finish strong with a nice mix in the middle; it'll be tough to beat this year. The Falcons have one of the mid-state's best heavyweights in senior Jerry Hiller, a legitimate district championship threat. And the insertion of tough freshman Bill Van Winkle at 103 gives the Falcons a nice opener. …In between, the Falcons can count on steady performer Ryan Koser at 112. …If a few new faces come through, look out…. **With its 7-0 record in the league last year, LD can claim never to have lost a Division II dual meet.**"

Even with only four returning seniors (Mike King, Chad Koser, Brian Moure, and Jerry Hiller), this year's team still won both of their pre-season tournaments. However, those victories were not enough to carry a winning season, regardless of the team's avowed focus on the need for discipline and development. Typically, such characteristics are better met by a larger group of experienced wrestlers; this year, however, L.D. simply did not have the experience, despite having the determination. Thus, the Falcons faced an uphill battle at every turn.

The early 1990s teams had captured several titles in Mid-Penn Division II and had begun to ascend the podium again at the District 3 Team Tournament in 1993-94 with a second place to defending champion Warwick. The first half of the 90s brought the team to a new level of success, even though individual titles were less common.

On December 15, 1993 the LD Matmen opened their season at Ephrata with a team title, three champions, and four runners-up. Falcon title winners included Bill Van Winkle (103), Travis Rogers (135), and Ryan Lutz (140). Eyes were on Jerry Hiller (HWT) to be a repeat champion. Rogers also was named Outstanding Wrestler of the tournament. This was followed by dominating the Dallastown Tourney (95 points) with **three individual champions,** and, to top it off, besting Dallastown (**90**), State College (**63**), and Cedar Cliff (**59.5**).

The team won their first Division II of the Mid-Penn Conference, coming up golden. Cassel was interviewed by Rod Frisco of the *Patriot-News*, "Now the Falcons are poised to make it two in a row. They have the muscle to grab their second straight Division II title."

To top off this successful year, the Cassel Company claimed **LD's 400ᵗʰ Victory**, which had occurred with the **win over Northern Lebanon** on December 23. (Of the total 400 victories, Cleon Cassel had coached the first 325 of those wins while Craig Cassel coached the most recent 25.)

LD wiped out CD East **44-11** in Division II, helped by Mark Woodring's 6-3 triumph at 160. The team had little trouble putting their 401st match win in the record books on Thursday, January 6. In early February the Falcons had two giant victories shutting out Milton Hershey **56-0** and blasting Middletown **66-3**. They were on a turn-around roll of wins.

Next, just as LD had figured they were on top, Hershey surprised them "with an effort that came straight from the deepest reaches of their wrestling souls." (*Patriot-News*, Feb. 3) Hershey led with the stunning score of **33-16**. This was followed by a loss to Cedar Cliff **29-21**, thanks to the Colts' Chris Cain who literally hung on in **double over-time** to win a **3-3** criteria decision over the Falcons.

As reported by *The Sun*, "L.D. Falcon Matmen Back on Top of the Hill …as the lights went up at the end of the February 12 confrontation with the Central Dauphin Rams for a mind-boggling **49-9** triumph by Lower Dauphin over C. D."

At Red Land things were a bit grim when Ryan Koser lost a tough 5-2 decision, but then things kicked in and the Falcons won the next six bouts.

We don't know which to commend, but Rod Frisco and Craig Cassel were vying as being the better orator:

Frisco: "Like the victorious Roman Gladiator, strained from Battle and flush with triumph after its **47-9** slaughter of Palmyra, Lower Dauphin must lift its eyes toward the Mid-Penn Conference's other emperors and await its verdict. Will it be thumbs up or thumbs down for the 9-3-1 Falcons' chances at the District 3-AAA Team Championships?"

Cassel: "I'm sure the coaches of the Mid-Penn Conference will make an enlightened and informed decision when they vote for the Class AAA representatives."

Cassel was smiling. Sort of. (You know, his "look!") And he did insist that the assembled media "Jot it down, Guys. **Verbatim.**" (The walls in the area of B-1 resounded.)

Winning brothers

For two seasons in the 1990s the LD wrestling lineup was anchored by brothers Kurt, Ryan, and Brin Koser, who at one point had 57 combined wins.

[see page 269]

Nick of time

In one of many Falcon clutch performances, from January 2006 Mid-Penn competition, Jon Crawford makes an escape with 12 seconds to go to force overtime, then gets a takedown with less than six seconds remaining in overtime to hand LD the win. [see page 304]

Getting accepted

"I will never forget how difficult it was for Lower Dauphin to be accepted at the long-running Christmas tournament," Coach Cassel remembers. "Central Dauphin finally allowed us to join their event at the last minute. We went on to win the title!"

[see page 283]

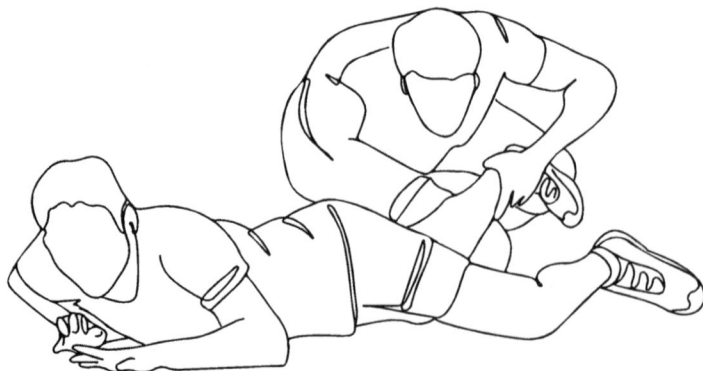

1994–1995 *(Record 19-0)*

Row 1. Louis Pavone, Clovis Crane, Bill Van Winkle, Ryan Koser, Joe Kulp, Bob Hahn, Eric Kessler, Brin Koser, Steve Polshuk, Kurt Koser, Adam Kopp, Eric Zedonis, Greg Verdelli.

Row 2. Coach Cassel, James Orwin, Matt Buerk, Matt Willard, Travis Rogers, Jason Burrows, Roy Warlow, Dan Floyd, Rick Good, Jeremy Burrows, Brian Minto, Mark Woodring, Ron Michael, Matt Weaver, Coach Youtz.

"The 1995 wrestling team is sometimes grouped with other spectacular teams and may have had the potential to go all the way to the finals of the State Championships if there had been one. The team finished the season 9-0 and defeated every team soundly on its way to a District 3 championship"[1]

January 15, 1995

LD stood alone, undefeated in the Mid-Penn. Early in the week LD made very quick work of Red Land (**57-15**), getting nine falls on the way to victory, continuing the path over Big Spring. Of those 13 matches, 11 ended in falls.

---

[1] See page 265 in *Loyal Hearts Proclaim: The 50th Anniversary of Lower Dauphin High School*, a publication (hardbound book of 500 pages) authored by Dr. Witmer.

January 18, 1995

LD's wrestlers made it look easy when they took the sport to Hershey, winning **38-18**. Two days later the match against Cumberland Valley was named by the *Patriot-News* as the "entertainment of the week," starting out just as billed. Hahn garnered nine take-downs and gained a technical fall. The match "continued as breath-holding when the Eagle wrestler took Ron Michael[2] to the mat and dusted him in 47 seconds." While this might have been simply entertainment night for Falcon fans, luckily it went their way, LD **38**, Hershey **18**.

Following the January 29 match, the *Harrisburg Metro* used a photo with the caption, **"The Falcons put the official stamp on their claims to be one of the wrestling powers when they stepped up against Cedar Cliff and earned a 34-22 match win."**

In early February the Falcons took a **41-18** win over Harrisburg and clinched at least a tie for the Mid-Penn II Division.

The wrestlers came back thrilling and victorious, as they earned an undefeated season, the District Team Tournament Championship, and the Mid-Penn Conference Championship! **The defeat of Cedar Cliff—the first time in 13 years—was remarkable in itself,** as was **LD's accomplishing their first undefeated dual meet season in 23 years.**

The press noted that the Lower Dauphin Falcon wrestling team of Craig Cassel did everything in their power to be ready for the District III team championships. Coach Cassel noted, "These guys improved greatly by their own hard work and determination and they already have **challenged next year's squad to do the same.**"

March 1, 1995. Lower Dauphin celebrated round one of the State Wrestling Tournament with **three champions**: Travis Rogers (135), J.D. Shuman (145), and Mark Woodring (160).

March 4, 1995. *The Patriot News.* It will be a big surprise if Craig Cassel is not the Class AAA winner of the 1995 Coach of the Year.

March 8, 1995. Following disappointments by all three champions at not winning States, 160 pounder Mark Woodring used the wrestle-back opportunity to gain entrance to the PIAA advance.

After the team became Mid-Penn Champions and District III Team Champions, Coach **Craig Cassel was named the District III AAA Coach of the Year,** with the press noting, "As coach at Lower Dauphin for five years, Cassel has led the Falcons to two Mid-Penn championships and a District III team title."

Rod Frisco added, "…the Falcons expected a decent year and a good run at the AAA dual meet title, but an unbeaten season? That was no sure thing. There were a number of other worthy candidates, and **Cassel**—humorous, a little self-effacing and already so successful that no one calls him Cleon's son anymore—**is** the name for this year." Frisco called it right!

[2] Son of legendary Ron Michael of the 1970s.

From the Sidelines on this Team:

- There are all sorts of heroes. **Eric Kessler** kept his pledge to stick it out.

- Eight of **Brin Koser's** 15 dual victories were by fall. Five of those pins were in the first period, and the announcers still can't get his name correct.

- For the second year in succession **Steff Poleshuk** would rather not know too far in advance just whom he'll wrestle and at what weight.

- **Roy Warlow** nailed a 2:27 pin at Red Land.

- **Kurt Koser** never quit. He gave a fine showing for a ninth grader.

- The oldest and lightest of the Koser trio, **Ryan Koser** was a **20 bout winner**. Only a Junior, he will add experience to his skills next year. Keep your eye out for him.

Another landmark from this team was a record 6 additions to the 30-Second Pin Club, with five of them belonging to senior LD star, **Mark Woodring**.

Also at this point in their wrestling history (about halfway to the present) the Falcons heralded five undefeated teams:

1963-64	14-0
1964-65	14-0
1970-71	13-0-1
1971-72	14-0
1994-95	19-0

Mark Woodring wrestling 1995

1995–1996 *(Record 10-4)*

The Sun, **Wednesday, January 1, 1996.** Lower Dauphin High School opened Mid-Penn II wrestling action with a **64-0** whitewash over Palmyra. The match was over when Palmyra forfeited the 103-pound match to Clovis Crane, giving the Falcons a quick 6-0 lead. Bill Van Winkle in the 112 pound match needed even less time than it took Crane to double the score to 12-0…in 52 seconds.

The rout became apparent as LD engineered a four-win string in response to Palmyra's forfeit. The victory run featured the successive **triple-threat Kosers—Ryan '96** decisioning Louis Chandler 6-2 at 119; **Brin '97** pinning Dave Koch in 3:06 at 125; and **Kurt '98** decisioning Chris Cowan 7-3 at 135. This is our second set of "**brothers in a row, one after another,**" and is certainly indicative of our legacies. In the case of the Kosers, their father Lamar is a ranking member of the Koser Clan, claiming Leon, John, and Joel as his brothers. (See our special listing in "Wrestling Fathers and Sons.")

Row 1. Clovis Crane, Louie Pavone, Will Tucci, Jeremy Jackson, Dan Smoyer, Brad Martz, Billy Van Winkle, Ryan Koser.

Row 2. Brin Koser, Jason Malecki, Joe Kulp, Kurt Koser, Steve Poleshuk, Adam Kopp, Eric Zedonis, Greg Verdelli, James Orwas, Dan Seiders, Matt Buerk.

Row 3. Cole Ebersole, Roy Warlow, J.D. Shuman, Mike Slatt, Dan Floyd, Seth Duncan, Dillon Kessler, Brad Shuman, Mike Slatt, Dan Floyd, Seth Duncan, Dillon Kessler, Brad Price, Brian Minto, Dan Kepner, Matt Thompson.

"Jason Malecki added a 10-8 squeaker win over Andrew Morgan at 130 and the lead was 27-0. Joe Kulp garnered the forfeit win at 140. Lower Dauphin led 33-0. At 145 Falcon Steve Poleshuk rolled over Dan Stauffer 14-6; J.D. Shuman (152) rolled Jerry Harby over on his shoulders in 1:33, moving the whitewash along to 43-0. Jason Burrows (160) worked Chris Jones for a 9-5 decision, while Seth Duncan (171) and Matt Thompson (189) garnered falls to move the score to 58-0. Duncan's pin came at 5:13, while Thompson's pin came in 1:44.

"Tim Bilger worked Frank Stump for a 10-3 score through three periods of grappling and finally forced Stump's shoulders to the mat for the victory. Final score, 64-0."

January 10, 1996. In a battle of the unbeatens (Susquenita and Lower Dauphin), the Falcons came out on the short end, 33-25. Our winners included the first match with Clovis Crane picking up an important 11-17 decision and Bill Van Winkle scoring a 1:49 fall. Brin Koser took a 12-3 major decision while Kurt Koser added a fall.

January 24, 1996. The header says it all: Hershey, Red Land are LD Grappling Victims! "Clovis Crane worked Lami for a 12-4 spread and pinned him. Van Winkle garnered a 7-1 verdict and LD added three more pins—from Brin Koser, Kurt Koser, and Steve Poleshuck." At the end the score was LD 42 and Hershey 14. Against Cedar Cliff Jake Lininger came back for a pin win against Cedar Cliff. Lower Dauphin was the meet winner at 40-28. Brin Koser advanced to the PIAA Championships.

January 31, 1996. "LD picked up a Mid-Penn victory, slipping by CD East and mauling Cedar Cliff, 45-23, including six pins."

Coverage on **February 14** focused on the team's winning the Mid-Penn title: "The Falcons escaped by the skin of their teeth, 29-27. Against Central Dauphin, it was the presence of mind by the last three Falcon wrestlers not to lose by any more than 3 points."

Dan Floyd, 1996 Season

Jason Malecki, 1996 Season

Mid-Penn II Champions

LD dominated the Mid-Penn II Division once again! Coach Craig Cassel summarized the team, "This year they worked well together while still having a lot of fun. Although they fell just short of qualifying for the District Team Tournament, they were a distinctive group with stalwart dedication, which led them to a tremendous season."

Much of the season occurred during a winter when there was an additional loss of a week's time at Christmastime because of snow. This disruption was followed by another week of two-hour delays and early dismissals. Mother Nature then sent a record snowfall and tremendous flooding which led to the destruction of the Walnut Street Bridge over the Susquehanna River in Harrisburg, only a few miles from Falconland. Finally, contaminated water became another negative factor—all of which contributed to making this an unforgettable season in many ways beyond wrestling.

Kurt Koser, Steve Poleshuk, and Jeremiah Shuman were selected as **Mid-Penn II wrestling All-Stars; Bill Van Winkle qualified for States.**

High water mark

A highlight of the 1999-2000 season was the defeat of Gettysburg, 33-28. [see page 276]

If you blinked, you missed it

Glenn Ebersole and Randy Umberger have tied for the fastest Falcon fall, pinning their opponents in just 12 seconds. [see page 424]

Win-Win

In the 2007-08 season, Nick Kristich broke a 24-24 deadlock against Cumberland Valley to achieve his 100th personal victory. [see page 310]

Pin wins

LD topped Cedar Cliff 38-22 in District 3 AAA action in 2008. "There's no way we're going to win a 7-7 match..." the Cedar Cliff coach admitted, "...not with LD's ability to pin." [see page 310]

1996–1997 *(Record 13-2)*

Row 1. Paul King, Chad Hoke, Chris Shertzer, Rusty Daubert, Billy Van Winkle, Brin Koser, Dan Smoyer, Louie Pavone, Cody Ebersole, Matt Miller, Will Tucci.

Row 2. Travis Warlow, Ryan Michael, Adam Kopp, Kurt Koser, Steve Christ, Jason Malecki, Brian Jones, Josh Gosik, Eric Zedonis, Matt Thompson.

Row 3. Seth Duncan, Tom Whiston, Dan Floyd, Roy Warlow, Justin Mease, Jake Lininger, unidentified, Jason Parmer, Tim Bilger, Joel Martin, Steve Knackstead.

From 1996-2000, the teams, coached by Sean Ahern, met with a great deal of success by individuals, including **state runner-up status by Kurt Koser** and **Jake Lininger.**

In December the Falcons placed second at the Ephrata Tournament, crowning four champions—**Louis Pavone, Bill Van Winkle, Kurt Koser,** and **Seth Duncan.** New Falcon coach Sean Ahern was pleased, as there were **six sophomores who had no previous record going in to the tournament unseeded.**

On December 5, Lower Dauphin "whooped" Middletown **57-6.** The nail-biter at 112 was LD's **Dan Smoyer** against Blue Raider Steve Seicher at 2-0. Kurt Koser made short work of Loren Davis at Manheim Central with a fast pin at 1:20. Close matches included LD's **Adam Kopp** vs. Manheim Central's Jesse Kopp (Yes, and it is reported that Adam and Jesse were 3rd cousins). In December LD rolled **over Red Land.**

John Crull's sports reports often included colorful—but appropriate—one-liners, as they do here: "Northern's top wrestler, Tim Sullivan, needed the first two periods to fathom Falcon Jake Lininger's wrestling style...."

At Milton Hershey School, "a lot of people saw a lot of wrestling, including a see-saw with Duncan working his way back to winning the match 9-6, only to have been beaten by the buzzer." LD won, however, **46-3**.

At Central Dauphin on January 3 Kurt Koser won 14-0, but we lost against CD.

Against Harrisburg's incomplete squad, Lower Dauphin won handily at **54-13**. The bigger news, however, was LD's **stopping** Cedar Cliff's legendary Coach Bob Craig's march toward his 500th win with a **35-30** victory by LD over the Colts.

"LD has a virtual lock on the Mid-Penn II championship after destroying CD East 52-6, with the score bulge coming on pins by Kurt Koser, Travis Warlow, Tom Whiston, Seth Duncan, and Roy Warlow." The February 12, 1997 article reported that against Hershey, falls were recorded by Louis Pavone, Bill Van Winkle, Kurt Koser, Ryan Michael, Adam Kopp, and Tom Whiston.

The team moved back into the Mid-Penn Division with success at the highest level that District 3 had to offer. They reached the state tournament and continued the strength that Lower Dauphin wrestling has always demonstrated. [*]

This team maintained its self-motivation and held its own, ending with a **13-2-0** season record. Achieving the Division II Championship fit them well, as the role of team captain was shared among four seniors who demonstrated they were "One for all and all for One." Later in life they noted just how important their comradery had been.

In March at the District 3 Tournament **Brin Koser** pinned Kevin Baum of Spring Grove and advanced to the PIAA Championships. Bill Van Winkle placed second at the tournament. Brin withstood a furious third-period rally to claim an 8-6 victory which earned him the **Outstanding Wrestler Award** as voted by the coaches.

Later, these team members recalled that they had once been told that "At Lower Dauphin, Students Create Unity." One noted, "We believe our team definitely demonstrated this strong friendship."

[*]Ibid.

Kurt Koser puts the pressure on.

Junior Adam Kopp, his opponent down.

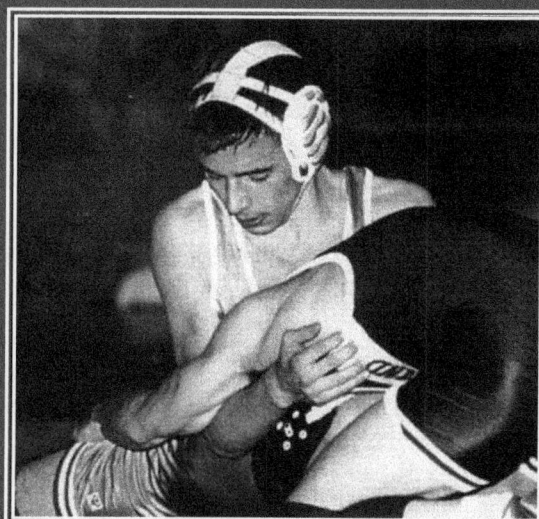

More strength from the Falcons!

267

Winning . . . a lot

Jarred Kane and Nick Kristich were the first LD wrestlers to have over 100 career wins. Kane was also the first LD wrestler to qualify for state championships three times.
[see page 315]

Short timer

In the 2007-08 season, eighteen of Nick Kristich's 19 pins occurred in the first period, with the average length of 56 seconds. [see page 310]

Maybe a little repetitive

In 2021 sophomore Griffin Barilla pinned all five of his opponents in the Dutchman Duals at Annville-Cleona. [see page 361]

1997–1998 (Record 14-3)

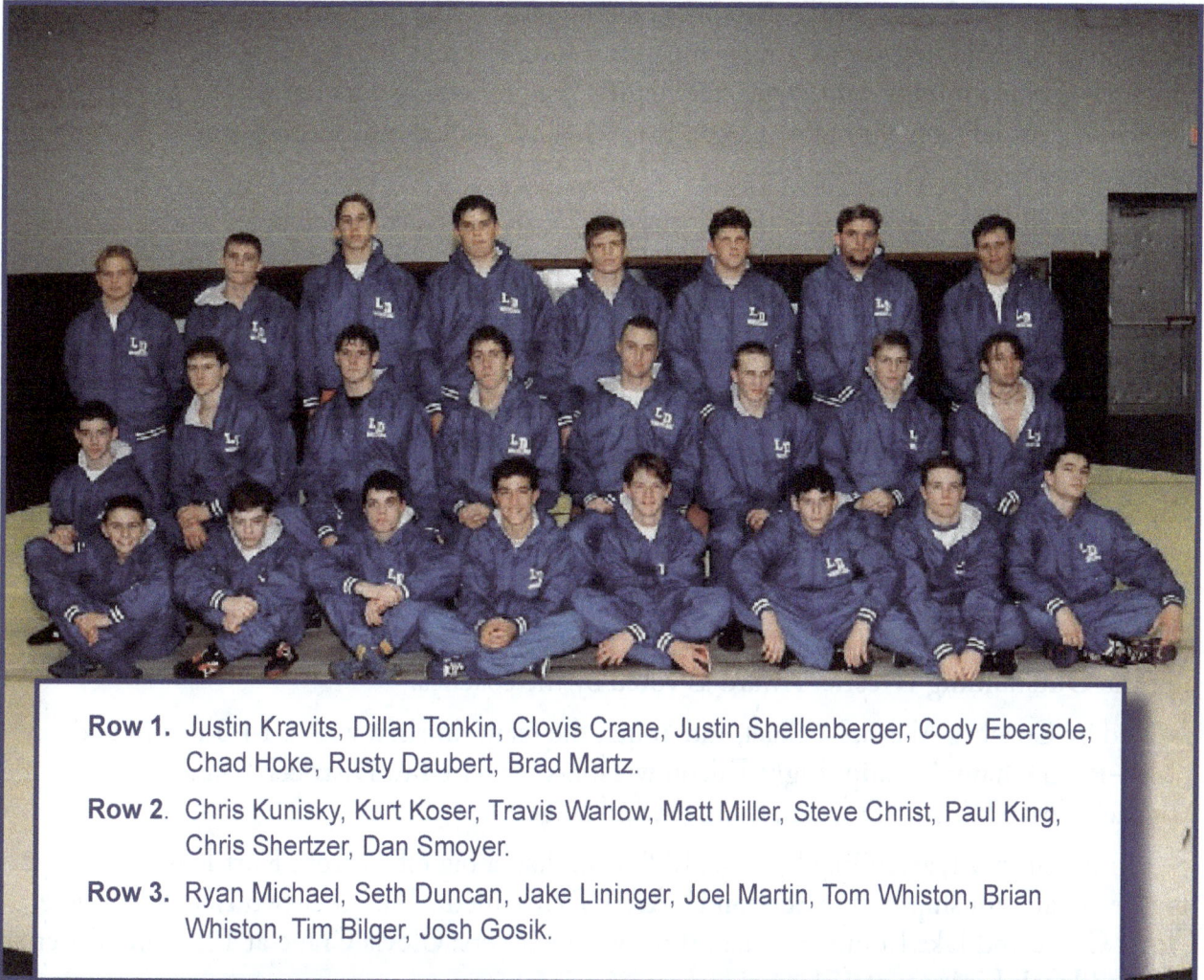

Row 1. Justin Kravits, Dillan Tonkin, Clovis Crane, Justin Shellenberger, Cody Ebersole, Chad Hoke, Rusty Daubert, Brad Martz.

Row 2. Chris Kunisky, Kurt Koser, Travis Warlow, Matt Miller, Steve Christ, Paul King, Chris Shertzer, Dan Smoyer.

Row 3. Ryan Michael, Seth Duncan, Jake Lininger, Joel Martin, Tom Whiston, Brian Whiston, Tim Bilger, Josh Gosik.

The Falcon's **Wrestling Tonight** *printed program* for spectators opened the wrestling season with its "Spot Light" on Kurt Koser, the youngest of the trio of brothers in the Falcon wrestling starting lineup. Thus, for two seasons the lineup **was anchored by Kurt, Ryan,** and **Brin Koser who last year had 57 combined wins.** Kurt alone held a dual meet record of **13-2 and an overall record of 28-4.**

Just as the 1970s had the three Fluman brothers who wrestled in sequential years and the four Camastas (mainly in the '80s) who covered a generation, as did the Umbergers—and many other sets of dedicated brothers (See the featured listing of *LD's Wrestling Brothers,*), the Kosers of the 1990s dominated that sibling slot for over six years. [1]

[1] Dupler, Ebersole, Etnoyer, Gessaman, Gosik, Hahn, Kelley, Kiessling, Koser (2 generations), Lutz, Michael, Mutek, Ricker, Salus, Sanders, Seaman, Tonkin, Vale, Verdelli, Watts, Zitch—**all had three or more brothers on the wrestling teams.**

Following a **48-15** win over Middletown in **early December** 1997, the Falcons held a winning streak of **13 consecutive matches** reaching back to the preceding season. The team had rolled over Middletown **48-15**, opening via a forfeit win at 103, pushing the lead to 12-0 on **Clovis Crane's minute-and-a-quarter victory**. And following a forfeit win by Kurt Koser, our **Ryan Michael** (son of notable Falcon Ron Michael) **nailed a 43 seconds pin** to push the leading score to 30-12.

John Crull (*The Sun*) reported on the meet in which the Falcons had opened with a quick 12-0 on pins in toppling **Manheim Central (36-24)**, rolled easily over Harrisburg, and stopped Cedar Cliff—all in the same week.

On **December 11**, the *Patriot-News* reported that **Northern** had ripped past Lower Dauphin, coming through for the 20th consecutive time, stinging LD in their home territory, 37-24. This intrusion served as an incentive for the Falcon team! Further, Harrisburg sportswriter Rod Frisco carried this information along in his column, "Lower Dauphin, all but guaranteed another Mid-Penn Division II title, *must win* to keep its Team Championship hopes alive," and **they did**.

At **Warwick** were the trio of Clovis Crane, Kurt Koser and Jacob Lininger. After building a 5-0 lead, Kurt "withstood a furious third-period rally to claim an **8-6** victory" which earned him the **Outstanding Wrestler Award** as voted by the coaches.

Led by Coaches Ahern, Michael, and Youtz, the team finished with a **14-3** record and a **Mid-Penn Championship**. Eight Falcon wrestlers advanced to Districts: Crane, Smoyer, Michael, Koser, Warlow, Duncan, Lininger, and Bilger.

On February 21, at Boiling Springs, LD's team had a big effort from Kurt Koser for one of its three championships at the **Section II-AAA** Tournament. The other two LD titlists were Clovis Crane and Jake Lininger and all three were winners: Clovis Crane at 103, Kurt Koser at 135, and Jacob Lininger at 171.

Koser fell to Reading's Kevin Maeir in the semi-final round at **Districts**, but wrestled back to a third place finish. Crane lost by technical fall. Lininger and Koser advanced to States.

Clovis Crane[2] was notable in his own right, taking detours during his years at LD, made possible by his academic success, wrestling, and his phenomenal skill as a horseman—all in a supportive school district that could help it happen.

Rod Frisco named Crane the "mysterious Mr. X" of Mid State wrestling this year. "…Crane took off last year to ply his trade as an apprentice jockey. He had more than 3,000 mounts and was the **nation's leading apprentice**." Yes. Our LD wrestler! And all within the rules. (See feature article on Clovis Crane in this chapter.)[2]

---

[2] Clovis Crane. See separate story in this section, Wrestler, Jockey, Entrpreneur. The following is an excerpt from that story: "Leaving LD to become an apprentice jockey, Crane booted home 95 winners during his first season as a jockey. In his second year, he rode 122 winners and earned good purses—all of this while still on the LD wrestling team and keeping up with academics."

Kurt **Koser** and Jake **Lininger** were named as members of the "**Big 13,**" along with Crane, giving LD nearly **40% of the slots in the Big 13.** Impressive!

Legendary Coach Bob Craig of Cedar Cliff commented on the dedication of LD's wrestlers, citing that at one point (even) LD's 103-pounder professional jockey **Clovis Crane has given up winning purses and four mounts at Penn National Racetrack to wrestle this match!!!!**"

Talk about Falcon commitment! And maybe that is the real key to Lower Dauphin's success. (Readers are invited in particular to read our special sections in this book's tribute to all areas of Lower Dauphin wrestling. We are more than a team. We are **Family.** We are **Legend.** We are a **Lifestyle.**

1998–1999 *(Record 7-6)*

Row 1. Ryan Michael, Jeff Beaver, Cody Ebersole, Kyle Meyer, Chris Kunisky, Josh Dimeler, Paul King, Rusty Daubert.

Row 2. Zach Jackson, Matt Verdelli, Tyler Snyder, Jared Prichard, Chris Shertzer, Steve Crist, Kevin Dupler, Tom Whiston, Jared Horn.

Row 3. Matt Miller, Travis Warlow, Jake Lininger, Joel Martin, Tim Bilger, Chris Long, Brian Whiston.

Early in the season Waynesboro's grapplers put the Falcons into a 13-0 hole when Chad Knott and Andy Spittle were decisioned on December 15. However, Lower Dauphin pulled to within one point on the work of Rob Melly, Max Bartlebaugh, and Casey Koons. In a tennis-like back and forth, the birds picked up the **33-27** victory on the strength of pins by Matt Verdelli, Chris Long, and Joel Martin.

On January 6, 1999 LD was ranked third at the State College Tournament, winning 8 medals. On January 20 LD lost to CV, but topped CD East in a match that initially had looked as if East would pull it out. However, LD "squirmed" back to **21-15** when Ryan Michael picked up a forfeit and Rusty Daubert garnered a decision. And LD trounced the big team, Cedar Cliff (**39-29**).

February 3, 1999. "The Falcons dumped the first five bouts against Manheim Central and found themselves at a 22-0 default. The Falcons then turned things around at 135 and motored to a **27-25** victory."

February 10, 1999. Against Elizabethtown, coming out of a tied score in the 125 bout, Michael and Daubert picked up decisions and King grabbed a pin. Losing the next few weights, a Hollywood Walk was the path for Lininger. Martin's pin at 4:16 sealed the Falcons' victory, **36-32.**

February 24, 1999. At Districts, Falcon wrestlers making it to the quarter finals were Ebersole, Michael, Daubert, Shertzer, Matt Miller, Tom Whiston, first seed Jake Lininger and Joel Martin. Daubert went on to a second place finish to advance. **Lininger was the only Falcon** to win a title, placing first, thus qualifying for States.

Despite various obstacles and injuries, this team put forth a sincere and dedicated effort in moving to a new division where they faced some of the best teams in the area, finishing with a record of 7-6. Seniors in this team included Captains Cody Ebersole, Chris Shertzer, and Tom Whiston. Senior Jake Lininger earned a place in the Patriot News Big 13 and Rusty Daubert and Tom Whiston were chosen for the Optimist Club Award. Six team members represented the Falcons in District competition.

Ryan Michael

1999–2000 *(Record 5-7)*

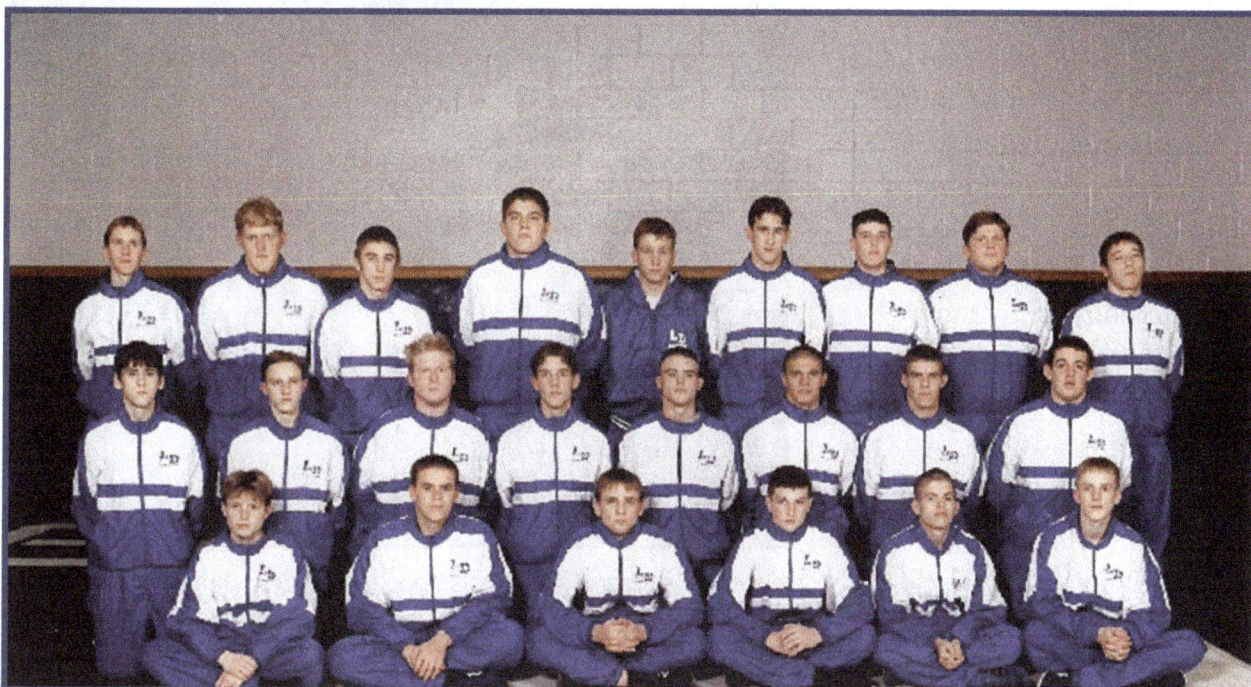

Row 1. Chad Knott, Ben Billet, Paul King, Rob Melly, Richie Swartz, Ben Hallam.

Row 2. Nate Sumner, Andy Spittle, Justin Krebs, Casey Koons, Kevin Dupler, Matt Gosik, Jeff Beaver, Ike Fullerton.

Row 3. Max Bartlebaugh, Chris Long, Tom Turner, Joel Martin, Ben Shertzer, Zach Jackson, Matt Verdelli, Brian Whiston, Jared Prichard.

Early in the season Lower Dauphin split wins with the West Shore, losing to Cedar Cliff (**51-16**) on Thursday, December 9, then coming back on Saturday to beat Red Land, **39-24**. Matt Gosik's 19-8 decision at Cedar Cliff was one of the bright spots for LD.

On Thursday, December 6, the Falcons traveled to Cumberland Valley where they came away with the short end of the **37-20** score. Then, on the 8th they pinned their way to victory over Carlisle **37-26**.

Sportswriter John E. Crull's colorful accounts included this early season description of January meets: "…the Falcons nailed last year's champion Gettysburg's hide to the gym floor and then followed on Saturday by adding Chambersburg to the stack. Bartlebaugh picked up a forfeit win and Casey nailed a 4:36 fall, leading to two wins."

Against Gettysburg, Jackson won by disqualification and Pritchard squeezed out overtime; Shaffer disposed and Joe was handed a loss. Foiling Chambersburg, Knott blew off Collier, Summer pinned Smith, Schwartz grabbed a decision, Melly nailed Peters; and decisions were claimed by Koons, Gosik, King, Jackson, and Pritchard."

Next, LD won **49-10** over Central Dauphin East, but later in the week we lost to Cumberland Valley **37-20**. The Falcons lost **35-29** against Central Dauphin and then fell to Manheim Central **43-21**.

Locking his arms around his opponent's waist, **Jeff Beaver** gets some leverage.

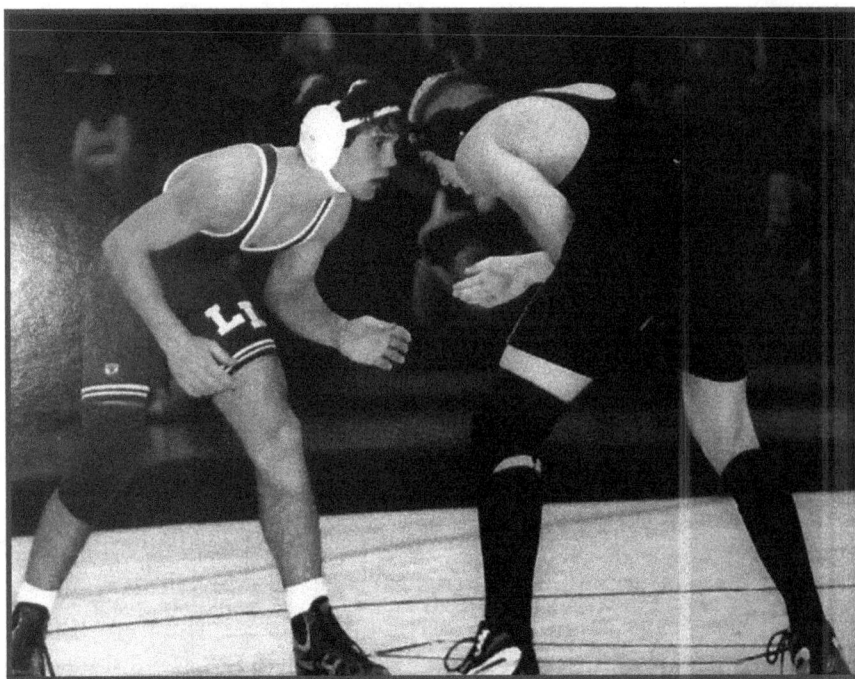

Casey Koons (*Casey at the Mat*)

Highlights in the Carlisle meet were Casey Koons who pulled off a squeaker 8-6 win and heavyweight Joel Martin who picked up a 3:43 pin. The Elizabethtown match at **36-31** closely mirrored the Carlisle contest. Rob Melly was dubbed as the "no-take-down" pin king.

The highlight of this season was the defeat over Gettysburg (33-28), whose team to that point had not lost a meet in two years. Paul King, Joel Martin, and

Matt Gosik advanced to Districts where Joel placed fourth. Martin also is quoted as saying, 'While we had our ups and downs, we did pretty well. Six freshmen started this year; they should be interesting to follow."

Lower Dauphin then closed out the regular wrestling season dropping a pair of closely scored matches to Carlisle (**37-26**) and Elizabethtown (**36-31**). At Carlisle the match began with four losses, all pins. LD did not score until Casey Koons "pulled off a squeaker win" at 8-6.

LD came away with three advancing wrestlers to the PIAA sectionals—Matt Gosik (140), Paul King (152) and heavy-weight Joel Martin who placed fourth at Districts.

Athletic Trainers

Lest we forget, Lower Dauphin also has had an exceptional crew of Athletic Trainers who devoted much time keeping the athletes ready for their respective sports.

Especially noted during these years is Head Trainer Mark French, who had initiated this program some years before.

Mark French

I Am a Lower Dauphin Wrestler and This is My Story
The Man and the Legend

Adapted from *A Tribute to Falcon Wrestling* (upon the team's reaching its 400th Victory, 1993)

> The name Cleon Cassel for many years was a synonym for Lower Dauphin Wrestling. At the helm for 25 years, Coach Cassel engineered the construction of a mighty wrestling program, whose foundations continued even after his retirement. —*Brian Kelly '94*

From the beginning, Cassel showed a flair for the mats. From the beginning of his journey first as a wrestler for Hershey High School, Cassel was successful, crowning his high school achievements with a second-place medal at the PIAA State Championships. That match was one of epic proportions, finally decided in overtime by a penalty point.

Following graduation from Franklin and Marshall College, Cassel seized the opportunity at newly formed Lower Dauphin High School where he accepted a position teaching Social Studies at the nearly completed, attractive, brand-new Lower Dauphin High School, and he could remain living in South Hanover Township.

Thus, Cleon Cassel began his coaching career, one that when finished would find him in the company of greats. Over his 25-year tenure, Cassel's teams compiled a record of 324 wins, 42 losses, and four ties. These statistics combine for an overall winning percentage of an astounding 88.1%! Alongside his team success, Cassel has coached many outstanding individual wrestlers, including 26 District Champions and 7 State Finalists. Other accomplishments include 15 league championship teams, and having the **number one team in the state in 1973.**

In 1980 Cassel was honored, along with Coach Randy Umberger, as the state's "Wrestling Co-Coach of the Year," an honor surmounted only by his 1986 induction in the Pennsylvania Wrestling Hall of Fame.

As the curtain fell on his last season of coaching in 1986-87, Cassel left behind a great legacy of both personal and team-wide achievements. Accomplishments of Lower Dauphin Wrestling have become known throughout the mid-state and further, along with the legend of their coach. Lower Dauphin Wrestling has gained many material honors under the leadership of Cleon Cassel; his lasting legacy to the program is its very foundation. As we have seen, this carefully crafted foundation is becoming an integral factor which gives Lower Dauphin wrestlers a unique drive, spurred on by the long standing tradition and continuing excellence in the program.

We are now celebrating the 400th victory of Lower Dauphin High School Wrestling. This milestone was achieved through the efforts of the many young men who dedicated themselves to the task of being the best they could be and the guidance of a committed coaching staff. The teams have left a legacy. Our wrestling history is rich. We are proud to remember it. And we are dedicated to a continuation of excellence in the future.

Wrestling — a Ray of Hope in a Sea of Chaos and Despair

—Eric Strunk 1993

I have come a long way since I first wore my blue and white. Growing up one of eight children, in a single parent household, I always knew what it meant "to scrape by." From sixth to tenth grade, I lived in the National Hotel, above a bar, in one room with my mother, three siblings, and all of our worldly possessions. Life was chaotic, undisciplined, smothering, and at times utterly unbearable. I was witness to many things that a young kid should never know.

The National Hotel was a common route for traveling to and from Lower Dauphin High School. This meant that if I didn't want to risk my classmates seeing me leaving for school from the National Hotel, I had to either leave early, or leave after I was sure everyone had passed the hotel, meaning that I would be late for school.

I got tired of hearing about my tardiness, so sometimes I would simply not go to school. The pattern would continue until late October or early November when wrestling season was starting. During the wrestling season, I would occasionally be late, but rarely be absent the entire day, as I needed to be in the wrestling room, on the mat. I had no clue why, but **it was just where I wanted to be.**

Moving to Senior High as a freshman taught me how to take a loss, pick myself up and keep moving forward. I was a 14-year-old boy who was wrestling against mostly 16 through 18-year-old young men. I spent time looking at names, records, and body types. What I learned was that the mat doesn't hear excuses; the mat doesn't lie; the mat doesn't take sides. On the mat YOU have only yourself to answer to.

Following my sophomore year of high school, the National Hotel caught fire, and my family awoke to fire fighters kicking the door in and leading us out of that inferno. Oddly enough, that was one of the best things to happen in my life.

For the remainder of the school year, I lived with the Duplers (the family of a wrestling teammate) in Grantville. God bless that family for taking me in and showing me what stability and structure were.

It was at this time that Craig Cassel became the coach and the father/uncle/big brother who helped me to learn how to direct my life. Through Craig Cassel's guidance, expectations, and support, both my attendance and my grades dramatically improved.

I was graduated from high school (one of four of the 8 in my family to have done so) and I went to Wilkes University. I then enlisted in the military, where I won the US Armed Forces Wrestling Championship in 1997.

I am able to be a loving father and husband, mentor, and a respected Corporal in the Norfolk Police Department due in no small part to a foundation instilled in me by having wrestled. This is how wrestling at Lower Dauphin led me to who I am today.

2000–2010: Strengthening the Dynasty

The LD Mat

The Grappler

The Falcon Grappler

The Coaches' Corner

How many of these publications do you remember?

The LD Mat and *The Falcon Grappler*

In the early years of wrestling the Lower Dauphin Varsity Club *mimeographed* programs for the fans attending the wrestling matches and also produced several newsletters. The first newsletter, *The LD Mat*, listed the evening's home and visiting wrestlers' names, along with the weight and the record of each wrestler, and included the name of the evening's referee. It also noted the scores in former encounters with the evening's opponent. On the back of some of these handouts was the score card for use by the spectators.

These early programs listed the Wrestling Captains and our District Wrestling Champions. One of the issues included "Mat Mutterings" with facts such as "...Falcons are 11-0-1 and have won their matches by an average of 31 points per match"...and that next year there will be available a record (yes, those round platters that preceded tapes and CDs and cell phones) of a rendition of the National Anthem to be used prior to the first match.

This author's own limited collection of these early programs began with Volume I, No. 3 of *The LD Mat* sold at the wrestling matches, price 10 cents. The front page carried the names of LD's wrestlers (by weight), beginning with Mike Kreiser '67 at 95 lb. and ending with Dan Verdelli, Hwt. Their respective opponents were Mechanicsburg's Roger Parks and Carl Shields. The referee's name was also provided, in this case Mr. Lew Gruber, a name perhaps still remembered by some readers. The front page included scores of previous meets between the two teams. It listed LD's highest team score, lowest team score, most points by an individual, fastest pin and most pins, as well as the same information for our opponent. It included the *Season Records to Date,* LD's *Wrestling Record Against All Opponents and* LD's *Sectional Wrestling Champions:* Ebersole, Kahler, Shellenhamer, Pinkerton, Sanders, Kopp, Rhone, Umberger, Hess, Cruys, Neidig, Ebersole, Smith, Ruggles, Koser, Boyer, Mutek, and Tritch, along with other records.

The LD Mat also included Carl Espenshade (who defeated William Costopoulas, later to become one of the top criminal defense lawyers on the East Coast) and Frank Neiswender who was the first of many LD wrestlers who would later return to coach at their Alma Mater.

Early issues of *The LD Mat* included the information that Randy Umberger had never before seen a wrestling match when the football and wrestling coaches talked him into coming out for wrestling after a successful Junior High football season in the fall of 1960. Another story featured Randy Kahler who had won Sectionals, Districts, Regionals, and was the first LD wrestler to qualify for the State Finals. (Can any of us fathom how uncommon this was for a novice wrestler to reach such heights?)

Stories from the third year of wrestling included the last matches LD would lose for the next 3 ½ years and our more than 40 wins. By far the most memorable match that year was that of an undefeated Mechanicsburg wrestler who had not lost in 5 years.

Years later *The LD Mat* was followed by a more polished publication, *The Grappler.* This newsletter was published for at least another decade, preserving stories of wrestling and wrestlers.

Later *The Falcon Grappler,* produced by Eric Stauffer '76 and Ed Neiswender '73, appeared again, with its first issue dated September 2005. From the "Coaches Corner" came a reminiscent mention of the old felt wrestling mat.

Another piece in *The Falcon Grappler* is Eric Stauffer's account of one of his favorite matches, a compelling story about his legendary older brother George who had provided "some of the most electrifying matches in LD history." George not only had been an outstanding wrestler, but also was a tremendous "crowd pleaser."

The November 2005 issue opened with an episode of LD Wrestling by Coach Cassel: "The **very first year** our bunch of 'inexperienced No-Names' (only two wrestlers had had previous wrestling varsity experience at Hershey) ended the season with a 6-4 record!"

Coach continued, "… and Glenn Ebersole, who anchored the team, was 'undefeated and pinned all but one opponent!' Glenn set a record still unbroken of pinning his opponent in only 12 seconds. Jay and Galen Kopp became the first set of brothers, something that became a trade-mark of L.D. wrestling—and they may be the first father-son succession with Jay's son (Adam) wrestling. We had many brothers and almost every team included a younger brother who had been taught to wrestle by his older sibling."

Cassel continued, "…and I will never forget how difficult it was for Lower Dauphin to be accepted at the long-running Christmas tournament; the athletic director (Jack Goepfert) contacted every tournament director in the state until Central Dauphin finally allowed us to join their event at the last minute. **We went on to win the title!**"

The May 2006 issue featured "The Most Unusual Matches," while February 2007 offered information such as "The 2006 and 2007 teams in many ways remind me of LD's 1964 and 1965 teams when the **Falcons dominated everyone** by winning every tournament and had the longest winning streak in the state—45 wins!"

Craig Cassel added, "The feeling of excitement throughout the match and the final outcome made me realize why we all love to hear the stories from the past. That match made my memories more vivid than ever. I think of my heroes on the mats in the wrestling room and gyms of my childhood and how I tried to emulate their moves and character. I still have **autographs** from Jockers, Young, Neiswender, Mutek, Stauffer, and Michael." Through the years typically there were individual programs for the matches, with the styles changing periodically. One of the series was named *Wrestling Tonight* and included short articles from both past and present.

In the early years of the 21st Century, a helpful newsletter appeared periodically. *The Coaches Corner* published much helpful information for the wrestlers as well as serving the general wrestling community, such as the Wrestling Boosters and their fund-raising events. However, its major purpose was well-served to promote the camaraderie among wrestlers, coaches, and parents.

Kudos to the coaches who cooperated in preparing this publication! It also is reassuring to note that a sports printed program continues. One cannot help smiling and it feels reassuring to see and hold the printed "Projected Lineup," "Falcons Roster," "Senior Spotlight" and coverage of the Alumni Night as found in a program dated January 5, 2023.

Falcon Pride
Fathers and Sons of Wrestling

The following list has been compiled to the best of our collective ability, checking information from many sources over the past nearly four years.

(We do not, by law, have access to the school's personnel records.)

Coach Ed Neiswender '73 and Son, Eddie Neiswender '08

Fathers	Sons	Fathers	Sons
Arndt, Roger	Matt	Gamber, Tim	Timmy Gamber and Clint Fackler
Barrick, Mike	Zach		
Bath, Chris	Andrew	Geesaman, Duane	Kyle, Eric
Camasta, Chris	Anthony	Gesford, Roy	Jacob
Cassel, Chris	Lee, Colton	Hahn, Mark	Jonathon
Cassel, Craig	Elliot	Harner, Walt	Garrett
Crick, Mike	Mike	Higgins, Tim	Robbie
Dupler, Brian	Kevin	Kiessling, John	Jake
Dupler, Sam	Jason	Kiessing, Mark	Matt
Dupler, Jason	Evan	Kopp, Jay	Adam
Ebersole, Bob	Bobby, Cole, Cody	Koser, John	Chad
Espenshade, Carl	Matt, Andy	Koser, Lamar	Kurt, Brin, and Ryan
Foreman, Jim	Matt, Jordan	Koser, Kurt	Clayton

Fathers	Sons		Fathers	Sons
Messick, Don	Tyler		Stoak, Joe	Joey, Hunter
Michael, Ron	Ronnie, Ryan, and Trevor		Tonkin, Barry	Dustin, Dalton, and Dillon
Neiswender, Ed	Eddie		Umberger, Keith	Dustin
Rhinesmith, Brian	Jesse		Verdelli, Dan	Greg, Matt
Rogers, Travis	James		Wallace, Craig	Matt
Shutt, Tim	Blaine, Bailey		Walters, Todd	Mitch
Smoyer, Dave	Mike, Dan		Watts, Jeff	Tyler
Stauffer, Eric	Kyle		Watts, Mel	Chris and Josh
Stahl, Ted	Marshall			

Koser Generations

BROTHERS OF WRESTLING

The Camasta Brothers

Craig '82   Chris '78   Mark '74   Keith '85

Dedicated to all siblings who ever had to share… a bedroom, clothing, ice skates, a bicycle or a car …

Alexander	Scott, Wade	Ebersole	Bobby, Cole, Cody
Bath	Chris, Andrew	Ebersole	Dennis, Bob
Book	John, Jacob	Elhajj	T.T., Elijah
Burrows	Jeremy, Jason	Espenshade	Matt, Andy
Burrows	Tom, Dick	Etnoyer	Bill, Greg, Clint
Camasta	Mark, Chris, Craig, and Keith	Fallinger	Sam, Matt
		Fluman.	Allen, Brandon, Eric
Cargas	Nick, Rick	Foreman	Matt, Jordan
Cassel	Craig, Chris	Gamber	Timmy Gamber & Clint Fackler
Cassel	Lee, Colton		
Christofes	Tom, Eryc	Geesaman	Warren, Duane, Galen
Costik	Brian, Steve	Geesaman	Kyle, Eric
Crawford	Justin, Jonathan	Gesford	Roy, Tim
Cruys	Ron, George	Gleim	Jason, Justin
Donnelly	JT, Sean	Goodwin	Ron, Dale
Dowhower	Steve, Tom	Gosik	Kirk, Matt, and Josh
Dupler	Sam, John, Robert	Gray	Cary, Ryan

Heagy	Mike and Sam	Myers	Robert, Rhys
Hahn	Matt, Mitch, Mark	Neiswender	Frank, Ed
Hertzler	Jim, Eugene	Reese	Derek, Kiel
Jackson	Jeremy, Zach	Remsburg	Marty, Mike
Kane	Jarred, Jason	Rice	Wayne, Curt
Kelley	Rick, Pat, Mike	Ricker	Kevin, Steve, Doug
Kessler	Eric, Dillon	Salus	Richard, Tom, John, James
Kiessling	John, Jamie, Mark	Sanders	Jim, Dan, Tom
King	Karl, Chet	Seaman	Darrel, Dean, Doug
King	Mike, Paul	Sharkey	Alex, Patrick
Klinger	Bryan, Mike	Shellenhamer	Harold "Buster", Bob
Kolaric	P.J., Kevin	Shertzer	Chris, Ben
Kopp	Jay, Galen, Ron*	Shutt	Blaine, Bailey
Koser	Kurt, Brin, Ryan	Smith	Bill, Keith
Koser	Leon, John , Joel , Lamar	Smoyer	Mike, Dan
Kotchey	Kevin, Keith	Snavely	Glenn, Jeff
Krebs	Justin, Jason	Stahl	Ed, Jimmy, Ted
Kreiser	Bob, Mike	Stammel	Ron, Rod
Kulp	Joe, Pete	Stauffer	George, Mark, Eric, Ed
Lehmer	Kirk, Craig	Stoak	Joey, Hunter
Lininger	Jake, Josh	Summy	Steve, Roger
Long	Ken, Chris	Tonkin	Barry, Rich (Butch)
Lutz	Randy, Ryan, Chad	Tonkin	Dalton, Dylan, Dustin
Martz	Brad, Marshall	Ulrey	Clayton, Gannon
Michael	Ed, Jim, Ron	Umberger	Randy, Keith, Lloyd Jr., Joel
Michael	Ronnie, Ryan, Trevor	Vale	Valerie, Jacob, Vivian
Minto	Brian, Mike	Valeri	Claudio, Peter
Morrill	Travis, Evan	Vance	Dan, Marty
Mutek	Tom, Fred, Ken, Mark		

---

* Ron wrestled from grade 7 to the beginning of his Junior year when a huge barn fire led to injury of Mr. Kopp. Ron left the team from necessity to help on the farm. Such actions reflect the duty prevalent among the LD wider family.

Vance	Dan, Marty
Verdelli	Dan , Ron, Tom , Mike
Verdelli	Greg, Matt
Wallish	Gary, Chris
Wallish	Chris, Rob
Walters	Rich, Doug
Warlow	Roy, Travis
Watts	Melvin, Jeff, Scott
Watts	Chris and Joshua
Weirich	Howard (Herc), Brad
Weneck	Matt, Mike
Whiston	Tom, Brian
Wuestner	David, Jr., Kyler
Zitch	Dwight, Jere, Jeff

Of note . . .

✓ The Kane Brothers—Jared (132 career wins) and Jason Kane (85 career wins) hold the record for brothers with the most combined wins of 217.

✓ Blaine (88 career wins) and Bailey Shutt (110 career wins) run a close second at a combined score of 198.

✓ In the mid-2010s, Valerie and Vivian Vale, two sisters, were rightful members of the Falcon team. Both earned varsity letters and Bri was close to .500 her senior year. She later wrestled at the college level. Jacob is their brother.

The Umberger Brothers:

Randy '65   Keith '75   Lloyd '77   Joel '81

HIGHLIGHTS OF THE MEETS: 2000-2010

The 2000s were exciting for the wrestling program. During this decade…

- ♦ LD twice sent 11 wrestlers to district championships.

- ♦ The 2006-2007 team set an LD record by qualifying five wrestlers for states and also tied another record with producing three state medalists.

- ♦ Jarred Kane and Nick Kristich were the first LD wrestlers to have more than 100 career wins.

- ♦ Also a first in this decade was establishing a website with wrestling history and "branching out," challenging state powers Easton, Reynolds, and Bald Eagle Area.

"Wrestling gives me the satisfaction of working hard and seeing an end result."
Jared Prichard, LD wrestler.

2000–2001 *(Record 6-7)*

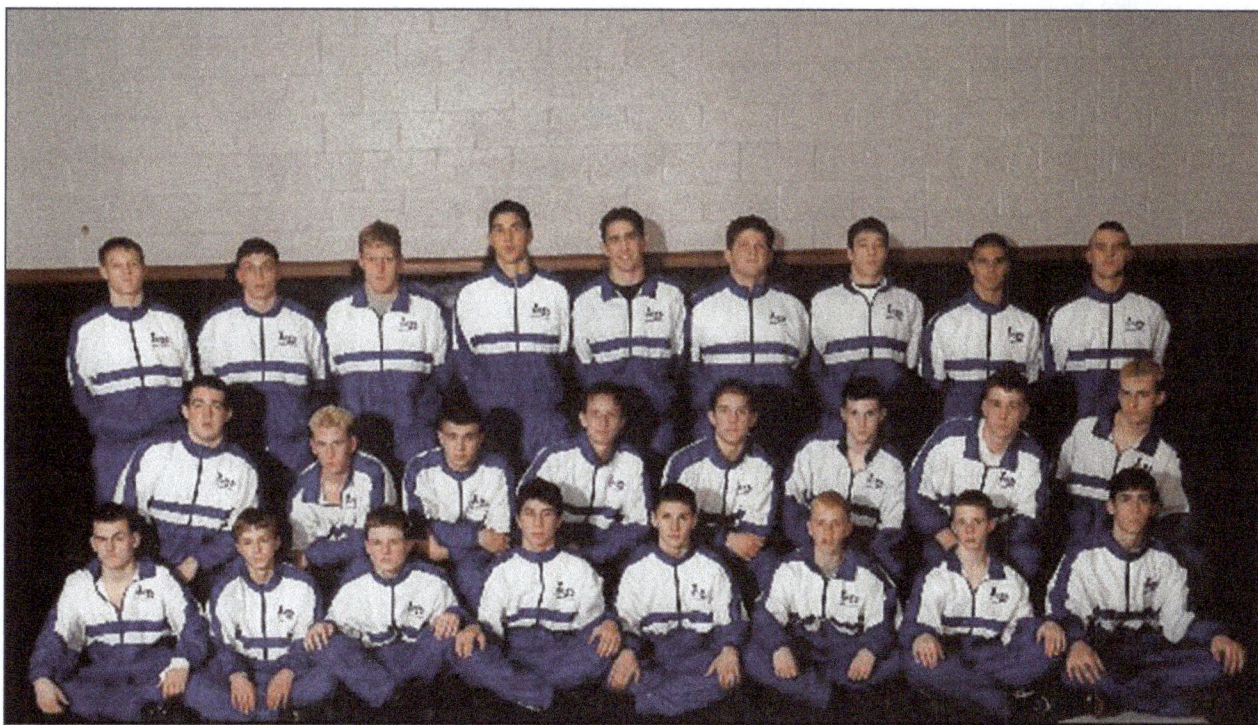

Row 1. Shawn Mead, Mike Adair, Chad Knott, Adam Sherlock, Kirk Gosik, Matt Arndt, Rusty Green, Nate Summer.

Row 2. Ike Fullerton, Max Bartlebaugh, Trevor Michael, Matt Moyer, Casey Koons, Rob Melly, Ben Shertzer, Marshall Martz.

Row 3. Clint Fackler, Hudson Hughes, Chris Long, Chris Watts, Zach Jackson, Brian Whiston, Jared Prichard, Matt Gosik, Kevin Dupler.

Thursday, **December 7, 2000,** *The Sun.* "135 pounder Casey Koons acquired the hold he wanted on his **Cumberland Valley** opponent and moved on for the pin win. Zach Jackson had a decision win over his opponent. The Falcons battled CV to a **31-31** match score only to see it go in the loss column on criteria because the Eagles had one more bout win than the Falcons did."

On **December 9** the team fell short against **Carlisle (37—27)** even with Matt Moyer's pin win that kicked off four straight wins until the momentum swung to Carlisle and with the pins from Rob Melly and Matt Gosik (who did the job in only 54 seconds). The Falcons continued with their pins, including those from Clint Fackler, Chris Watts, and Ben Shertzer.

On **December 14,** this young Falcon team faced undefeated **Cedar Cliff**. However, their determination for a win was not to be, despite the rally from Casey Koons to get an individual win at 135. Cedar Cliff: 43; LD: 18.

As reported by *The Sun,* "On Saturday, powerhouses State College, Dallastown, *and* Cedar Cliff all came to town. When the smoke had cleared, the Falcons found themselves in the cellar of their own tourney, fourth with just 51 points against 111 for State College, the winner." A high point, however, was Casey Koons pinning Cedar Cliff's notable Ryan Shaffer!

The Falcons came out winners against CD East **(53-18),** Waynesboro **(34-25),** Chambersburg **(66-6),** Hershey **(38-15),** Manheim Central **(33-22),** and Red Land **(29-24).**

In the post season, five wrestlers placed at sectionals. These included Brian Whiston in 1st place, Zack Jackson, Matt Gosik & Rob Melly in 2nd place, and Casey Koons in 3rd.

2001–2002 *(Record 11-2)*

Quite a Crew!

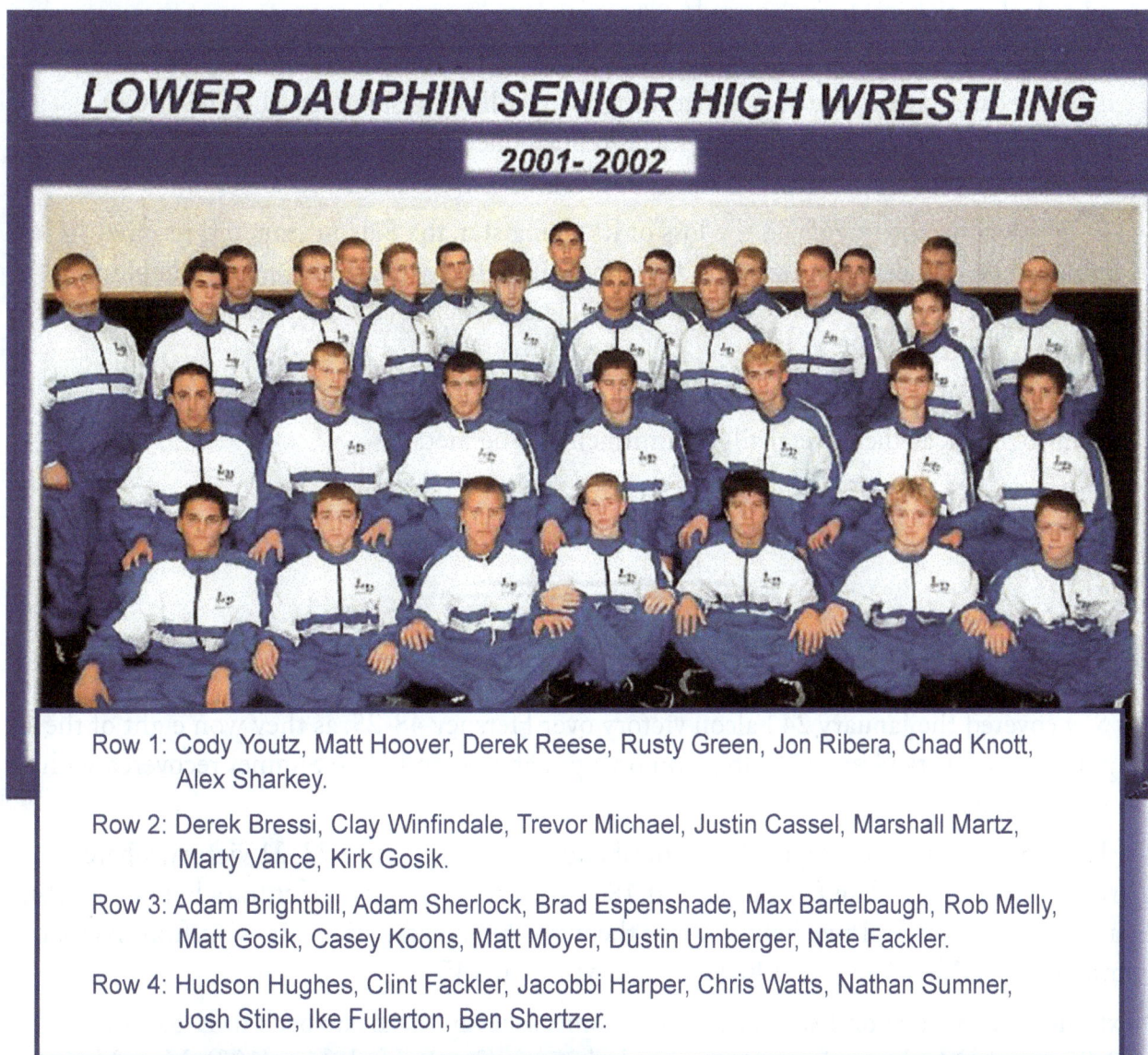

LOWER DAUPHIN SENIOR HIGH WRESTLING
2001- 2002

Row 1: Cody Youtz, Matt Hoover, Derek Reese, Rusty Green, Jon Ribera, Chad Knott, Alex Sharkey.

Row 2: Derek Bressi, Clay Winfindale, Trevor Michael, Justin Cassel, Marshall Martz, Marty Vance, Kirk Gosik.

Row 3: Adam Brightbill, Adam Sherlock, Brad Espenshade, Max Bartelbaugh, Rob Melly, Matt Gosik, Casey Koons, Matt Moyer, Dustin Umberger, Nate Fackler.

Row 4: Hudson Hughes, Clint Fackler, Jacobbi Harper, Chris Watts, Nathan Sumner, Josh Stine, Ike Fullerton, Ben Shertzer.

In a sport by which the competitors challenge themselves to reach greater heights of personal success, it is essential that they possess endurance, vigor, and passion for the particular sport. Throughout the season this team encompassed the true meaning of being willing and **ready to work hard and carry on through hardship.** They did this to a final record of 11-2. In the course of those matches, they experienced thrilling exhibitions with Big Spring (31-28) and CD East (42-9) when both times LD pulled away with the victory. In addition, Coach Sean Ahern accomplished a personal milestone as he won his 200th dual meet.

Newspaper, December 12, 2001:

Casey J. Koons, 17, of Grantville, died Tuesday, December 11 as a result of a traffic accident in Derry Township. He had stayed home that morning and was driving to school when the accident occurred.

Later the newspaper announced: Rocked by the loss of team member Casey Koons in a one-car accident, the Falcon wrestling team will not resume its schedule at CD East until Thursday, December 20. The two postponed meets with Cedar Cliff and Dallastown have not as yet been rescheduled.

With all of the tragedy in the loss of its young star, the Falcon team did resume its schedule to meet its obligations, traveling with a heavy heart to Central Dauphin East on December 20 (**42-9**) and hosting Waynesboro (LD, **39**; Waynesboro, **18**) on Saturday, December 22.)

The coaches did what they could throughout the rest of the season to hold the team together, as there were still commitments to be met.

The Sun covered the **January 24** Falcon victory over Hershey **48-25**, as they won eight of the 13 weight classes. Rusty Green (112 lb.) won on a pin at 1:54 and Nate Sumner recovered with a pin win at 4:13.

On **January 31** LD visited Manheim Central and came away with a **33-21** victory, where Chris Watts had earned an 8-2 decision at 180, shattering Manheim Central's hopes of getting a pair of pins in the final two bouts. Along the way LD gained critical pin wins from Nathan Sumner at 119, Matt Gosik at 140, and Matt Moyer at 145.

Next, the Falcons took on Elizabethtown at home, sending the Bears back to E-town with a **40-25** loss. LD had five pins and a major decision as Dustin Umberger (103), Matt Moyer (145), Max Bartlebaugh (160), Clint Fackler (171) and Chris Watts (189) all showed their opponents the lights. Matt Gosik earned a major decision at 140.

On **February 7** the Falcons topped the Red Land Patriots **42-16** with a pin from Rusty Green and a decision by Adam Sherlock.

On **February 22** LD entered the championships at Wilson High School, but lost in the consolation semi-finals on **February 23**.

Matt Moyer working to get his opponent on his back.

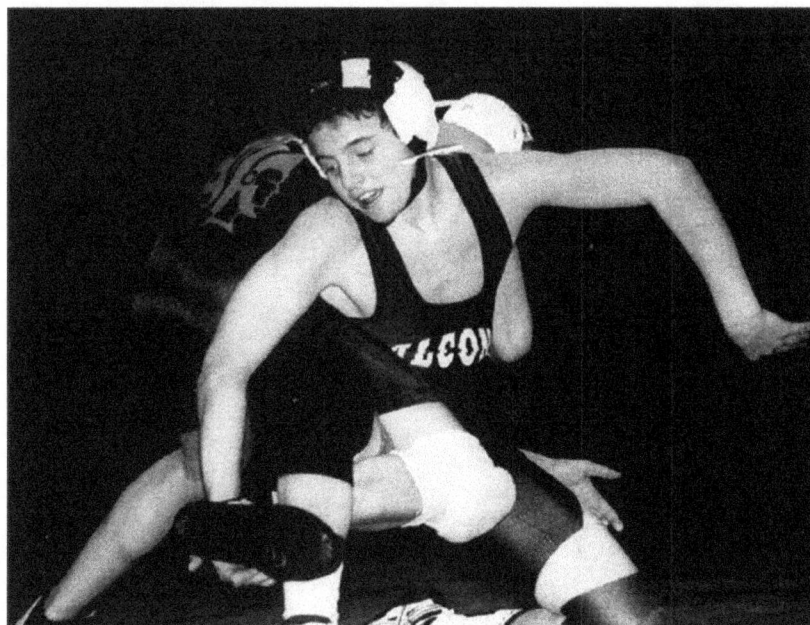

Dustin Umberger gaining control of the match.

In post season five wrestlers placed at Sectionals and advanced to Districts. Jared Prichard was named to the Big 15.

2002–2003 *(Record 10-6)*

Row 1: Hudson Hughes, Bradford Espenshade, Christopher Watts, Adam Brightbill, Clint Fackler, Matthew Moyer, Jacobbi Harper.

Row 2: Marty Vance, Derek Reese, Marshall Martz, Adam Sherlock, Jack Hileman, Rob Melly, Jonathon Ribera, Trever Michael, Clayton Winfindale.

Row 3: Chad Knott, Alex Sharkey, Matthew Hoover, Kirk Gosik, Joshua Stine, Matthew Coyne, Rodney Still, Patrick Lister, Cody Youtz, and Dustin Umberger.

Under a new coaching staff led by one of Lower Dauphin's own champions, former coach, and mainstay in the wrestling program, Ed Neiswender returned as head coach. This team's goal was to make a name for the complete team, working singly to achieve a high cumulative score. To prove their prowess during the season they beat arch-rival Middletown (46-24) and led a close match with Cedar Cliff (LD **27** and CC **30**).

The team had opened their 2002-2003 season on **November 30** at the Big Spring Duals. On **December 7** they topped Reading, **42-29**, with pins from Rob and Trevor Michael. This was Melly's second pin—and early in the season. Michael pinned in 1:42 following a quick takedown and Matt Moyer's forfeit win cinched LD's win.

On **December 13** LD's Melly took 5th place in the Mid-Penn Conference Meet held at Milton Hershey School.

In the January 15 issue of *The Sun* Tony Joseph reported LD wins: January 9's handling of Susquehanna Township (**56-12**) and the **39-19** rout of previously unbeaten Red Land. After Clint Fackler's pin gave LD a 13-9 lead, the Birds never looked back. Dustin Umberger earned a decision between forfeits to Kiel Reese and Cody Youtz. This was followed with decisions scored by Derek Reese and Jack Hileman. Melly topped it all off with a technical fall.

After dropping a close decision to Cedar Cliff in the Mid-Penn Duals, the Falcons were manhandled by Cumberland Valley in the quarter-finals at Mechanicsburg. Seniors Chris Watts and Clint Fackler had the only wins for LD against the Eagles (who eventually lost to Northern in the finals). Thanks to their upper weights, LD then handed losses to Manheim Central (**42-26**) and Elizabethtown (**46-21**).

Rob Melly, a senior, became the **first district wrestling champion from Lower Dauphin since 1994** when he reversed top-seeded Chris Murray (Central Dauphin) with 45 seconds left on the clock for a 4-3 win at 145. Melly noted, "I honestly don't remember what I did. I just kept going."

In **2003** an addition, to be known as the 1,000 Wing, was built to accommodate an increase in student enrollment. Much needed, this facility housed state-of-the-art fitness and conditioning equipment and an expanded sports medicine facility. **Later,** an added area would also serve as the venue for wrestling practice and other after school activities, freeing up valuable—and coveted—gymnasium space for its original uses.

Matt Coyne is about to reverse his opponent

Coach Ed Neiswender with Kirk Gosik (2004)

2003–2004 *(Record 11-4)*

Row 1: Peter Kulp, Matt Coyne, Zach Wakefield, Matt Hoover, Rusty Green, Jarred Kane, Kiel Reese.

Row 2: Corey Snyder, Kyle Geesaman, Kirk Gosik, Marty Vance, Kevin Gerhart, Derek Reese, Adam Bainbridge, John Ribera.

Row 3: John Turns, Jacob Book, Matt Moyer, Jacobbi Harper, Josh Watts, Jimmy Miller, Mark Wise, Cody Youtz.

A sports writer, covering a tournament held December 10-11, at Solanco, raised some interesting questions in his article—a series of "What If's" regarding the tournament that LD likely could have won handily under different conditions. He noted that LD showed once again that "You make it happen with what you have." And the Falcons did just that, **claiming eight of the 14 weight classes:** Nick Kristich and Jarred Kane, 1st place; Mark Wise, 4th; Peter Kulp, 5th; Jonathan Crawford and Jimmy Miller, 6th; Matt Coyne, 7th; and Zack Wakefield, 8th place.

At the New Year's holiday break the Falcons were matched against the top team in the Mid-Penn Commonwealth Division—the Central Dauphin Rams who definitely showed their strength. Only Jarred Kane (119), Matt Hoover (130), Matt Moyer (171) and Mark Wise (275) of LD were individually victorious as the Rams posted a **47-16** win over the Falcons.

On January 8, 2004, Lower Dauphin had an easy **72-6** win over Susquehanna Township where the Falcons won four of the six bouts, all by pins from Mark Wise (275), Cody Youtz (130), Derek Reese (135), and Matt Moyer (160).

Many of the wrestlers did admirable jobs filling in for those who had been ill or injured throughout the season. This was most beneficial when major matches were on the line. One of the most memorable is the team coming from behind and winning their final three bouts to claim a **37-29** win over Red Land on January 10. Another strike was a satisfactory destruction of nemesis Cedar Cliff (**47-22**) to become second seed in the Commonwealth Division. The Falcons racked up six pins against the Colts to finish at 7-1 in the division.

On January 15 the Falcons easily disposed of the Harrisburg Cougars (**54-21**) and were ready for Middletown (**32-31**) on Saturday, January 17. The pin from Mark Wise at 275 sealed the Mid-Penn Commonwealth Division win.

On January 28, while within a minute of advancing to the Mid-Penn Conference Duals semifinals, LD was unexpectedly upended by Big Spring, **36-27**.

First team selections in this Commonwealth Division were two wrestlers from Hershey. The second team selections—all Lower Dauphin—were Jarred Kane (119), Rusty Green (125), Cody Youtz (130), Derek Reese (135), and Matt Moyer (160). However, only Moyer made it to the state tournament.

2004–2005 *(Record 11-2)*

Row 1: Peter Kulp, Nick Kristich, Matt Coyne, Jarred Kane, Mitch Walters, Zach Wakefield, Jonathan Crawford.

Row 2: Kyle Bohn, Dustin Umberger, Alex Sharkey, Matt Hoover, Dalton Tonkin, Corey Snyder, Cody Youtz.

Row 3: Mark Wise, Jared Phoenix, Jimmy Miller, Josh Stine, Andrew Williams, Kevin Gerhart.

This 2005 team became known for its ability to rally, remaining focused, confident and intense, whatever the odds. This worked to their advantage when the scores looked grim. As one team member noted, "I get knocked down, so I get up again."

During many of the matches this year when scores looked grim, LD garnered the same fortitude as the team rallied for a victory. Perhaps the best example of this resilience is the many close matches through the years against Middletown. This year the Falcon's **27-26** score over the Blue Raiders earned them second place in the Commonwealth Division with **eight LD wrestlers advancing to Districts.** The only **losses** during the season were **very close matches** with Central Dauphin (CD-**28**; LD-**25**) and Northern (**31 -28**).

Author's Note: The following are excerpts from *The Sun* whose coverage of area sports continues to deserve our thanks. The newspaper receives no compensation—not even through advertising from the school events it covers—so remember this the next time you consider renewing your subscription. The schools do not write their own narratives of their meets, matches, bouts, and tournaments….and often school yearbooks barely acknowledge sports scores…. Thus, most of **LD sports history—and 98% of the narrative—would be lost without the local newspaper.**

At the beginning of the **2004-05 season** Lower Dauphin took a **74-6** win over Harrisburg with five pins. Four LD wrestlers earned weight titles in placing second to Dallastown in the invitational tournament on December 16. On January 4 at Central Dauphin East, **LD won nine bouts,** four through pins by Nick Kristich, Peter Kulp, Jarred Kane, and Dustin Umberger, who won his bout in 68 seconds.

On January 6 LD's team placed a disappointing 12th at **Manheim's** holiday tournament (**35-26** score). Jarred Kane placed 2nd, defeated in the finals after he had posted an 8-5 decision, a 15-0 technical fall, and a 3-2 decision.

On January 13 Jonathan Crawford and Jarred Kane gave LD an 8-0 lead after two bouts in route to a **47-24** victory over Red Land. This brought LD's division record to 4-0.

On January 24 LD's unbeaten wrestling season "came to an end at the hands of still-unbeaten Central Dauphin in the battle for first place." (CD-**28;** LD-**25**) John Crawford delivered a come-back that led to the Falcons' 25-21 lead, but this was still their first loss of the season.

On the 27th LD defeated Susquenita, **51-12.**

On **February 3** a major decision by Jarred Kane and a decision by Matt Coyne in the final two bouts held off Manheim Central **35-26.** This was followed by a pair of non-league wins, defeating Elizabethtown and Carlisle.

On **February 11** a newspaper noted, "Mark Wise's pin of Zach Stosius ignited Lower Dauphin to a **45-22** win over West Perry." Nick Kristich's pin in 33 seconds certainly added to the win, followed by a continuous see-saw score, until the last three matches produced a major decision and two pins led to the final winning score for the Falcons.

Eight Falcons qualified for Districts 3's AAA Championships. Of those 8, **Jarred Kane qualified for states with his second place finish at 125.**

2005–2006 *(Record 9-2)*

Row 1: Jake Keissling, Derrick Sweigart, Jason Kane, Taylor Rudy, Nick Kristich, Jonathan Crawford, Taylor Stuart, Matt Foreman, Peter Kulp, Zach Wakefield.

Row 2: Matt Blosser, Eddie Neiswender, Corey Snyder, Mitch Walters, Matt Coyne, Jarred Kane, Kevin Gearhart, Dalton Tonkin, Matt Wallace.

Row 3: Kyle Cassel, Tyler Watts, Mark Wise, Jimmy Miller, Josh Watts, Kyle Geesaman, Andrew Williams, Jared Phoenix.

December 16, 2005. As only a sportswriter can describe it, "Kevin Gearhart pinned Harrisburg's Leroy Armstrong in the 160-pound bout and Zack Wakefield decisioned Andy Efflong in the 152-pound bout as the Falcons *de-clawed the Cougars*, **64-7**, last Friday in a Mid-Penn Conference Commonwealth match."

Further, Lower Dauphin finished second in the Wildcat Invitational Tournament at Dallastown with the following champs: Nick Kristich (with a 47-second pin), Jon Crawford, Matt Coyne, and Jarred Kane.

January 11, 2006. In the Mid-Penn Conference Commonwealth Division, LD had pins from Nick Kristich at 112, Jimmy Miller at 189 and Mark Wise at 275. Kristich is top-ranked at 112 in District 3 AAA. Freshman Jason Kane won a major decision in his first bout at 130 while Jarred Kane is third-ranked in the Division.

January 25, 2006. The press took a deep breath to summarize the first five Mid-Penn Conference Commonwealth matches where "Lower Dauphin had things pretty much its own way, winning by an average of 40 points. The Falcons showed area wrestling fans they could handle the pressure of a close match as well, as they kept their record clean while handing previously unbeaten and second-ranked Central Dauphin a stunning **27-23** setback, the first dual-meet loss for the Rams in 47 matches, covering more than five years. In the many highlights of the Mid-Penn showdown was Jon Crawford's heroic overtime decision over Walt Peppelman who is the reigning PIAA bronze medalist. Crawford's escape with 12 seconds left forced overtime and prevented what would have been a 26-24 CD victory. Crawford's takedown (with less than six seconds remaining) **handed LD the win.**"

In a **51-16** triumph over Susquenita Eddie Neiswender (152) had a pin and Jarred Kane wrapped up his opponent in a technical fall.

On **February 1** Peter Kulp (119) had a 20-4 technical fall at Cocalico at the quarter-finals of the District 3AAA Team Championships. Nick Kristich (112) pinned in 1:13 minutes.

The **2006 yearbook** did not include scores in their publication; however, the photography is sharp, so if you just like to see pictures of wrestlers and have no interest in the scores, the *2006 Falconaire* is for you!

2006–2007 *(Record 15-2)*

Row 1: Danny Vance, Taylor Rudy, Peter Kulp, Jonathan Crawford, Jacob Bashore, Taylor Stuart, Zach Barrick, Blaine Shutt, Matt Kiessling, Mike English.

Row 2: Nick Semancik, Jason Kane, Chad Savage, Matt Foreman, Jake Kiessling, Mitch Walters, Josh Gipe, Jarred Kane, Kevin Gearhart.

Row 3: Kyle Wright, Matt Wallace, Eddie Neiswender, Nyles Rife, Jimmy Miller, Jared Phoenix, Eric Geesaman, Dalton Tonkin, Tyler Watts. (Missing: Nick Kristich, Justin Crawford, and Garrett Harner.)

Coach Cassel noted, "The 2006 and 2007 teams in many ways remind me of LD's 1964 and 1965 teams when the Falcons dominated everyone by winning every tournament and had the longest winning streak in the state—45 wins!"

LD has **two District 3 dual meet championships—the undefeated 19-0 1995 team and the 2007 team that was undefeated at 14-0.** The 2007 team also was Lower Dauphin's first PIAA state dual meet qualifier, but this saw many changes during the years. The only other qualifying team was 2009. That team entered the district tournament with a 20-1 record and finished 3rd place. That was the first year that District 3 sent the top 3 teams to state championship. Even though eliminated, they finished 23-3—the most wins by a team in LD history.

In **December 2006** against Middletown, LD won seven of the first 11 bouts and cruised to a pivotal **36-22** Mid-Penn Division win over Middletown. *The Sun* reported, "Waiting in the wings in the final weight class was District 3 AAA champ Jarred Kane, and while Middletown could muster only eight points in the next two bouts, Kane was awarded a forfeit."

On **December 21**, LD registered nine pins on its way to a rout—a **60-9** wrestling victory over **Red Land**. This annihilation of Red Land **left the Falcons in complete control of the Mid-Penn Conference Commonwealth Division**. The Falcons next won a showdown victory over the Rams, after Jarred Kane's eye-opening 9-2 decision at 140 over Walter Peppelman (Central Dauphin), the returning PIAA runner-up. CD's Tony Dallago escaped Jake Kiessling to tie the match. The next six bouts went to L.D. which built a 33-3 lead, cruising to the end.

Commonwealth crown

...was simply look-...to get on the mats ...in a competitive Falcons performed ...nderstatement, as ...ch has outscored ...l and are the only ...team in the Mid-

...on just a six-point ...hrough Thursday's ...ook the opening ...s via a major deci-...eiswender put the ...nt with a 17-5 tech

...k on top after a 7-5 ...n LD's Kevin Ger-...n midway through ...a 5-2 decision.

...CHAMPS
...8-2

TECH FALL - Lower Dauphin's Eddie Neiswender helped LD win the Mid-Penn Commonwealth Division title with a 20-5 tech fall victory in Hershey on Thursday.

This was the 2nd year in a row that an LD wrestler defeated Peppleman, the 2-time state runner up, to defeat the Rams in a dual meet. Beaten by Crawford the year before (2005-06) in the final bout of the match and beaten by Kane in the first bout of the match. Both victories were on the Falcons' home mat.

On **January 31** the *Press and Journal* shouted that the *Falcons had wrapped up the Commonwealth crown*, and for the 7th time this season the Falcons scored **50 or more** team points.

At the AAA District Championship finals against four-time champion Cumberland Valley, Kristich had turned the lesson of that loss into a virtual meet-clenching victory when he pinned Busler. (The *Press & Journal* noted the goals the team had made in November, ultimately resulting in a **perfect 14-0 record and both titles**.)

The Falcons toppled CV, finishing unbeaten, topping Middletown and CD for the second time. "Months ago in November Coach Ed Neiswender and his squad had set their sights on some lofty goals—including a Commonwealth division crown and Division 3 gold, and now they had achieved both."

The Falcons assured at least a tie for the Division title with a **43-22** victory over **Cedar Cliff with pins from Kristich, Neiswender, and Phoenix**, then took a 15-0 lead on Kulp's major decision, Crawford's technical fall, and Kristich's pin.

Eleven Falcons qualified for Sectionals and came home with three Sectional Champions: Jarred Kane, Jon Crawford, and Kevin Gerhart. Kane and Crawford continued on to win District Crowns.

February 4th's *Patriot News* headlined "**District 3-AAA Wrestling Team Champions: Lower Dauphin wraps up AAA crown**," in coverage by master sportswriter Rod Frisco. "… the pain that has been accessory to Kristich for nearly a year was exorcised…last night. At the District 3-AAA competition, the undefeated Falcons (14-0) turned Middletown back **36-26**, edged Central Dauphin, **33-29**, then cruised to a **34-21** title win over four-time champ Cumberland Valley, delivering their first district title since 1995." Simply put, CV head coach noted, "Lower Dauphin beat us because they were the better team—tonight."

But that was not the end of it.

The 2006-2007 team set an LD record by **qualifying 5 wrestlers** to compete at the state championships. This same team tied another record with **3 state medalists**.

The February 10th *Patriot News* screamed, "LD LOCKDOWN: LD's Jarred Kane, firms up a fall at 140 pounds, but the Falcons lost **41-13** to Nazareth in the PIAA Championships quarterfinals."

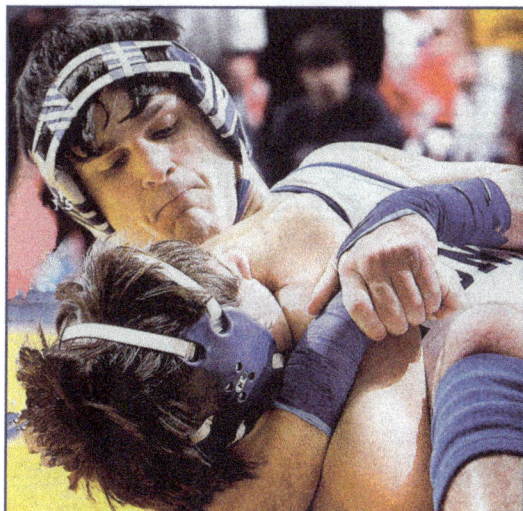

BIG OPPONENT - Lower Dauphin's Dalton Tonkin wrestles at the District 3-AAA tournament at Hersheypark Arena on Friday.

won his first two matches via decision and pinfall before losing to eventual 130-pound champ Tyler Nauman of Middletown.

Jason Kane won a 10-5 decision over Manheim Township's Tim Duke in first round consolations at 135

pounds. Eddie Neiswender Jr., won a forfeit in first-round consolations at 152 pounds. Dalton Tonkin lost his first-round match at 215 pounds, but then won a forfeit and a 13-1 major decision over CD East's Kenny Terry.

Dalton Tonkin on the right in dark uniform

February 28: "Jarred Kane and Jonathan Crawford Claim District 3 Crowns." With undefeated Lower Dauphin slowly strengthening its grip on the District 3 AAA Wrestling Team Championships final against CV, LD rebounded nicely from its second-round defeat to eventual champion Nazareth in the PIAA Class AAA Team.

Four of the Birds earned a spot at the District III Southcentral Regional Championships: Kane, Crawford, Barrick and Gerhart. Those four settled for a third (Crawford), fifth (Kane), and eighth (Gearhard) place finishes two weeks later at the PIAA State Championships.

The headline announced that the **Raiders and Falcons Own Section II!** Middletown crowned the most Section II Champions with five winners. Wednesday's headline shouted "Middletown & LD send five each to PIAA." A secondary title followed: "LD's Kane and Crawford win District 3 titles." The Falcons broke another record at the above District tournament, advancing five wrestlers to the PIAA tournament for the first time in team history where they finished with the second-most team points.

To cap it off, District 3 coaches named LD's Ed Neiswender as Coach of the Year and three Falcons placed, with Jon Crawford as LD's top finisher with a third place medal.

2007–2008 *(Record 15-3)*

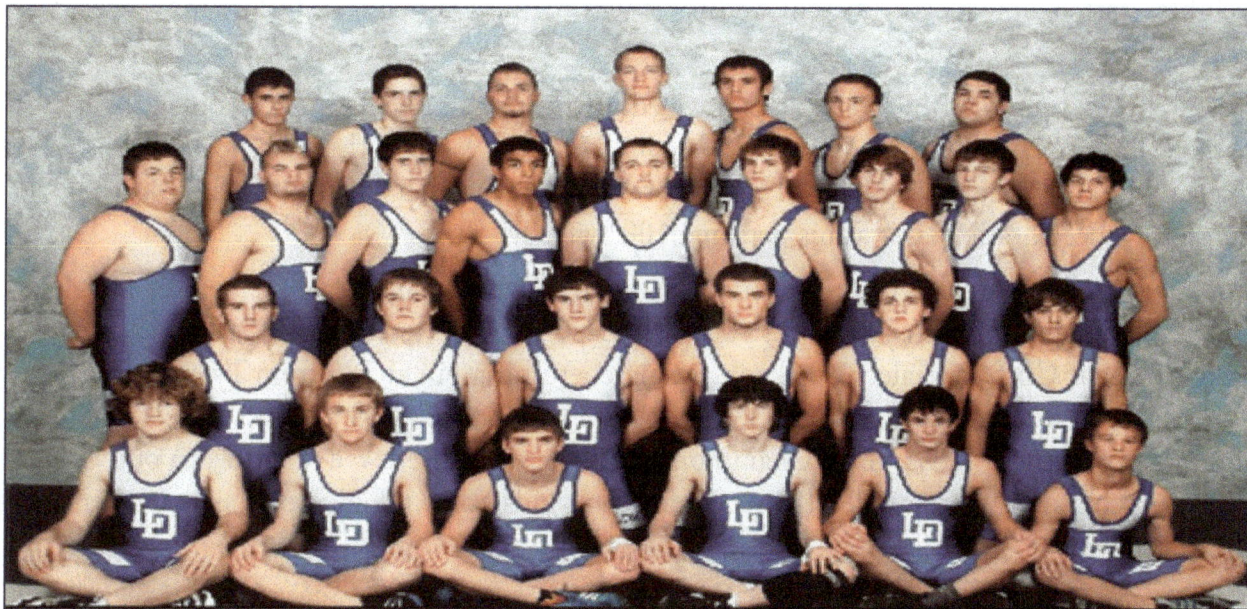

PIAA's Roster for 2007-2008:

Row 1: Jason Kane, Taylor Stuart, Zach Barrick, Blaine Shutt, Calvin Wright, Robbie Higgins.

Row 2: Jake Kiessling, Matt Foreman, Mike English, Ed Neiswender, Garrett Harner, Jake Bashore.

Row 3: Tyler Watts, Ryne Johnson, Andrew Bath, Chad Savage, Kyle Wright, Danny Vance, Ryan Boline, Kyle Stauffer, Nick Kristich.

Row 4: Nick Vozzella, Eric LaFleur, Matt Wallace, David Hahn, Tim Gamber, Nyles Rife, Paco Ramos.

Thursday, December 20, 2007, LD opened by drubbing Red Land **63-6**.

Against CD's formidable team, according to Sportswriter Rod Frisco, the biggest match was at 130 when Nick Kristich wrestled a smooth, solid match to score a 7-1 decision over PIAA medalist and 3-AAA runner-up Kenny Stank.

Two days later, Kristich marked his **100th win** at the match against Cumberland Valley.

From *The Falcon Grappler*, "The Coaches' Corner" …Wow, did these guys ever impress everyone by the way they worked and put together a very tough team …perhaps over-achievers. Even the coach found himself saying, "I can't believe you did that."

First-time varsity included Calvin Wright, 25 wins; Blaine Shutt, 20; Mike English, 17: Chad Savage, 25; Matt Wallace, 23; and Tyler Watts, 24. The regulars kept pace with Taylor Stuart, 31; Zach Barrick, 25; Nick Kristich, 37; Jason Kane, 31; and Eddie Neiswender, 28. Most of the matches were won by pins. The Seniors alone had 96 falls among them while **Nick Kristich shattered LD's fall records** with his deadly cross face cradle.

Two very inexperienced freshmen (David Hahn and Tim Gamber), as well as the heavier weights, started almost every match. And there was Blaine Shutt, a true 112 pounder who wrestled most of his matches at 125.

At the beginning of the season, LD traveled to Cumberland Valley "for a nonleague contest (which) left the fans wanting more." The Falcons won **30-29**, but with much post-match fodder to clean up. A particular highlight of the event was **Nick Kristich's** breaking a 24-24 deadlock that led to a celebration later as his personal **100**th victory.

Always reliable sportswriter Rod Frisco featured LD in the *Sports* supplement of January 18, "Lower Dauphin hasn't yielded its 2007 District 3-AAA Wrestling title yet. …down 13-0 early to **Cedar Cliff**, the Falcons picked up a match-turning pin at 285 from Tyler Watts and a key decision from Zach Barrick at 119 to stop the Colts **38-22**. LD all but secured a second straight trip to the 3-AAA Team Champions…." "We're not tired. We're not worn out," LD Coach Ed Neiswender reminded the reporters. "Our kids know the big goals are at the end of the season…."

There was little doubt that LD had the better matchups, something Cedar Cliff Coach Rapsey recognized in noting, "There's no way we were going to win a 7-7 match, not with LD's ability to pin." A fair warning.

Frisco's narrative continued, "The Colts got off to a fine start at 171, and Cedar Cliff's Dan Schreffler turned in a pin in 3:37 over David Hahn. CC followed with Tom Heckman's 12-6 decision over Tim Gamber and 3-AAA champion Keith Dickey's 13-4 major win over Matt Wallace. This not only gave the Colts a 13-0 lead but produced genuine eccentricity. With 17 seconds gone in the third period and Dickey leading 9-3, Wallace took an injury timeout after hitting his head…. At that point, match official Rick Trimmer called Dickey over and raised his hand for the default. But Neiswender and Wallace, stunned by the action, said that Wallace could continue. Trimmer reversed his decision, citing the rule that says (only) a doctor, and not a certified trainer, can make the stoppage decision. Following all the fuss, the bout ended with a win by the Falcons **38** to the Colts **22**.

Nick Kristich was named to *The Patriot-News Big 14 Wrestling Team*. While he had yet to qualify for the PIAA Championships, eighteen of his 19 pins occurred in the first periods with the average length of his pins at 56 seconds!

At the end of the season the (defending champions, 14-2) Falcons had to scrap against Dallastown (7-6), getting a key pin at 215 from Matt Wallace to advance to the quarterfinals.

The team finished 15-3 but was bumped from the district playoffs by a **very close** loss to runner-up Cumberland Valley. The LD team had worked hard to rebuild itself and to make its own mark in the history of LD wrestling. It was one tough team.

Individually, Nick Kristich was third at the PIAA state championships with a 37-2 record. His only losses were to nationally-ranked Jordan Oliver in the state semifinals. **Nick broke LD's fall season record at 28 and the career record with 90 falls.**

Nick also became LD's second 100 career match winner with 122 wins. Other state qualifiers with Nick were juniors Taylor Stuart and Jason Kane.

Kane and Nick Kristich were champions at the sectional tournament. In consolation finals the team did not lose a match and came away with seven 3rd place finishers.

Mid-Penn all-stars included Taylor Stuart, Nick Kristich, Jason Kane, Mike English, Eddie Neiswender, and Tyler Watts, by now **all familiar names** to sports readers.

LD's final dual meet this year was also the last coached by Ed Neiswender. It ended perfectly with his **100th win as coach.** Congrats to "Neis" for his unorthodox journey through a memorable, successful career (1) beginning by following all of the meets in which his older brother had competed, (2) being a grappler himself as part of the second set of LD's glory years, then (3) as a successful head coach at his Alma Mater, including coaching his own son.

The wrestling year closed with an agreement to use seeding in one half of District 3, Class AAA. LD scored a pair of titles from senior Nick Kristich (29-1) at 130 and junior Jason Kane (26-4) at 135. In addition, LD's Kristich earned a bronze medal at States.

The printed Wrestling program for this year garners kudos with its appealing inclusion of a team picture from **each decade** of LD wrestling.

Later, a newspaper headline announced *Raiders and Falcons Own Section II!* Middletown was crowned with the **most Section II Champions** with five winners and a main headline shouted "Middletown & LD send five each to PIAA." A secondary title followed: "LD's Kane and Crawford win District 3 titles."

The Falcons also broke another record at the above District tournament, **advancing five wrestlers to the PIAA tournament for the first time in team history.** There, they finished with the second-most team points.

To cap it off, District 3 coaches named LD's Ed Neiswender as Coach of the Year and three Falcons placed, with Jon Crawford as LD's top finisher with a third place medal.

And yes, all of them—black-haired together—celebrated Crawford, Gearhart, and Kane's capture of titles at the end of the season.

2008–2009 *(Record 23-3)*

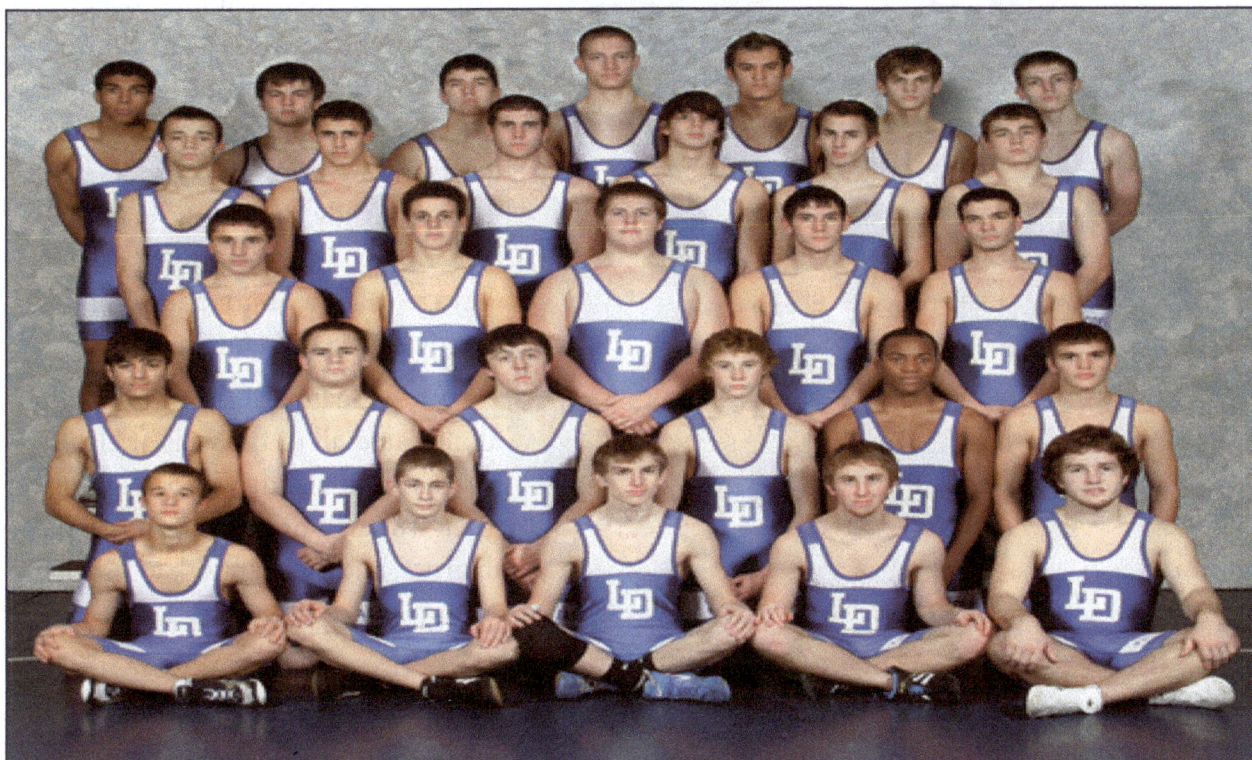

Team Members (These following names are from the PIAA list; they are not in order of wrestlers as they are shown here, rather, they are in alphabetical order): Zach Barrick, Jacob Bashore, Andrew Bath, Ryan Boline, Anthony Camasta, Justin Crawford, Hayben Ehrlich, Mike English, Tim Gamber, Jon Germany, David Hahn, Garrett Harner, Robby Higgins, Jason Kane, Gavin Miller, Taylor Mozingo, Daniel Mummau, Aaron Naccarato, Marco Palermo, Jesse Rhinesmith, Zachary Rinaldi, Chad Savage, Kyle Savage, Joe Scerbo, Jack Shope, Blaine Shutt, Zachary Smith, Kyle Stauffer, Taylor Stuart, Danny Vance, Nick Vozzella, and Tyler Waltz. Perhaps at one of the Wrestlers' Reunions a correct list identifying each wrestler can be made and given to the Wrestling Boosters and members of this team. There is no doubt you will all remember every name!

January 2009, *Patriot-News*

On December 16 (2008) Rod Frisco of *The Patriot-News* light-heartedly had projected that Lower Dauphin would rank third behind Central Dauphin and Middletown and would be followed by Cedar Cliff. A day or so later, in the same humor mode, Frisco noted, "Oops. It looks like everyone was a little too quick to declare Neiswender retired at the end of last season; he's had a change of heart and returns as head coach. He has good reason: The Falcons, while thin at a couple of weights, are still a **potent dual team starting eight seniors.**" Three days later was the headline "**LD reaches 10-0.**"

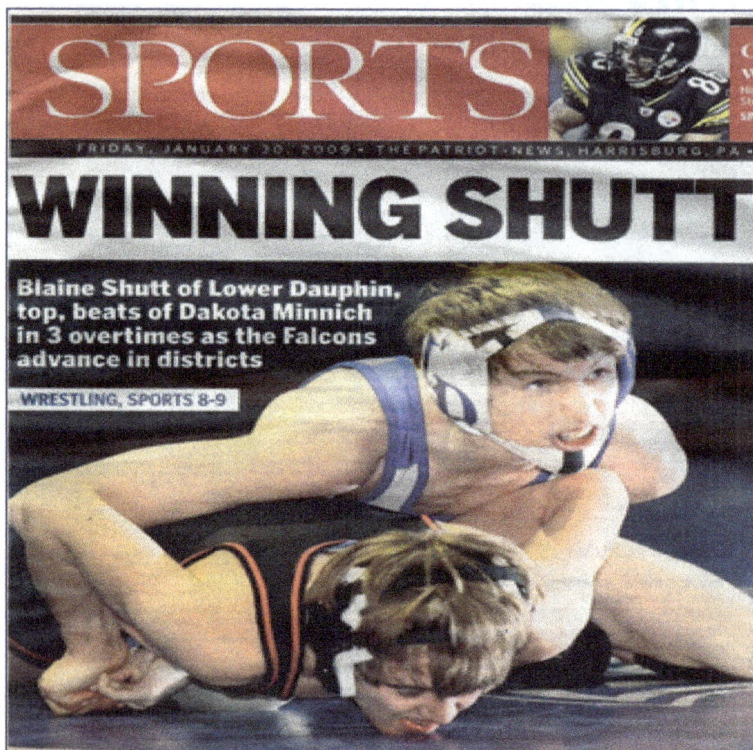

SPORTS

FRIDAY, JANUARY 30, 2009 • THE PATRIOT-NEWS, HARRISBURG, PA.

WINNING SHUTT

Blaine Shutt of Lower Dauphin,
top, beats of Dakota Minnich
in 3 overtimes as the Falcons
advance in districts

WRESTLING, SPORTS 8-9

On January 7th the Falcons had a solid **55-12** triumph over Mechanicsburg. This was followed by a **62-16** drubbing of Harrisburg. At Mechanicsburg the following had pins—Justin Crawford, Garrett Harner, Andy Bath, Tim Gamber and Robby Higgins, while Chad Savage, Blaine Shutt, and Zack Barrick racked up technical falls.

On January 10th Lower Dauphin dominated all of the weight classes against Red Land, **57-15**, bagging their **18th win** of the season. Barrick, Harner, and Naccarato had pins.

In an insightful commentary Rod Frisco wrote, ".....we're not bedazzled by LD's fat record ...but **we are impressed with Lower Dauphin's balance.**"

Regarding the drubbing by Central Dauphin, Coach Ed Neiswender said, "The fight was there. Our kids battled in every match. We told the kids that we were going to go strength-on-strength tonight, and whatever happens, happens."

Not surprising, then, that as the Falcons neared their goal, they rolled over Hempfield (**34-22**) which propelled LD into the semi-finals for the **third time** in four seasons.

A highlight for this team was Blaine Shutt's defeating Dakota Minnich in **3 overtimes** as the Falcons advanced. "Battles were everywhere," noted Rod Frisco, as LD held off Middletown, "...there was a bunch of good wrestling.... Frisco concluded, "The Falcons do not always win—it just seems that way."

LD was eliminated from the PIAA AAA Team Wrestling Championships on February 3 by Blue Mountain, **38-30.** While LD won six bouts, only one was against an Eagle with a winning record and that came at a key moment in the match when Blaine Shutt posted a 3-2 win, his 16th straight win, hiking his record, 29-1.

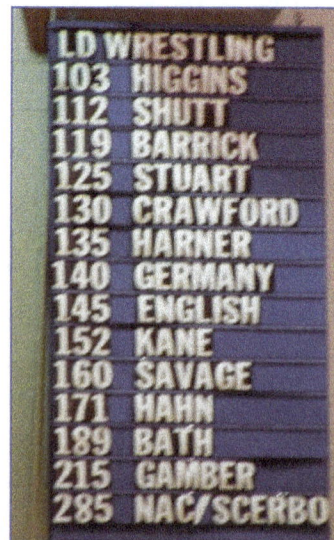

LD WRESTLING	
103	HIGGINS
112	SHUTT
119	BARRICK
125	STUART
130	CRAWFORD
135	HARNER
140	GERMANY
145	ENGLISH
152	KANE
160	SAVAGE
171	HAHN
189	BATH
215	GAMBER
285	NAC/SCERBO

A compliment followed from Rod Frisco in his column (February 14), congratulating Central Dauphin, yet lauding Lower Dauphin as he recalled their history, "…Lower Dauphin was essentially a start-up at the beginning, kicking off its varsity

Blaine Shutt and Robby Higgins, wrestling teammates and best friends

program in 1960. **The Falcons just might have developed better and more rapidly than any other school in District 3 history,** this year sending **two** to States, Jason Kane and Mike English."

The following is from an original article published in the *Grappler*, Nov. 20, 2009: Last year the **08-09 team set a LD dual meet win record with 23 wins. Jarred Kane and Nick Kristich were the first LD wrestlers to have over 100 career wins. Jarred** was tied (as of this date) with only a few wrestlers, by winning 3 sectional championships and 2 district titles. He is also **the first at Lower Dauphin to qualify for the state championships three times. Nick Kristich** set the season fall record at 28 falls and the **career fall record at an incredible 90 falls.** Amen.

(Thanks to whoever is responsible for the exemplary wrestling program for this year—creative and complimentary to various individual achievements. It is a keeper! As is the Banquet Program!! True Evidence of *Falcon Pride!*)

2009–2010 *(Record 16-5)*

Row 1: Hayden Fox, Sean Maguire, Spencer Rhoad, Dan Mummau, Gavin Miller, Robbie Higgins, Blaine Shutt, Dalton Deimler

Row 2: James McElwee, Ryan Gelnett, Patrick Sharkey, Sean Birriel, Jesse Rhinesmith, Taylor Mazingo, Aaron Naccarato, Kyle Savage, Jack Shope

Row 3: Zach Smith, Ryan Lewis, Jon Hahn, Kyle Stauffer, Nick Vozzella, Andrew Bath, Jon Germany, David Hahn, Tim Gamber, Joe Scerbo, Matt Rico

The Varsity Roster as listed by PIAA also includes the names of Michael Joyce and Zachary Rinaldi.

With a young team, wrestling started off the 2009-2010 season on a strong foot. Lower Dauphin placed **ninth out of 14 teams** in the Manheim Central Holiday Wrestling Tournament on December 29-30, led by runner-up finishes by junior Robby Higgins and senior Blaine Shutt. The Falcons totaled 78.5 points. Easton won the team title with a score of 193.

Next at Conestoga Valley, L.D.'s Tim Gamber took third place at 285 with an overtime decision and David Hahn took fourth.

In Mid-Penn action, Cedar Cliff handed LD a **52-13** loss on January 7, 2010 in a Commonwealth Division match, and the Falcons fell to Mechanicsburg, **40-19**, in a non-divisional bout.

It was also during the early years that Lower Dauphin began garnering huge fan support, both at home and away games. Some of the same individuals who doubted the team in the beginning became the sport's most avid fans. Thus, even sixty years after the program was initiated, Lower Dauphin wrestling was as exciting as ever.

On Saturday, January 9, 2010, in the first round of the Hamburg Hawk Mountain Duals against Abington, LD recorded the school's 600th wrestling victory, 59-12.

In the match that produced the actual 600th win, LD had pins from Robby Higgins, Blaine Shutt, Kyle Savage, Jon Germany, Andrew Bath, and Tim Gamber; a technical fall from Kyle Stauffer; and decisions from Jack Shope at 152 and Aaron Naccarato. Joe Scerbo won both of his matches.

Heavyweight Tim Gamber pins CD East's Darius Solomon in Lower Dauphin's MPC Commonwealth Division victory Dec. 17. Photo: Geno Simonetti.

From *The Sun*, 2010: "Along with cheering about the wrestling squad's current athletes, this year Lower Dauphin wrestling is **celebrating two milestones**—the 50th anniversary of the school, its own 50th anniversary—and, its 600th win."

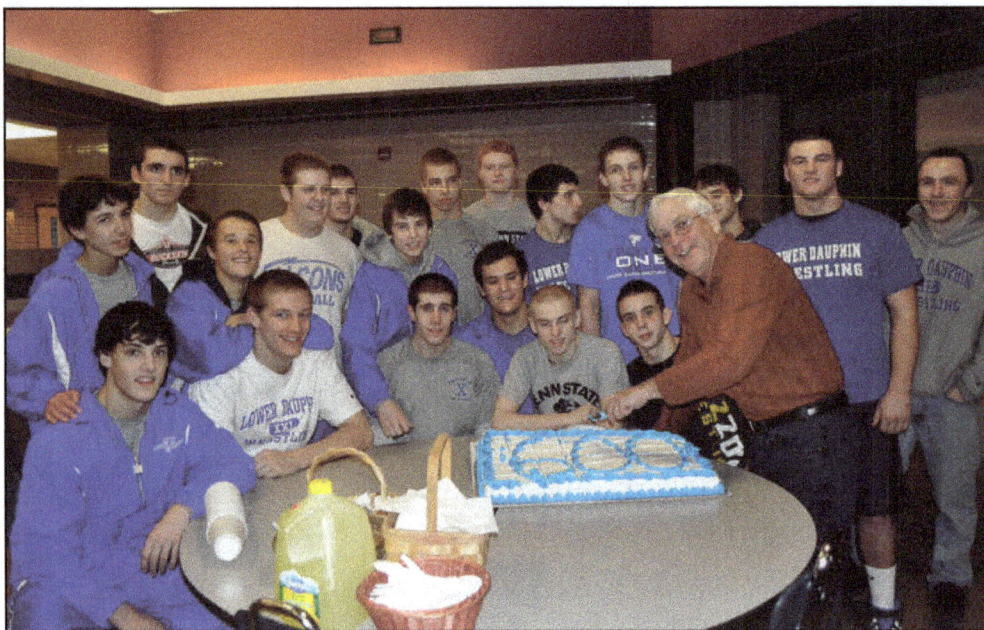

In the title match at 135, LD fell behind 22-0 before senior Jon Germany began the comeback at 160 with a 6-2 decision. Junior Kyle Stauffer picked up a decision at 171 but Hamburg answered with a decision at 189 to retain its 19-point lead.

That's when junior Tim Gamber (215) began a string of four straight pins that put LD on top. Junior Aaron Naccarato at 285 and sophomore Daniel Mummau at 103 brought the tie within a point at 25-24. That set the stage for undefeated junior Robby Higgins to put LD ahead for good with his third pin of the day. A forfeit at 119 was followed by senior Blaine Shutt's 4-3 decision at 125 to assure the win. Shutt had two pins, raising his own overall record.

Blaine Shutt '10

January 14, 2010. Lower Dauphin improved to 3-1 in the Mid-Penn Conference Commonwealth Division with a 52-15 verdict over Harrisburg. The Falcons scored the first 30 points as Joe Scerbo ignited the meet with a pin at 215. Dan Mummau, Robby Higgins, Jonathan Hahn and Jack Shope also registered pins for the Falcons, while Tim Gamber, Blaine Shutt, Gavin Miller, Jon Germany, and Kyle Stauffer posted decisions.

Above is Blaine Shutt wrestling Jordan Murray from Middletown; Blaine later defeated Murray at **Sectionals and at Districts,** for a total of three wins.

Blaine is LD's only professional wrestler, in itself a distinction. LD has had any number of wrestlers compete at the collegiate level, but only Blaine has made wrestling a successful career.

Lower Dauphin's Dan Mummau, above, pins Harrisburg's Mike Duncan during the Falcons' 52-15 victory Jan. 14. Lower Dauphin's Jack Shope, right, registers a pin over Jarrell Aikens on Jan. 14. Photos: Geno Simonetti.

Central Dauphin's 49-12 wrestling victory over Lower Dauphin on Saturday, January 16, put the Falcons in a must-win situation against Middletown on Thursday, January 21, to finish third in the Mid-Penn Conference Commonwealth Division. Middletown's Shyheim Brown defeated previously unbeaten Robby Higgins, 2-1 in three overtimes at 112. Next, at 119, freshman Nick Varndell improved to 16-2 with a 2-1 decision over our Blaine Shutt.

Following were two forfeits and by the time Kyle Savage scored a 3-2 decision over Colton Peppelman at 140, LD was in a 24-0 hole. The Falcons' other points came from Jon Germany, with a major decision at 152; Kyle Stauffer and David Hahn won with decisions at 171 and 189, respectively.

District 3-AAA Wrestling Rankings in the *Patriot News* included only one Falcon. Blaine Shutt ranked third in the 119 weight.

January 28, 2010. LD completed a 4-3 season in the Commonwealth Division under first-year coach **Josh Lininger**, and on **January 30** LD finished a close second to its host Elizabethtown.

Five Falcons reached the finals and four were victorious. Champions were Dan Mummau, Robby Higgins, Jon Germany, and Tim Gamber. Finishing second, after dropping a 2-1 final decision, was Blaine Shutt.

A compliment goes to the Booster Club whose 2010 Wrestling Banquet printed program was particularly well-done with its lists of records. Would that every year's team had been so honored with the listing of individual tournament results: Mid-Penn All Stars, Most Takedowns, Most Pins, Fastest Pins, Most Escapes, Most 2-Point Nearfalls, Most Reversals and Most Team Points Scored (Tim Gamber, Robby Higgins, Blaine Shutt).

600 Wins for LD Wrestling Program

Self-effacing, Coach Lininger's take on this achievement is that while six-hundred wins was the important number for the Falcons this season, they viewed it first as achieving a **team goal.** Lininger noted, "Reaching 600 is a testament to the program. The coaches before me did a fabulous job of building the path to success. **We are here to carry it forward.**"

AAA Sectional Titles To LD's Shutt, Higgins

Lower Dauphin senior Blaine Shutt and junior Robby Higgins were crowned District 3-AAA Sectional champs Saturday, Feb. 20, at CD East on a day that saw nine Sun Country wrestlers extend their seasons. Next up is this weekend's South Central Regionals in Hersheypark Arena.

Shutt needed four overtimes before knocking off top-seeded Nick Varndell of Central Dauphin, 3-2, to capture the 119-pound title.

Higgins also needed extra time to get past CD's Shyheim Brown, 2-1, in the semifinals before taking down top-seeded Dan King of Susquehanna Twp., 3-1.

Both Shutt and Higgins [lo]st 2-1 decisions to Varn[de]ll and Brown, respective[ly] [b]ack on Jan. 16 in a dual [me]et.

[L]D's Kyle Savage, a [seni]or who wrestled most of [the] season at 145, finished [secon]d at 140 after Mar[k] [C]lement of Cedar Cliff [beat] him, 3-2.

[T]hird-place finishers [were L]D's Joe Scerbo at 215 [and Jo]n Germany at 152, [Pal]myra's Jake Martin [...] while settling for

Lower Dauphin's Robby Higgins registers a tense 2-1 victory over CD's Shyheim Brown in the 112-pound semifinals. Photo: Geno Simonetti.

With the indication that Shutt and Higgins were best friends, as well as teammates in high school, this headline is even more an achievement to remember!

A tribute to all such wrestling friendships!

I am a Lower Dauphin Wrestler: This is My Story
Champions All : A Tribute to Casey from Melley
——*Coach Ed Neiswender*

Wrestlers are the toughest athletes I know. They can also be the most passionate. Casey Koons died in an automobile accident his junior year during wrestling season. I could write volumes on how we struggled to keep going and make it through that season. Casey was one tough brute.

It's strange how close you become to the people you beat up and get beat up by. In our sport this person is our workout partner. With the loss of Casey, however, we all were hit unexpectedly hard. Somehow we made it through the season, but not without shedding tears at every practice. The following year when the season rolled around again, we were without our great friend, teammate, and tough wrestler. It was impossible to not be constantly aware that this would have been Casey's senior year.

One of Casey's best friends and workout partner, Rob Melly, had not been himself since the accident that took Casey's life, as Rob emotionally struggled through that first year. The following year we still felt the loss of Casey as everything was a reminder. Rob in particular continued to mourn. I believe he worked even harder as wrestling became the catharsis. This, along with the intensity of all who had been close to Casey, left Rob struggling through the season, yet we went on to take our first district championship in four years—but that was only the beginning.

Winning districts put Rob in the state tournament. He was two and out, with two close matches.

The following, however, is what the spectators did not know. We coaches were on the floor awaiting the call over the PA system for Rob's consolation mat assignment when we realized that Rob had disappeared from his spot where he had been warming up. I said, "Where the heck is Rob?"

We looked around and spotted him in the stands! Following our first reaction of panic, we saw he had made it to the mat in time. There he wrestled a tough match … but lost.

Much later I asked him, "Rob, what the heck were you doing in the stands?" He quietly replied, "I knew this might be my last match at states, so I went up to the stands where I had placed Casey's wrestling shoes and put them on so they could touch the state championship mats where I was wrestling, where Casey would have been."

Wrestling's Cycles of Life:

▸ *Seated is Superintendent David Emerich who introduced the sport of Wrestling in the First Year of LD*

▸ *Junior High Schoolers who became livelong members and supporters of Lower Dauphin Wrestling: our dear friend and contributor to this book, the late Dan Dorsheimer '66, flanked by wrestling pals, teammates, and lifelong friends, Marty Remsberg '66 and Keith Smith '67*

▸ *Left, Paul Hoffman, Faculty and faithful follower of his Junior High 8th graders.*

2010–2024 ✦ *Endorsing the Dynasty*

History:

Sports Writers and Newspaper Coverage from:

- ✎ *The Falcon Flash* (LDHS)

- ✎ *The Sun* (Hummelstown)

- ✎ *The Patriot News* (Harrisburg)

We live in an area that respects newspaper reporters and, in this particular instance, their Sports Writers. From its first wrestling match, Lower Dauphin High School has been covered by the local and city newspapers. On the following page are the names of those publications that we found in our quest for coverage of school sports, and we list here the names of writers we culled from scrapbooks and news clippings, both in the school newspaper and local and city papers. We are indebted to all of them.

We are, however, most grateful to *The Sun* in Hummelstown for providing electronic access to all newspaper issues since 2016 and for microfiche access to earlier issues of the publication. These were made available for our use by the Hummelstown Historical Society through the aid of Chad Lister.

Student Sports Writers

Most of the following reporters were on the staff of the school newspaper "The Falcon Flash" and a few others were contributors to the local and city newspapers during their years at LD. Year of graduation is provided for those whose names are listed in the LD Alumni Association Directory. (We had no source to confirm graduation dates.)

Tyler Angeloff '06
Barb Baxter '78
Steve Bobb
Dave Bowser '74
Karen Camasta '80
Martha Ann Costik '76
George Cruys '70
Ron Cruys '66
Patti Detweiler '80
Joe Elliott
Eric Fluman '78

Barbara Gebhart '82
Joe Heinzman '65
Dave John 2013
David M. Jones
Jennie Jones '94
Brad Kane '09
Joanna Manders '97
Tammy Manoogian '80
John Neidinger
Jim Neidinger '73
Tom Orsini '72

John Pagano '71
Jeff Peyton
Barbara Saylor '73
Bill Sheaffer
Dennis Shope '74
Bill Tonkin
John Tuscano
Amy Wallish '87
John Williams '66

Professional Sports Writers

This list was created mainly from the sports section of the Harrisburg daily newspapers and from the weekly local papers "The Sun" and the "Press and Journal." We have included the names we found.

Bob Black
James M. Bryant
Bruce Carey
John E. Crull
Jeremy Elliott
Chuck Ercole
Charley Frey
Rod Frisco
Marce Graybill

John C. Hartwell
Skip Hutter
Dave Jones
Tony Joseph
Mike Nortrup
Josh Orlandi
Ed Ponessa
Joe Sauffley
Daryl Simione

Geno Simonetti
Sean Simmers
John Tuscano
Drew Weidman

Behind the Scenes
Coach Ed Neiswender

It takes many people to make a successful wrestling program. Here we acknowledge many "behind the scenes" wrestling supporters through the years.

The first would be those who volunteered as members of the booster clubs which play a very important role in developing and rewarding our student athletes. Fundraising is an essential part of making this happen. It is by far the least "glamorous" aspect of a total team effort.

The boosters meet regularly, in season and out of season and a smooth running booster club works tirelessly inventing and organizing various fund raisers. You name it; we've probably tried it: Sub sales, candle sales, apparel sales, chicken BBQs, golf outings, wrestling tournaments, program sales, refreshment stands, basket bingo, where I was forced to be the "Price is Right" model and carry the baskets around to show to the bingo players. If you were one of those many volunteers, you know how much work it is. Although, we DO make it fun!

These efforts provided funding for wrestlers to participate in developmental activities such as the NHSCA national duals, the Disney duals, the NHSCA individual nationals, various MAWA and AAU tournaments, Fargo freestyle and Greco nationals, team camp, specialized camps, and numerous local tournaments. The Boosters also supply wrestling "spirit" apparel, which was sold at the matches.

At the end of the year the Boosters hold a banquet to celebrate the season and to honor the graduating seniors. They also prepare for summer camp and any off-season tournaments the wrestlers may be participating in.

Parents, especially those involved in the Booster Club, are an essential part of our program. It is especially helpful to the coaches when parents get involved in the wrestlers' weight management. Being a parent of athletes, I also know how many miles one can put on a car! I was fortunate to have parents who carpooled and put together some outstanding cheering sections at home and away. Several parents took vacation time from work, and helped drive wrestlers to team camp. Most importantly, the many fundraisers we have during the year would not be possible without their help.

Lower Dauphin wrestling also has a large alumni backing. We have our "die hard" supporters who are at almost every match. We also have a variety of different graduation classes attending matches. We appreciate their support and their stopping by to say "Hi!" after the match. I want to give a shout out to the custodians as well. The mats must be cleaned and sanitized every day, as an outbreak of skin disease could affect the entire season! It is quite the chore to keep up with that massive wrestling room.

All of these persons, and, of course, the students, make up an awesome fan base. **I can sum this up with an example of one of the greatest matches I coached: LD vs CD 2006.** It seemed everyone in the area decided to attend this event day. By the time the national anthem was finished, I don't think there was a seat available! The staff was looking for places where people could stand. The school was turning people away. The score went back and forth with every match. It felt like 100 degrees in the gym. And just like a Hollywood movie, winning the match came down to the last two wrestlers! Not just any two wrestlers, but two who were ranked top in the state. Winner takes all! As if it couldn't get any better, the match went into overtime. The noise was so loud I could not communicate to my wrestler only a few feet away.

Then we got a takedown in overtime to win the match and the championship. **I must give compliments to our fans.** No one was ejected from the match. I did not hear vulgar language or vulgar cheers—just "good old" cheers from both sides, supporting the wrestlers. What an experience for our team, feeling the tremendous support of our fans!

Defeating CD—the last bout of the meet. Center, Coach Ed Neiswender.

HIGHLIGHTS OF THE MEETS: 2010-2024

2010–2011 (Record 6-4)

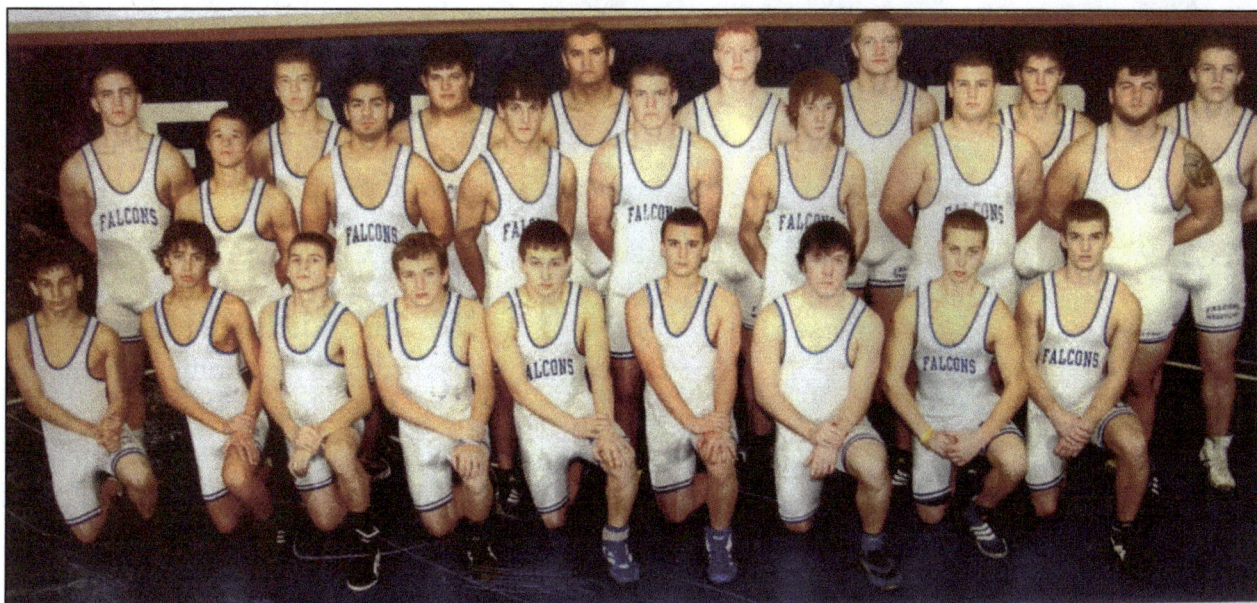

Row 1. Michael Gonzalez, Daniel Mumau, Dalton Deimler, Tyler Messick, Alexande
Nicholas Dippery, Jack Shope, Nate Miles, Sean Birrel.

Row 2. Robert Higgins, Matthew Rico, Jonathan Hahn, Patrick Sharkey, Jesse Rhinesmith,
Taylor Rice, Joseph Scerbo.

Row 3. Stanley Morril, Ryan Gelnet, Christian Brand, Timothy Gamber, Zachary Smith,
David Hahn, Matthew Rissmiller, Kyle Stauffer.

January 20, 2011. The Falcons had pins from David Hahn at 171, Kyle Stauffer at 189, and Tim Gamber at 285, along with a major decision from Dalton Deimler at 112.

January 27. Lower Dauphin spotted Red Land an 18-0 lead through five bouts, then scored 40 straight points for a **40-24** Mid-Penn Conference Keystone Division victory.

January 28. LD completed a 4-3 season in the Commonwealth Division under first-year coach Josh Lininger, and on January 30 LD finished a close second to its host Elizabethtown. Five Falcons reached the finals and four were victorious. Weight champions were Dan Mummau, Robby Higgins, Jon Germany, and Tim Gamber. Finishing second, after dropping a 2-1 final decision, was Blaine Shutt.

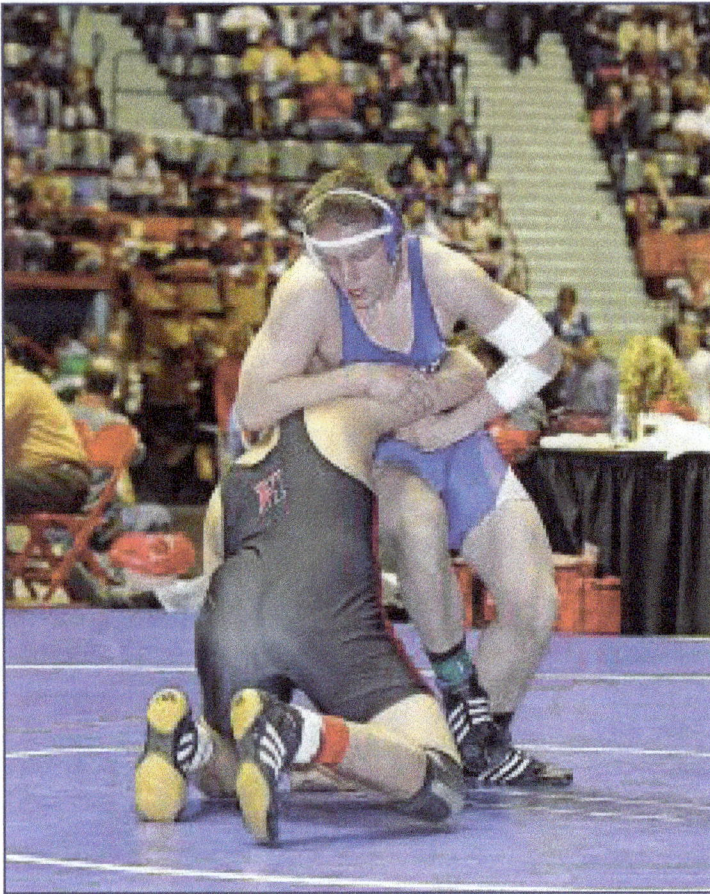

Lower Dauphin's Kyle Stauffer tries to free himself from the grasp of Hempfield's Nate Kulp during their 189-pound bout.

Photo: Geno Simonetti.

On Monday, **February 7**, Lower Dauphin defeated Hershey **59-12**; at the Sectionals, Lower Dauphin grabbed three runner-up finishes and two third-place slots.

LD Senior heavyweight **Tim Gamber** raised his record to 23-6 with a pair of pins before falling to Susquehanna Township in the finals at 285. At 119, Senior **Robby Higgins** (9-3) won over E-town, then pinned Susquehanna before being stopped by CD's Dippery.

The other LD Sectionals runner-up was senior **Kyle Stauffer** who fell to an injury in his 189 lb. title bout with CD's Kenny Courts after pinning Elizabethtown's Kyle Embly in 2:29 and upsetting Palmyra's Jake Lehman 13-1. Area third-place finishers were LD Junior Dan Mummau at 103 and senior David Hahn at 171. Mummau had opened with a 8-2 decision, lost to the eventual runner-up, and bounced back with a 7-0 win over Bradley Focht of Susquehanna and a pin in 2:30 over Jamie Lewis of E-town.

LD's **Hahn** took a similar path with a 10-7 decision over East Pennsboro, a 13-4 loss to eventual runner-up Tyler Rhoads of CD East, and a pair of pins. Meanwhile, Lower Dauphin senior **Kyle Stauffer** won five straight elimination bouts in the Class AAA South Central Regional to grab third place and **advance to the State Tournament**. That set up his third-place bout with Conestoga Valley's Delis Krupp, who was sporting a 36-6 record. Stauffer outlasted Krupp 11-8 to extend his season two more weeks and closed out the season with a 25-16 record.

2011–2012 *(Record 7-7)*

Row 1:   Aaron Gordon, Travis Morrill, Dalton Deimler, Ryan Gelnett, Zach Smith, Patrick Sharkey, Daniel Mummau, Christian Brand, Tyler Messick

Row 2:   Mike Gonzelez, JT Donnelly, Amanda Vale, Jordan Foreman, (Unknown), Calvin Nolt, (unknown), Alex Dill, Nick Dippery

Row 3:   (Unknown), Kalob Ware, Josh Gelnett, Lee Cassel, (Unknown), David Wuestner, Troy Spencer, Freddy Maines

As happens periodically in most school-level sports, this was a re-building year. The signature win came against Northern York County whom the Falcons defeated **33-29**. However, LD had seven **Section II place winners** in Dalton Deimler, Lee Cassel, Troy Spencer, Patrick Sharkey, David Wuestner, Christian Brand, and Zach Smith.

LD was especially busy during late December with two dual meets and a tournament within eight days. On December 21 Wilson came to Falconland and left with a tightly-contested **44-21** victory without head coach Josh Lininger, sidelined by a torn ACL.

Meanwhile, on December 22 the **6th grade wrestlers** were busy defeating Susquehanna Township 84-14. Among these young winners were those whose names would, in turn, become legendary in LD Wrestling. And among the confident high school JVs was **Amanda Vale** who at 106 took a third place against Elizabethtown.

In the 2010s, these two sisters were rightful members of the Falcon team. Amanda Vale was a member of the 2014-2015 squad and **Brianna (Bri) Vale** a member of the 2015-2016 squad. Both earned varsity letters and Bri was close to .500 her senior year (2016). She later wrestled at the college level.

Lower Dauphin's Daniel Mummau during the 120-pound match against Kennard-Dale

LD ran over Susquehanna Township **43-32** with **Patrick Sharkey** hammering his way to an 18-2 tech fall and **Ryan Gelnett** with his own 19-4 tech fall over Susquehanna. **Foreman** and **Deimler** pinned, giving the team early momentum that proved valuable. **Zach Smith** at 285 continued his impressive senior year with a fourth-place finish in the Manheim Central Tournament while Freshman Troy Spencer at 160 took sixth place.

February 9, 2012. Lower Dauphin drew an end to its mildly successful season with a thorough dismantling of Kennard-Dale. The Falcons strolled through their **65-15** win, which featured a 13-second fall by sophomore **J.T. Donnelly** (138), his second fall in less than a minute this year. **Lee Cassel** (126) and **Troy Spencer** (152) also recorded pins for LD. Josh Lininger's crew won four of its final five matches.

2012–2013 *(Record 5-7)*

Row 1: Calvin Nolt, Chase Mader, Peter Mummau, Jordan Foreman, Amanda Vale, Alex Dill, J. T. Donnelly.

Row 2: Troy Spencer, Kalob Ware, Kolby Straw, Tyler Messick, Nick Dippery, Josh Gelnett.

Row 3: Bailey Shutt, Freddy Maines, David Wuestner, Travis Morrill, Christian Brand, Omi Ramos, Lee Cassel, Caleb Koval.

Hummelstown Sun, December 13, 2012. **Bailey Shutt** (152) began his Lower Dauphin wrestling career with several statement wins in the Cumberland Valley Kickoff Classic. **This freshman battled throughout the weekend,** earning bronze and leading the Falcons to a 10th-place finish in the 16-team field.

Christian Brand (Hwt) took third place, while Travis Morrill (195) grabbed fourth. Other placers included Tyler Messick (145) and David Wuestner (182), both of whom brought in fifth-place finishes.

The Grappler, Volume I, Issue 1 noted, "Not knowing what to expect, we performed as well as we could have. None of our boys were seeded, so we hit the tough wrestlers early on and had to wrestle back to place."

The team then geared up for Hershey, a meet televised on the local ABC station.

333

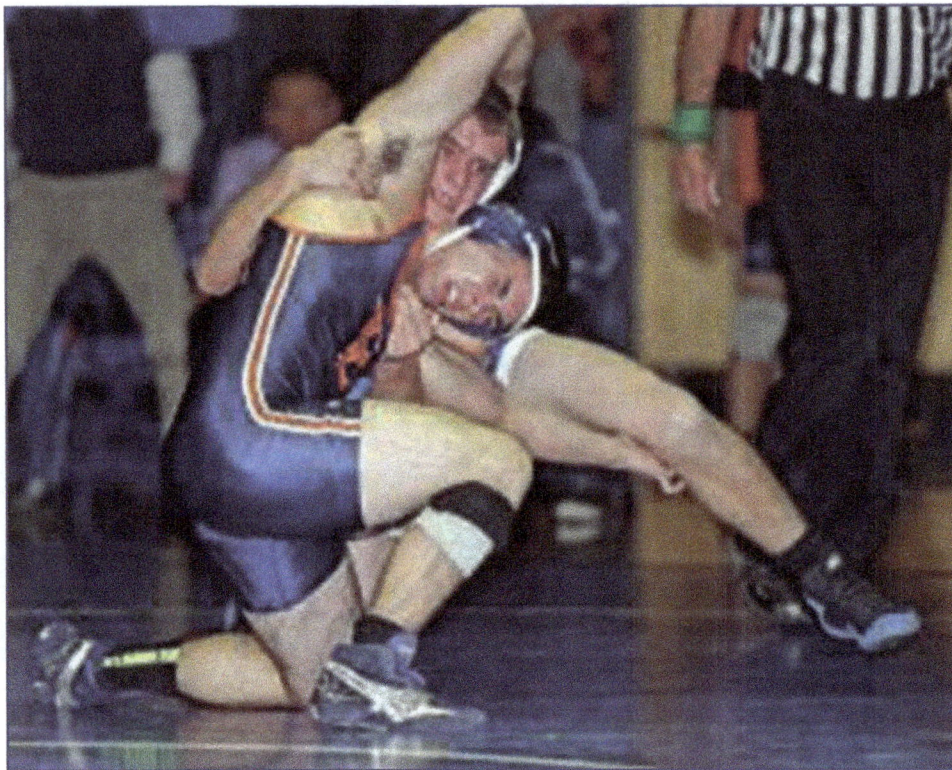

Above: Lower Dauphin's Troy Spencer and Hershey's Tyler Loraw go at it in the 170-pound match Thursday, **December 13.**   (Photo: Geno Simonetti)

On **December 20**, 2012, Joe Saufley wrote, "**Hershey** won its first match against Lower Dauphin in 17 years." He then neatly summed up Hershey's wrestling history against LD over the past two decades as "Unimpressive, Mediocre, Laughable...." *However,* the group of Trojan wrestlers that strode into Lower Dauphin High School last week were **not** joking around. They looked anything but mediocre. *And they certainly left quite an impression.*" The score was **38-20** led by second-year head coach Brandon Bucher and a fistful of gritty lightweights. Their rare triumph snapped the program's 17-year losing streak against the Falcons!

Lower Dauphin rebounded from its difficult loss to Hershey, scoring a **50-22** triumph over Susquehanna Twp. on Dec. 20. The match opened at 145, where senior Tyler Messick set the pace with a 6-4 decision. Bailey Shutt (152) and Kolby Straw (160) followed with pins. Troy Spencer (182) added six points, and Peter Mummau (106) earned a tech fall to cap the onslaught.

January 3, 2013. Joe Saufley reported, "While usually it is hard to find worth in defeat, LD's effort against the Mid-Penn Keystone kingpin **Cedar Cliff** is noteworthy. The wrestling crew managed to piece together its **best performance of the year,** capturing four of the first six bouts. While the Colt middleweights went on to secure a victory, sealing a **39-15** lead, this did not dampen the Falcon heavyweights who closed the match with a 14-point run—enjoyable for LD fans to watch."

January 17, 2013, again with **Joe Saufley** reporting. While his report was focused on Hershey's team who "has already exceeded expectations and defied history," Saufley gave plenty of written attention to Lower Dauphin even in their **loss against Middletown**, ending with "The match closed on a positive note for the Falcons. After Travis Morrill grabbed six points via forfeit, David Wuestner and Christian Brand pounded out a pair of pins."

January 24, 2013, *The Sun.* A week later, Saufley wrote, "The entire Lower Dauphin wrestling squad had good reason to celebrate a solid **59-9** triumph over **Palmyra** on January 17. **Lee Cassel** (132) and **Troy Spencer** (170) delivered pins while **J.T. Donnelly** (126) and **Bailey Shutt** (152) contributed majors to the rout. By the time **David Wuestner** hit the mat, the Falcons had already clinched victory. Even so, **Wuestner found a way to steal the show** by leveling Ben Martin 10-3, a top contender for a state berth this year." And he added "… it may be time to add Wuestner to the list of competitors who remain undefeated in PM-Keystone matches and should be able to navigate sectionals with relative ease." An astute prognosis from Saufley!

Wuestner continued his success against Mechanicsburg, but the Falcons failed to extend their team-win streak, falling to the Wildcats **43-24** on Jan. 22. LD took six bouts, but was undone after relinquishing five pins.

Unfortunately, the loss overshadowed excellent performances from several top wrestlers, with **Travis Morrill** (195) working a 6-3 decision and **Wuestner** a 4-2 OT win.

LD struggled at HW and 106, but junior **Jordan Foreman** revived the Falcons with a 7-4 win at 113. After a forfeit widened the Wildcat lead to 22-9, **Donnelly** (126) and **Cassel** (132) belted consecutive falls to draw LD within one. However, Mechanicsburg took over from there, collecting 21 points over the final five bouts.

End of season remarks from Sportswriter Saufley included: "This year was rather different for LD wrestling, finishing with an uncharacteristic record of 5-7 with a roster of **only 20 wrestlers.**" Individually, four of the wrestlers had more than 20 wins, surprising perhaps, as the wrestlers needed to be placed at various weights in the weight line-up—a challenge to any coach—and wrestler! Even with this handicap, **four wrestlers qualified for Districts:** David Wuestner, Kalob Ware, Lee Cassel, and Travis Morrill. A good year—it was amazing as to what the coaching staff and team achieved with the small number of wrestlers on the team."

2013–2014 *(Record 12-4)*

Row 1: Jordan Foreman, Cody Wagner, Brianna Vale, Chase Mader, Peter Mummau, Amanda Vale, Joey Kilgore.

Row 2: Taylor Steigerwald, Liam Maguire, Angel Cruz, Tristan Phillips, Will Puderbaugh, Lee Cassel, Evan Morrill, Bailey Shutt.

Row 3: Calvin Nolt, Freddy Maines, Kalob Ware, David Wuestner, JT Donnelly, Troy Spencer, Omi Ramos

Both challenges and cooperation were needed when the wrestling season began this year, with **half of the wrestling team on the football team, playing football well into December.** Yes, the football team had made State Finals! Fortunately, only the opening wrestling tournament needed to be canceled and, when the full team was intact, they hit the ground running, **together as a team.**

Mader, Mummau, and the rest of the squad turned the tables on Hershey as LD rode away with a **41-29** victory. It was a crowd-pleasing event, one hard-fought battle after another. Even Senior David Wuestner said the lightweights took him by surprise. It was a match for which "you had to have been there" to fully appreciate. As new coach Kemal Pegram noted, "Our lightweights were important for us and they have been working out in the mat room from the beginning of the school year."

On December 19 against Susquehanna Township the Falcons collected seven pins on their way to a **63-9** triumph that left them at the top of Mid-Penn. They then did well in tournament competition, and at Sectionals placed 4th and advanced to Districts. There, Wuestner placed third, **qualifying for PIAA States.**

However, as Joe Saufley noted, "A loss that occurred in a packed West Shore gymnasium on January 13 stung quite a bit more than the rest because "Kemal Pegram's bunch was in position to knock off an incredibly talented Cedar Cliff, earn a signature win, and take control of the division title race. …and **they** *misfired*." The result was a hard-fought **36-23** loss. A 7-2 win at 152 stirred up the Cedar Cliff side, but then Bailey Shutt pinned the Colts' star senior J. Colello, which gave LD's experienced heavyweights a chance to take command of the match. Although, as can happen, not a single bout broke the way the Falcons had wanted.

January 23, 2014, with Saufley …"LD took care of business against Palmyra on January 16. Shutt (160), who stands as **one of the top District contenders for the crown,** pinned his opponent in 30 seconds. Calvin Nolt (132) and Chase Mader (106) also came up with pins for LD, while JT Donnelly (45) and Angel Cruz (152) posted decisions."

LD placed six wrestlers in the top three in the Elizabethtown Challenge Tournament on January 18. In their **first** tournament, four wrestlers placed and two were champions. Not doing as well in the **second** tournament, by the **third** at Chambersburg, LD had reversed, placing ten wrestlers in the top eight of their weight classes.

To add to it, out of our **14** starters at Sectionals, **13** placed in the top 6, good enough for LD to move to Districts. Lee Cassel finished fifth in his weight class and **Bailey Shutt came out a District Champion, qualifying him for States.**

January 24 and 25. "At the New Oxford Tournament LD held a 7th place finish in the 28-team tournament. The Falcons crowned a champion with sophomore Bailey Shutt (160) who squeaked out a pair of decisions to earn the title. David Wuestner (285) stormed through consolations to finish third after dropping his quarter-final bout. Lee Cassel (132) took sixth, Evan Morrill (195) seventh, and Calvin Nolt (126) with a solid showing."

We revisit here coverage of the **2013-14** season with the appointment of David Wuestner as wrestling coach in 2021 and have added information from the March 13th *Patriot's* coverage of the District 2-AAA wrestling tournament which headlined, "Lower Dauphin's David Wuestner has impressive showing… (2/25/2014)" and *The Sun's* " Wuestner Earns State Berth" where Joe Saufley notes, "High school athletes dream about having a memorable senior season, but few receive the opportunity to actually live out that dream. …" Saufley continues, "David Wuestner stands out as an exception. In the fall, Wuestner had played a pivotal role in the football team's remarkable run to the state semifinals.

Over the winter Wuestner brought his gridiron success to the mats, where he led his team to a 12-win season and captured an individual sectional title. In February Wuestner look his talents to Hersheypark Arena in hopes of claiming a state wrestling berth, his final goal. He overcame a 220 bracket littered with top competitors to take **third** at Districts, guaranteeing him a spot in the state tournament. He held on for a tense 4-2 win against Seth Janney who had ranked 10th in the state. Wuestner also had four victories at states, an outstanding showing, but lost in the end against Shikellamy's Dwayne Pepper. …however, "Wuestner will be graduated as the Falcons' **most impressive wrestler this decade,** ending his school career on a 30-plus win season that included more than 20 pins and a sectional championship."

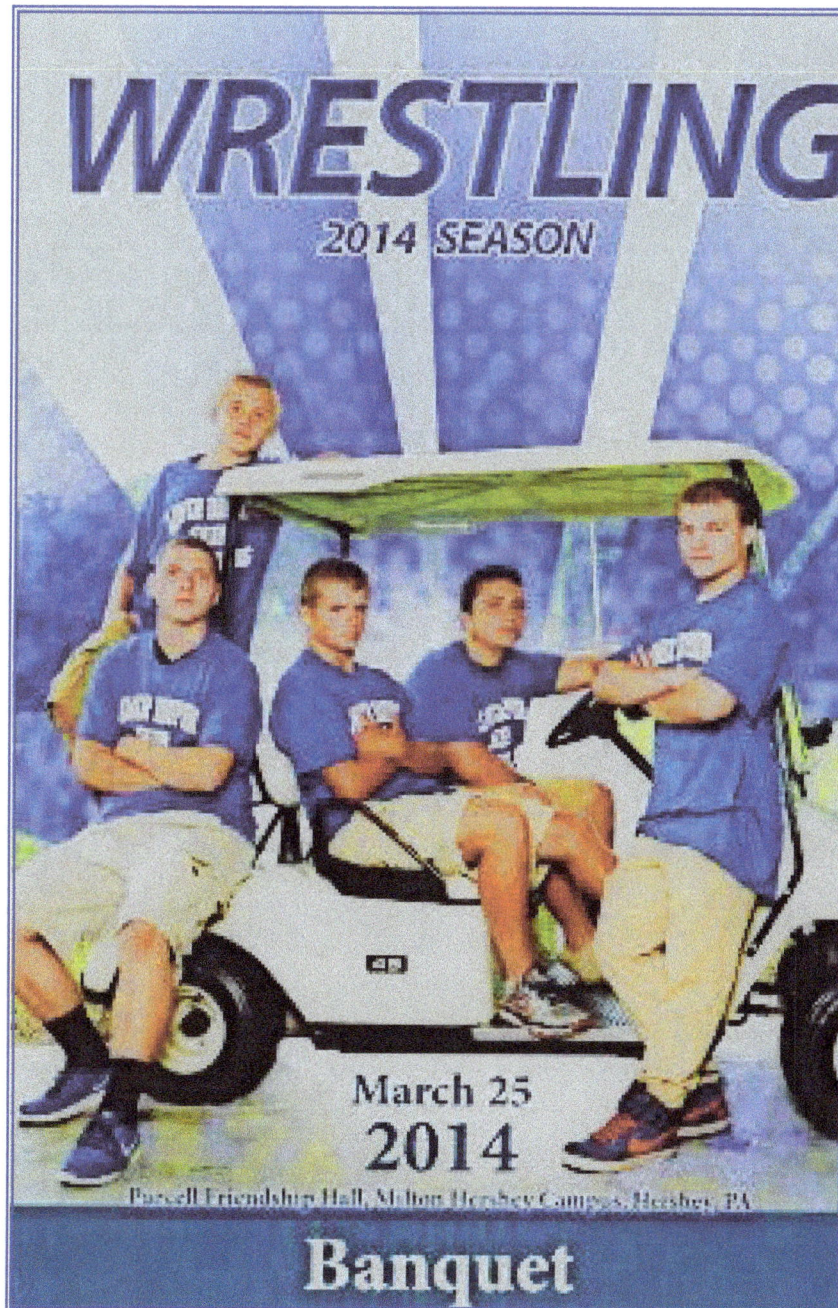

Wuestner at the wheel

2014–2015 *(Record 11-6)*

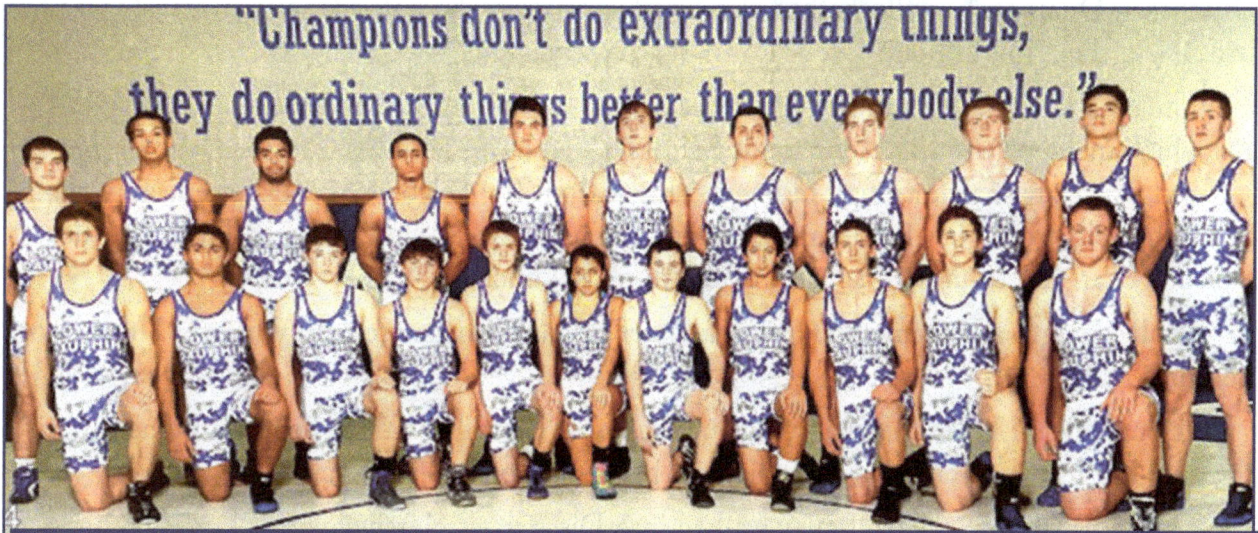

Front row: Elliot Cassel, Christian Vaughn, Cody Wagner, Adam Hoy, Chase Mader, Brianna Vale, Tyler Walters, Peter Mummau, Dilan Dreibelbis, Hunter Smith, Will Puderbaugh.

Back row: Jordan Foreman, Collin Ware, Angel Cruz, Chris Martin, Taylor Steigerwald, Lee Cassel, Nathan Bucks, Evan Morrill, Bailey Shutt, Hunter Harnish, Brendan Shaffer.

December 7, 2014, *Sunday Patriot-News,* John Tuscano. "The Falcons undoubtedly have a lot of hard work ahead of them, but the effort put forth by Kemal Pegram's team is a step in that direction." After coming away empty-handed at this tournament a season ago, on Saturday the Falcons crowned a pair of champions and finished 10th of 19 teams. Senior Lee Cassel downed Mechanicsburg's Brayden Wills 6-2 in the 138-pound final while **Bailey Shutt captured the title** at 160 over Frankie Krauss. **Cassel,** a District 3-AAA qualifier a year ago, made the early take-down stand up and never trailed. "Bailey wrestled a smart match," Pegram noted. **Indeed Bailey did.**

December 11, 2014. LD wasted no time knocking down the Blue Raiders with LD's freshman Joey Stoak and senior Lee Cassel. **Stoak** pinned in 4:32 and **Cassel** in 1:27 for a strong beginning.

January 3, 2015. LD took home four wins at the Wilson Duals. However, they lost to West Chester, a minor blip. They did well at Chambersburg's tournament with Shutt taking second and Lee Cassel and Tyler Walters nabbing third.

January 8, 2015. LD's shot at a division title hit a snag against a talented Cedar Cliff (36-28). Despite this loss the Falcons came away with four wins and a second place finish at the Dutchmen Duals at Annville, helped also by LD's Shaffer who battled Cedar Cliff's Gause to win 8-1 in their 152 lb. bout.

January 14, 2015. LD had two heartbreaking losses at home, then defeated Red Land (43-27) which included five LD pins. As Joe Saufley noted in his account, "Lower Dauphin has suffered its steady share of rough moments this season. The Falcons are inexperienced in spots and have dealt with a few key injuries, factors that have contributed to losses. However, the fans do get an LD team that is **really, really tough to knock off.**"

A full strength LD team ended its dual meet season with a statement win over Hershey on Senior Night.

At Sectionals LD led the charge, advancing six to Districts with **Bailey Shutt** emerging as the only champion, as he remained poised in his championship bout.

According to Joe Saufley, "Bailey walked into Districts at Hershey with a target on his back. He weaved through his bracket on Feb. 20 and 21, posting two wins on Friday night before sealing the deal Saturday afternoon. **Shutt came away as LD's first District 3-AAA champion since Nick Kristrich had accomplished the feat in 2008.** His effort was a testament of his approach all week-end: "Get ahead early, stay collected, and polish off the win late." … Lee Cassel also performed well and nearly joined Shutt at States, finishing just one spot shy of a bid at 138.

2015–2016 *(Record 10-5)*

Front row: Christian Vaughn, Dilan Dreibelbis, Brianna Vale, Chase Mader, Cody Wagner, Tyler Walters, Peter Mummau, Elliot Cassel

Back Row: Brendan Shaffer, Hunter Smith, Bailey Shutt, CJ Silsky, Nathan Bucks, David DeNotaris, Taylor Steigerwald, Will Puderbaugh, (Not pictured, Evan Morrill)

December 10, 2015, **LD Wrestling** *Preview:* "Eight seniors are seasoned, led by **reigning District champ Bailey Shutt who had stormed through the district brackets on the way to States where he finished sixth.** This feat gave the Falcons back-to-back state qualifiers (David Wuestner in 2014, Shutt in 2016).

Brendan Shaffer and Lower Dauphin began their season by doing one of the things they do best: **defeat Hershey.** Shaffer opened the match with a declaration win and his comrades followed suit, locking down the Trojans to a **51-18** win on December 10.

LD sent six place winners to the wrestlers' podium at the Trojan Wars Invitational, but had a rough showing on the mat at CV Duals on January 9, followed by a **44-30** loss to Northampton. Two other defeats came from Cumberland Valley and Mifflin County. On January 14 Lower Dauphin improved to 3-1 in the Mid-Penn Commonwealth Division with a 45-30 verdict over Harrisburg.

Bailey Shutt captured his **100**th win during LD's **40-32** triumph over Mechanicsburg on January 28. He had steadily improved through a quality sophomore season with 30-plus wins. In his junior year he closed with 77 total wins and felt confident to attempt 100 wins with a solid team behind him. **From a team perspective Shutt was instrumental in guiding the Falcons to a** second-place finish in the Mid-Penn Keystone even with the 100 landmark in sight. At Mechanicsburg the stage was set and, with

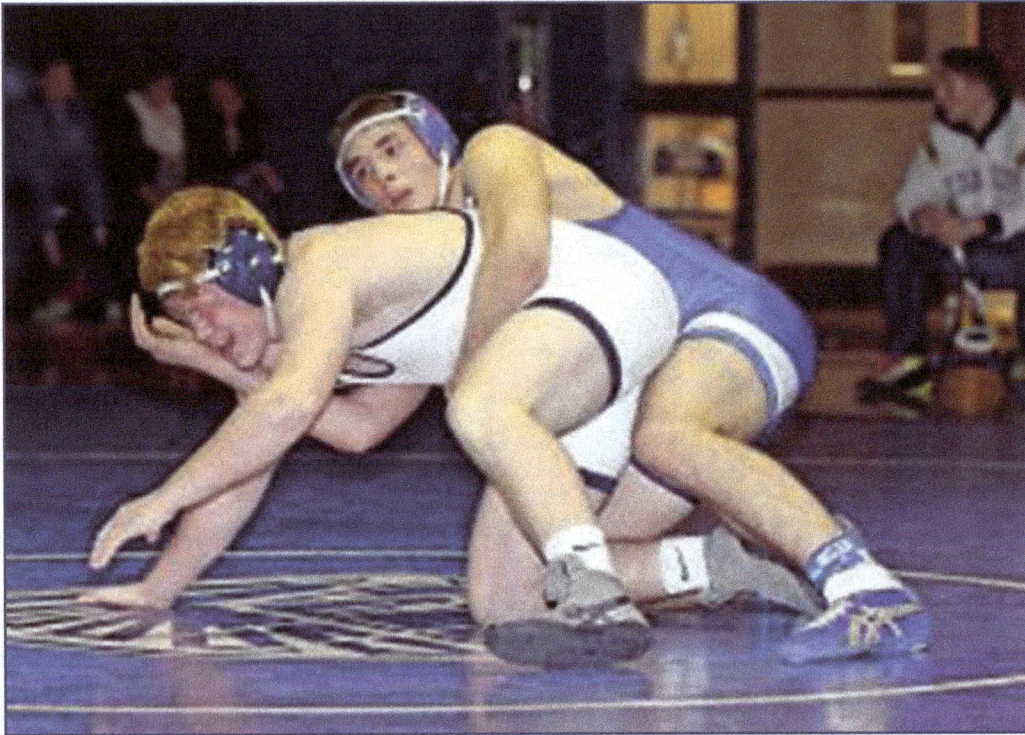

Hunter Harnish won his match against Cole Whalen in the 195-pound bout. — Photo: Geno Simonetti.

a pin, Shutt brought a fitting close to LD's solid team season.

On **January 24** a full strength LD team ended its dual meet season with a statement win over Hershey. LD's first match of the season 2015-16.

During the post-season run at Sectionals, LD had two champions, with five qualifying for Regionals where they placed ninth of 51 teams. Bailey Shutt earned a championship with Evan Morrill placing 4th, **qualifying the two for the PIAA State Tournament. Shutt and Morrill both made the semi-finals for the second year.**

February 04, 2016. Joe Saufley wrote a profile of **Bailey Shutt** including an explanation of Shutt's popular phrase "Keep it 100" (work hard, perfect a skill/goal, and commit to what one does). No one embodies the description better than Bailey himself, who had earned his **100th win** on January 28.

According to Saufley, Shutt had steadily improved from an injury-riddled freshman season he was unable to finish. The commitment to his craft paid off during a quality sophomore campaign that resulted in 30-plus wins and a spot in districts. In his junior season, **Shutt** captured sectional and district titles before **finishing sixth at states.**

Behind every 100-win wrestler is a solid team, and Bailey Shutt will be the first to admit that his biggest motivation and aid has been the **Falcon family working together in the mat room.** "My team is on my side with support, such as pushing me in the practice room, and my coaches correct all I do wrong to keep me from repeating a mistake."

From a team standpoint, **Shutt** was instrumental in guiding the Falcons to a second place finish in the Mid-Penn Keystone competition. **He achieved a**

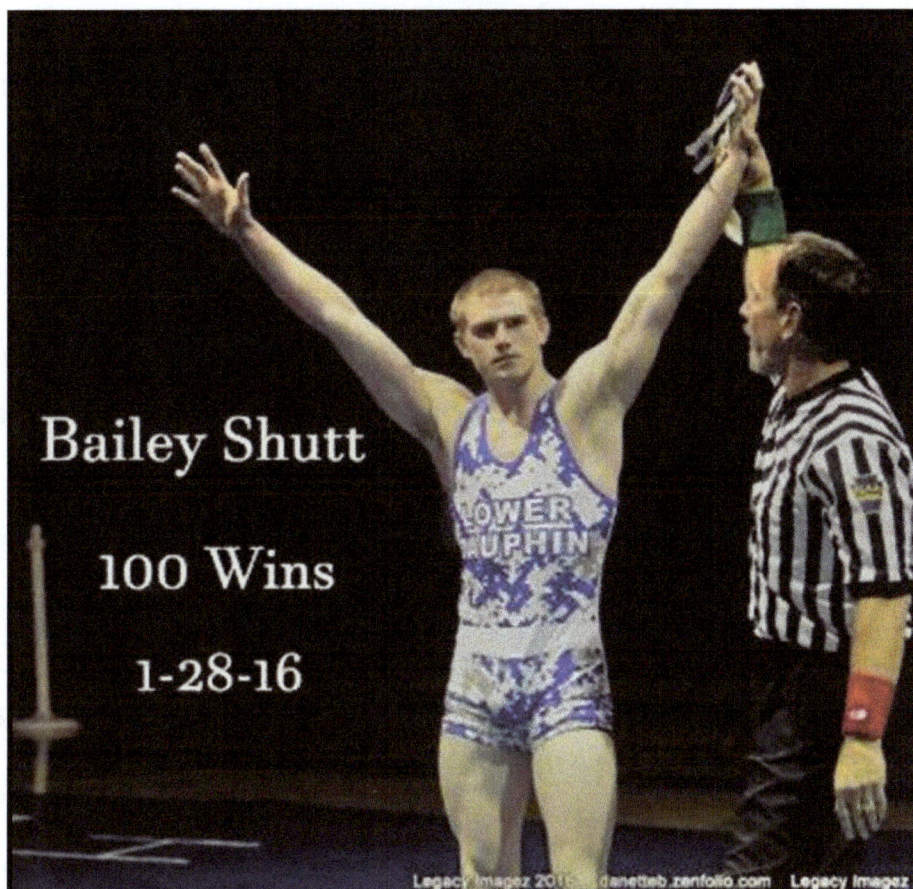

Above: Shutt's secured both the victory and his **100th win** at Mechanicsburg with a first-period pin bringing a fitting close to LD's solid 10-5 team season.

perfect record in division duals, with a memorable effort coming in crunch time against Mechanicsburg's Cruz Manatt.

At the PIAA SC **Regional Tournament,** the Falcons placed 9th of 51 and had a **champion** in Shutt, a **4th place** in Evan Morrill, and a **6th place** with Hunter Harnish.

Shutt and Morrill both qualified for the PIAA State Tournament where Bailey was a fourth placer taking his spot on the winners' podium. This was the first time since 2007 LD had more than one qualifier and placed 2 wrestlers for the 3rd time in program history. Further, for **the first time in LD history, a wrestler made the PIAA semifinals two consecutive years.**

Get up and go
"Moving to Senior High as a freshman taught me how to take a loss, pick myself up, and keep moving forward." [see page 279]

Winning tradition
In December 2023 LD out-pinned Hershey in a 50-23 dual meet, the latest development in a rivalry that began when LD was founded in 1960.

[see page 373]

How do we keep them down on the farm
"As I reflect on my wrestling career, I give Coach Cassel and Lower Dauphin credit for being a major part in my development as a person. I was the only one in my family to go to college. I do not know if I would have gone without wrestling.... Wrestling helped me mature from that poor, bashful country boy."
[see page 87]

This says it all
The plaque presented to Coach Cleon Cassel upon the 200th Cassel victory in 1977 notes, "You're only as tough as you think you are; you're only as good as you want to be."

[see pages 137 and 396]

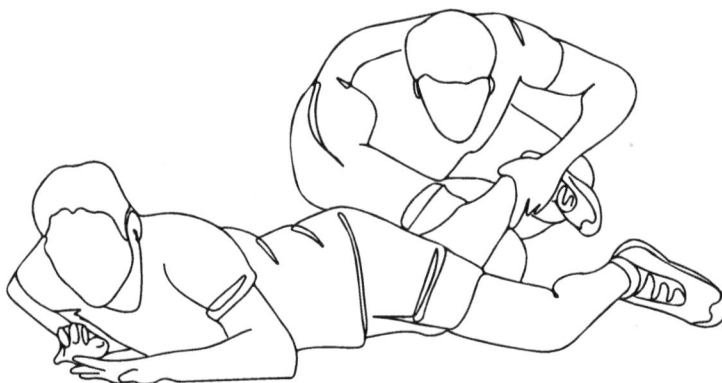

2016–2017 *(Record 14-5)*

Front Row: Christian Vaughn, Jacob Vale, TT Elhajj, Matt Herniak, Kyler Wuestner, Gannon Ulrey, Clayton Ulrey, Sean Donnely.

Back Row: Brendan Shaffer, Dylan Dodson, Cody Wagner, Etwarth Bernal-Noriega, Hunter Harnish, David DeNotaris, Carlos Merced, Allen Armenta, Tyler Walters.

During the second week of January the team banked another perfect week on the mats **scoring over Red Land and a 5-0 weekend sweep at the Annville-Cleona Duals.** At the Duals, LD rolled through. Harnish highlighted the Falcons' performance at 220 with five falls. Wuestner had three; Shaffer, five; DeNotaris, two; Vaughn, four; Ulrey, four; Elhajj, two; Walters, three; and Donnelly, five.

Wrestling's Alumni Night had a "full house" with the Falcons in control on the mat and on their feet when Wuestner took advantage of his off-balanced opponent, bringing him down at the mat's edge with a surprising **pin at 1:44.**

In late January the team also soundly defeated CD East **48-18** (although there were reports by sports writers of 48-23 and 38-18). The season boasted a 14-5 record which included qualifying for individual District III championships for the first time since 2008.

Clayton Ulrey became the first freshman in LD Wrestling History to qualify for the PIAA Tournament.

Hunter Harnish perhaps best expresses the feeling that, while shared many times over through the years, is always heart-warming for team members and fans to read: "With such a special group of guys on the team, I personally feel that this year's team was one of the best I have been part of."

2017–2018 *(Record 11-8)*

Front Row: Leonardo Bueno, Clayton Ulrey, Tito Moreno, Mason Clingan, Joey Stoak, Danny Pascale, Alex Merry.

Back Row: Taylor Walters, Sean Donnelly, Brendan Shaffer, Kyler Wuestner, Luis Armenta, Ricky Skidmore, Gannon Ulrey, Luis Pendolino.

Early on, the season was pegged with high expectations with two returning state qualifiers, **T.T. Elhajj** and **Clayton Ulrey**. Even though this was a young team across the board, Coach Kemal Pegram was pleased with their prospects. Another plus was Kyler Wuestner, a junior with a knack for clutch finishes.

Joe Saufley, writing for *The Sun*, noted LD's continued division dominance over Hershey (**57-21**) and Mechanicsburg (**39-27**). At Hershey, Ulrey dug in against their district qualifier.

LD carried a 51-0 advantage into the final five bouts which Hershey managed to tilt in its favor. **Sean Donnelly (120) grabbed LD's only win,** a fall in 2:41 in the lightweights.

In the Trojan Wars tournament, LD sent four wrestlers to the finals, where they placed fifth as a team—(1) T.T. Elhajj, (2) Joey Stoak, (3) Clayton Ulrey, and (4) Brendan Shaffer— to their respective finals, but **Ulrey emerged as the team's lone champion.**

Ulrey breezed through his first round and quarterfinal matches before claiming an 11-2 decision in his semifinal bout. He capped this with a 5-3 finals victory over Chambersburg's Drake Brenize (who, along with Ulrey, was ranked in the state's top 12 at the 152 lb. weight class).

Elhajj reached his final on a 12-6 decision before tumbling Korbin Myers (Boiling Springs) in the first place match.

The test, as usual, for the Falcons would be their showing against Cedar Cliff (winner of five straight division titles).

LD forfeiting at 106 and 113 gave Cedar Cliff an early 12-0 lead. The closest overall that LD would get to CC's ruling the bout would be pins by Elhajj and Stoak—both which came in first periods, while Ulrey took a 15-1 major win. This tightened LD's deficit to **30–16,** but the Falcons would get no closer, losing **46–24.**

Coach Kemal Pegram summarized the season, "LD finished the year 11-8 and wrestled one nationally ranked team and nine of the top eighteen teams in District III. We finished third in the PIAA Section II tournament, 2nd in the PIAA South Central Regional Tournament, and 16 in the PIAA State tournament with Clayton Ulrey finishing 5th and Brendan Shaffer finishing 7th."

The Falcons were a force to be reckoned with, despite missing a key starter from time to time in the team line-up. They showed the state what they were capable of in the post season.

2018-2019 *(Record 5-10)*

Front Row: Elijah Elhajj, Luis Armenta, Matt Rodriguez, Max Klingensmith, Denver Kalenevich, Alec Merry, TT Elhajj

Back Row: Bethany Bonham, Clayton Ulrey, Ricky Skidmore, Thomas Carney, Kyler Wuestner, Gannon Ulrey, (missing), Sean Donnelly, Carter Powell, Haley Smith

While the Falcon grapplers had an uneven year due to injuries, **they had outstanding performances in some of the toughest tournaments on the East Coast.** Clayton Ulrey and Kyler Wuestner claimed their second consecutive individual tournament win in Chambersburg at the end of December at the Trojan Wars.

Seeded seventh to open, Wuestner won all four of his bouts via pin, a **combined** 11.57 minutes of mat time to put away his opponents—three of whom were ranked in the top 10 among heavyweights in New Jersey.

Meanwhile, Ulrey opened his title run with a pair of falls, cruising to a 21–5 tech fall in the semis and claiming the title with a 9-4 decision in the title bout. T.T. Elhajj wrapped up a third-place finish in the 138-pound bracket, earning three consecutive pins in the consolation round before claiming a wild, 15-13 decision in the third-place match.

Clayton Ulrey and Kyler Wuestner claimed their second consecutive individual titles after winning titles in Chambersburg.

The trio of **Elhajj, Ulrey,** and **Wuestner** picked up medals at the prestigious Escape the Rock at Council Rock South High School on January 19-20. Elhajj rebounded from an 8-4 loss in the 138 lb. quarterfinals to earn a spot in the seventh-place bout, where he pinned Jake

Niffenegger of La Salle in 2:50. Elhajj went 4–2 for the tournament, pinning his lone in-state opponent when he took down Joe Dolak of Parkland in the first round.

Ulrey came away with three pins and a decision on the way to a third-place finish at 160 pounds, but suffered his first loss of the season in a 7–3 thriller in the semifinals. In the loss, Ulrey orchestrated a second-period takedown of Bethlehem Catholic's Luca Frinzi and later went ahead, 3–2, following a third-period escape.

According to Coach Pegram regarding junior Ben Snyder: "Ben has the heart of a lion. He doesn't care who he's wrestling, he doesn't care where he's wrestling. The name of the game is **win by pin**, and Ben is going to do that whoever's hand is raised." Snyder won the clinching bout against Hershey, turning an even battle with the Trojan Hibbert with an upper-body takedown and pin, giving the Falcons a 36-22 cushion in an eventual **36–28** victory.

The post season was a success with exceptional performances in the regional and state tournaments. At the PIAA State Championships we had a **state finalist in Ulrey** for the first time we had done so since 1999. The coach also notes, "Kyler Wuestner blends size, strength, and athleticism to overwhelm his opponents. In the rare case when his physical skills aren't enough, he relies on **his superior mat sense and match management to find a way to win.**"

One notable example of Lower Dauphin's True Blue Families

Kyler Wuestner with his parents (1) Lynn Wuestner, South Hanover Township Manager and former President of the Lower Dauphin Wrestling Boosters and (2) Dr. David Wuestner, Principal at Conewago Elementary School. Kyler's older brother is Wrestling Coach David Wuestner.

In the regular season on December 22 the Falcons dropped a dual meet against Sun Country rival Palmyra, **38–35**. Ben Snyder and Gannon Ulrey joined Elhajj, Clayton Ulrey, and Kyler Wuestner with **pins**, while Sean Donnelly (145) recorded a tech fall.

Clayton Ulrey won 6–0 at the Trojan Wars Tournament at Chambersburg on December 29 with heavyweight Kyler Wuestner at 285 matching Ulrey's first-place finish at 160.

The Falcons topped Middletown **39–37** at home on January 2, with pins from Elhajj, Skidmore, Clayton Ulrey, Snyder, Gannon Ulrey, and Kyler Wuestner, along with a hard fought victory from Sean Donnelly.

On January 4 the Falcons **won five** of the first seven contested bouts, but lost the meet victory to Cedar Cliff 49–25.

The Falcons were seeded seventh in a tournament in New Jersey on January 5. **Wuestner won all four of his bouts with pins**, while **Ulrey** opened his title run with a pair of falls, cruising to a 21–5 tech fall in the semis and **claiming the title** with a 9–4 decision in the title bout.

On the 17th the Falcons dropped a **40–35** team dual to perennial foe Red Land.

At the prestigious "Escape the Rock" Tournament at Council Rock South (January 19–20) TT Elhajj, Clayton Ulrey, and Kyler Wuestner all picked up medals.

In a rare instance, Daryl Simione, sports contributor to *The Sun*, profiled one of LD's many outstanding wrestlers, noting LD Junior, **Ben Snyder,** "who has proven every bit worth his weight this season, **earning victory after victory** while bracketing the dynamic duo of Clayton and Gannon Ulrey at upper middleweight." (The entire account is well worth reading in *The Sun's* archives.)

25 years, outstanding record

In the spring of 1987 Coach Cleon Cassel ended his 25th year as a wrestling coach, never having had a losing season. His tenure as coach included four undefeated teams and nine teams that were defeated only once. His dual meet record was an outstanding 324-42-4.

[see pages 203 and 229]

More career wins

In 2020 two LD seniors, Clayton Ulrey and TT Elhajj, ended their high school careers with a combined 270 wins, 141 pins, six sectional championships, five district titles, a pair of state runner-up finishes, state fifth-and eighth-place medals, and a total of 13 stage tournament victories. [see page 357]

In case it sounds easy

In 2009 Blaine Shutt defeated Dakota Minnich of Hempfield after three overtimes and the following year he beat CD's top-rated Nick Berndell after four overtimes.

[see pages 314 and 321]

2019–2020 *(Record 2-8)*

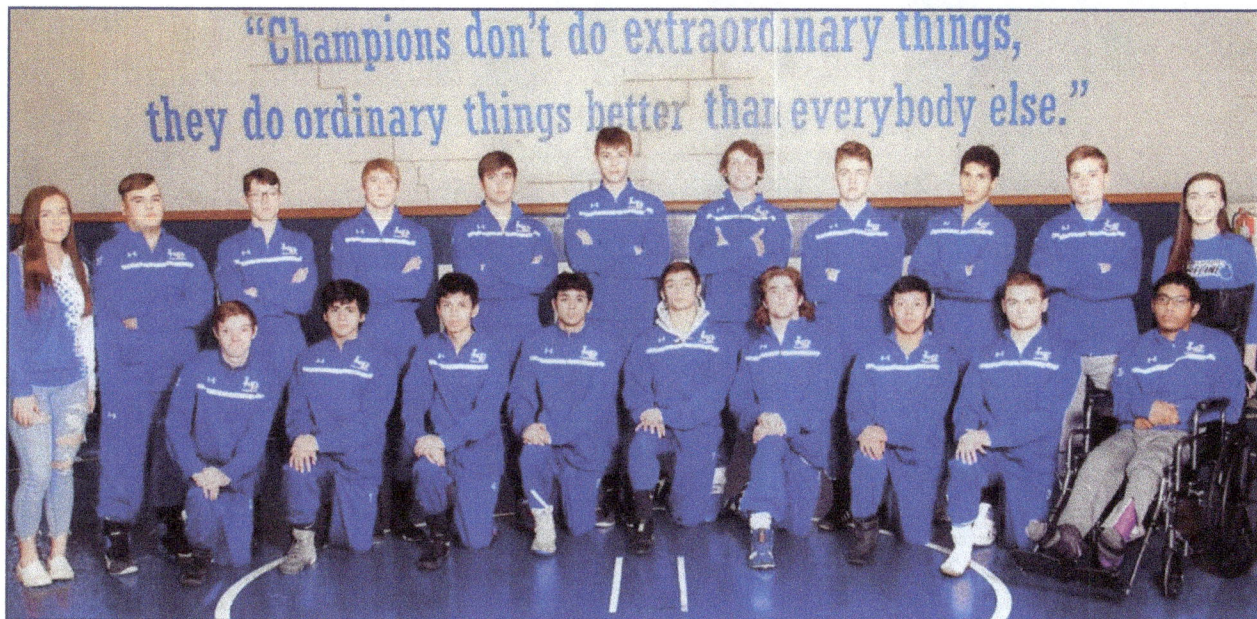

Front Row: Thomas Myers, Matt Rodriguez, Jason Tierney, Andrew Carmona, TT Elhajj, Clayton Ulrey, Tate Ingram, Alec Merry, Carter Powell.

Back Row: Manager Bethany Bonham, Aaron Moyer, Ayden Minnich, Sean Donnelly, Dylan Godert, Domenic Defrank, Ben Snyder, Blake O'Brien, Moustafa Elfawal, Max Klingensmith, Manager Haley Smith.

At the December 12th season opener, the team began with a thrilling 45–34 victory over Central Dauphin East with returning state runner-up Clayton Ulrey leading the way. On December 14 at the Carlisle Christmas Tournament Elhajj and Ulrey came away with tournament titles. LD dropped a **62–15** match to defending District 3 Class 3A champion Cedar Cliff with victories from Klingensmith, Donnelly, and Ulrey.

The Lower Dauphin wrestling team continued to test their grit against the best wrestlers in the Mid-Atlantic, traveling to the prestigious Sam Cali Invitational in New Jersey where Ulrey added a championship to the record. Ben Snyder placed fourth and TT Elhajj placed third. Elhajj, at 138 pounds, was upset 6–3 by Al De Santis of Shore Regional in the quarter-final. Elhajj fought his way back with a pair of falls and a major decision to reach the third-place match where he picked up a fall in 1:11 to place third.

Following these grueling tournaments, LD went back to the team aspect in a home match with Mechanicsburg (January 9) which the Wildcats won **51–28**; LD then had a loss to Northern, 43-27.

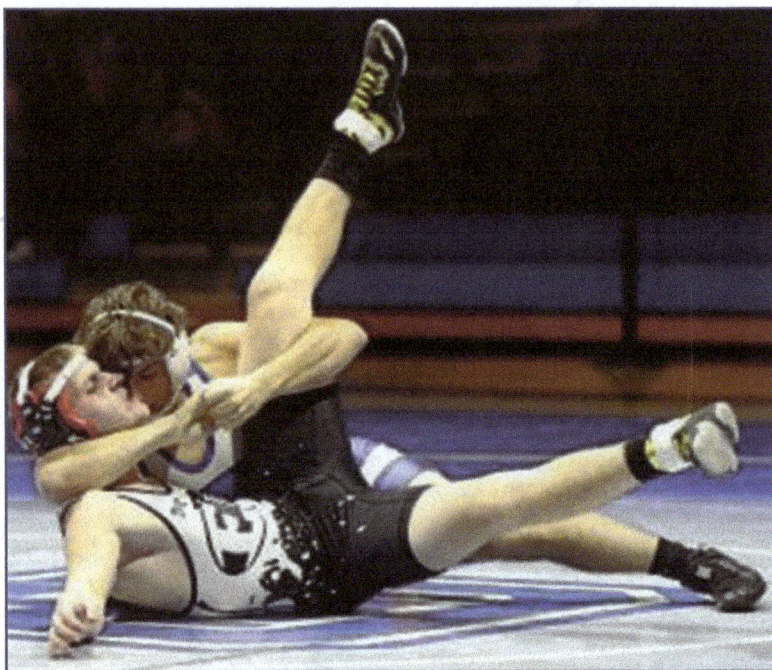

TT Elhajj grapples with Central Dauphin East's Mike Dunleavy in the 152-pound match. Photo: Geno Simonetti.

LD then lost against Red Land who limited the Falcon trio of TT Elhajj, Clayton Ulrey, and Ben Snyder to a combined 13 points. However, **in the match of the night**, Elhajj knocked off Red Land's Bryce Brennan 2–1.

LD went 1–1 for the week with the **42–22** victory over Hershey on Thursday, January 23. On Saturday January 25 Palmyra and LD met in Hummelstown for a mat showdown that the Cougars won, **44–36**. On Saturday, February 1, the Falcons met Susquenita for a non-league match, losing **48–28**. On the 5th, LD, Hershey, and Palmyra closed out their team dual season. LD then finished duals at Governor Mifflin, dropping a **60–18** match. It was there that **Ulrey at 170 had his fastest victory in 1:44.**

The "Road to Hershey" Meet started February 14 with Sectionals. Teammates Ben Snyder (182) and TT Elhajj (138) brought home gold medals.

Ulrey won the District 3 Class AAA 160 title on Saturday, February 22, to become the **18th four-time champion in District 3 history. Teammates Ben Snyder and TT Elhajj finished fourth and third respectively.**

Clayton Ulrey was ranked 9th in the nation as he approached States.

Ulrey was ready for his second shot at it when the match ended abruptly. With Ulrey facing Chambersburg's Luke Nichter, the two were locked in a scramble when Nichter caught Ulrey in a cradle, turned him on his back and completed the fall in 3:43. **It was the first time in his career that Ulrey had ever been pinned….**

Lower Dauphin sent three wrestlers to the medal stand at the state tourney. They are, from left, Clayton Ulrey, Kyler Wuestner and T.T. Elhajj. Photo: Geno Simonetti.

The Sun

The two seniors (Ulrey and Elhajj) ended their careers with a combined 270 wins, 141 pins, 6 sectional championships, 5 district titles, a pair of state runner-up finishers, a state fifth-place medal, a state eighth-place medal, and a total of 13 state tournament victories in eight combined appearances.

Three Lower Dauphin wrestlers stood at the state tourney: Clayton Ulrey, Kyler Wuestner, and TT Elhajj.

Clayton Ulrey won the District 3 Class AAA 160-pound title on Saturday, February 22, at Spring Grove. He also avenged a 3-1 loss to Chambersburg, turning it into a 7-5 victory to become a **four-time** District III Champion:

Congratulations to Clayton Ulrey, who became the 18th four-time District III Champion ending his high school career with a total of 144 wins.

Ulrey noted, "Perhaps the best thing is that our season was finished before the shutdown caused by Covid-19. Above all, we have learned that **there is nothing like being on a team,** especially wrestling, whereby one is alone on the mat, but fighting (to win) for the entire team."

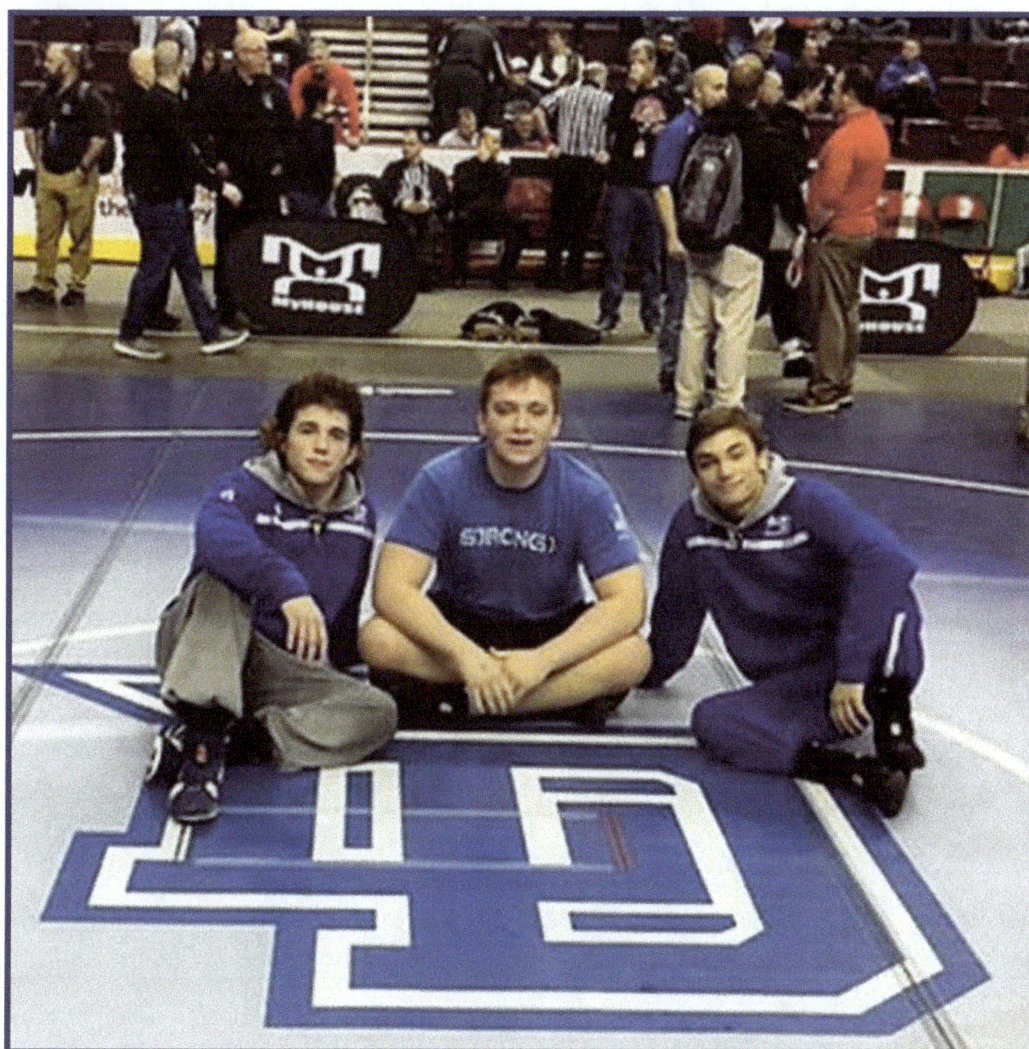

The Big Three: Ulrey, Wuestner, Elhajj

2020–2021 *(Record 6-11)*

Row 1: Cheyanne Calloway, Manager Cali Mease, Alex Merry, unknown, Luke Mease, Jacob Gesford, Jorge Borgos.

Row 2: Manager Bethany Bohnam, Griffin Barilla, Thomas Myers, Lewis Fisher, Joey Swartz, Aaron Moyer, Clayton Koser, Manager Haley Smith.

Row 3: Blake O'Brian, Cody Dent, Tanner Webb, Domenic DeFrank, Carter Powell, Marshall Stahl, Max Klingensmith.

As sportswriter Mike Nortrup noted, "Lower Dauphin's wrestling team opened its new season Saturday, January 9, at Manheim Central with a really tough **33-31** loss. The Falcons had had a big push from their middleweight wrestlers to overcome an early deficit and take a 13-point lead. But they could not hold on. The Barons would win four straight bouts to open an insurmountable gap before forfeiting six points to LD in the final weight. The highlight came when **freshmen Clayton Koser and Griffin Barilla had successive pins** at 126 and 132 over opponents who had more experience than they. These two pins put LD ahead and, with wins by **Merry** and **Swartz,** things were looking good. However, the Barons won (and garnered three pins) at the heavier weights even with 215 lb. **Tanner Webb taking the final six points for LD** via another forfeit.

As might be expected, Covid-19 restrictions and postponements (along with bad weather) wreaked havoc with the wrestling team's practice schedule. After losing eight of its first nine bouts, the team won four of its next six matches. While that didn't entitle them to bragging rights, it was far better than their record of last season.

In the imaginary "Ways to Win" manual, the Falcons, while managing to physically win only three of 13 bouts at Warwick, **took the overall win, thanks to six forfeits by Warwick at the February 6 meet.**

Coach Pegram noted, "As tough a season as we've had with as many competitions as practices along with Covid-19 restrictions and snow days, my greenhorns are having to "learn on the fly."

From the team: "Indeed, we did learn new shortcuts and games of challenge, pretending this was all normal. *Wasn't it?*

Resiliency became our mantra."

"Humor helped as well. We laughed like fools sometimes, to hide our fears of many unknowns—family, school and, particularly, our teammates. Everyone understood, and **no one left the room until we all did.**"

Coach Pegram gave much credit to the senior wrestlers and the two senior managers who displayed the needed leadership under what had to have been overall a stressful season.

Kudos to Managers Alec Merry, Bethany Bonham, and Haley Smith.

This . . . was . . . a . . . challenging . . . year . . . to . . . say . . . the . . . least.

2021–2022 (Record 9-9)

Give this team a round of applause for valor. These young men "took what was given and made the most of the opportunity to compete—which oddly enough was engaging in more competitions than in (dual) matches."

Front Row: Lewis Fisher, Clayton Koser, Evan Dupler, Jorge Burgos, Griffin Barilla, Jacob Gesford, Gabe Hutchman, Thomas Myers.

Back Row: Elijah Elhaj, Aaron Moyer, Max Klingensmith, Marshal Stahl, Domenic DeFrank, Moustafa Elfawal, Joey Swartz, Luke Mease.

The Falcon mural on the gymnasium wall was created by local artist Cig Stroman in the mid-70s. In the late-80s a sign noting "Falcon Pride" was sponsored by the Alumni Asociation and created through the donated talent of Kurt Stoner Signage.

LD reaches its 700ᵗʰ Victory

On December 8 (2021) Griffin Barilla, who wrestled at both 132 and 138, **had as big a day as one could have.** He pinned **all five** of his opponents—and, yes, he was only a sophomore. The sports reporter evidently enjoyed this pinning romp of Barilla at the Dutchman Duals at Annville-Cleona. As a matter of fact, the Falcon Team also had their day there as well, finishing on a high note, ripping host Annville-Cleona, **47-23.**

In his sports report in *The Sun* on January 19, Mike Nortrup wrote, "Lower Dauphin suffered through a rough week on the mats. It has lost four of its five matches since **January 11**, falling to 6-7. On **January 18**, against a gloomy stretch of losses, Red Land defeated LD, as did Carlisle. Then came **Griffin Barilla** with a pin at 132, the only bright spot during that otherwise disappointing string of meets.

LD's Clayton Koser grapples with Hershey's Ben Farr in the 126-pound match, Thursday, Jan. 27, 2022.   — Photo: Geno Simonetti.

On January 20 the Falcons were defeated by Northern (**48-27**); at Shippensburg the Falcons won four of the first five bouts, but the Greyhounds took three straight to cut LD's margin to **33-28**. At that point Aaron Moyer at heavyweight took a 3-2 overtime decision to give his team three crucial points and the win. A sophomore, Jacob Gesford, had opened the match with a pin. Coach Wuestner complimented him, "… Jake is very aggressive and just keeps attacking until he gets his shot."

At Hershey the Falcons lost the opening bout, but then swept 10 straight for an easy romp.

That "easy romp" was the road to **Lower Dauphin's 700th win.**

We were!

Prominent figures standing in the back row are Coach Dave Wuestner on the left and former AD/Coach/ still Record-Holder Randy Umberger on the right. (*To the best of our collective knowledge the back row klatch includes, l to r:* David Wuestner, Kurt Koser. Lamar Koser, Ryan Koser, Tim Gamber, Jerry Hiller, Randy Umberger .) Coaches Craig and Cleon Cassel are holding the banner. Front Row standing are Jason Dupler, Craig Cassel, Joe Stoak, Travis Rodgers, and Cleon Cassel. In the front are Coach Zach Barrick and Roy Gesford.

The press had it right: "LD is pleased to have two of the winning wrestlers among local schools—Max Klingensmith 160 at 22-5, and sophomore Griffin Barilla, 20-5."

Unfortunately, neither the records of the teams of Hershey, nor Palmyra, nor Lower Dauphin qualified for District Championships. However, individuals did the vetting with pins by Jacob Gesford, Clayton Koser, Griffin Barilla, and Elijah Elhajj. LD **had two top contenders** among all the wrestlers from surrounding high schools as named above.

According to Mike Nortrup, sportswriter for *The Sun*, Palmyra sophomore Josh Smith and Lower Dauphin Senior **Max Klingensmith** had the best regular season records among area school wrestlers for this year's season. (photographer unconfirmed)

In an interview with Klingensmith, Coach Wuestner noted that Max, who grew up in a wrestling family, is the strongest man on the team. In his sophomore year Klingensmith tore his meniscus "and was shut down the rest of the year." If that wasn't bad enough he re-injured the knee during the pre-season practice the following year. Between that and Covid-19, he missed all but the final few

ALL STARS – 1ST TEAM
KEYSTONE DIVISION
MAX KLINGENSMITH

matches and failed to make the post-season. "Thus, he was approaching his third year (2021-2022) under a great deal of pressure. Amazingly, he was able to reel off a **12-bout winning streak**, eventually taking down 15 of his final 16 opponents." Klingensmith, 22-5 in this year's Sectionals, pinned his first two opponents, and finished second at the competition. Clay Koser finished third.

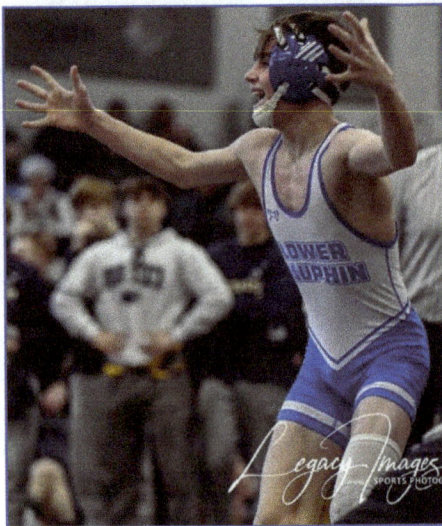

Jacob Gesford

New Coach Wuestner summed it up, "We were better than I thought we'd be. We lost some close matches I thought were winnable. I'm proud of how far we've come this year considering we were a young team. Not many teams have **eight** sophomore starters, and I am excited about what is yet to come."

Klingensmith paced the group, taking a second place finish at Sectionals. He pinned his first two opponents before being pinned by Bruscino even though it was noted that "Klingensmith opened with two tough matches and wrestled very smart."

Coach Wuestner also commented that Elijah Elhajj and Jacob Gesford faced competitors who eventually became the champions, with Elhajj pinning three straight opponents through the consolation rounds before falling to Central Dauphin East's Thaddeus Krebs in the battle for third place. Gesford had a pin in the quarterfinals, but lost in the semifinals to eventual sectional 113-pound weight champ Rylan Carter.

2022–2023 *(Record 16-4)*

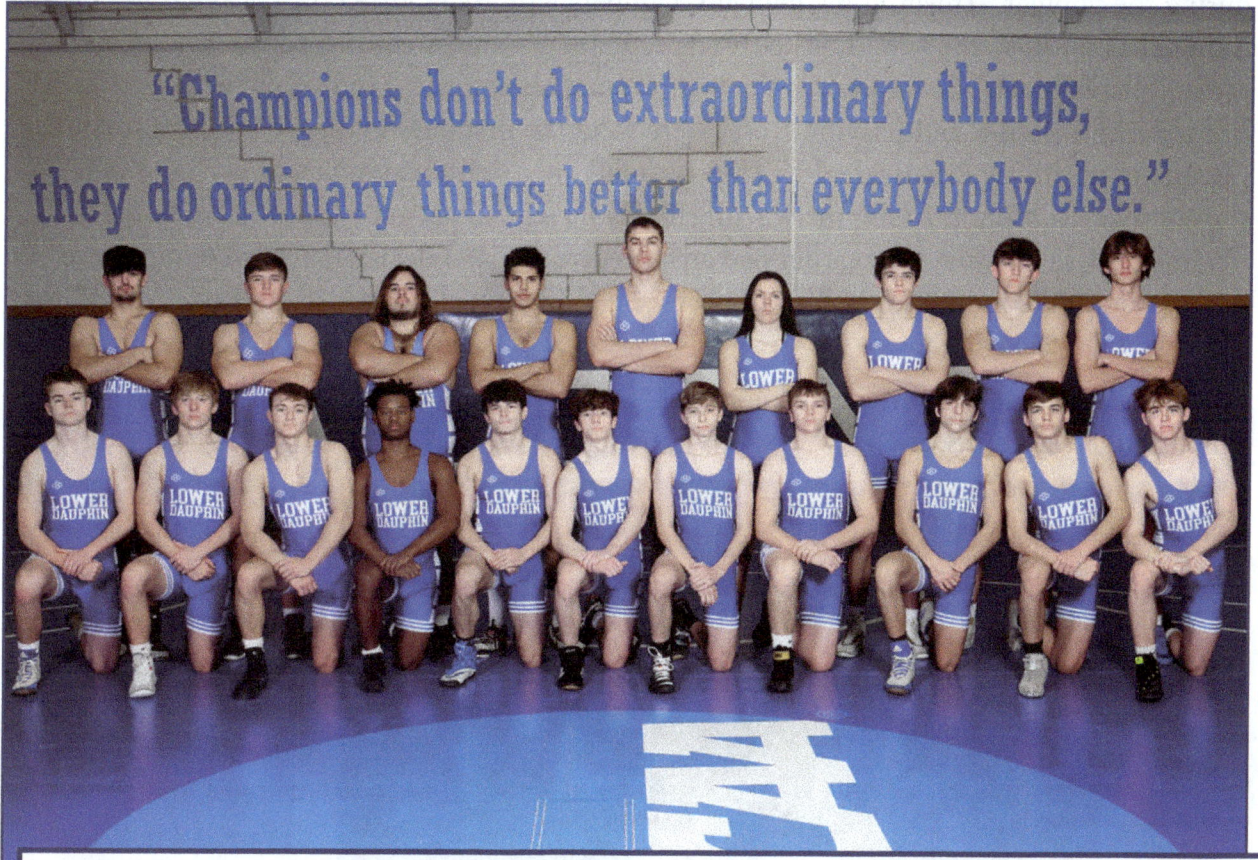

Front l to r: Carter McQuiddy, Joey Swartz, Clay Koser, Gerald Sanders, Griffin Barilla, Cael Rossi, Hayden Bohensky, Evan Dupler, Cole Warren, Jacob Gesford, and Luke Mease.

Back to r: Marshal Stahl, Will Gray, Aaron Moyer, Moustafa Elfawal, Domenic Defrank, Ivy Hiatt, Isaac Ulrich, Nathan Stuckey, and James Rogers.

The 2022–23 team lost to Northern York 30-34 on December 8, and took part the following week-end at the Penn Manor Holiday Tournament highlighted by a 2nd place finish by Clayton Koser who beat Hershey's Joseph Parks by a fall. Cael Rossi and Griffin Barilla placed 3rd. Rounding out the podium finishes were Will Gray and Marshall Stahl.

A highlight was Isaac Ulrich bringing the Falcon fans to their feet with a tightly contested 4–3 decision over Hershey's Salem Essis.

On December 21 LD topped **Mechanicsburg 36-21** where Barilla, Koser, Ulrich and Aaron Moyer notched pins and the following night tripped up **Hershey 40-24!**

12/22/2022[*] is a date Jacob Gesford should not forget for his winning a first day victory during the popular "Trojan Wars" held at Chambersburg. As reported by *The Sun* (with Geno Simonetti's photos), the team finished a respectable 32nd and, according to the newspaper account, LD's coach was pleased, as the team strengthened several individual wrestling vitae. Rossi, Griffin Barilla, and Clayton Koser were solid the first day, holding off the consolation placement until Day 2. Rossi had an 18–3 tech fall, then, with teammates, bowed out in the consolation rounds. Along the way **Barilla** had a second period fall over Lamirande of Perkiomen while **Koser**, who earlier had advanced with a 4–3 decision, had a second-place finish. Additional individual match winners were **Will Gray, Jacob Gesford, Luke Mease, Joey Swartz**, and **Isaac Ulrich**.

Further, 8th grader **Hunter Stoak** placed 1st at 250 in the Junior High Division, pinning his way through the competition.

Lower Dauphin's Jacob Gesford battles with Carlisle's Garrett Pedrick in the 127-pound match. The Falcons knocked off visiting Carlisle 41-28.

On January 5, 2023 LD hosted its home opener against front-runner **Red Land**. Nathan Stuckey wowed the crowd in his battle with Caden Gibson of Red Land as he thwarted a takedown attempt in the first period. A crowd pleaser, Stuckey then fought off Gibson, remaining **"unstuckey,"** and with 11 seconds to go in the period, was awarded a stalling point as his opponent tried to maintain control. Through a tight see-saw, Stuckey worked a pull and takedown with 15 seconds left for a hard-won, **4-2** decision.

Cael Rossi was impressive in building a 16–2 lead, including four takedowns and two near falls, reversing his opponent onto his back in the third period for a pin in 4:27. **Barilla**

[*] Easy to remember with six "2♂."

In the 189-pound match, Will Gray of Lower Dauphin defeated Lane Rhoads of Carlisle.

earned a fall at 133, throwing his opponent in the first period before completing the pin in 3:03. **Jacob Gesford** and **Clayton Koser** both had forfeits, but, as noted, Red Land pulled out the win.

January 5 also was the date of this year's annual Alumni Night, an event that draws many to the meal and the match, as well as serving as a time to recognize alumni in a setting for all decades to be honored, where the alum gather to evoke the friendships, and whose conversations cover every decade, both the memorable matches of yore and the current season. And these men together gather around banners honoring the teams. Heart-warming and very fitting!

The Lower Dauphin and Palmyra matmen pulled significant upsets last week to flip the Keystone Division standings on its proverbial back."

On **January 12**, the Falcons knocked off visiting Carlisle **41-28**. The match got off to a rousing start at 215 pounds.

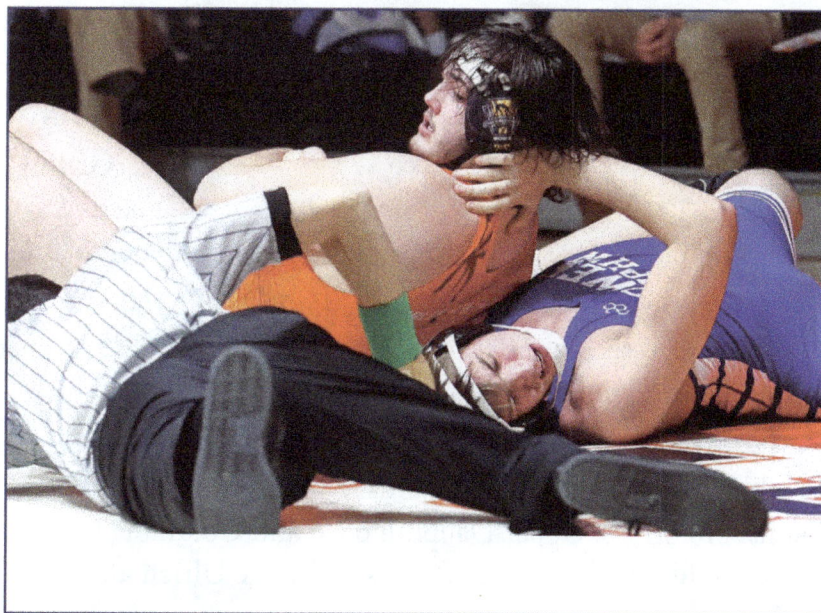

Palmyra's Jayson Albright does battle with Lower Dauphin's Domenic DeFrank in a January 26 match. — Photo: Geno Simonetti

Lower Dauphin Coach Dave Wuestner bumped **Nathan Stuckey** up from his customary spot at 189 to take on Carlisle's Bradyn Jumper. Working on top to begin the second period, Stuckey completed a cradle for a fall in 3:08.

367

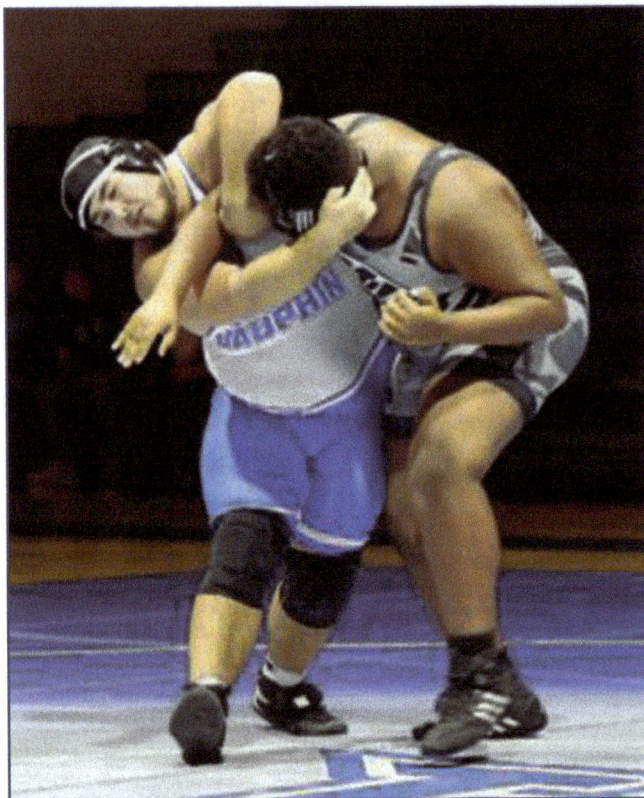

Lower Dauphin heavyweight Aaron Moyer, above, defeats Central Dauphin East's Miles Davenport in less than a minute in a Jan.19 match.

After Carlisle knotted the contest with a pin at 285, **Lower Dauphin took control by winning the next six bouts.**

First, **Hayden Bohensky** won a war of attrition over Carlisle's Jarrett Lynch, who led 2-0 after the first period and 3-0 following a second-period escape. Lynch responded with takedowns in the second and third for a 4-3 lead. On a restart with just eight seconds to spare, Bohensky made another escape to force the extra period. At this point, a score by either wrestler would end the bout. A pair of stalemates only increased the tension. With seven seconds left, Bohensky brought his opponent to the mat for a thrilling 6-4 decision.

Riley Winsett followed suit with a throw and pin in 1:30. **Cael Rossi** received a forfeit, and **Jacob Gesford** worked consecutive tilts for a fall in 1:50.

Griffin Barilla notched a pair of takedowns for a 4-0 decision, and Clayton Koser completed an 18-3 technical fall to cap the Falcons' run.

Carlisle would rally with falls at 145, 152, and 160. But LD's **Marshal Stahl** (172) stayed off his back to secure the team win, and **Will Gray** (189) turned his opponent for a first-period fall to top off the victory.

January 14, Dutch Duals: Lower Dauphin (3-2) routed the competition at the Dutchmen Duals at Annville-Cleona on January 14. The Falcons topped Middletown 62-3, East Pennsboro 66-10, Upper Dauphin 65-6 and Columbia 61-9. Barilla, Bohensky, Gesford, Koser, Rossi, Stahl, Stuckey, James Rogers and Isaac Ulrich all went **4-0.**

The team celebrated Senior Night in style by getting four pins from its upperclassmen during a **57-9** romp over visiting **Central Dauphin East** on January 19. Falcon senior **Aaron Moyer** highlighted the night with his fall at 285 pounds. Moyer lifted East counterpart Miles Davenport in the air—no easy feat at heavyweight—and threw him down for the initial takedown. From there, Moyer worked to turn Davenport for the fall in 0:57.

(Fellow seniors Domenic DeFrank, Moustafa Elfawal and Thomas Myers all notched pins during a series of exhibition bouts prior to the match. The audience was enthralled.)

Jacob Gesford had an easy fall at 127 to give LD a 12-6 lead. **Griffin Barilla** had a little more work to do in facing East's Niy Niy Soe. Barilla scored with an initial trip and takedown, building a 7-2 lead after one period. Starting at neutral in the second, Soe's takedown attempt was stymied and countered by Barilla, who finished off the pin in 3:28.

LD's **James Rogers** received a forfeit at 139 pounds and **Clayton Koser** consolidated the run of wins with a cradle at 145. **Isaac Ulrich** and

In the 133-pound match, LD's Griffin Barilla, right, defeats CD East's Niy Niy Soe by fall. *Photo: Geno Simonetti.*

Marshal Stahl earned narrow decisions at 160 and 172 pounds respectively. Ulrich led 4-2 after the first period and 9-3 in the second, before holding on for an 11-7 win.

Stahl reversed for two points and worked a late near fall to close out the first period leading 5-2. His opponent earned a pair of escapes but Stahl made the lead standup for a 5-4 win. At 189, **Will Gray** scored a single-leg takedown and led 3-1 entering the third period. When his opponent chose (being on) top to begin the period, Gray reversed and scored a two-point near fall to finalize a 7-2 decision.

On the 26th the Falcons visited **Palmyra**, winning 8 of the contested matches, highlighted by winning five of the first six bouts, including falls from James **Rogers** at 145, Marshall **Stahl** at 172, and Nathan **Stuckey** at 125. **Ulrich** added a 16-2 major at 160. Will **Gray's** 5-1 decision at 189 for LD, and Clayton **Koser** with a first period pin at 139—all added to the rout.

In one of the more exciting bouts of the night, LD's Domenic **DeFrank** moved up to heavyweight to battle Palmyra's Jayson Albright. DeFrank scored a first-period takedown plus a headlock for a 4-0 lead entering the second period. Albright reversed to open the second, and trailing 5-2 in the third, worked from the top to tilt his opponent into a fall in 4:57. Tyler **Detwiler** followed suit with a first-period pin at 107, LD forfeited at 114, and, suddenly, Palmyra was down just 25-21 with four bouts to go.

However, Rossi regained the Falcons' momentum with a 14-4 major decision at 121. Palmyra's Xavier Hoffer scored four reversals in his 12-6 decision versus **Barilla**. The match was decided by a Cougars forfeit at 133; **Koser** then set the final margin with a first-period pin at 139 (41-24).

The team competed in the inaugural Rumble in the Jungle at Red Lion on January 28, finishing 2nd which ultimately gave them the winning percentage needed to qualify for the District III Team Tournament as the 12th seed.

January 31. A successful regular season earned Lower Dauphin the right to compete in the opening round of the District 3 tournament held at Elco High School. Making their 10th District Tourney appearance—the first since 2017—the 12th seeded Falcons gave powerhouse Chambersburg an early run before falling, **37-24**. The match began at the lower middleweight with **Cael Rossi** winning a hard-earned 5-3 decision at 121; **Clayton Koser** followed with a 4-1 decision at 133. **Griffin Barilla** tallied a second-period pin at 139; **Joel Swartz** earned a 6-2 decision at 152. When **Isaac Ulrich** pinned his opponent at 160, Lower Dauphin had a 21-10 lead.

Three straight defeats put Chambersburg on top to stay, however. Aaron Moyer recorded a 7-3 decision at heavyweight to get within 25-24, but a Trojan pin and Falcons forfeit ended the match.

The team won the League Division Championship (first since 2007) with a perfect 7-10 record. They qualified for the District III Team Championships for the 2nd straight year, advancing to the Elite 8. David Wuestner, Jr. was named Keystone Division Coach for 2023-2024.

2023–2024 *(Record 16-4)*

Front Row: Evan Dupler, Griffin Barilla, Cael Rossi, Jorge Burgos, Christian Madden, Tommy Oswald

Second Row: Carter McQuiddy, Leonard Moreno, Isaiah Allen, Hayden Bohensky, Clay Koser, Rylan Ulrich, Joey Swartz, DeVon Jackson, Jacob Gesford

Back Row: Noah Goniea, Will Gray, Hunter Stoak, Marshal Stahl, James Rogers, Nate Stuckey, Issac Ulrich, Kaiden Keddy, Braeden Heckard

"Champions don't do extraordinary things, they do ordinary things better than everybody else."

2023-2024 Wrap-up from the Hummelstown Sun

December 7. LD's match with **Northern** was a back-and-forth affair. Knotted at 26-all, Griffin Barilla and Clayton Koser recorded consecutive pins to give the host Falcons a 38-26 victory. "Our motto all week was 'do your job,' from the bottom of the lineup to the top," Coach Dave Wuestner said. "…All of our hammers did their job and we got it done. That's a really talented bunch over there and it was nice for us to come out on top." Stuckey put the Falcons on the board with a 4-1 decision—the decisive points coming at the third period buzzer. Gray, Rossi and Jorge Burgos added pins for LD. Jacob Gesford rounded out the winner's circle with a 19-4 tech fall.

December 8-9. The Falcons then had a stellar showing at the **Penn Manor Holiday Tournament** at Penn Manor. LD dominated the opening rounds, soaring to the team lead with 88.5 points after Day 1. The second day of action was equally exciting, as the Falcons placed five wrestlers during the marquee event. Nathan Stuckey led the way with a second-place finish at 189 pounds. Cael Rossi (127 pounds) and Clayton Koser (145) took home third-place trophies, Will Gray (215) earned fifth place and Griffin Barilla (139) earned seventh place. In all, the Falcons finished fifth among 31 schools with 130.5 team points.

December 14. LD thumped visiting **Mechanicsburg**, 58-12. Barilla, Koser, Swartz, Stahl, Stuckey, Gray and Rossi each won via fall.

December 16-17. The Falcons made hay at the **Howdy Duncan Classic** at William Penn High School in Delaware. LD finished second among 32 schools with a whopping 243.5 team points. Thomas Oswald (113), Cael Rossi (126) and Will Gray (215) won titles. Griffin Barilla (138), Clayton Koser (144), and Marshal Stahl (175) were runners-up. Joey Swartz (152; 3rd) and Nathan Stuckey (190; 4th) also placed for the Falcons.

December 21. LD out-pinned **Hershey** in a 50-23 dual meet victory over the Trojans. The rival schools split the first six bouts, with all six victories coming via fall. But Rossi gave the Falcons the lead for good with a pin of his own, and Gesford, Barilla, Koser, and Joey Swartz consolidated the effort with a series of dominant victories to help the Falcons pull away. Stuckey, Oswald, Jorge Burgos, and Marshal Stahl all recorded falls for LD.

December 29-30. LD placed two wrestlers at the prestigious **My House Trojan Wars tournament** at Chambersburg High School. Seniors Cael Rossi and Jacob Gesford finished fourth and sixth, respectively, while counting themselves among the nation's best wrestlers in the Atlantic region. In all, LD finished 21st among 51 schools, with 87 team points. Thomas Oswald (114), Griffin Barilla (139), Clayton Koser (145), Nathan Stuckey (189) and Will Gray (215) had multiple wins for the Falcons.

January 11, 2024. LD doubled up **Carlisle**, 42-21.

January 13. The Falcons upped their record to 10-0 with a dominant effort at the **Dutchmen Duals** at Annville-Cleona. LD went 4-0 in bracket play with wins over Middletown (57-15), Columbia (59-12), West Chester Henderson (50-15), and Halifax (39-25). The Falcons then ousted the host Dutchmen 55-18 to claim the tournament title.

January 25. The Falcons put the wraps on their first division title since 2007 with a 42-16 Senior Night victory over local rival **Palmyra**. They answered Palmyra's early challenge in order to complete a 7-0 run through **Mid-Penn Keystone Division** play. "That was one of our main goals this year," Coach Wuestner said after the meet. "We knew we had the team to do it, but it's really hard to run a clean slate. It's a testament to all the kids." The division title not only provides a worthy tribute to the Falcons' eight seniors, all of whom were honored prior to the met, but also puts into context what Wuestner calls the team's "resurgence."

January 30. LD entered the **District 3 3A (3AAA)** tournament as the No. 7 seed and traveled to No. 2 Conestoga Valley for a pair of dual meets. The Falcons fought through some early jitters to defeat Keystone rival **Red Land** 40-14 in the opening round. It was LD's first District tournament victory since 2009. The win advanced the Falcons into a quarterfinal matchup against Lancaster-Lebanon League Champ Conestoga Valley, which they lost 36-23.

February 1. A few tough breaks wound up costing the LD team in a **District 3 AAA consolation match** at Spring Grove High School. The seventh-seeded Falcons wrestled aggressively up and down their lineup against No. 3 Central York before losing in heartbreaking fashion, 35-33.

February 17. Cael Rossi nabbed his second-straight sectional title, this time at 127 pounds, to lead a bevy of Falcons' medalists at **District 3 AAA Sectionals** at Mechanicsburg High School. LD finished fourth in the team standings with 132.5 points. In all, the Falcons would send seven wrestlers to the regional tournament: Rossi, Clay Koser (2nd, 145), Griffin Barilla (4th, 139), and Joey Swartz (4th, 152) were all back-to-back qualifiers. They were joined by 2022 qualifier Jacob Gesford (3rd, 133), as well as first-timers Will Gray (3rd, 215) and Thomas Oswald (4th, 114).

February 23-24. Two third-place finishes equaled success for LD wrestlers at the **District 3 3A South Central Regionals** at Spring Grove High School. Seniors Cael Rossi and Clay Koser earned the bronze medal in their respective brackets and wrapped up berths in the PIAA state tournament.

March 7-9. Cael Rossi clinched a spot on the podium, finishing in seventh place at the PIAA state wrestling championships in Hershey. "It means the world to me," Rossi said afterward. "I wasn't ranked, I wasn't seeded to place, but I got the job done."

Meanwhile, as friends and family watched from the stands, Clay Koser achieved his 100th career victory at the state tournament. "It's something I've dreamed about since elementary school" Koser said, finishing the season with a career 100-34 record.

What a Way to Close a Senior Season!

Clayton Koser:
Our most recent "100 Wins" Winner

Wrestler's Personal Story of 2012

Pinned, Not Beaten: Dalton Deimler 2012

(Edited from an account in *The Sun* first written by Joe Saufley, January 2015)

Dalton Deimler is an example of the importance of physical stamina and mental endurance learned in wrestling, which likely saved his life after a terrible automobile accident in December 2014.

On his way home at dusk, following a hunting trip in Liverpool, a deer jumped in front of Dalton's truck, forcing him to swerve off the left side of the road. With his Ranger heading straight for a guardrail, Deimler whipped into a median littered with trees and bushes, bringing the barreling Ranger to a sudden, forceful stop. He went into survival mode when he realized both legs were broken—every single bone with the exception of his left shinbone, he later learned. Every movement was painful and he had no workable lights or horn—his Ranger totally dysfunctional. Through the pain and cold (set to dip near 15 degrees), he was able to grab his college laundry in the seat behind him to pile on his chilled and immobile body. Five hours later he was able to retrieve his flashlight which he waved, hoping to catch a passing eye.

No one stopped.

At 11:25 p.m. Dalton dragged a hanger across the front seat, touching what he thought was a large piece of glass, but realized with great elation that it was his cell phone. Following a 911 call, he was rescued near midnight. Responders used the Jaws of Life to free his trapped front leg. He was rushed to Geisinger Hospital and following two surgeries (a total of 20 hours) and later rehabilitation. He returned home and later made a full recovery, possible in large measure by his strength and fortitude, much of which is attributed to his being an athlete. "Back then, as a wrestler, I would go through the grind, but I am still telling myself the same thing, that I can make it. I will say it until I have conquered it." And so he did.

How do we keep them down on the farm

"As I reflect on my wrestling career, I give Coach Cassel and Lower Dauphin credit for being a major part in my development as a person. I was the only one in my family to go to college. I do not know if I would have gone without wrestling.... Wrestling helped me mature from that poor, bashful country boy." [see page 87]

Great upbringing

In his February 14, 2009 column, sportswriter Rod Frisco said, "Lower Dauphin was essentially a start-up, kicking off its varsity program in 1960. The Falcons just might have developed better and more rapidly than any other school in District 3 history....

[see page 315]

More than good wrestlers

"Lower Dauphin Wrestling and proper leadership can and does result in much more than only good wrestlers and championships. It results in solid Americans who continue the legacy. I am proud to be part of the exceptional Lower Dauphin Legacy." [see page 216]

Wrap-Up

Continuing the Journey and the Legacy

David Wuestner Jr.
Wrestler and Coach

Fall 2023

The start of the 2023-2024 season marks the conclusion of the Resurgence! The program has significant numbers and is competitive at all levels, and the seven senior wrestlers who populate the 2023-2024 roster are geared up for a fantastic run.

As a 12 year old, I remember coming to Lower Dauphin wrestling matches with my father to watch the Falcons compete against some of the best in District III. Often the gym was standing room only to watch the likes of Johnny Crawford, Jarred and Jason Kane, Kevin Gerhart, and Robbie Higgins just to name a few. That generation of wrestlers inspired me in my own wrestling journey. The rowdy and vocal crowds, electric atmosphere, partisan fans, all fired me up and caused me to dream about reaching the position I so proudly hold today.

The sport of wrestling at Lower Dauphin holds a very special place in my heart. Wrestling helped shape me and my younger brother Kyler into the men we are today. Wrestling is a unique sport, in that you wrestle as an individual, but you come together as a team.

Having individual success at LD was great, but the team goals I strived to attain did not come to fruition. After witnessing so much success growing up, I am hungrier than ever to reach the district and state team level once again. The last three years have been focused on program building, team building, and providing energy to a proud history of wrestling that will result in future prominence across the state landscape.

Last year we had a glimpse of what this community and what this team is capable of doing. We achieved a record of 15-4 (17-4 if you count the forfeits) and qualified for the District 3 wrestling tournament. We proved that we belong and are excited for what the future holds. There are exhilarating things happening in our program and we want everyone to be a part of it.

THE RESURGENCE!

This
We
Most
Remember

- *The gut-wrenching matches.*

- *The guys who wrestled while injured, exhausted, but never afraid.*

- *The obstreperous middle weights who were lovable and took on everyone.*

- *Parental support, unflaggingly loyal.*

- *The sacrifices parents made to be able to attend meets.*

- *The legacy families of wrestling.*

- *Rides home after victories.*

- *Families who became "camp followers," driving from one end of the state to the other.*

- *Wrestlers who prayed before a meet.*

- *Wrestlers who missed a holiday (and sometimes daily) meal to "make weight."*

- *Faculty who wished the wrestlers "good luck" the day of an important meet or made an appropriate comment the next day.*

- *The school nurses, always supportive medically and personally, and who often helped with travel clothing for the team.*

- *Those team members who were soundless before a match, those who had to openly display (or work off) their abundant energy, those who prayed, and those who never showed the fear they felt.*

- *Mr. Mark French, Trainer*

- *Our Coaches, FOREVER*

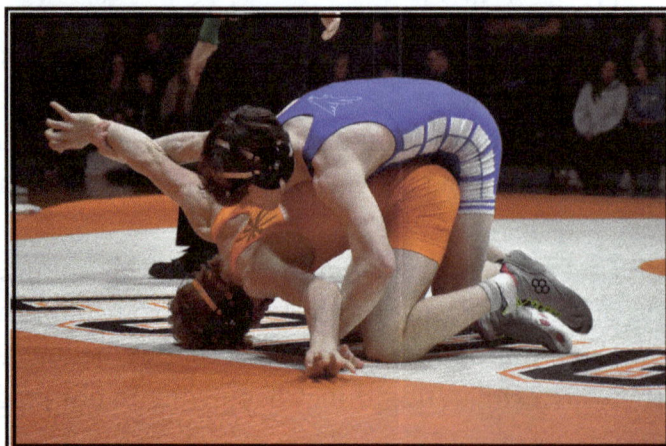

Representing the 1960s

With Trust in their Coaches, their Teammates, and their Teachers

Yesterday, Today, and Tomorrow

Forever Wrestlers (January 2023)

Front Row. Lamar Koser, John Koser, Sam Dupler, Dan Dorsheimer, Lynn Grimm, Galen Kopp, Ed Neidig, Bill Pinkerton, Ron Cruys.

Back Row. Randy Umberger, Brian Lesser, Keith Umberger, Leon Koser, Fred Foreman, Ron Kopp, Carl Espenshade, Ed Neiswender, Ron Michael, and Glenn Ebersole.

Mostly 1980s:

L to R: Chris Cassel, Barry Tonkin, Joel Umberger, Greg Etnoyer, Eric Stauffer, Lloyd Umberger, Mel Watts, Larry Cobaugh, Craig Cassel, Craig Hetrick, unconfirmed, Tim Shutt, Keith Camasta, Jeff Hollenbush, unidentified.

Mostly 1990s:

L to R: Kyle Geesaman, behind Kyle, Jason Kane, behind Jason with hat, Bryan Whiston, Jason Dupler (blue shirt), behind Jason to the right, Kurt Koser, Tom Whiston Ike Fullerton, Ryan Koser, Brin Koser.

The 2000s:

Eli Elijah,
Carter Powell,
Max Klingensmith,
Alex Merry,
TT Elijah,
Sean Donnelly,
Nate Bucks

History may little note, but we will long remember....

And for *Generation Tomorrow,*

below we see them ready to head home

following a day of wrestling . . .

To dream of being a Falcon Varsity Starter!

Waiting in the Wings

and counting . . .

In Memoriam

Mark Camasta	Jay Kopp	Jim Sanders
Jerry Crick	Ken Long	Tom Sanders
Bill Crick	Don Messick	Harold Shellenhammer
Mike Dean	Ed Michael	Mike Smoyer
Bill Divel	Jim Michael	Ronnie Stammel
Dan Dorsheimer	Fred Mutek	Mark Stauffer
Jay Ebersole	John E. Neagle	Chris Wallish
Jim Faber	Frank Neiswender	Craig Wallace
Eric Fluman	Carl Patrick	Tyler Watts
Matt Hahn	Bob Plouse	Brad Weirich
Rick Kelley	Kevin Rodgers	Mike Weneck
Casey Koons	Dan Sanders	Kevin Wolf

CONTRIBUTORS

Lower Dauphin Wrestling: An Uncommon Heritage

PIAA wrestlers warm up at the Giant Center in Hershey
(photo by Sean Simmers, PennLive.com)

The Press

In 1960 when Lower Dauphin came into existence the area was served by several newspapers. As not many homes had a television set in the early sixties, townspeople relied on the local newspaper and/or or newspaper(s) from the nearest city for news or entertainment. These included Harrisburg which until 1996 was served by a morning newspaper, *The Patriot*, and an evening newspaper, *The Evening News*. In 1996 these two newspapers merged into a single morning paper, *The Patriot-News*.

There were also three local newspapers in the area surrounding Lower Dauphin High School—all who were generous in their local coverage: *The Hummelstown Sun, The Hershey Chronicle* (which closed in 2009) and *The Middletown Press and Journal* (which folded in 2020.)

The Hummelstown Sun has become an exemplary regional weekly newspaper with a very positive history of its own. Now known as *The Sun*, extending coverage to Hershey, Palmyra, and Lower Dauphin sports, it is to be celebrated for its generous coverage given to sports in our geographic area. *The Sun* has provided extensive coverage of Lower Dauphin sports from the time the high school opened its doors in September 1960.

Sports coverage was greatly increased when Bill Jackson came to our community in 1968, and sports reporting expanded as new sports were added in the school districts served by *The Sun*. David Buffington, Publisher and Drew Weidman, Editor, further expanded sports coverage.

We are also grateful to those wrestlers who had saved news clippings of the meets many of which serve as the basis for what is written here.

Contributors

A special note of gratitude goes to the following who shared the nearly four-year journey in order to tell the story and preserve the story of a successful sport for which there had been no formal collection of sports records or individual remembrances:

♦ **Ann and Jay Kopp**, book sponsors who provided information and wrestling memorabilia.

♦ **Anonymous Donors** who made it possible to expand the book's initial contents by helping to defray printing costs.

♦ **Bill Jackson** for donating copies of *The Hummelstown Sun* (from its beginning to 2006) to the Hummelstown Historical Society and to the Society for purchasing a microfiche processor which made it possible to review the accounts of wrestling meets from the early years.

- **Carl Espenshade,** book contributor and part of the first year's notable wrestling success.

- **Chad Lister** who donated his time in accessing some of the earlier accounts of the wrestling matches, painstakingly retrieved from microfiche.

- **Coach David Wuestner,** notable wrestler and newest "home-grown" wrestling coach serving his Alma Mater.

- **Claudio Valeri,** wrestler and experienced coach, an enthusiastic follower of LD wrestling who has shared a number of his favorite memories.

- **Dan Dorsheimer,** among the first responders to the author's search for information. Dan served as an early historian/story-teller for the book, and was very much a devotee of his Alma Mater. He is profoundly missed by teammates and by members of this close-knit community.

- **Don Heistand,** well-respected and skilled wrestling coach; one of the first to offer materials for this book.

- **Drew Weidman,** General Manager/Editor and **David Buffington,** *The Sun,* who provided access to all articles from their Archives.

- **Ed Neiswender,** award-winning wrestler who loaned personal memorabilia and provided many behind-the-scene memories.

- **Elaine Royer** and **Kathy Weber** whose culling of artifacts from Lower Dauphin Alumni Association's sports collection has made items easier to review.

- **George Cruys,** a major contributor to this book.

- **Glenn Ebersole,** one of our first "sports stars" with valuable information and treasured, detailed remembrances of Year One.

- **LD Wrestlers,** the substance and soul of this book, wrote their personal stories for this memoir, providing keen and caring insight into what otherwise would not have been known. It is this respect and humility from wrestlers in their classroom interface that first caught the author's attention to the sport that has resulted in this tribute to them.

- **Lamar Koser,** scrapbook lender and member of a dynasty wrestling family.

- **Lloyd Umberger,** Book Sponsor from a family engrained in LD.

- **Randy Umberger,** Book Sponsor and Sports History Reviewer. A champion wrestler and coach himself, Randy's name is synonymous with LD sports and more in almost every area.

- **Ron Cruys,** wrestling historian and content reviewer, acknowledged as a notably skilled wrestler, keeper of wrestling stats, relentless in his searches for vetted material.

- **Hummelstown Historical Society** which provides storage space for LD High School artifacts collected, catalogued, and preserved by the Lower Dauphin Alumni Association.

- *The Hummelstown Sun* which has provided extensive coverage of Lower Dauphin sports from the time the new high school opened its doors in September 1960. Coverage was increased when **Bill Jackson** purchased the newspaper. **David Buffington,** as new Owner, and **Drew Weidman,** Editor, further expanded sports coverage.

- **Lower Dauphin Alumni Association,** founded by the author, is dedicated to preserving LD history and by Alumni who donated funds some years ago to build the large showcase in which to display memorabilia and promote school activities. The active Board members of the Association continue with service to LD. Current President is **Kris Eisenbise.** **Elaine Mater** and **Kathy Weber** create the delightful displays in the LDAA Showcase.

- **Tim Shutt,** keeper of detailed scrapbooks and father of champion wrestlers.

- **Tom Elling,** State and National Wrestling Notable, who gifted a copy of his *PA Wrestling Handbook* to this publication.

What Would Pat Have Done?

Mrs. Patricia M. Lanshe was one of the original faculty at Lower Dauphin Junior-Senior High School, and is being remembered here as representative of those faculty who, whatever their title, provided good advice—and sometimes a haven—for students. Pat Lanshe was the person to whom students—and teachers—most turned for a trusted, objective opinion.

Arriving to LD as an eighth grade English teacher in the fall of 1960, Mrs. Lanshe later became a guidance counselor in the high school, heading the department following the retirement of student advocate Kenneth Staver.

Pat's stories of living in New York City during World War II are unforgettable, as was her distinctive but quiet laughter, almost a subdued giggle! She befriended countless students and many faculty members, offering practical advice, never wasting time on pipe dreams. She did not "suffer fools gladly."

Patricia Lanshe was a person of integrity and worked diligently behind the scenes to "right a wrong," skillfully guiding students in making good decisions, whether the incident involved a classroom encounter, applying for college admission, or perhaps a situation in which a student could not go home because there was no home.

Not many people knew how much both teachers and administrators also counted on Mrs Lanshe's keen insight, wise advice, and judgment of character, as they asked themselves, "What would Pat do?" And wrestlers knew that the only accepted reason for being late to practice or a class was to admit that, "I needed to see Mrs. Lanshe." No questions asked.

I particularly remember an incident when one day after school two male students rushed into my classroom after having been followed and taunted by a group of classmates (not wrestlers) who were gathering in the wide yard between B and A Wings. This inconspicuous grassy area would not be noticed by passers-by walking or driving from the school's major entrance into the parking lot.

There were no cell phones at that time and no communication system in any of the classrooms. Had these students left B-1 to exit to the parking lot they easily could have been harmed by those who would have rushed from yard. Wrestlers, of course, could physically defend themselves but they also realized that would not be the best choice for this situation. And had they waited until dusk, they could have been ambushed.

Thus, the first thing I did was to take Pat's advice and lock the classroom door to the hallway and then close the blinds in the windows facing the yard. Outside the window, shouting and name calling continued until dusk when the bullies finally tired of hoping for a response to their taunts. They sulked away from the area, mumbling expletives. The novice wrestlers then headed for the safety of the practice area. They quietly apologized to their coach for their late arrival and, only later, relayed their tale, as they had not wanted to lose the team's allotted time on the mat....

Records and Rules
A Review of 64 Years of LD Wrestling

(Wrestling seasons span two years. They are listed in this summary by the second year of each season. For example the 1960-61 season is listed as 1961.)

1961: A winning season in its first year (6–4). Fifteen wrestlers took second place in the seasonal tournament to close out the season. Six wins and 4 losses. **Glenn Ebersole, Captain,** was undefeated.

1962: 10 wins, 3 losses and a tie, earning the first wrestling trophy. "...maintaining their power in the league, earning their first trophy in Central Dauphin's Christmas Tournament."

1963: Their spirit, determination, skill, and training are what it took to make LD's wrestling squad one of the best, with four seniors in a team of 12. There were only 12 weight classes at this time.

1964: Undefeated and Division I title. The team's first win over the defending champion Cedar Cliff was followed by a record 13 straight wins. **This was our first undefeated season.**

1965: Consecutive undefeated seasons. Seven sectional champs out of 12—and the only consecutive back-to-back undefeated season in our 64 year history. At the Williamsport Invitational Tournament, the team earned seven weight championships in **Ron Cruys, Harold Shellenhamer, Jim Sanders,** and **Randy Umberger.**

1966: For the third consecutive season LD captured the Sectional Tournament Championship and gained the Capital Area Co-Championship. Longest winning streak in Pennsylvania history ends at 40 wins.

1967: Despite maintaining their winning style by ending the season with a 13-1 record, LD lost the championship to Cumberland Valley in a 20-19 squeaker, bouncing back to end with wins.

1968: The team brought the CAC championship back to LD. Team spirit, determination, and wrestling skill under the supervision of Coach Cassel was the combination for the winning team. The Falcons are the only team in the state to have both District and Regional Championships for seven consecutive years.

1969: The team again had a winning season (13-1), capturing the Capital Area Conference crown after an exciting match with Cumberland Valley, winning 20 to 17. Five LD wrestlers selected to attend U.S. Olympics camp. Three make the *Wrestling News* honor roll—making LD the only high school in the nation to have more than one wrestler to make the list.

1970: The grapplers began the season by winning the Christmas Tournament, captained by Steve Dowhower and Dan Verdelli, and by concluding with another winning 13-1 season. Also, in the 1970s, Lower Dauphin was named the number one high school wrestling team in the state of Pennsylvania.

1971: The 1970-71 wrestling team did it again. They brought home another CAC Championship with ability, determination, and pride (13–0–1).

1972: …an undefeated season. The sectional tournament saw **Mark Stauffer, Tom Mutek, Ron Michael, Ed Neiswender,** and **Fred Foreman** qualify for the District competition.

1973: This year's team again proved to be just as great, if not greater, as in other years. They produced a season record of 13-1 and three state runners-up **Mark Stauffer, Tom Mutek** and **Ed Neiswender.**

1974: Valentine's Day was palpable, with emotions at a fevered pitch for the most dramatic match of the season: two teams undefeated, fighting for the CAC Championship.

1975: LD faced Cumberland Valley in a packed gymnasium in a showdown. While hearts were set on a victory, confidence weakened as the match progressed… their goal was unattainable.

1976: Spartans were crushed. Colts were left in the dust. E-town JVs, 58-0 and Varsity breezed by; best match was **Mel Watt's** upset over Pfautz. Defeated Palmyra; Mutek and Watts go to States.

1977: The season began with six underclassmen in the starting line-up with three straight victories. At season's end, three champions and a tie for the championship with Cedar Cliff. December 2, 1977, Coach Cassel's 200th Falcon win.

1978: The Falcon wrestlers continued to show their dominance in the CAC. **Charlie Cole** and **Chris Camasta** were both district champions.

1979: 14-2-1 record, including defeating nemesis Cedar Cliff and scoring an amazing total of 728 points (opponents 230) and tying Mount St. Joseph (27-27), the four-year reigning National Prep School Champions on December 15, 1978.

1980: *Wrestling USA* in its May 1 issue featured District III AAA Coach of the Year honors shared by Cleon Cassel and Randall Umberger. The team had captured its eleventh league championship and in the process ended District III's second-ranked Warwick High School's 32-match win streak and third-place Cumberland Valley's 27-win run as well as halting Shikellamy, District IV's top team at 32 wins.

  Headlines: Matmen Win Debut; Grapplers Have Good Season; LD Does Well in Week-end Wrestling; LD Takes Cedar Cliff Tourney; Crowned Sectional & CAC Champions.

1981: The road ahead seemed rough and unending; however, victorious triumph was their reward. LD doubled the score of their opponents and clinched the CAC title.

1982: For the third consecutive year the CAC wrestling trophy rests upon the shelf of the trophy case with a record of 15 wins and one loss. LD had many outstanding grapplers.

1983: A Championship from the newly formed Mid-Penn Conference. A second consecutive record of 15-1 season brought the 4th successive league championship and sent Stumpf and Sadler to States.

1984: A young team with one Senior in the starting line-up, LD ended with a winning season holding a record of 8-6. Five of the wrestlers qualified for the first round of District 3.

1985: Another winning season, with 16 meets, defeating our opponents by wide margins, closing only to our nemesis, Cedar Cliff, and a powerful Shikellamy team. First place at the Christmas Tournament and the 300th victory.

1986: Before the close of season the wrestling record was an impressive 310 wins. **Matt Moore** remained undefeated in dual meets. Three-quarters of the varsity were underclassmen.

1987: This team surpassed expectations while being labeled the mid-state's best group of "No-Names." They finished with a successful season led by the coach who had started it all.

1988: Young, inexperienced wrestling team members were hard-nosed and well-coached, wide-eyed, not quite knowing what to expect. They won over Dover, CD and Susquenita.

1989: Even with fewer wrestlers, the tradition was maintained through a successful year. Senior **Jamie Eberhard** was rated first in District 3 and **Jeff Hollenbush** was named to the Big 13.

1990: With mostly underclassmen, many first-year varsity, and a new head coach, the team rose with steady and consistent performances, ending with a clearly winning season.

1991: This young team gave it their all with great spirit and grit, never putting out less than 100%. **Andrae Lewis** had the spectators loudly cheering.

1992: Another change, another head coach steeped in LD history at the helm. A young squad established a sound record, building the stepping stones to future success.

1993: A REVERSAL leading to an undefeated Mid-Penn II Championship is just what this empowered team did. The magic captains included **Strunk, MacLeod, Lininger,** and **Udlehoven.** Three former LD wrestlers and coaches inducted into the PIAA District III Wrestling Coaches Hall of Fame. LD's 400th wrestling win.

1994: After winning two pre-season tournaments, but with only four returning seniors, the team focused on discipline and development, building for the future.

1995: A thrilling season—undefeated no less—District Team Tournament Championship and the Mid-Penn Conference Championship defeating Cedar Cliff for the first time in 13 years. Coach Craig Cassel named District III AAA Coach of the Year. In the 19–0 season Falcon wrestlers become Mid-Penn Champions and District III Team Champions.

1996: Defeating Harrisburg, Hershey, and Palmyra met the team's goal, and claiming the Mid-Penn II Championship was the reward.

1997: This was an exciting season—leading to a Division II Championship. **Adam Kopp** summarized it well, "All the tough hours in the mat room—LD Wrestling is the Best!"

1998: *The Falconaire*, "...the Falcon matmen destroyed one opponent after another," finishing with a 14-3 record and a Mid-Penn 2 Championship. Eight Falcon wrestlers advance to Districts.

1999: Moving up to a new division brought yet another challenge which the team met well. **Jake Lininger** was a *Patriot News* Big 13 choice.

2000: Into the new season the Falcons had some tough opponents, defeating Gettysburg. **Joel Martin** placed in the district match. A record six freshmen were starters.

2001: The team placed five wrestlers at sectionals, all of whom advanced to Districts, including senior **Brian Whiston** who had taken first place at Sectionals.

2002: Boasting a 11-2 record with exhibitions with Big Spring and CD East, Head Coach Sean Ahern won his 200th dual meet with the team's victory over Elizabethtown.

2003: Highlights of this season included defeating arch-rival Middletown and nemesis Cedar Cliff. Several of the team qualified for Districts with **Rob Melly** advancing to States.

2004: The team took second in the league and sectional tournaments and Matt Moyer went to states. They came from behind to defeat Red Land and stomped arch-rival Cedar Cliff.

2005: The 27–26 win over the Middletown Blue Raiders earned the Falcons second place in the Commonwealth Division with eight LD wrestlers advancing to Districts.

2006: Mid-Penn Champions–the team who rolled out the mats, strapped on the headgear and dominated the Conference once again, defeating Harrisburg, Hershey, and Palmyra.

2007: **Jason Kane** and **Nick Kristich** were champions at the sectional tournament. In consolation finals we did not lose a match and had seven 3rd place finishers.

2008: An unforgettable season as the Falcon matmen destroyed one opponent after another, finishing with a 11-3 record and a Mid-Penn Championship.

2009: **Mike English** and **Jason Kane** both qualified for the PIAA State Tournament where English placed 8th.

2010: The wrestling team reached its 50th anniversary and 600th win, the result of grueling training and year-round practices.

2011: After a winning season, LD manhandled Hershey in dual meets 59–12 at sectionals Falcon wrestlers took three runner-up finishes and two third-place slots. Senior Kyle Stauffer won five straight elimination bouts in the Class AAA South Central Regional to grab third place and advance to the state tournament.

2012: In a rebuilding year with an even record, LD's signature win came against Northern York County 33–29. LD also had seven Section II place winners.

2013: Freshman **Bailey Shutt** began his Falcon career with statement wins in the Cumberland Valley Kickoff Classic, leading the team to a 10th place finish. Hershey snapped a 17-year losing streak against the Falcons.

2014: After a strong season, 13 of the 14 LD Sectional starters placed in the top 6, good enough for LD to advance to Districts. **Bailey Shutt** is District Champion and qualifies for States.

2015: Six LD wrestlers advanced to Districts from the Sectionals and **Bailey Shutt** came away as LD's first District 3-AAA champion since **Nick Kristrich** won that title in 2008.

2016: **Bailey Shutt** was instrumental in leading the Falcons to a second-place finish in the Mid-Penn Keystone event and at Mechanicsburg captures his 100th win with a first period pin. For the first time in LD history, a wrestler makes the PIAA semifinals two consecutive years.

2017: The season boasted a 14-5 record including qualification for individual District III championships for the first time since 2008. Clayton Ulrey becomes the first freshman in LD wrestling history to qualify for the PIAA Tournament.

2018: Coach Kemal Pegram summarized the season:"LD finished the year 11–8 and wrestled one nationally ranked team and nine of the top 18 teams in District III. We finished third in the PIAA Section II Tournament, second in the PIAA South Central Regional Tournament, and 16th in the PIAA State Tournament ..."

2019: The Falcons had an uneven season due in part to injuries, but they wrestled some of the toughest tournaments on the East Coast. **Clayton Ulrey** and **Kyler Wuestner** claim their second consecutive tournament win at the Trojan Wars. At a New Jersey tournament, **Wuestner** wins all four of his bouts with pins. **Ulrey** goes on to become the first Falcon state finalist since 1999.

2020: In a rare losing season there were many bright performances. **Clayton Ulrey** won the District 3 Class AAA 160 title to become the 18th four-time champion in District 3 history. Teammates **Ben Snyder** and **TT Elhajj** finished fourth and third, respectively. Ulrey was ranked ninth in the nation as he approached States and ended his high school career with 144 wins.

2021: In another challenging season resiliency became the mantra, according to Coach Pegram, who gave much credit to the senior wrestlers for their leadership. "Everyone understood and no one left the room until we all did."

2022: On January 27, 2022, the wrestling team achieved its 700th win of a proud wrestling legacy, a testament to all of the proud Falcon wrestlers who have been part of this amazing wrestling tradition since its first season in 1960-61. *(Coach David P. Wuestner, Jr.)*

2023: A successful regular season earned LD the right to compete in the opening round of the District 3 3A team wrestling tournament held January 31, their 10th district tourney appearance and the first since 2017.

2024: At the close of another successful 16-4 season LD finishes 4th in Sectional team standings, sending seven wrestlers to Regionals. At the PIAA State Championships, unranked **Cael Rossi** clinches a podium spot and **Clay Koser** achieves his 100th victory.

This year (2024) we won our first League Division Championship since 2007 with a perfect 7-0 record, qualifying for the District III team Championship for the second straight year. Coach Wuestner was named Keystone Division Coach for 2023-24.

Lower Dauphin Win-Loss Records:

(LD scores are listed first following the season year)

1960–1961:	6-4	1982–1983	15-1	2004-2005	11-2
1961–1962:	10-3-1	1983–1984	8-5	2005-2006	9-2
1962–1963	12-2	1984–1985	14-2	2006-2007	15-2
1963–1964	12-2	1985–1986	11-5	2007-2008	11-3
1964–1965	14-0	1986–1987	13-3	2008-2009	23-3
1965–1966	3-1	1987–1988	11-3	2009-2010	16-5
1966–1967	13-1	1988–1989	10-7	2010-2011	6-4
1967–1968	12-2	1989–1990 `	10-4-1	2011-2012	7-7
1968–1969	13-1	1990–1991	1-14	2012-2013	5-7
1969–1970	13-1	1991–1992	6-12	2013-2014	12-
1970–1971	13-0-1	1992–1993	17-4	2014-2015	11-6
1971–1972	13-1	1993–1994	12-4-1	2015-2016	10-5
1972–1973	13-1	1994–1995	19-0	2016-2017	14-5
1973–1974	12-2	1995–1996	10-4	2017-2018	11-8
1974–1975	12-2	1996–1997	13-2	2018-2019	5-10
1975–1976	13-1	1997–1998	14-3	2019-2020	2-8
1976–1977	14-2	1998–1999	7-6	2020-2021	6-11
1977–1978	14-2	1999–2000	5-7	2021-2022	9-9
1978–1979	14-2-1	2000-2001	6-7	2022-2023	16-4
1979–1980	16-1	2001-2002	11-2	2023-2024	16-4
1980–1981	13-4-1	2002-2003	10-6		
1981–1982	15-1	2003-2004	11-4		

Lower Dauphin Sectional Champions:

Year	Name	Weight
1961	Glen Ebersole	165
1962	Randy Kahler	165
1963	Harold Shellenhammer	95
	Bill Pinkerton	103
	Jim Sanders	112
	Galen Kopp	120
	Randy Umberger	180
1964	Bob Hess	95
	Harold Shellenhammer	103
	Jim Sanders	112
	Jim Rhone	138
	Randy Kahler	165
	Randy Umberger	180
1965	Ron Cruys	95
	Ed Neidig	103
	Harold Shellenhamer	112
	Jim Sanders	120
	Bill Pinkerton	127
	Jay Ebersole	133
	Randy Umberger	180
1966	Ron Cruys	95
	Bill Smith	112
	Jack Ruggles	180
1967	Dan Sanders	95
	Leon Koser	127
	Jay Ebersole	133
1968	Dan Sanders	95
	Gene Boyer	120
	Fred Mutek	138
	Craig Tritch	165
1969	Dan Sanders	95
	Fred Mutek	138
1970	Sam Dupler	103
	Bob Kreiser	120
	Steve Dowhower	138
1971	Sam Dupler	103
	Joe Umbrell	112
	Bob Kreiser	120
	Ron Michael	138

Year	Name	Weight
	Ed Neiswender	145
	George Stauffer	180
1972	Mark Stauffer	133
	Tom Mutek	138
	Ron Michael	145
	Ed Neiswender	155
	Fred Foreman	UNL
1973	Bill Divel	119
	Tom Mutek	138
	Mark Stauffer	145
	Ed Neiswender	155
	Wayne Jockers	UNL
1976	Dale Hixon	112
	Mel Watts	185
1977	Chris Camasta	138
1978	Charlie Cole	119
	Bryan Klinger	132
	Chris Camasta	138
1979	Mike Kelly	126
	Jeff Watts	167
1980	Chuck Deibler	98
	Craig Hetrick	132
1981	Craig Hetrick	132
	Joe Radwick	167
	Joel Umberger	185
1982	Cary Gray	98
	Sam Fallinger	112
	Craig Cassel	119
1983	Dan Sadler	145
	Tom Stumpt	155
1985	Ed Arnold	112
1986	Matt Moore	185
1987	Pete Valeri	98
	Tom Salus	145
1990	Randy Lutz	103
	Jason Dupler	112
	Nick Kargas	125
	Chuck Via	145

Lower Dauphin Sectional Champions (continued)

Year	Name	Weight	Year	Name	Weight
1991	Randy Lutz	112	2008	Nick Kristich	130
1993	Jerry Hiller	275		Jason Kane	135
1994	Michael King	112	2009	Jason Kane	135
	Jeremy Burrows	189	2010	Robbie Higgins	112
	Jerry Hiller	275		Blaine Shutt	119
1995	Travis Rodgers	135	2014	Kabob Ware	171
	Jeremiah Shuman	145		David Wuestner, Jr.	220
	Mark Woodring	160	2016	Bailey Shutt	160
1996	Bill VanWinkle	112		Hunter Harnish	195
1997	Bill Van Winkle	112	2017	Clayton Ulrey	138
1998	Jacob Lininger	171	2018	Thomas-Troy Elhajj	138
1999	Jacob Lininger	189		Joey Stoak	145
2000	Joel Martin	275		Clayton Ulrey	152
2001	Brian Whiston	275		Brendan Shaffer	182
2004	Matt Moyer	160	2019	Thomas-Troy Elhajj	138
2005	Jarred Kane	125		Clayton Ulrey	160
2006	Nick Kristich	112		Kyler Wuestner	285
	Jarred Kane	135	2020	Thomas-Troy Elhajj	138
	Kevin Gerhart	160		Ben Snyder	182
2007	Jonathan Crawford	125	2023	Cael Rossi	121
	Jarred Kane	140			
	Kevin Gerhart	171			

PIAA State Qualifiers:

Year	Wrestler	Weight	Year	Wrestler	Weight
1962	Randy Kahler (2nd)	165	1995	Mark Woodring	160
1964	Jim Rhone (2nd)	138	1996	Billy Van Winkle	112
	Randy Kahler	165	1997	Billy Van Winkle	112
1965	Jim Sanders	120		Brin Koser	119
1966	Ron Cruys	120	1998	Kurt Koser (2nd)	135
1967	Jay Ebersole	133		Jake Lininger	171
1968	Dan Sanders	103	1999	Jake Lininger (2nd)	189
1969	Dan Sanders	120	2003	Rob Melly	145
1971	Bob Kreiser	120	2004	Matt Moyer	160
1972	Ron Michael	145	2005	Jarred Kane (8th)	171
	Fred Foreman (2nd)	Unl.	2006	Jonathan Crawford	125
1973	Tom Mutek (2nd)	138		Jarred Kane	135
	Mark Stauffer (2nd)	145	2007	Zac Barrick	103
	Ed Neiswender (2nd)	154		Jonathan Crawford (3rd)	125
1974	Roger Witmer	167		Jarred Kane (5th)	140
	Dave Graybill	145		Kevin Gerhart (8th)	171
1975	Karl King	138		Jimmy Miller	189
1976	Dale Hixon	112	2008	Taylor Stuart	112
	Ken Mutek	132		Nick Kristich (3rd)	130
	Eric Stauffer (4th)	145		Jason Kane	140
	Mel Watts	185	2009	Jason Kane	145
1977	Charlie Cole	119		Mike English (8th)	145
	Lloyd Umberger	145	2011	Kyle Stauffer	189
1978	Charlie Cole	119	2014	David Wuestner	220
	Chris Camasta (3rd)	138	2015	Bailey Shutt (6th)	160
1979	Mike Kelley	126	2016	Bailey Shutt (5th)	160
	Bryan Klinger	132		Evan Morrill (8th)	182
	Jeff Watts	167	2017	TT Elhajj	132
1980	Chuck Deibler (3rd)	98		Clayton Ulrey	138
	Craig Hetrick	132	2018	TT Elhajj	132
	Eryc Christofes	167		Joey Stoak	145
1981	Craig Hetrick	132		Clayton Ulrey (5th)	152
	Joel Umberger	185		Brendan Shaffer (7th)	182
1983	Dan Sadler	145		Kyler Wuestner	285
	Tom Stumpf	155	2019	TT Elhajj (8th)	138
1985	Ed Arnold	112		Clayton Ulrey (2nd)	160
1987	Pete Valeri	98		Kyler Wuestner (7th)	285
1989	Jamie Eberhard	171	2020	TT Elhajj	138
	Jeff Hollenbush	112		Clayton Ulrey (2nd)	160
1991	Randy Lutz	112	2024	Cael Rossi	127
1993	Eric Strunk	119		Clay Koser	145
1994	Jerry Hiller	275			

State Place Finishers

Year	Name	Weight Class	Place
1962	Randy Kahler	165 lbs	2nd
1964	Jim Rhone	138 lbs	2nd
1972	Fred Foreman	UNL	2nd
1973	Tom Mutek	138 lbs	2nd
	Mark Stauffer	145 lbs	2nd
	Ed Neiswender	155 lbs	2nd
1976	Eric Stauffer	145 lbs	4th
1978	Chris Camasta	138 lbs	3rd
1980	Chuck Deibler	98 lbs	3rd
1998	Kurt Koser	135 lbs	2nd
1999	Jake Lininger	189 lbs	2nd
2005	Jarred Kane	140 lbs	8th
2007	Jonathan Crawford	125 lbs	3rd
	Jarred Kane	140 lbs	5th
	Kevin Gerhart	171 lbs	8th
2008	Nick Kristich	130 lbs	3rd
2009	Mick English	145 lbs	8th
2015	Bailey Shutt	160 lbs	6th
2016	Bailey Shutt	160 lbs	5th
	Evan Morrill	182 lbs	8th
2018	Clayton Ulrey	152 lbs	5th
	Brendan Shaffer	182 lbs	7th
2019	TT Ehajj	138 lbs	8th
	Clayton Ulrey	160 lbs	2nd
	Kyler Wuestner	285 lbs	7th
2020	Clayton Ulrey	160 lbs	2nd

The (Almost) Perfect Season

Wrestler[1]	Season	W	L	D
Camasta, Chris	1977-78	15	0	0
Camasta, Chris	1976-77	15	0	0
Christofes, Eryc	1979-80	14	0	0
Cole, Charlie	1977-78	16	0	0
Cruys, Ron	1964-65	12	0	0
Dupler, Sam	1969-70	14	0	0
Ebersole, Glenn	1960-61	10	0	0
Fallinger, Sam	1981-82	10	0	0
Jockers, Wayne	1972-73	12	0	0
Kreiser, Mike	1971-72	13	0	0
Lutz, Randy	1990-91	15	0	0
Michael, Ron	1970-71	13	0	0
Michael, Ron	1971-72	13	0	0
Moore, Matt	1985-86	16	0	0
Mutek, Fred	1968-69	11	0	0
Mutek, Fred	1967-68	12	0	0
Mutek, Tom	1972-73	13	0	0
Mutek, Tom	1971-72	14	0	0
Neidig, Ed	1963-64	9	0	0
Neiswender, Ed	1972-73	14	0	0
Neiswender, Ed	1971-72	13	0	0
Rhone, Jim	1963-64	13	0	0
Rice, Wayne	1979-80	17	0	0
Salus, Tom	1986-87	16	0	0
Sanders, Jim	1964-65	11	0	0
Sanders, Jim	1963-64	13	0	0
Shellenhamer, Harold	1965-66	12	0	0
Shellenhamer, Harold	1964-65	12	0	0
Shellenhamer, Harold[2]	1963-64	13	0	0
Stauffer, Eric	1975-76	14	0	0
Stauffer, George	1970-71	14	0	0
Umberger, Randy	1964-65	14	0	0
Umberger, Randy	1963-64	12	0	0
Verdelli, Dan	1969-70	12	0	0
Walters, Rich	1961-62	13	0	0
Watts, Mel	1975-76	13	0	0
Yavoich, Dave	1974-75	14	0	0

[1]**Almost Perfect Season** here indicates dual matches. None of these wrestlers won a state championship; thus, technically, the season was not perfect. It is, however, a highly meritorious achievement and set the bar high for those who followed.

[2]According to our records, there was only one LD wrestler in the first thirty years who had THREE Seasons in which he won all dual matches: Harold Shellenhammer '65.

100 Match Winners

By weight:

2020	Clayton Ulrey	144
2007	Jarred Kane	132
2020	Troy Thomas Elhajj	126
2008	Nick Kristich	122
2016	Bailey Shutt	110
2018	Joey Stoak	103
2024	Clayton Koser	145

By date:

2024:	Clayton Koser	145
2020:	Clayton Ulrey	144
2020:	Troy Thomas Elhajj	126
2018:	Joey Stoak	103
2016:	Bailey Shutt	110
2008:	Nick Kristich	122
2007:	Jarred Kane	132

Most Pins in a Season

By number of pins

Nick Kristich	28	2007-2008
Nick Kristich	23	2005-2006
Nick Kristich	22	2006-2007
Nick Kristich	17	2004-2005
Matt Moore	17	2003-2004
Tyler Watts	17	2007-2008
Ed Neiswender, Jr.	16	2007-2008
Matt Gosik	13	2000-2001
Randy Umberger	12	1964-1965
Chuck Via	12	1988-1989

Most Pins in a Career

Nick Kristich	90
Ed Neiswender, Jr.	29
Tyler Watts	28
Jerry Hiller	27
Chuck Via	26

Fastest Pins of Record

Glenn Ebersole	12 seconds
Randy Umberger	12 seconds
Nick Kristich	16 seconds
Peter Kulp	17 seconds

The Kane Brothers (Jarred and Jason) together have a total of 217 wins, the most by brothers.

The wins together by the Shutt Brothers (Bailey at 110 and Blaine at 88) are a close second at 198.

Evolution of Scoring Wrestling

Classifications

THEN ▶ One classification to two classifications: A & AA

NOW ▶ Two classifications: AA & AAA

Number of Weight Classes

THEN ▶ 12 to 14

NOW ▶ 13

Order of Wrestling

THEN ▶ Begin at lowest weight class to heaviest

NOW ▶ Random draw to start match followed by next weight

District and State Championship Opportunities

THEN ▶ Only Individual

NOW ▶ Individual and Team

Individual Post Season Advancement

THEN ▶ Finish 1st at Sectionals, Districts, Regionals to advance to States

    Sectional: 8-man bracket

    District: 8-man bracket

    Regional: 2-man bracket (District 1 *vs* District 3)

    State: 4-man bracket

NOW ▶ Sectionals: AA–2 sections top 6 each section advance to District 3
                (12-man bracket)

                AAA–4 sections top 4 each section advance to District 3 SE Region
                (16-man Bracket)

    Districts: AA–7 advance to SE Regional 14-man bracket

                AAA–No District 3 Tournament. Sectional winners advance to
                SC Regional 16-man bracket

    Regional: AA–advances 5 to State 20-man bracket

                AAA–advances 4 to State 20-man bracket

    State: Went from 4-man bracket to 8-man bracket to 16-man bracket before
                present day 20-man bracket

Individual Match Scoring Summary

Takedown

THEN ▸ 2 points for 1st period- 1 point for each in 2nd & 3rd periods

NOW ▸ 2 points for all

Escape

THEN & NOW - 1 PT.

Near Fall (based on how long held in fall position)

THEN ▸ 3 points

NOW ▸ 2 or 4 points

Predicament

THEN ▸ 2 points

NOW ▸ no longer used

Reversal

THEN & NOW - 2 PTS.

Riding Time (time spent in top/offensive position vs opponents time in top position)

THEN ▸ 1 match point

NOW ▸ No longer used

Team Scoring (Dual Meets)

Fall or Pin

THEN ▸ 6 points for 1st period; 5 points for 2nd or 3rd period

NOW ▸ 6 points 1st, 2nd, 3rd periods

Technical Fall (defeating opponent by greater than 15 points)

THEN ▸ Not used

NOW ▸ 5 points

Major Decision (defeating opponent between 8-12 points)

THEN ▸ Not used

NOW ▸ 4 team points

Decision (defeating opponent between 1–7 points)

THEN & NOW 3 points each team

Draw or Tie

THEN ▸ 2 points each team

NOW ▸ not used - wrestle overtime until a winner

Gender Participation

THEN ▸ Only males to females with males

NOW ▸ Starting 2023-24 established girls as a separate sport from boys

THEN = When Lower Dauphin started Wrestling in 1960–61

NOW = Current. Some other modifications not noted between then and now.

Judith T. (Ball) Witmer
The Author

7:30 a.m. every week-day morning, beginning in September 1960

Growing up in central Pennsylvania in a town smaller than Hummelstown, the author earned a Bachelor of Arts degree from Penn State's College of Liberal Arts where she was a member of the Penn State Thespians. Despite having had public performance experience from the age of three, she was awed by the size of Penn State and was welcomed as the keyboardist in the "pit orchestra" in Schwab Auditorium.

She became part of the faculty at Lower Dauphin High School when the doors first opened on a rainy day in the fall of 1960 after a delay of about two weeks, as the finishing touches were being applied to the building's interior. In the peak of the Baby Boomers explosion, the ninth grade classrooms were overflowing with teen-agers filled with uncertainty. In most English classes the average number of students was in the low-to-mid thirties. Desks were squeezed in the already crowded classrooms and we sighed as each additional desk was pushed through the door.

Three years later Mr. David J. Emerich, Supervising Principal, asked this teacher to accept an assignment in the senior high school that would include British Literature and Public Speaking. There she created a number of innovative courses, most notably award-winning English Enrichment, a team-taught, three-year rigorous course for self-selected students. During the heyday of "mini courses" (which focused on special topics of interest), she taught "The Lesser Known Plays of Shakespeare." In addition, she was the director/ producer of six musicals, where she recruited LD athletes to give the stage a try. She also directed a number of dramatic productions and served as advisor to seven yearbooks.

In the mid-1960s she initiated student-centered Commencement and Baccalaureate services which were produced until the end of the 1980s. She also originated the inclusion of alumni in graduation programs, as well as the formality of Junior Class Marshals.

Later, as an administrator, Dr. Witmer was the Director of the Coalition of Essential Schools, a model school-within-a-school concept using an integrated curriculum designed by a faculty task force on school improvement, guided by the PA Department of Education. She initiated a Student Advisory Board; the Senior Awards Family Night; Elementary and Secondary Parent Advisory Boards; a revamped Superintendent's Forum for students; Spirit Club; an alumni network to serve in resource and partnership capacities which became the Lower Dauphin Alumni Association—and for a short time she was editor of "Know Your Schools."

She also served as chairman of the Publications Committee for Hummelstown's Bicenquinquagenary celebration and editor of its resulting book. She was a founding member of the Lower Dauphin Falcon Foundation and, at present, continues as an ex officio in the Lower Dauphin Alumni Association, which she had initiated in 1989.

Witmer's Masters and Doctoral degrees were earned at Temple University with additional credits from Harvard where she spent a summer in residence studying ethics in education (which led to an invitation to serve on the Ethics Committee at Penn State's Medical Center). Her doctoral dissertation was the first qualitative study to be honored by the International Association for Moral Education. Witmer was offered a faculty position at Temple, but not wanting to relocate to Philadelphia, she chose to remain with Lower Dauphin, agreeing to accept a faculty adjunct position with Temple, and two years later was accepted at Widener School of Law. The sitting superintendent then asked that, instead of law school, Dr. Witmer accept a position as assistant to the superintendent, a position she held until leaving LDSD.

Her last years before leaving LD to accept an appointment at the PA Department of Education were spent as an assistant principal followed by district-wide administrative positions. It was a time of internal turmoil at LD, and leadership faced uncertainty. As a result, Dr. Witmer resigned and established her own consultancy with clients such as the Pennsylvania Department of Education, Milton Hershey School, and Penn State Harrisburg where later she served as the Director of the Capital Area Institute for Mathematics and Science.

She served as co-chair (with Jerry Kling) of the fund-raising committee for constructing the Alexander Library in Hummelstown and she authored the book based on the 175th year of the founding of Hummelstown, as well as serving as co-chair (with Randy Umberger who most capably took the lead) of the fundraising campaign for the construction of the Fields and Field House at the East End of the Lower Dauphin campus).

TEMPLE UNIVERSITY, doctoral papers

- *A Day in the Life.* (A) "Excellent report."
- *I Stood Among Them, But Not of Them.* (A+) "...and I don't give A+'s! Excellent Report"
- *A Review of the Literature.* (A) "Very impressive—a lot of fine readings."
- *Leadership: A Personal Profile.* (A) "You write so well!"
- *Leadership: A Profile of the Superintendent.* (A) "Beautifully written."
- *An Oral Report on Mastery Learning.* (A) "In the 13 times I've taught this course no one has contributed this total effort.... you ultimately are the winner and I suspect so will be the teachers you will lead as an administrator."
- *A Case for the Liberal Arts.* (A) "What a conclusion! ... Extraordinary documentation—absolutely excellent! ...Yours is one of the finest papers ever submitted, perhaps the cleanest, most logical presentation I've ever read. ... I suspect no one will excel this work of yours."

♦ *Final Exam.* "Good grief, what an answer. Excellent! ...Superior responses."

♦ *Final Exam.* "Superior response. Out of a high of 55 points, I'd deduct a mere 1, total 54, and would even feel a bit guilty doing that."

♦ *"This same philosophy is a good horse in the stable, but an errant jade on a journey."* (A+) "Well-written."

♦ *"Do I dare to eat a peach? or The Prufrock in Us All.* (A) "Excellent introduction. ... Superbly written paper with many excellent ideas. I thoroughly enjoyed reading it."

♦ *The Best and the Equal: A Synthesis or "May I have this waltz?"* "Very interesting intro... excellent 'stuff' on Hegel. ... Superbly written and interestingly done."

♦ *Won't You Come Home, John Dewey?* "Excellently put...Great job–a superbly written and, unfortunately, accurately described portrayal."

♦ *He Who Commands the Language Commands the World* – some thoughts on emotivism. "As usual, beautifully portrayed."

♦ *Would Beowulf Eat Quiche...and other musings about the virtue of heroism.* "... excellent references...nicely done...interesting point ...cleverly related...Your papers are always great to read—so informative and so very well put."

♦ *Ab Absurdo: Ad Veritatem—A Creed.* A+. "Simply, thank you!"

PERFORMANCES, a sampling

2006—2015: Acoustic and Electronic Piano, occasional vocals: Weddings, Reunions, Receptions, Special Events, including Hummelstown High School All Class Reunions and Lower Dauphin Falcon Foundation Blue and White Galas

December 1988: Hershey Community Chorus, "An Afternoon Christmas Party" and "An Evening Christmas Concert," Producer

May 1988: Hershey Community Chorus, "Music America Loves," Producer

December 1987: Hershey Community Chorus, "An International Christmas," Producer, Stage Production: Community Theatre

June 1970: Pipe Organ Recital, Hershey Theatre

1965—1970: Acoustic Piano and Vocals, Various venues

BOOKS AUTHORED

Some High Schools are Just Better

- *Wrestling: An Uncommon Heritage—All about Lower Dauphin Wrestling and its Wrestlers*; for everyone who loves Lower Dauphin Wrestling, 2024.

- *The Informal, Incomplete and Random History of LD High School, According to the* Falcon Flash, *Right or Wrong*, 2022.

- *Memorable Moments: L. D. High School Classes*, special highlights, 1960-2020, 2020.

- *The Lower Dauphin Falconaire, A Sampling of Yearbooks*, 2019.

- *The English Students in B-1: An Odyssey with the Baby Boomers*, 2018.

- *A Son's Letters to His Father, WWII*, November 2016 – a collection of World War II letters written by William Calhoon, father of Bill '61, June '66 and Dr. Janet Calhoon '66.

- *Loyal Hearts Proclaim: Lower Dauphin High School: The First Fifty Years*, December 2013.

Small Towns: Big Dreams

- *It's the Berries: The Story of a Small Town Flapper* (the mother of Bill Jackson of *The Sun*), a 1920s Coed at Drexel University, a member of the first Class at the college that admitted women into a four-year degree program, 2021.

- *We Have Always Loved You: A Remembrance of John Elensky, Our Classmate and Leader*, private printing, June 2021.

- *Our Town: Supplement to The Bicenquinquagenary of Hummelstown*, Editor, Picture Perfect Productions, Fall 2012.

- *Bicenquinquagenary of Hummelstown*, Editor-in-Chief. Picture Perfect Publishing, 2012.

- *Kay: A Woman Before Her Time*, private printing.

- *Genealogy and Story of the Thompson Sisters*.

- *Kate and Howard: A Retrospective*.

- *Growing Up Silent in the 1950s: Not all Tailfins and Rock n Roll*.

- *All the Gentlemen Callers: Letters Found in a 1920s Steamer Trunk*.

- *Jebbie: Vamp to Victim—The True Story of the Beautiful Miss Pifer*, Elementary School 3rd grade teacher.

- *I Am From Haiti: The Story of Rodrigue Mortel, MD*, A Biography, Mortel Foundation, December 2000. (French edition, *Je Suis D'Haiti*)

Creative Development: Fresh Ways to Learn

♦ *Memorable Moments: A Snapshot of Yearbooks, 1961-2020.*

♦ *Team-Based Professional Development: A Process for School Reform.* First Author; co-authored with Steven A. Melnick. Rowman & Littlefield, January 2007. Promoted in Australia, 2010.

♦ *Moving Up,* second edition, Rowman & Littlefield, Lanham, MD, co-published with the American Association of School Administrators, 2006.

♦ *The Keystone Integrated Framework: A Compendium.* Pennsylvania Department of Education, 1997.

♦ *The Keystone Integrated Framework, a Case Study in Curriculum Integration.* First Author; co-authored with Steven A. Melnick. 1997, Alexandria, VA: Association for Supervision and Curriculum Development.

♦ *Moving Up! A Guide for Women in Educational Administration.* Lancaster, PA: Technomic Press, 1995. This was the first book published on this ground-breaking subject. (Optioned by Scarecrow Press, Inc., Lanham, MD, 1999).

♦ *How to Establish a Service-Learning Program.* Witmer, first Author; co-authored with Carolyn Sandel Anderson '65. Alexandria, VA: Association for Supervision and Curriculum Development, 1994.

♦ Numerous plays, scripts, speeches for corporate leaders, pageants, choralogues, and editing books for other writers.

Yesteryear Publishing—Providing Writing and Publishing Services to authors

Dr. Judith T. Witmer, Yesteryear Publishing
jtwitmer@aol.com
www.yesteryearpublishing.org

Education

BA; English Literature, Penn State's College of Liberal Arts; MS in Science and Humanities, Temple; Doctorate Administrative Ethics, Temple; Graduate Credits, Harvard.

Professional Work History

- CEO, Educon Consulting and Yesteryear Publishing
- Director, Capital Area Institute for Mathematics and Science, Penn State Harrisburg
- Project Manager, PA Department of Education
- Evaluator, Hershey Medical Center and other entities
- Consultant and Program Designer, Milton Hershey School
- Speechwriter for various national presenters
- Editor for the U.S. Department of Education's National Arts Standards
- College Professor (Adjunct: Temple, Millersville, and Penn State)
- Assistant to the Superintendent; High School Principal for Academic Improvement; Director, Coalition of Essential Schools; English Instructor (Initiated English Enrichment, Developed Special Topic Courses; Department Chair)

Community Service

- Co-Chair, fundraising for Lower Dauphin School District's Field House
- Chair, Editor and Chief Contributor for *A Bicenquinquagenary: 250ᵗʰ Celebration of Hummelstown's Founding*
- Chair, Golden Jubilee, celebrating the first 50 years of Lower Dauphin H.S.
- Co-Chair, fundraising to build the Alexander Library in Hummelstown
- Chair, fundraising for the imposing Alumni Display Case at Lower Dauphin H.S.
- Founding Board Member of the Lower Dauphin Falcon Foundation
- Chair, Board of Pennsylvania Governor's Schools of Excellence
- Founding Member of the Lower Dauphin Alumni Association

Honors

- Lower Dauphin Falcon Foundation Honoree for Lifetime Service
- Penn State DuBois Outstanding Alumna
- Class of 1965, Life Service Award
- Lower Dauphin Alumni Association, Initial Honoree
- Scholarship established by the Class of 1965
- Dissertation Award, Association for Moral Education, Harvard University
- Mensa International Inductee

Administrative Contributions to LDSD

Initiation and development of several Student Assistance Programs, including an early plan for coping with crises; creation of Student Advisory Board; redesign of Student Forum; initiation of plan and process for Class Gifts to the school; design for New Teacher Induction Plan; proposal for School Governance/Fairness Committee; institution of Senior Awards Family Night; founding of Secondary and Elementary Parent Advisory Boards; formation of student Spirit Club in response to negative incidents; establishment of administrative committee for professional supervision & evaluation.

Director/Producer of 8 school musicals; Director of 7 plays and other performances; Advisor for 7 Yearbooks; Director/Producer and Script-writer for 24 student-centered Commencement Productions and 24 Baccalaureate Programs; Initiator of Junior Class Marshals and Alumni participation in Commencement; Advisor to various clubs and the Class of 1965; Dinner music for several proms; Editor and Voice of Daily Announcements at LDHS, 27 years.

And to confirm the dedication of the Lower Dauphin High School faculty, its students were involved in many varied areas and almost every adult was involved in at least one of the activities, be it sports or music or simply walking, which, yes, was a club as were many other extra-curricular activities. The result was well-rounded graduates. (I believe, however, that English Enrichment was the only class in which we went to the woods for a full day and the assignment was to "pack for survival and then narrate your day," and English Enrichment was also the only class invited by an alumnus for a week-end at West Point!)

My own extra-curricular involvement was mainly—but not exclusively—the arts and I was part of the school musicals beginning with the first year when, it still is fun to say, "I was one third of the orchestra" comprised of piano, bass, and drums....in 1961 and 1962. In the late 60s, I served as producer. In 1980 I assisted with *The Sound of Music*, followed the next six years as director or producer with *Annie Get Your Gun*, *Guys and Dolls* (our first year with a bona fide external choreographer), *South Pacific*, *L'il Abner*, *Bye, Bye Birdie* and a breathtaking *Camelot* (all included student athletes as actors). And for many years I hosted a "Christmas Open House" for my students who had become alumni.

We were a faculty involved with musicians and athletes, clubs and other extra-curricular activities! There was no manufactured lesson plan for this. It was called "learning, guidance, friendship, and devotion."

For further information:

Win/Loss statistics for this book are drawn from the Lower Dauphin Wrestling Booster Club's online file at https://www.ldsd.org and search Wrestling History.

Sources for individual match scores are the PIAA Wrestling pages at www.piaa.org and PA-Wrestling.com at https://www.pa-wrestling.com/index.htm

To order copies of "Lower Dauphin Wrestling: An Uncommon Heritage, 1960-2024," visit amazon.com and search "Lower Dauphin Wrestling."

The more than 400-page book Lower Dauphin Wrestling: An Uncommon Heritage, 1960-2024 by Dr. Judith Witmer is a non-profit, volunteer venture in support of Lower Dauphin Wrestling.

Proceeds from the sale of the book, beyond production costs, will be donated to the Lower Dauphin Wrestling Boosters to a minimum of $1,000.